# Clever
# Girl

# Clever Girl

Elizabeth Bentley,
the Spy Who Ushered in
the McCarthy Era

## LAUREN KESSLER

HarperCollins*Publishers*

HarperCollins books may be purchased for educational, business, or
sales promotional use. For information please write: Special Markets
Department, HarperCollins Publishers Inc., 10 East 53rd Street,
New York, NY 10022.

FIRST EDITION

Designed by Elliott Beard

Printed on acid-free paper

Library of Congress Cataloging-in-Publication Data

Kessler, Lauren.
Clever girl : Elizabeth Bentley, the spy who ushered in the
McCarthy era / Lauren Kessler.
p.   cm.
Includes bibliographical references and index.
ISBN 0-06-018519-8
1. Bentley, Elizabeth.   2. Women communists—United
States—Biography.   3. Communism—United States.
4. Intelligence service—Soviet Union.   5. Espionage, Soviet—
United States.   6. Informers—United States—Biography.
I. Title.

HX84.B384 K47 2003
327.1247073′092—dc21
[B]

2002038740

03 04 05 06 07 NMSG/RRD 10 9 8 7 6 5 4 3 2 1

To Tom,
again, and always

# Contents

PART ONE
## The Romance

PART TWO
# The Reality

PART THREE
# The Ruin

# Clever Girl

# Introduction

ER CODE NAME was "Clever Girl," but some contacts knew her as "Myrna," and others called her "Helen." To the New York City tabloids in the late 1940s, she was the "Red Spy Queen." She ferried secret documents from covert communists in the federal government to her Russian lover, a KGB operative. She recruited informants. She debriefed agents. During the "golden age" of Soviet espionage, Elizabeth Turrill Bentley, the well-bred, Vassar-educated descendant of Puritan clergy, ran two of the most productive spy rings in America. And then, one day in 1945, she "turned"—and started naming names.

Bentley's lengthy statement to the FBI awoke the Truman White House to the possibility that Soviet spying was more than just J. Edgar Hoover's paranoia. Bentley's testimony before grand juries and at House and Senate subcommittee hearings exposed scores of Communist Party members working for the federal government who were passing confidential information and secret documents, and otherwise aiding the Soviets. Harry Dexter White, assistant secretary of the Treasury and a member of one of the spy rings Bentley managed, was one of them. So was FDR's assistant, Lauchlin Currie. And so was Duncan Lee, a top aide in the OSS, the precursor to the CIA. Bentley's statement to the FBI helped point the way to Julius Rosenberg, and her testimony as the last witness for the prosecution at the Rosenbergs' trial sealed their fate. Her disclosures and accusations put a halt to Russian spying for years and helped to set the tone of American political life for nearly a decade.

But who really was Elizabeth Bentley? Was she a smart, independent woman who made her choices freely—right and wrong—and had the strength of character to see them through, or an emotionally unstable and needy spinster in search of love and excitement? Was she shrewd and self-possessed, a woman who calculated her moves and called the shots, or had she been used and manipulated by others? Was she protagonist or victim? Saint or sinner? Traitor or patriot?

Two generations of writers and historians have largely steered clear of her story, and it's not hard to understand why. The excesses of the McCarthy era, a period Elizabeth Bentley helped to usher in, have until recently blinded most of us to the more complex realities of that time. Senator McCarthy made headlines claiming, with much malice and little proof, that communists had infiltrated the government, that hundreds, even thousands of people who believed in perfectly legitimate liberal and progressive causes were in fact dangerous radicals intent on disabling democracy and killing capitalism. McCarthy's faked evidence, his egregious tactics, his smear campaigns that ruined innocent lives, the often offensive and sometimes clearly unconstitutional behavior of the House Un-American Activities Committee and its Senate sibling, the Internal Security Subcommittee, made anticommunism not just a dirty business but a highly suspect one.

What many people who witnessed that era and many historians who wrote about it later came to believe was that communist subversion was a myth invented by Joe McCarthy, that communist spies were a figment of J. Edgar Hoover's overheated imagination, that the entire "communist conspiracy" was a fabrication born of paranoia and right-wing political intrigue. Because McCarthy was wrong about so much, because he was so visibly and dangerously out of control, it was easy to believe that he, along with the congressional committees that paved the way for his excesses, was wrong about this, too. Given this understanding of history, of what importance could Elizabeth Bentley be? How could she be taken seriously? How could her life be anything more than a sad footnote to an indefensible time?

But history is not immutable. Sometimes the present rewrites the past, and the story we thought we knew, the story we were so sure of, begins to unravel and reweave itself into different cloth. It can happen in an instant: documents no one knew existed are discovered or declassified; secret archives are opened; people who had been silent speak out. And we are forced to reevaluate, to literally re-view history. This is what happened when suddenly, dramatically, in the mid-1990s, the United States government first revealed the existence of a top-secret project, code-named Venona.

Venona was a World War II–vintage, Army counterintelligence scheme that set a group of ace cryptographers to work trying to break coded cablegrams sent from Russian embassies in the United States back home to Moscow. That Army intelligence was intercepting and working to decipher messages sent by our then staunch wartime ally speaks to the flimsiness of the friendship between the two countries. And it says much about the basic distrust and fear that underlay the relationship between the most powerful capitalist country and what was the most powerful communist nation. Few people beyond those directly involved knew of the Venona project at the time. FBI director Hoover guarded the secret zealously, cutting the CIA, the Congress, the cabinet, the White House, and almost, but not quite, the president, out of the loop.

By the early 1940s, the extraordinarily complex Soviet code had been broken, and slowly, painstakingly, nearly three thousand cables were decrypted and translated. When the job was done, there was little doubt to the meaning of the cables: The Soviets had been spying on the U.S. government throughout the 1930s and 1940s, aided by a number of American citizens working within the government who had passed information and documents to both American and Russian contacts. The cables detailed who was spying, making clear the

tie between the American communist party and the Russian espionage effort. And the cables highlighted the critical work of an
American-born woman operative who rose to a position of power
greater than that of any other American spy. Her code name was
"Clever Girl." Her real name was Elizabeth Bentley.

And so, a half century after the fact, the story began to reveal
itself. The Venona cablegrams coupled with documents found by
U.S. scholars in fleetingly accessible archives in Moscow show that
the Soviets established a productive espionage apparatus in the
United States that made use of American communists and sympathizers. A "communist conspiracy" did, in fact, exist. Spies were real.
Elizabeth Bentley did what she said she did. She was near center
stage in a drama few knew had even taken place. She was an important part of this moment in history. She *made* this history.

Hers is a story of danger, intrigue, romance, treachery, hope,
despair, betrayal, and redemption. It is tempting to see Bentley as a
pitiable, unregenerate character. She was deeply flawed, yes, but her
story is more complicated—and far more interesting—than the sum
of her personal imperfections. It is a story of good intentions gone
bad, of skewed loyalties, of a past that could not be outrun no matter
how long the race. It is the story of a woman who lived a life much
bigger than the one to which she was born—and who paid the price.

# Prologue

SHE KNEW THEY were following her. She could feel it with that sixth sense Yasha had helped her develop. The man in the dark suit idling at the street corner when she left work in the late afternoon. The man at the back table at Schrafft's on Fourth Avenue. The man reading the paper in the lobby of the Hotel St. George. The man at the bar. She shouldn't have talked to him. She shouldn't have taken him up to her room, she knew that. But she was lonely and on her third martini, and he was attentive, very attentive. What had they talked about? What did she tell him? She couldn't quite remember.

She knew they were following her. She just didn't know who "they" were. Sometimes she thought it was the KGB. The Russians wanted her out. They had made that clear. But did they also want her dead? It had happened before. People had disappeared. Yasha had told her stories. But "Al," her KGB contact, seemed genuinely concerned for her security when they rendezvoused in a darkened movie theater in Washington, D.C., a few weeks earlier. He warned her that the situation was extremely dangerous. He told her to take a vacation, to go to Canada or Mexico where she didn't need a passport. From there, the Russians would smuggle her out to safety. So maybe the KGB had her best interests at heart. Or maybe not. Maybe it was a plot. Yasha would know. He understood the way things worked. But Yasha was gone.

Sometimes she thought it was her own people, people in the American communist party, who were setting her up for a fall. The company she worked for, her "cover," United States Service and Shipping, had originally been funded with party money, and now it seemed the party wanted it back. One party official told her he would "blow her to hell" if the money wasn't returned. Was that a serious threat or a bluff? Was the man just trying to scare her or was the party really after her? She didn't know.

Mostly, though, she figured it was the FBI. Agents had tailed her before, back when Yasha had that trouble with the Dies Committee and almost went to jail. That was years ago, but maybe they were back on the trail. They were certainly back on *some* trail. Two months ago, the papers were full of details about an FBI raid on the offices of a magazine with ties to the party. The agents found stacks of confidential documents, letters, memos, and reports from the offices of governmental agencies. The documents had to have come from someone inside, a government worker passing secret information to the party. The FBI was zeroing in. The papers said it was the work of spies. How soon would it be before some trail led to her?

And then there was Louis Budenz, a long-time party member and former editor of *Labor Age*. He had been involved in espionage activities and had known and worked with Yasha. She had met him several times. Now Budenz had publicly denounced communism. He was making headlines. Would he start naming names? And would hers be one of them?

Her nerves were shot. When she wasn't at work, she was alone in her hotel room, alternately pouring herself stiff drinks and pacing the floor. The Russians had told her to leave her apartment. They thought it was being watched. So now she was camped out in a single room at the St. George, lonely, confused, afraid. Even the alcohol, as much as she was drinking, wasn't taking the edge off.

Yasha hated the FBI, but they might be her best hope. If she could get to them before they got to her, if she could get to them before the Russians got to her, she might have a chance. If she told her story first, she might save herself. She might not be hounded by the party or killed by the KGB or imprisoned as a spy. But how to do it? She couldn't just stroll into the FBI's New York office down on Foley Square. They would be watching that, whoever "they" were. If the Russians saw her, that would be the end of it. If someone from the party saw her, even if no one was really after her for the money, she would be branded a traitor, and that could mean trouble.

She thought about taking the train to Washington, D.C., as she had done so many times before, when she went to check on her sources and gather the documents they had for her. But she couldn't imagine herself marching into FBI headquarters. Where would she go once she got in the door? It wasn't worth thinking about anyway because, of course, the KGB would be watching there, too. She would have to go to some small field office, some place more discreet, some place where no one knew her, where she could sneak in and out without being noticed.

Through that spring and into the summer, she had weighed her options. She was in over her head, she knew that. And she was scared. But she couldn't let fear get in the way of being careful, of thinking ahead, of planning. She had to keep her wits about her. Her life could depend on it. Finally, she made up her mind. She would go to New Haven. She knew the town—Connecticut was home turf—and there was a field office there. The address was familiar. She would take the train up from Grand Central. If she didn't panic, if she paid close attention and followed the routine, she could lose the tail, if there was one, on her way to the station. Yasha had taught her how. He'd pointed out restaurants and movie theaters and subway stations where she could slip in one entrance and out another. Macy's was always a good bet, with all those doors and all those shoppers. In a pinch, there was the ladies' room at Grand Central. She'd done it before.

It could work, she decided. She could get herself to New Haven safely and unnoticed. But once there, she would have to play it close to the chest. She'd figured it all out. She wouldn't tell them her story. She wasn't going to confess. Not yet. She had to see if they knew about her, see if that man in the bar—the one she shouldn't have talked to, the one she was sleeping with—really was an FBI agent. She had to meet these Bureau men face to face, see if they were the monsters Yasha told her they were. Then later, maybe, if it seemed right, if it felt safe, she would talk.

# Part One

# The Romance

# Chapter 1

# Connecticut Yankee

*I*N THE ROLLING hills of western Connecticut, at the foot of the Berkshires, where the Housatonic River cuts a wide swath south to the Long Island Sound, sits the self-possessed, quintessentially New England town of New Milford. Bucolic, picture-postcard pretty in all seasons, it is a town that could have been engraved by Currier & Ives, with its expansive village green, its tall, white-steepled churches, and its quiet, leafy lanes. Up from the river, on Main Street and Bridge Street and Bank Street, the houses are wood-frame colonials, impressive Greek Revivals and elegant Queen Anne Victorians, one historic building after another, built to last by merchants and farmers, cavalrymen and clergy, doctors and bankers, the solid, and stolid, New Englanders who made this place their home since the early 1700s.

But New Milford is more than a comely village. It is a town with a pedigree. It was the birthplace of Roger Sherman, a leading colonial statesman and politician who signed the Declaration of Independence and the Articles of Confederation and the Constitution, and served as one of Connecticut's first senators. A hundred years later, the town was an important stop on the Underground Railroad. By the beginning of the twentieth century, it was a diverse and prosperous commercial center, with two banks, three hardware stores, four blacksmiths, five hotels, six dry-goods stores, seven doctors, eight churches, and one billiards parlor. Its population of five thousand made it the largest town in the Berkshire Valley. Still, it was largely a rural community, the few, well-manicured downtown streets surrounded by rolling farmlands. Out in the countryside, there were one-room schoolhouses to serve the farm families. In town, there was the New Milford Center School, housing grades one through eight, and presided over in 1906 by a bright, well-read, plain-faced, twenty-nine-year-old spinster named Mary Charlotte Turrill.

The Turrill family had the deepest of roots in New Milford. Daniel Turrill, Mary's great-great-great-great-great-grandfather, was one of the original purchasers—from "the Heathen," as town records indicate—of the New Milford townsite in 1702. But he was not the first Turrill in the colonies. That was his father, Roger Tyrrell, who came to America from Hereford, England, on the ship *Lion* in 1632 as part of the great Puritan migration. By the time of the Revolutionary War, in which nine Turrill men fought, the family had already been in Connecticut for five generations. John Turrill, Mary's great-grandfather, was a private who fought at Germantown and survived the winter at Valley Forge. After the war, he married the niece of colonial statesman Roger Sherman, thereby connecting two of the "first families" of Connecticut. Mary's father, Frederick Jay, a member of the eighth generation of Turrills in America, was an ardent trout fisherman, a vestryman of St. John's Episcopal Church of New Milford, and owner of one of the finest tobacco farms in the area. He and his wife, Julia Frances Smith—a "conscientious Christian, a devoted wife and mother"—had seven children, the oldest of whom was Mary Charlotte, born in the summer of 1877.

She was a bright child and an eager learner, a girl of both strong character and strong faith. The Turrills lived close to town, with its venerable public library, its active civic and cultural life, and its laudable public schools, which, by town meeting decree, distributed textbooks free to all "scholars." Her parents must have encouraged her educational ambitions, for when Mary finished eight grades of public schooling in New Milford, she was sent to Northfield Seminary for Young Ladies in the hills of northern Massachusetts. A college preparatory boarding school founded by a free-thinking evangelist preacher, Northfield Seminary—commonly referred to as "Mr. Moody's School"—was famous for having graduated a former slave in 1889 and enrolling Choctaw and Sioux students. Mary Charlotte returned to New Milford a young woman enlightened, and a young woman with a vocation, teaching, which she found deeply rewarding. By the age of twenty-nine, she was a veteran teacher at Center School in the village and, by the standards of the day, a confirmed spinster.

There was, however, a man in town who caught her eye, a thirty-seven-year-old bachelor named Charles Prentiss Bentley. He was a long-faced, jug-eared man with a strong chin and intelligent eyes. The son of a Baptist minister, he was the direct descendant of a dissident English clergyman who had arrived in Boston Harbor in 1637. His ancestor had preached from the pulpit of the church attended by Mary Charlotte's ancestor Roger Tyrrell.

Charles Bentley had spent his early adulthood trying to distinguish himself in a career outside the church. He was still trying. He had worked in New York City for a number of years, moving from one dry-goods establishment to another, while also serving on the staff of the *Dry Goods Economist,* the leading trade paper in the industry. At the end of 1900, he moved to New Milford to take over management of C. H. Booth's store on Bank Street. Booth had been selling everything from clothing to carpets, hats to "fancy crockery," from a small establishment just off the town green for more than forty years. It was time, he told his customers in a letter published in the local newspaper, to "lay aside some of the care and responsibility of business." In January of 1901, the store was renamed Booth & Bentley Company, with Charles the junior, but more active, partner.

The schoolteacher and the merchant wed in the spring of 1907, setting up their home in one of the well-kept, clapboard houses on Terrace Place, a lovely, tree-lined street near the center of town. The homes were not grand, but the street was one of the most respectable in town, home to a number of long-time New Milford residents. It was here, on January 1, 1908, almost exactly nine months after their wedding, that Mary and Charles welcomed their first and only child, a daughter, whom they named Elizabeth Turrill Bentley.

Mary's life, still lived in the comfortable confines of her hometown among her large, stable family, nonetheless changed dramatically. She had been a self-supporting career woman. Now she was a mother and the wife of a man who was fast becoming, or trying to become, one of New Milford's leading citizens. Charles had taken on civic responsibilities, acting as a committee chairman for the town's bicentennial celebration during the summer before his daughter's birth. He donated, with some fanfare, a large American flag that was ceremoniously hoisted up a new eighty-foot flagpole constructed on the town green for the occasion. He worked hard at Booth & Bentley, using his knowledge of jobbers and manufacturers in New York City to bring new merchandise to the store. He advertised aggressively, tempting customers with inventory sales, Christmas sales, spring sales, and half-price sable fox neckpieces. But Booth & Bentley was one of a half dozen dry-goods stores serving the area, and there just wasn't enough business to go around. Old Mr. Booth was quite old by then and, although Charles had taken over the daily operation of the business, Booth didn't want the responsibility of ownership in his dotage. When Elizabeth was just about to start grade school, the store was sold to a Danbury businessman, leaving Charles temporarily unemployed.

But Charles Bentley was a man accustomed to the vagaries of employment. Early in 1914, he signed on as business manager of a new weekly newspaper, *New Milford Times,* which promised to serve "every man, woman, boy and girl in the community" and run competition to the already established *Gazette.* "Tell It to the Times; We Tell It to the People" was the spirited motto. The paper seemed to flourish under Charles's management, offering a lively compendium of local news with a healthy dose of advertising. But less than a year and a half after taking the position, Charles left, and in 1915, when Elizabeth was eight and just finishing second grade at Center School, the Bentleys moved to Ithaca, New York, where Charles had apparently secured a position at another store. Elizabeth would leave behind not only her school companions and Terrace Place neighbors but also her grandparents, her many aunts, uncles, and cousins—the entire Turrill clan. It would have been a difficult move for any little girl. But for Elizabeth, who had inherited her mother's quiet temperament and studious ways, it was especially so. It was not easy for her to make friends, and the sudden move to a new town in a different state didn't help. Ithaca, it turned out, was only the first of many moves that would disrupt her childhood.

The Bentleys lived in western New York for barely two years before the peripatetic Charles, always looking to better himself, moved the family down to Poughkeepsie and then, three years later, in the summer of 1920, to McKeesport, a western Pennsylvania steeltown. While Charles was alternately finding and losing his occupational footing, Elizabeth attended four different grammar schools in five years. It was a lonely childhood spent reading books and following the stern dictates of her mother, who, regardless of where they lived, focused on giving her daughter an old-fashioned New England upbringing. Elizabeth may have chafed under the rules, but her mother was her role model. From as early as she could remember, Elizabeth Bentley wanted to be a schoolteacher.

Life in McKeesport, just south of Pittsburgh, couldn't have been more different than her first seven years in peaceful, prosperous New Milford. McKeesport in 1920 was in the throes of a post–World War I depression, with steel mills shut down, hundreds of men out of work, and families homeless and hungry. Evidence of poverty was everywhere. Even if it were possible for a twelve-year-old bookworm to miss what was going on around her, Elizabeth was made directly aware of the problems of McKeesport when her mother began volunteering at a small, private relief agency in town. Every afternoon, Mary would come home weary and grim after a day of visiting tenements, listening to sad stories, and dispensing the little aid made available to the agency by local donors.

One evening she returned white-faced and shaken. She had spent the afternoon investigating conditions at a filthy tenement whose rickety stairs had collapsed and injured one of her clients. Back at the agency office, Mary discovered that the owner of the building was a leading citizen of the community, a wealthy man who sat on the executive board of the relief agency. With one hand, he had donated money to the agency. With the other, he had extracted rent payments for deplorable housing from families who could barely afford to feed themselves.

How could anyone be so greedy for money that they'd make it that way? Mary asked her daughter. A rock-ribbed Republican, Mary made a connection for Elizabeth that the girl would not forget: the greed of the wealthy tied to the poverty of the working class. But Mary was not a political person. She dealt with the problems she saw in quiet ways. She worked for the relief agency until it ran out of money. She invited people into her home to eat hot meals. She nursed the sick. Meanwhile, Elizabeth finished eighth grade in McKeesport, graduating first in her class and earning the top award, the Golden Eaglet, in Girl Scouts. She started high school, but at the end of her sophomore year, the family moved again, for the fourth time, to Rochester, New York.

In Rochester, Charles Bentley finally found a stable—and quite lucrative—position as general superintendent of McCurdy & Company, a large, fashionable, downtown department store. Mary took a job as an eighth grade teacher. The family moved to a new home on East Avenue in a respectable neighborhood south of downtown. All along East Avenue, a half-mile to the north, were the mansions of Rochester's elite. This is where George Eastman, of Kodak fame, lived. The Bentleys were not of this class, but Charles's new job meant they were living better than they ever had before. Elizabeth enrolled for her final two years in East High, a big, imposing school with a junior class larger than the entire eight grades of New Milford Central. It would have been easy for her to get lost there, a new girl, quiet and bookish, wandering the long corridors of the massive three-story building. But she made an effort to become involved in high school life. She played field hockey during her junior year and also joined the swimming and riding clubs. As a senior, she joined the Literary Club and worked on *The Orient,* the school's yearbook.

She tried hard, but she remained essentially a loner. She had a nick-name, "Terry," a playful, lighthearted name that belied the serious, almost dour young woman she had become. She stared out from her senior picture, her eyes guarded under heavy brows. Her dark brown hair hung short and straight. Her lips formed a thin, taut line. She looked both resolute and unhappy.

Partway through her senior year, Elizabeth decided to cut back on her extracurricular activities. She wanted to concentrate on academics, raise her already laudable grades so that she could qualify for a college scholarship. She wanted a good college education, one that would prepare her for a position teaching school, like her mother. She set her sights on Vassar, in Poughkeepsie, New York, an elite school with an elite price tag. Tuition and residence fees totaled $1,000 a year, a sum that exceeded the financial wherewithal of her parents, even with their respectable jobs. She studied hard her senior year, shunning both school activities and any social life she might have had. In the spring of 1926, the good news came. Vassar would award her a scholarship covering half her yearly expenses. She would enroll in the fall.

# Chapter 2

# Sad Sack

OUT OF THE one million babies born in 1908, it is the happy fate of 337 to attend Vassar [as the] class of 1930," the esteemed Professor Mills told Elizabeth Bentley and her classmates when they gathered in the college chapel for the fall 1926 convocation. The faculty took places in the choir, dressed in colorful academic robes. The senior class marched in procession to the side pews, in premature caps and gowns. The freshmen, wide-eyed and white-gloved, sat in front listening to the professor exhort them to live their lives not as "Flaming Youth"—a reference to the lurid, "Roaring Twenties" depiction of their generation—but as "youth aflame with zeal for all that is self-sacrificing, beautiful, noble, spiritual."

You are a privileged group, Professor Mills told the Vassar girls. And he was right. Few girls went to college those days, and fewer still were admitted to what was considered to be one of the country's most elite women's colleges, an institution that prided itself on delivering an education equal to the best of the men's Ivy League, a school that called its graduates "a breed apart." But with the privilege of going to Vassar, the professor was careful to remind them, came a great obligation, an obligation to live a meaningful life.

The college was a lovely, brick-and-ivy place. Just seventy-five miles north of Manhattan, it was in a rural, Hudson River Valley world of its own, with a graceful, grassy, old-fashioned campus established in the years before the Civil War. The library looked like an English cathedral. A number of the buildings, impressive, Elizabethan structures of brick and stone, were courtesy of Vassar's most famous and generous trustee, John D. Rockefeller. Although its reputation for rigorous intellectual pursuits was well established, Vassar was, in other ways, a typical aristocratic female academy, patrician, mannerly, and genteel, with rules and regulations, proscribed behavior, codes of etiquette. Every Thursday afternoon, from four to six, the president and his wife hosted a formal tea at their campus home for the freshman girls. Every evening after dinner, there was mandatory chapel. After seven, no girl could be seen in the company of a man unless the couple was escorted by an approved chaperone. There was no riding in cars, no smoking in public, no inappropriate dress, no indecorous behavior, no unladylike language. Yet under the surface, Vassar brimmed with female intrigue, intense friendships and intense rivalries, confidences sought and betrayed, shifting allegiances, competition and jealousy, relationships both platonic and otherwise. There was a rich emotional texture to life at Vassar for those who lived it fully.

College life meant rites and traditions, proms, plays and parades, grand marches, the selection of class trees, the ice carnival, Founder's Day, the passing of Chinese lanterns. In a popular spring ritual, twenty-four of the most popular girls, dressed in white heels, white pleated skirts, and long-sleeved white blouses, paraded across campus with a one hundred–foot garland of daisies draped over their shoulders. Vassar girls could participate in any number of activities from the drama club to the field hockey team, from the debate society to the birdwatching league. There were foreign-language clubs, political clubs, glee clubs. There were opportunities to write for the college newspaper, the college magazine, the yearbook. There were opportunities, every day for four years, for the girls of Vassar to build a close, female society, to form the friendships and the attitudes that would define the rest of their privileged lives.

Elizabeth Bentley started her life at Vassar in a room on the second floor of Lathrop House, one of a matched set of four dormitories built around a grassy quadrangle. Her room, a single, faced north away from the quad, away from campus and into the dark woods. The light coming through the windows was thin and weak. Elizabeth kept to herself. She made no close friends and shunned the rich mix of rituals and activities that made up campus life. She joined only one club during her four years at Vassar, and that for just a few months. She played no sports. She attended neither her junior nor her senior proms. She majored in English and minored in Italian, also taking a number of French classes. But if she spent her solitary time at Vassar studying, it was not reflected in her grades, which were steadfastly mediocre. Elizabeth Bentley, the scholarship student, the brainy girl who had graduated first in her eighth grade class, was a C-plus student at Vassar. At various points in her college career, she received Ds in English, Italian, and Latin. In studies as diverse as chemistry, history, and drama, she was a C student. She excelled at nothing.

The work was undoubtedly challenging, and competition from classmates at such an elite school could have been fierce and intimidating. But Elizabeth's lackluster performance at Vassar probably also had something to do with her general mental health, with the energy and enthusiasm she was unable to muster in living her everyday life. Perhaps her solitary, standoffish ways were a symptom of depression or maybe they were a result of it, but either way, she was not a happy person. At Lathrop House, she was known simply as "Bentley," probably a function of the fact that there were twenty-six Elizabeths in the class of 1930 but also perhaps an indication of the distance she kept from others. There would be no engaging nickname for her, as many of the girls had. She was, in the eyes of one of the other Elizabeths, a girl who lived across the hall from her during freshman year, a plain, dull, lonely girl, listless and pitiable, a sad sack who, the other Elizabeth was quick to point out, didn't have a single boyfriend.

But even Elizabeth Bentley, for all her reclusive ways, could not have been unaware of the maelstrom of provocative ideas circulating around Vassar in the late 1920s. Underneath its finishing-school veneer, with its teas and proms and daisy parades, Vassar was alive with the progressive ideas of the decade. College president Henry Noble McCracken, a liberal thinker and an ardent women suffragist, promoted the notion that political indifference was a "mental defect" and made sure that the intellectual foment of the time found full expression in the lecture halls on campus. During Elizabeth's freshman year, there were campus lectures on the Equal Rights Amendment, the World Union movement, and "Racial Understanding for Negroes." There were mass meetings to discuss world issues like the British coal strike and the China "situation." In her junior year, the president of the American Federation of Labor headlined a weeklong roster of "Economics Week" speakers. In her senior year, there were lectures by social critic Lewis Mumford, historian Will Durant, and Socialist Party presidential candidate Norman Thomas, who had also visited campus the year before Bentley enrolled. Civil rights leader W. E. B. Du Bois came to speak on racial segregation. Socialist and pacifist Scott Nearing lectured on Soviet Russia. And, amid the Granddaughters Club (open only to those girls whose mothers were Vassar graduates), Le Cercle Français (French Club), and the Classical Society (which featured productions by students of Greek and Latin) was the campus chapter of the League for Industrial Democracy (LID), a left-wing, reformist group whose motto was "production for use not for profit." The campus group, which was small but active, was home to student progressives, socialists and communists alike.

Although she felt no affinity to any particular left-wing party and did not consider herself a political person, Bentley joined the League. Its philosophy—that greed and profit-grabbing underlay much of the suffering of the world—was the view espoused by her own mother, the hard lesson Mrs. Bentley had learned working with the poor in McKeesport. This did not seem like radical or revolutionary thinking to Elizabeth. It was common sense. It was what her mother told her. But she quickly lost patience with the group's endless discussions of social ills. Everyone seemed to know what was wrong with the world, but no one knew what to do about it. She found her LID compatriots to be impractical dreamers with no plan, no goal, and no vision. Later, she would say that her years at Vassar had served to expose her to so many social injustices that she came away feeling that democracy had failed. She was, she said, left high and dry, not believing in anything.

But some who came to speak at Vassar did have a vision. They talked about what was considered by many forward-thinkers to be the greatest social experiment of the day, a political philosophy that redefined the individual, reordered society, and revolutionized everyday life. The Bolshevik Revolution was not even ten years old when Bentley started college, and both the causes of the uprising and its outcome were topics of intense interest and debate. Russian counts and barons came to Vassar to give talks about pre- and postrevolutionary education, philosophy, and legislation. Homegrown socialists touted the ultimate triumph of communism over capitalism. Three Vassar professors who had recently visited Russia came back to report improved education for peasants, improved conditions for factory workers, and, as Professor Drake told his youthful audience in the fall of 1928, "a seriousness of purpose, a widespread earnestness." To drama professor Hallie Flanagan, Russia was a living stage upon which a mighty social drama was being enacted. She called it a struggle against disease, dirt, poverty, and ignorance. More than anyone else at Vassar, Hallie Flanagan was a true believer. She opened many eyes at Vassar, including those of Elizabeth Bentley.

Hallie Flanagan was a four-foot-eight-inch dynamo with dark wavy hair, intense eyes, and a soft, pretty face. President McCracken, who hired her away from Grinnell College where she had been developing an experimental theater program, called her a "pocket Venus." She had graduated Phi Beta Kappa from Grinnell, received a master's degree in drama from Radcliffe, and, at the time she was hired in 1925, was considered a bright and rising star. A dynamic speaker with a charismatic personality, a woman who always had something interesting to say and was never afraid to say it, she broke creative and curricular barriers at Vassar and quickly became a campus cult figure. In the spring of her first year at Vassar, while busy revamping the drama department, she learned she was the first female recipient of a Guggenheim Foundation grant that would fund a yearlong study of European theater. She left that fall, Bentley's freshman year, and, after a tour of western Europe, spent time studying the productions of the Moscow Art Theater and Riga Experimental Theater. When she returned to campus, it was with revolutionary ideas in both theater and politics, and with enormous and contagious enthusiasm about the Soviet Union.

Hallie Flanagan became a one-woman political movement at Vassar, writing and producing plays about labor, poverty, free speech, and fascism, and gathering around her a group of similarly committed students who called themselves "Hallie's Girls." Inspired by their teacher, Hallie's Girls were involved in most of the left-wing causes that found expression on campus. Elizabeth Bentley, the perennial wallflower, watched from the wings. She wasn't one of Hallie's Girls, but she took Dramatic Production from Professor Flanagan and was so taken with Hallie's stories of Russia that she wanted to go abroad and see for herself. In the meantime, she enrolled in two more drama classes.

In the spring of her junior year, Bentley received word that her mother had suddenly taken ill. Mary was rushed to Genesee Hospital in Rochester, New York, in great pain, unable to keep down food and running a high fever. The doctors diagnosed her with peritonitis, a severe and life-threatening bacterial infection generally caused by a tear somewhere in the gut. On March 25, when she underwent exploratory abdominal surgery, the reason for the peritonitis became clear. Mary Bentley had late-stage intestinal cancer. The tumor had perforated her intestines. She died a week later, four months shy of her fifty-second birthday.

The Bentleys were not an emotionally demonstrative family. Still, Elizabeth must have been devastated by her mother's sudden and untimely death. If she was close to anyone, she was close to her mother, the woman after whom she modeled herself, the woman who had imbued her with a social conscience, the woman to whom she owed her love of learning and her desire to teach. The dutiful daughter returned to Vassar after the funeral, throwing herself into her schoolwork as never before. Except for a C in chemistry, her grades were all Bs that term, the best she had ever done, the best she would ever do. All around her, Vassar bustled with activity, but Bentley ignored it all, distancing herself both from the excitement of college life and the intimacy of female friendship. Now her class, nearing graduation, was abuzz with talk of love affairs, of who was engaged to whom. There was, in fact, an epidemic of engagements, for a good marriage was what naturally, seamlessly followed a good education for these young women of Vassar. But Elizabeth had no fiancé, no boyfriend, no marriage prospects.

After graduation, she went on a musical tour of Europe conducted by one of her Vassar professors. The group visited England, France, Germany, and Italy, going to concerts, plays, and museums, experiencing the language and culture and history the young women had learned in the classroom. It was the perfect, fashionable way to polish off a quality education. But to Elizabeth Bentley, it was something more. It was a revelation. On the voyage to Europe, she had her first romance, a shipboard fling with a British engineer. It was almost as if she couldn't wait a moment longer to lose her innocence, to begin experiencing the emotionally charged world from which she had kept herself so distant. A thousand miles at sea, a thousand miles from her New England upbringing, she could dare to be something different from the woman she had been brought up to be.

Touring Europe, and especially Italy, the country whose language she loved and had studied for four years, she was awakened to the possibilities of her own life. Rome was thrilling. Florence was magnificent. The music was big and lush, the sights and smells intense and intensely felt. For a New England girl who had spent the last four years in a Vassar dormitory, it was a wild, wonderfully unsettling experience. Her depression lifted. When the time came to leave, she did so regretfully. She did so knowing that she would find a way to come back. But for now, she had a job waiting back in the States, exactly the kind of position for which she was trained. She would teach English, French, and Italian at Foxcroft, an aristocratic girls' boarding school in Virginia.

# Chapter 3

# Awakenings

FOXCROFT, WHERE ELIZABETH Bentley began teaching in the fall of 1930, was one of those small, exclusive boarding schools to which the well-heeled sent their well-bred daughters. Nestled in the hills of Virginia among the old-money horse farms and ample country estates of the gentry, the school was a world of its own, more than four thousand manicured acres of orchards, fields, and farmlands through which flowed a tributary of the Potomac. Foxcroft enrolled eighty very privileged young ladies of high school age, a significant number of whom brought with them their own horses. The riding program was reputed to be one of the best in the country. But Foxcroft considered itself more than an elite finishing school. It was a serious college preparatory academy that offered a number of courses in Elizabeth Bentley's specialties. It was just the place for a blue-blood from Vassar. In fact, schools like Foxcroft were where those Vassar girls who had to work ended up working.

But after her experiences abroad, after the freedom of travel and the awakening of her independence, and especially after her shipboard fling, it was difficult for Bentley to fit back into the cloistered, girls-school life. Like all unmarried teachers at Foxcroft, she was required to live in the student dormitory, in a small faculty apartment. She was expected not only to teach but also, by her presence on campus, to be a twenty-four-hour-a-day example for the girls, comporting herself in the genteel manner that would be expected in the upper-class circles from which her students came. Miss Bentley did her job well and even put her Vassar drama class experience to work acting in a faculty production of *Robin Hood*. She played the venal Guy of Gisbourne, the corrupt nobleman who crossed swords with Robin Hood and was, later in the play and much to the delight of the Foxcroft audience, stuffed into a chest by Friar Tuck. "Miss Charlotte," founder of Foxcroft and headmistress, played the part of Friar Tuck, with the aid of a number of pillows and a clown's red nose.

Charlotte Haxall Noland had founded the school on the values of determination, courage, and character. The possibilities before you, Miss Charlotte used to say, are measured by the determination within you. Miss Bentley, the English, Italian, and French teacher, had seen those possibilities and was determined to go after them. After her first year teaching, she returned to Europe in the summer of 1931. Her desire to go back was cloaked in academic terms—she would study Italian at the University of Perugia—but it was still desire. In Europe, she was free to be, she would give herself permission to be, another kind of woman entirely. In Europe, on her own, she could take up where she left off the summer before. She did study in Perugia. She was serious about furthering her education. But she was hungry for something more. That summer she lived with a Hungarian army officer who was stationed in Italy. He was an older man, a man with a rich and unknowable past, which she undoubtedly found thrilling in that way a young woman of twenty-three would. And he was, on top of that, a European, with European manners and an accent she must have found charming. He was an experience she had to have. When fall came, the Elizabeth Bentley who left to teach once again at Foxcroft was a woman of the world.

Her second year in Virginia passed uneventfully. She was grateful to have a job in increasingly tough economic times. She needed the work. Unlike for many of her former classmates at Vassar, for her employment was not a hobby; it was a necessity. But the lovely little upper-crust school was a little too lovely, a little too insular for the person she was becoming. She would have to break away, take her career in hand, perhaps aim for something with more freedom and more possibilities, like a position on a university faculty. In the summer of 1932, she began studying for her master's degree in Italian at Middlebury College in Vermont. That fall, instead of returning to Foxcroft, she moved to Manhattan and enrolled at Columbia University, where she continued her studies full-time. Her father died the following spring, leaving her a small sum of money that helped to pay tuition bills. But she had hardly settled into the graduate program when she started applying for several scholarships to study abroad. Of course, it made sense to go back to Italy. She would be surrounded by the culture and the language, which was the best environment in which to pursue her graduate studies. But she knew a trip to Europe would offer considerably more than academic opportunities. In the spring, Bentley was delighted to learn that she had been offered funding to either return to the University of Perugia or study for a year at the University of Florence. She chose Florence, where she was one of four exchange students sponsored by the Institute of International Education.

Once again, as she hoped it would, as she *knew* it would, Italy transformed her. Miss Bentley, the erstwhile prim and proper New Englander, lunged at the opportunity to live a life unfettered by either past or pedigree. She drank heavily. She enjoyed numerous liaisons. She was rumored to have seduced one of her professors. Among the other Americans studying in Florence, she was known as wild and promiscuous, a naughty young woman with a sometimes foul mouth. She was having fun at a breakneck pace.

But she was also experiencing firsthand what it was like to live under fascist rule. Mussolini's control not only of politics, but also of education, the press, health care, even family life, was extraordinary. A little more than a decade before, Il Duce's black-shirted squads had come to power by raiding the political headquarters of his opponents, destroying trade union offices, torching cooperatives, smashing left-wing presses, assaulting socialists with brass knuckles, and force-feeding communists castor oil. Now *fascismo* ruled, and Mussolini maintained control by encouraging violence, suppressing civil liberties, and imprisoning people without trial. No newspaper dared criticize his increasingly harsh policies. Free elections disappeared. Voters were given color-coded ballots so that poll-watchers could monitor how each person voted. Schoolchildren were required to use state-issued notebooks decorated with fascist cartoons and slogans.

Men who had not fathered children were taxed for their "celibacy" because Mussolini wanted big families to build national strength. On the first official Mother's Day in 1933, Il Duce himself presided over a national rally in Rome during which the most reproductively prolific mothers from each of Italy's provinces were paraded before the crowd as the number of their live births was announced to all. As an American university student, Bentley was undoubtedly insulated from many of the direct excesses of fascist rule. She even joined a university students' fascist group, not out of any ideological affinity with the repressive regime, but because it was a way to secure various discounts and privileges—another of Mussolini's successful attempts to control young people. Bentley was no fascist. On the contrary, she was deeply affected by the mood of the country and by what she saw around her in the streets every day.

In between her political and sexual awakenings, Bentley managed to finish writing her master's thesis, an analysis of a fourteenth-century poem, early in the summer of 1934. Her faculty adviser at Columbia thought it was a sophisticated piece of work—maybe a little *too* sophisticated, a little too intellectually mature for a graduate student. He wondered if she had had special help writing it, perhaps from one of her Italian professors.

In July of 1934, with her year of funded study over and her meager personal finances depleted, Bentley boarded the SS *Vulcania* and headed home to New York. She had a semester of work left to complete her master's degree, and she would have to find some kind of employment, and quickly, in order to support herself and pay tuition. But there could not have been a worse time to come home. America was reeling from the full force of the Great Depression, with more people out of work—20 million in 1933—than at any other time in U.S. history. In New York City alone, 650,000 people were unemployed. In the Help Wanted section of the Sunday *New York Times* that summer, the summer Bentley was hunting for work, the prospects were dim. She could read through the section faster than she could gulp down a cup of lukewarm coffee. Most of the jobs advertised were for maids. There were a few postings for department store models, and a few more for office stenographers.

Elizabeth Bentley was a teacher with a diploma from a prestigious college, an almost completed master's degree, a year of study abroad, and two years of classroom experience at an elite academy. But in New York, in the mid-1930s, those credentials didn't get you anywhere. The only teaching job listed in one Sunday *Times* that summer called for an instructor of shorthand and typing. Otherwise, employment possibilities for teachers were nil. More than a hundred candidates for public-school teaching jobs—some of whom had been on a waiting list for four years—had marched on City Hall that winter in an attempt to plead their case to Mayor Fiorello La Guardia. He sent out an underling to deal with them. Now it looked as if three hundred or more teachers would be laid off by the city in a money-saving consolidation move.

The city was spending more than six million dollars a month on relief efforts, but hundreds of thousands were still jobless, homeless, and hungry. Three-quarters of a million New Yorkers were living on relief payments that averaged $8.20 a month, about a fifth of what it took to feed and house a person in those days. And things were getting worse. The city was running out of money—the crooked Tammany machine was siphoning off federal funds faster than Washington could send them—and was unable to make a tenth of the contribution to relief work that was required. During the summer of 1934, the city cut its contribution by almost half a million dollars and threw more than six thousand relief workers out of work. All along Riverside Drive, crowded on a narrow strip of park by the Hudson, was the city's Hooverville: hundreds of shacks made of oil barrels, scrap lumber, corrugated tin, and cardboard. Beggars lined the streets. People were desperate. Two young men applying for work with the city collapsed from hunger in the mayor's reception room at City Hall. Earlier that day, a woman, disheveled and tearful, had lapsed into hysteria in the stairwell. She had come to see the mayor about getting food and coal for her family. Her children had been cold and hungry for three weeks. Armies of the homeless and the jobless took to the streets carrying placards that read FIGHT OR STARVE. It was a grim and miserable time.

Jobless and broke, Elizabeth Bentley, like so many others, was desperate. But she kept her head. She had to. No one was going to step in and rescue her. She had to come up with a plan, and she did. That fall she enrolled in business classes at Columbia to learn how to type and take shorthand, hoping that she might be able to land part-time secretarial work. She was angry that all her education had come to this and saddened that the dreams she had for herself now looked so unattainable. And she was scared. She had no idea how she could manage to pay next month's rent, let alone that night's dinner. With the fear and anger came something even more difficult to handle: loneliness. Both her parents were dead. She had no close friends and little social life. That may not have bothered her a few years before at Vassar, but now that she had experienced excitement and romance, now that she knew how it felt to be fully involved in life, she was, by contrast, lonelier than she'd ever been.

She was also stunned by the conditions around her, aghast at how people were being forced to live. Every day there were more tragedies reported in the newspapers, more hungry children, more desperate mothers, more out-of-work men, more misery, less help, less hope. It reminded her of the poor families her mother had tried to help in Pennsylvania when she was just a girl. Why were so many people starving and homeless? Her mother had told her it was because the wealthy were so greedy. Maybe she was right. Certainly it seemed to liberals of that generation that the great American experiment had failed, that capitalism itself had failed.

Scott Nearing, who had lectured at Vassar when Bentley was a student there, wrote a powerful, argumentative book in 1932 called *Must We Starve?* In it, he presented a point of view becoming increasingly popular—that the current economic system could not and should not be saved. The future of capitalism, Nearing wrote and so many others believed, was just more frequent and more severe periods of hardship. The Depression was the death agony of an entire social system. But there was a way out of this disaster—*one* way out, as Nearing titled the final chapter of his book—and that way was a revolution by the working class followed by a planned socialist economy. It was the way being forged by the Soviet Union. It was a radical idea, a revolutionary idea, but somehow, in the mid-1930s, in the throes of the Depression, it didn't seem all that radical. The American dream was vaporizing. Critics of the system had never sounded more persuasive. Good-hearted liberals, just a tick left of center, found it possible to read Marx and Lenin and believe they were right.

Elizabeth Bentley was not politically savvy enough to argue the fine points, but she knew what she saw, and she knew what she felt: Something was very wrong in America. Her social conscience, piqued when she was a child, nourished at Vassar, and reawakened in Mussolini's Italy, was now aroused by the conditions around her. The Depression opened her eyes. It was for her, as it was for many of her generation, a clarifying experience, a crucible. But for Bentley, the Depression was more backdrop than direct motivation. She was neither an activist nor a joiner. In truth, it was her own condition that worried her most.

Her future was murky, and not just because of the Depression, not just because she couldn't find a job. It was because she had strayed from the path, because the direction she had been headed—from New Milford to Vassar to Europe to Foxcroft—was no longer the direction she *was* headed. The Depression made it impossible for her to resume the life she had been brought up and educated to lead.

But she had strayed from that path before the Depression blocked her way. After the year in Europe, she could not have resumed her old life, even if it had been possible to do so. There was something in her, something that craved a different kind of life, a part of her that seemed more than ready to flout the values and traditions of her upbringing. There was something in her that was restless and reckless and needy.

# Chapter 4

# Circle of Friends

ELIZABETH BENTLEY FOUND accommodations in a cheap rooming-house on the Upper West Side, just a few blocks from Columbia University where she was dutifully and unhappily enrolled in secretarial courses. In six months, she would have the skills to apply for an office job—if she could find one—a prospect she, a twenty-six-year-old Vassar grad only a term away from a master's degree, did not relish. But it was work, and she needed to support herself. The only bright spot that fall was her growing friendship with a woman who lived down the hall.

Lee Fuhr was a nurse taking courses at Columbia's Teachers College. She had grown up poor and had lived a tough life, working in cotton mills to make enough money for school, weathering the death of her husband while she was pregnant with their child, and now struggling to support the both of them as she continued her education. Bentley did not make friends easily, or even try to, but it was more than she could bear, sitting alone in her shabbily furnished room thinking about her uncertain and downwardly mobile future.

And there was something about Fuhr that drew her in. Her new friend had a definite goal in life and was headed toward it with a sense of purpose Bentley herself no longer felt. Fuhr was tough but not toughened. For all her bad luck and difficult circumstances, she was not embittered. She was not cynical. She would always tell Bentley that although things were bad today, the future would be different. How? Bentley would ask her as they shared a cheap, hot-plate meal together. Fuhr would just smile.

As their friendship progressed, Bentley told Fuhr about her year in Italy under fascism, about what it was like to live in a totalitarian state with liberties curtailed and the threat of violence ever present. Bentley was afraid—many people were afraid—that America was headed in that same direction. The Depression was breeding deep unrest. There was an army of unemployed out there, hungry and angry and increasingly desperate. They were living on the streets. They were gathering in front of City Hall. They were marching on the mayor's mansion. Homeless, jobless, hopeless, they had nothing to lose. It was not difficult to imagine that soon there would be chaos in the city and that martial law would follow. And then, Bentley told her new friend, we wouldn't be far from what was happening in Italy. Fuhr listened with great interest. She too most emphatically saw fascism as ugly and dangerous, a threat to both individual freedom and international peace. In fact, she was a member of a relatively new group called the American League Against War and Fascism. Would Bentley like to come to the next meeting? She could find out what the organization was doing to prevent fascism from coming to the United States.

Bentley had never heard of the League, but when Fuhr listed for her some of its more illustrious members—a roster that included Sherwood Anderson, Theodore Dreiser, Reinhold Niebuhr, and a number of other writers, religious leaders, and university professors—she was impressed. These were intelligent, thoughtful people who wrestled with big ideas in their work. If they thought enough of the league to join, then surely she should go see what it was all about.

One night that fall, Fuhr took her to a meeting of the League chapter that had been formed by students and professors at Teachers

College. Bentley was immediately taken with the energy and hope she found there. The members seemed smart and articulate, passionate about politics, somehow both clear-eyed about the present and optimistic about the future. They believed in something. They had spirit in spiritless times. She went to another meeting, and another. She felt her own discouragement ebb in the face of such enthusiasm and fervor.

Fuhr suggested that she might get more involved by helping the league with research on Italian fascism. She could do volunteer work at the League's Manhattan headquarters, located in a loft on lower Fourth Avenue. Bentley decided to give it a try. But when she walked up the three flights of rickety wooden stairs and into the office, with its battered furniture, bare light bulbs hanging from the ceiling, and windows so grimy you could hardly see out of them, she almost turned around and walked out. A young man spotted her. "Come on in," he said, "and don't mind the mess. We don't have money to spend on fancy fronts."

His name was Harold Patch, one of the editors of the League's publication, *Fight*. He was immediately assigned to take Bentley under his wing. He was a voluble, enthusiastic soul who, despite being a few years younger than Bentley, had a long history of political activism. He told her he had been an anarchist and a socialist and had once belonged to the American Association for the Advancement of Atheism. Bentley thought he was a curious character—shabbily dressed, with rarely enough money to buy proper food, but full of good humor and high spirits. She liked him. She liked being around the office with its oddly engaging atmosphere, simultaneously casual and intense, financially impoverished but intellectually rich. She started showing up regularly, doing whatever needed to be done. Soon she joined the League and began attending weekly chapter meetings.

What she found in the organization was not just a group of young intellectuals who hated fascism as much as she did but also a warm and hospitable circle of friends. They were unpretentious, generous, and kind. They were easy and relaxed with one another, dropping by each other's apartments, going to the movies together, going out for coffee. She was drawn to them, but at the same time, she couldn't quite figure them out. They appeared to lack the usual prejudices—racial, religious, and economic. In the midst of their own poverty and the despair around them, they seemed to have found an inner sureness. They seemed to have an anchor where she had lost her moorings. She didn't know what their secret was, how they managed to find so much to be hopeful about, but she did know that the more time she spent with her league friends, the less despondent she became. The busier she was with League activities, the more she forgot about her own problems. Bentley was alternately irritated by and envious of her new friends. She was also never happier.

What she didn't know was that the sense of purpose and sense of certainty she perceived in Fuhr and Patch and many of the others came not just from their commitment to antifascism. It came from their attachment to a much larger, grander, more encompassing ideology. Although many in the League were antifascist liberals deeply concerned with what was happening in Germany and Italy, those who controlled the organization were something more. They believed not just in liberal causes but in radical ideas. They believed in a classless society, in a worker-run state in which the means of production were owned by the people. They believed most fervently in the social and political experiment they saw unfolding in the Soviet Union. The league was, in fact, a communist front, an organization set up by the Communist Party to draw good liberals into the revolutionary cause. But Bentley didn't know this in the winter of 1935. If she had any reservation about the League at all, it was, ironically, that the organization seemed to have a very definite program *against* war and fascism but was rather vague about what it stood *for*. She was thinking seriously about politics for the first time in her life and seeing her neighbor Lee Fuhr more often these days. Invariably, their conversations turned to the economic disaster they were living through.

"There's no use trying to kid ourselves that conditions in this country are good," Fuhr told her one night after they had eaten dinner together. "Our economic setup is rotten clear through . . . But I don't need to tell you that. You seem to know already."

Bentley did know. Or thought she knew. She read the papers. She saw the beggars on the streets. She remembered vividly the victims of an earlier economic depression, the starving families in McKeesport. Now she was the one out of work. She was the one living close to the bone in a little room in a bad neighborhood.

"But it's not a hopeless situation," Fuhr told her. If we can ward off fascism, she said, we may be able to evolve into a good, equitable society where everyone is guaranteed the essentials for a decent life. Bentley thought that sounded just fine, but she saw it as impractical. Greed would get in the way, she told Fuhr. As long as men were greedy, there would be social injustice. But Fuhr disagreed: Greed was *not* an essential part of human nature, she said, it was a by-product of the profit motive.

"That's the trouble with our present civilization," she told Bentley. "People have been taught to work only to accumulate money for themselves, without regard to the welfare of their neighbor." Why not, she asked, eliminate the profit motive? Why not produce for use and not for profit? It can work, she said. Bentley was dubious. It went against what she knew, or thought she knew, about human nature. It was a fine dream. But that's all it was.

But Fuhr insisted it was no dream. This is what they're doing right now in the Soviet Union, she told her.

Elizabeth Bentley was a woman with a social conscience. Her ancestors may have been Puritans, her family may have been rock-ribbed Republicans, but she was—the times had made her—a liberal. She wanted to believe that it was possible to build a society without greed, without poverty, without starvation, without the terrible inequities she saw around her. She listened to Lee Fuhr, and she remembered Hallie Flanagan's enthusiasm about Russia. Maybe this kind of society *was* possible. Perhaps, she said to Fuhr, the League can become the center of a movement to work toward a new society.

Fuhr said she didn't think so. The League was too big and unwieldy. Its organization was too loose. What was needed, she told her friend, was a core group of well-trained, well-disciplined people, people with energy and vision and commitment who would be in it for the long haul.

"But where are you going to find such a group?" Bentley asked.

"You don't have to find them," Fuhr told her. "They already exist." They're the communists, she said, the ones who will rally around them the progressive forces and lead them to a new society. I am one of them, she told Bentley. I am a communist.

So was, Bentley came to learn, her friend Harold Patch. So were many of the league members she most admired. And maybe, she began to think, so am I. After all, she seemed to agree with just about everything Fuhr said. Fuhr had lived a life of poverty. She had worked in the mills. She knew what she was talking about. Bentley understood now what buoyed Fuhr's spirits, what gave meaning and direction to her life. It was her friend's faith in communism. Bentley wanted to have faith in something.

If you believe in equality, if you believe in full employment and an end to poverty, then you're one of us, Fuhr told her. And if you're one of us, you ought to join the party. Bentley felt instinctively that her friend was right. Everything she learned about the party through Fuhr made sense. The party understood the threat of fascism and stood squarely against it. In fact, Georgi Dimitrov, head of the Comintern, the directing body for communist parties worldwide, was just about to proclaim a "popular front" against fascism. With Hitler and Mussolini on the rise, and the United States and other democracies otherwise occupied struggling with the devastating effects of the Depression, it looked as if the communists were the only bulwark against fascism. That was important to Bentley, very important. Through the late-night talks with Fuhr, she was coming to believe that communism stood for what she stood for: a decent education, a decent job, a decent chance for all. Fuhr and her league friends, unlike the muddle-headed, ineffectual liberals Bentley saw around her, were people who seemed to know where they were going and seemed to know how to get there. In these dark and confusing days, the people she now knew to be communists were the ones speaking with power and moral imagination.

But not all her thoughts that long winter were logical—or ideological. She was also caught up in a maelstrom of emotions. She was living, untethered and alone, through frightening and confusing times. She had no work to believe in, no career to which to devote herself, no family. She had long ago turned away from the Episcopal church of her childhood because she saw little connection between the well-rehearsed sermons of well-fed ministers and the tenets of Christian brotherhood her mother had taught her. So she had no religion to fall back on, no spiritual home to come home to. Maybe the party could be that home with the tenets of communism providing a scripture to live by. Communism could provide that meaning she was searching for, that something-bigger-than-herself to believe in. The emotional and psychological appeal of communism was particularly powerful for rudderless people like Elizabeth Bentley. It was an anchor for those adrift, a place of healing for the wounded, a family for the lonely, a home for the homeless. It was where an unemployed and powerless nobody could become a somebody.

For Bentley, there was yet another attraction, although she might not have admitted it to herself. There was the risk. Joining the party would be a daring venture, like going off to Europe for a year, like taking a lover. There was an excitement to it, a kind of titillation. Lee Fuhr had asked her months ago not to tell anyone else that she was a party member. She was not ashamed, she said, but she wanted to keep her affiliation secret. Communists were really just people with well-developed social consciences, she told Bentley, but they were not in good standing in this country. People seem to think we're bomb-toting terrorists, Fuhr said. But of course, we're not.

The disreputable image of communism may have appealed to Bentley's risk-taking side, but it may also have been the reason she found herself reluctant to take the plunge. Whatever else it was, membership in the Communist Party was a long way from membership in the Daughters of the American Revolution, a long way from a girlhood in New Milford, and a long way from the manicured lawns of Foxcroft. She turned twenty-seven that January, but she felt no wiser about herself, no surer about where she was headed. Maybe I am just a hypocrite, she thought. I believe, but I don't have the courage of my convictions. The more she waffled, the more she doubted herself.

"I thought you said that you had a New England conscience," Fuhr said to her one night. It was an accusation, not a statement.

Bentley heard the contempt in Fuhr's voice and was stung by it. The two had been meeting and talking for months, Fuhr full of energy, full of good words to say about the party, Elizabeth alternately enthused and hesitant. Now Fuhr was losing patience. "If you have a conscience, it ought to be bothering you pretty badly right now," she said. Then she left Bentley's room, slamming the door behind her.

Fuhr had moved out of the rooming-house and taken a cheap walk-up apartment on West 124th Street just off Amsterdam Avenue. Bentley visited her there many times as she continued to struggle with whether to join the party. Sometimes Fuhr would be friendly and talkative, discussing politics and the party with equal enthusiasm. But other times, it seemed as if her friend had given up on her. Increasingly, she was testy or annoyed, or silent. Perhaps as much as Bentley felt twinges of conscience, she also felt the removal of Lee Fuhr's friendly affection. Having a close friend, having a social life, was new to Bentley, but she had gotten used to it quickly. The relationship with Fuhr had sustained her through the dispiriting winter, but now it looked as if that friendship was contingent on Bentley joining the party.

She had many reasons to join. But ultimately, what caused her to walk over to Lee Fuhr's apartment one gray Tuesday afternoon in March of 1935 and sign her name to the party application was simple despair. She had just returned from yet another fruitless job search and was sitting in a chair in her room, staring out at the bare trees on Riverside Drive. It was a bleak day. The calendar said spring, but there was a raw wind off the river, and the skies were iron gray. Bentley sat there, stiff-backed, feeling sorry for herself. How many times had she gone over the same thing in her head: how unhappy she was that she was living in a little rented room, how unhappy she was that she couldn't find a teaching job, how unhappy she was that she was taking secretarial classes, how unhappy she was with her life. I am part of the "lost" Depression generation, she thought to herself. There will never be any great personal future for me. And now, on top of it all, her only friend thought she was spineless, that she didn't have courage enough to stand up for her convictions.

She thought of Fuhr's apartment a few blocks away. It was warm and friendly there when the living room was full of league and party comrades. It was a hedge against despair, a reason to keep caring. Fuhr had said Bentley would never be happy until she acted on her beliefs, until she stopped talking and started doing. That day in March, that afternoon, Bentley felt keenly that her friend was right. She had to *do* something. She had to do *something*. The party was the place for her. She grabbed her hat and coat and hurried over to Fuhr's apartment.

That evening, Elizabeth Turrill Bentley joined the Communist Party of the United States of America. She used the name Elizabeth Sherman. It was, she told Fuhr, to honor her colonial American ancestor. Lee Fuhr held out her hand warmly.

"Welcome to our ranks, comrade," she said.

# Chapter 5

# A Steeled Bolshevik

TENS OF THOUSANDS of professionals, artists, and intellectuals joined the Communist Party along with Elizabeth Bentley during its "Popular Front" heyday. The party was never more moderate, never less revolutionary than it was in the mid- and late 1930s when it publicly and earnestly embraced FDR and the New Deal. Like many of the mainstream reformers and progressives it attracted in those Depression-haunted days, the party stood for full employment and strong unions. Like most Americans, it stood against fascism abroad and discrimination at home. Popular Front communism was a far cry from the fiery Bolshevik sentiments of the early days, when American communists issued statements like this 1919 screed: "To hell with the teachings of peaceful revolution. The bloody seizure of power by the working classes is the only possible way."

But by the mid-1930s, communists in America espoused a progressive agenda that opened the door to alliances with liberals and progressives. In fact, the party was becoming a significant political force in a half dozen states, including New York, Wisconsin, and California. Even the news from the Soviet Union was temperate and upbeat. Stalin, wrote a party member in 1935, was directing "the building of Socialism in a manner to create a rich, colorful, many-sided cultural life among hundreds of nationalities . . . united in common work for a beautiful future." Most American communists had no idea that millions had already died during Stalin's collectivization of agriculture in the early 1930s and that millions more were dying as a result of his unending purges. What they did know was that the party said it stood for social justice for all, that the party was a bulwark against Hitler and Mussolini. Many believed that the communism was, as it was publicly proclaiming to be, "just twentieth-century Americanism."

During the Popular Front of the late 1930s, party membership in the United States tripled, reaching an all-time high of a hundred thousand by the end of the decade. But even more startling than the increase in members was the transformation of the membership. For the first time, native-born Americans like Bentley outnumbered the foreign-born members who had been the party's backbone. In 1919, when the Communist Party—actually two competing parties—was founded in the United States, fewer than ten percent of its thirty-four thousand members even spoke English. Most of these new communists were recent immigrants from Czarist Russia. Many of the others were the children of Eastern European Jews who had grown up poor and on the ragged fringe of American society. But now communism was, ironically, acquiring a middle-class patina. Well-educated, assimilated Americans, especially idealistic—and unemployed—young people were flocking to the party in record numbers.

Bentley attended her first communist cell meeting the same night she signed her application at Lee Fuhr's apartment. Fuhr had scribbled an address on a slip of paper. "We meet at different comrades' homes," she told Bentley. "We change every week to ensure that no outsiders get in." That Tuesday night the meeting was in a sixth-floor walk-up on West 123rd Street just off Broadway. At eight P.M.

Bentley knocked on the door of the apartment. She could hear voices within, then silence. The door opened a crack. A short, stocky man stuck his head out.

"Yes?" he said, looking her over.

Bentley was nervous, almost giddy from her first brush with the clandestine. This is just like a speakeasy in the Prohibition days, she thought. It crossed her mind to answer: "Charlie sent me." Instead, she said, "Lee told me to come here."

The man smiled and opened the door wide. "Come on in," he said.

The small living room was packed with more than two dozen members of Unit 1 of the Harlem section. They were perched on windowsills, sprawled on the arms of chairs, sitting cross-legged on the floor. A comrade stood up to give her his seat. She walked across the room, trying not to feel too self-conscious. There was really no reason to. Everyone was focused on the meeting. There was a lengthy discussion of world news and the presentation of earnest reports; there were debates, analyses, arguments, strategy sessions, self-criticism sessions, the airing of grievances. The meeting was four hours long, and Bentley sat through it all, transfixed. She was impressed with how organized they were, how articulate, how knowledgeable. She was even more impressed that the chairman of the group, which included Columbia professors and graduate students, was a food worker in one of the dormitory cafeterias. Past midnight, after the meeting broke up, she went out with a group of comrades to a nearby diner where they smoked cigarettes, drank coffee, and talked politics for hours. She was exhausted and exhilarated. Will I ever have their energy? she wondered. Will I ever be able to live up to their standards?

At another meeting a few weeks later, an eight-hour marathon that lasted until four A.M., she listened as member after member criticized a certain comrade Land, one of the old standbys in the party. He was not shouldering his fair burden. He was difficult to work with. He was accused of calling one organizer an "idiot" and another a "numbskull." That night no one had anything good to say about him. Bentley watched as the man sank deeper and deeper into his chair, eyes downcast, shamed by his comrades. The unit voted unanimously to expel him. But then the chairman stood up and said that Land should be given a chance to rehabilitate himself. Another vote was taken. It was, again, unanimous. Land would get a second chance. Bentley was struck by this whole episode. She was impressed with the application of party discipline. These people were serious about themselves and their work. She marveled at the detachment of the criticism. There was no yelling, no name-calling, no rancor. And then, when the chairman said Land ought to have a second chance . . . wasn't that the epitome of compassion? Didn't it show how much the party cared about its members? She was more convinced than ever that this was the place for her.

Almost overnight, she went from attending one meeting a week to four. There were lunches at the Columbia cafeteria, unit meetings, unit bureau meetings, weekly parties for fund-raising and recruiting. She started taking an active role in her unit, serving variously as financial secretary, educational director, organizer, and agitprop officer. As financial secretary, she collected party dues, kept the books for the unit, and went to an extra meeting a week. As the agitprop officer, she spent her evenings poring over stacks of party literature— pamphlets, brochures, special reports—reading the *Daily Worker,* front to back, every day, and preparing summaries for the unit. That position also meant another meeting each week. And she participated in what were considered the "usual activities": walking picket lines, helping out during strikes, carrying banners in parades, attending protests and demonstrations where she linked arms with comrades and sang "The Internationale."

She was told that she must "study incessantly" and "had a long way to go." She was sure that was true. I can't very well be a communist without knowing in detail just what it stands for, she told herself. So, soon after joining the party, she began taking courses in Marxist political economy and the philosophy of communist theory at the Communist Workers School, located in the same down-at-the-heels building on East 13th Street that housed the party's national and district offices and its official bookstore. She signed up for her first class under an alias, which was standard practice in the party. Cloaked identities, secret meeting places, coded phone messages, special knocks—they were all a part of this new world. Bentley was late to class that first evening. Attendance had already been taken, and the teacher had begun to talk when she tiptoed into the room and found a vacant seat in the front row. The teacher paused, scanned his class list, and looked down at her.

"What's your name, Comrade?" he asked.

She hesitated. She was nervous and rattled, and couldn't remember the alias she had used. "I don't know, Comrade Professor," she stammered.

The classroom erupted in laughter. It was an absurd remark, but they all knew exactly what she meant. They were all new to this clandestine life.

Bentley was impressed with the school. The teachers were friendly and helpful. They didn't lecture at you; they led spirited discussions. The students were eager and enthusiastic. Most worked hard all day, but they still filled the classroom with energy and passion in the evening. By the end of the first course, she felt she understood history better than she ever had before, and she had no doubt that the Marxist-Leninist interpretation was correct.

Although she had labored over her decision to join the party for months, once she took the plunge, she dove deep. Lenin had written that men and women must devote "not merely their spare evenings, but the whole of their lives" to the cause. And that's what Elizabeth Bentley was beginning to do. The new world she found herself in was bracing, and all-embracing. Life was full, a whirl of activity, an almost feverish busyness. It was a heady change, this transformation from the futility of searching for a job to the utility of making plans to save the world, from inertia to action, from loneliness to instant camaraderie. There was no time to doubt. There was no time to feel sorry for herself. There was, however, time to enjoy the forbidden fruits of radicalism.

Drinking, profane talk, and "loose morals" were seen as positive steps toward breaking the bourgeois code of behavior, making for a social life simultaneously salacious and politically correct. Bentley soon discovered that she no longer had to escape to Europe to live a sexually liberated life. She had an affair with a Greek worker who was a comrade in her unit. She had an affair with an Iraqi student at Columbia. Over the course of several months, she offered accommodations to fifteen or twenty men, all good communists who needed a place to sleep for the night. Some of them undoubtedly shared her bed. Later, when there was reason to find fault with her, one fellow traveler sniped that Bentley had "launched herself into party life with a zeal for the horizontal." There were rumors that she had an abortion, perhaps more than one, aided by her friend, nurse Lee Fuhr. Whatever happened, she felt both free and secure. The party answered her questions. The party took away her despair. The party gave her permission to be "bad" and feel good about it. There was an all-in-oneness to party life, a completeness, a lulling insularity. This was, she thought, the very best time of her life.

She was also coming to see her Columbia comrades not merely as intelligent, interesting people with lofty goals but as modern-day Good Samaritans, as self-sacrificing humanitarians who were putting into practice the old Christian ideals on which she was raised. She met a Union Theological Seminary student who was applying for party membership, and he told her that Christianity was dead. Christ came to earth to preach the brotherhood of man, but men are too busy making money to listen anymore, he said. "I am convinced," he told her, "that communism is the Christianity of the future." The more she thought about it, the more it made sense. Christianity had arisen as the advocate of the poor and oppressed. But now it had degenerated into a pastime of the wealthy. Communism could—and should—take its place.

Still, it was not easy to convert oneself from a strong individualist to a good communist, and Bentley struggled with that. She was an educated woman who had always harbored her own strong opinions. She considered herself thoughtful, reasonable—and independent. She was proud of her free-thinking Revolutionary War ancestors. But a good communist had to believe, not question. A good communist had to stay in step. A good communist had to sacrifice individual rights for the good of the whole. It was not so much belief in the ideology—that came relatively easily to her as she read the *Daily Worker* and sat in classes at the Communist Workers School—but rather the mind-set, the notion that she must trust the party above herself, that she must give herself up to the party. Still, as she became immersed in a whirlwind of party activity, inundated with communist literature, and increasingly insulated from ideas and people outside the party, Bentley's convictions grew stronger. If discipline and order and obedience were necessary to build a new society, if free thinking got in the way of the ultimate goal, then she would toe the line. She would become a communist in spirit as well as in name.

Bentley had been looking for a job, at first a teaching job, then a secretarial job, then any kind of job, since she returned from Europe. Finally, after almost nine months, something came through in the spring of 1935. Just a few weeks after she joined the party, the Columbia University Placement Center found her a position as an investigator with New York City's Emergency Home Relief Bureau, a welfare agency established to give aid to some of the city's neediest. She would work out of the Bureau's Harlem office at 150th Street and Amsterdam Avenue, spending her days visiting indigent clients in the neighborhood and determining their needs. It was a physically and emotionally draining job, much like her mother's dispiriting volunteer work in McKeesport, but on a larger and sadder scale. Every day she would walk endless blocks and climb long flights of stairs to the top floors of crumbling, fire-trap buildings. Every day she saw unlivable conditions—entire families crammed into a single room, apartments with no heat and no ventilation, the only light a solitary bulb hanging from the ceiling. Often there was one toilet down the hall serving a half dozen families. And every day she would hear heartbreaking stories of illness and unemployment, hunger and cold, desperation. Here again was proof that capitalism had failed, that greed had triumphed over humanitarianism. And even though she was working for a humanitarian operation, it seemed to her as if success on the job was measured by how many cases an investigator could close out and not on how much aid the agency could disburse or how many people could be helped.

Her caseload was so heavy that she skipped lunch to make home visits and did her paperwork—reams of it, it seemed, detailed studies and follow-ups, reports in triplicate—at home, after hours, squeezed in between her party meetings and her Workers School classes. She was horrified by the amount of red tape she and her clients had to go through, the number of weeks or even months it took to get a blanket for a young mother living in an unheated room. One day she went to visit an elderly black man living in a tiny furnished room. He had been employed as a Pullman porter most of his life. Now he was just another penniless man applying for relief. In order to process his application, Bentley needed to see proof that the man had lived in New York long enough to qualify for aid. Did he have a gas bill or a telephone bill, anything official showing his residence and a date? He didn't. She told him he would have to go to a notary and sign a statement. It would cost him a quarter.

"Miss," he said quietly, "if I had a quarter, I'd have eaten it."

Bentley's frustration with relief efforts was nothing compared to the frustration felt by those the agencies were supposed to help. More than 150 men and women marched on the relief office on East 149th Street, demanding aid for their families. Twenty people picketed the office on East 136th Street, parading with banners that called for the abolition of fire-traps, and clothes for the unemployed. People were collapsing on the street. Bentley felt increasingly helpless in the face of so much need, so much poverty. She herself was close to exhaustion.

But she had to pay attention to her party duties. When she got the job with the Relief Bureau, she had to leave the communist cell she originally joined, the Columbia University unit, and join a "shop unit" at her place of employment. But nothing was simple in the clandestine world. She was told to make contact with "Comrade H" at the Relief Bureau, but she knew enough not to be obvious about it. She arranged to accidentally run into her in the office hallway one afternoon. The woman looked at her sharply, clearly suspicious, clearly uncomfortable, told her to come to a meeting the next night, and hurried away. But Bentley had no idea where the meeting was, and Comrade H had made it obvious she didn't want to be contacted again. Ever dutiful, Bentley stopped by Lee Fuhr's place after work to ask her. Fuhr told her to go to an apartment on Lenox Avenue near 131st Street in Harlem. Bentley was scared to go to Harlem alone at night and was confused by the strange, conspiratorial arrangements that attended her change from one unit to another. But she ignored the voice in her head. She went against her own judgment. She was now enough of a communist that she trusted the party more than she trusted herself.

The communist unit at the Home Relief Bureau numbered only five people, including Bentley, all of them new to the party. The main job of the unit was to build support for a workers' union, a tough assignment given that social workers were white-collar professionals who knew little about unions—and that people lucky enough to be employed were more interested in holding on to what they had than agitating for more. At the first meeting, over her own objections, Bentley was elected educational director. She had no idea what the job entailed and no idea how she would find time to do whatever it was she was supposed to do. But she said yes.

Between her party commitments and her relief work, her late-night, coffee-fueled sessions with the comrades, and her love affairs, she ran herself into the ground. One day she fainted at the office. The doctor she visited told her she needed a rest and "a more peaceful occupation." She applied for a leave of absence, but while the paperwork was inching its way through the bureaucracy, she collapsed one night at the home of friends. The next day, she sent in her resignation.

Meanwhile, one of her comrades had introduced her to a woman calling herself Juliet Glazer, who said she was interested in doing research on Italian fascism and needed the assistance of a translator. Bentley was intrigued. She needed the money, and the work would be meaningful. The two women met several times at Glazer's apartment. Bentley expected to learn more about the job and when she could start, but the conversations were exasperatingly vague. Still, Glazer kept contacting her, asking her to come to her apartment or meeting her for dinner or drinks. At one point, Glazer offered to pay Bentley's graduate tuition in exchange for services rendered, but she never got around to saying what those services might be. During another conversation, Glazer asked Bentley if she would like to travel to Italy, informing her that her assignment would be to sleep with men to get information. Bentley was no prude, but she was shocked by the proposal and told Glazer so. A few days later, Glazer showed up at Bentley's apartment, called her a Trotskyist—the ultimate insult one could level against a communist in those days—and threatened to kill her. Alarmed, Bentley told Lee Fuhr about her encounter. It was Bentley's opinion that Glazer was a counterrevolutionary. Fuhr, on the other hand, thought she was a lesbian on the prowl.

They were both wrong. Juliet Glazer, whose real name was Juliet Stuart Poyntz, was a Barnard- and Oxford-educated, Moscow-trained member of the Soviet secret police. Ten years before, she had been a prominent member of the American communist party, running for Congress on the Workers Party ticket in 1924 and serving as the director of the Communist Workers School for several years. But she had left the open party to go underground and was in New York to recruit espionage operatives. Bentley had been targeted as a prime recruit.

Through Poyntz, Bentley met "Joseph Eckhart," a Lithuanian who said he was a businessman looking for a secretary. They had dinner together at Longchamps several times, but although Eckhart repeated his need for help, he never offered her a job. Over the course of several months, he went in and out of her life, calling frequently, then disappearing suddenly, then reappearing and taking her to dinner again. Bentley was confused by his odd behavior but flattered by the attention. At some point during their peculiar relationship, Eckhart introduced her to a man he called Marcel. A voluble and dramatic sort, Marcel told Bentley that he was a member of an organization similar to the Catholic Church, except, he told her pointedly, "if you left the Catholic Church, all you lost was your soul." Bentley couldn't help but be titillated by the mystery, the implied danger. After Eckhart disappeared again, Marcel started taking her out to dinner, and she began to learn more about what he did. One time, he told her he had been in Paris "terrorizing a communist who had gone astray of the party." He had called the man from a phone booth every five minutes, hanging up each time.

"I don't like this kind of work," he told her grimly.

"Why don't you get into something else?" Bentley asked. He stared at her for a long time.

"You don't know what you're saying," he said. "No one ever leaves the organization." Both Eckhart and Marcel, whose real name was Michael Endelman, were KGB agents.

Bentley might have suspected something, or she might have thought that the overly theatrical Marcel was just being overly theatrical. At any rate, she was just a neophyte who knew relatively little of Soviet politics or secret organizations or underground operations. What was important to her was that odd and interesting things were happening to her, that strange men were treating her to expensive dinners, that her life was suddenly quite exciting.

It was not difficult to see why Poyntz, Eckhart, and Marcel had all apparently considered recruiting Bentley into the espionage business. She was a willing and enthusiastic new party member. She was smart. She was unattached. She had an impeccable background, a Vassar grad with a DAR pedigree. And she wasn't Jewish. A woman with these "credentials" would be among the last to be suspected of undercover work, not to mention communist affiliation. But nothing came of it. The moment passed without Bentley even knowing that there had been a moment.


After she resigned from the Home Relief job, Bentley went back to Columbia to finish her master's degree while working part-time at a succession of odd jobs. She found work typing manuscripts, translating, and tutoring. She did publicity for the Brooklyn Institute. She did research for the Consumers Union. She did temp work at *Cue* magazine. She was a telephone operator at Macy's. During the summers, she worked as a counselor, one year at an upstate New York camp for the children of Soviet nationals, another summer for Macy's Fresh Air Fund camp. All of the jobs were temporary, and none of them paid well, but she managed to support herself, take classes, and faithfully pay her party dues. She was persistent and indefatigable, a woman who had to take care of herself and did. Gone was the despair and lethargy of those terrible months back in the fall and winter of 1935 when it was all she could do to drag herself out of bed each morning. Her life wasn't easy now, and it wasn't the life she imagined she was going to live. But she was making her own way. She was part of something. She had comrades and lovers.

In June 1938, the Columbia University Placement Center came through with another full-time job, this one with the Italian Library of Information on Madison Avenue. Hired to do research and secretarial work, she soon discovered that the library was part of the Italian government's Ministry of Propaganda whose purpose was to spread positive information about Mussolini's regime. She saw stacks of fascist literature. She saw anticommunist and anti-Semitic pamphlets. She was appalled. Antifascism was the bedrock of her own progressive beliefs. This was not the kind of place where she wanted to work. *Or was it?* When she stopped to think about it, maybe she could do some good being there. Maybe this job was more than it seemed. Maybe it was an opportunity to find out what propaganda the fascists were foisting on the American people. Perhaps the party would like to know, too.

She asked a comrade, a woman she knew from the party and the American League Against War and Fascism, whom she might talk to about all this. The woman gave her a letter of introduction to "F. Brown," a high-ranking party functionary, and Bentley went downtown to headquarters to talk to him. He listened carefully and told her to keep an eye on what was going on at the library and collect copies of any anticommunist or anti-Semitic material she saw. Bentley took her assignment seriously, making it her business during the next few months to bring Comrade Brown all such material. She had essentially taken herself undercover, using her legitimate position as secretary to secretly gather documents she thought would be embarrassing or compromising to the fascists.

Through the summer of 1938, she dutifully stuffed her handbag at work and ferried the material to Brown at party headquarters. But after a while, she saw that he was not all that interested. She, however, remained convinced of the importance of what she was doing. She hoped to expose the library for being a propaganda machine. She hoped to expose fascist propaganda for the lies she knew it was. The clandestine work she was doing was not only meaningful to her, it was also exciting. There was always the possibility that she would be caught with material in her handbag, always the chance she would be unmasked as a communist. There was a thrill to that.

If Brown wasn't interested, perhaps the Italian leftist underground might be, she thought. When she couldn't find a contact there, she asked Brown to put her in touch with someone in the party with ties to the Italian labor movement in the United States. He gave her a name, but that man proved unreliable, missing arranged meetings and neglecting to call her back. Still, she didn't drop the matter. She went back to Brown and asked for a new contact, someone dependable, someone who would take her and her information seriously.

In this way, she met the man who would change her life.

# Chapter 6

# Yasha

IN MID-OCTOBER 1938, Comrade Brown instructed Bentley to meet him in Greenwich Village in front of a little restaurant on University Place. He had a new contact for her, a top man in the communist movement, he told her, a man she could trust. They rendezvoused at the appointed hour and began walking slowly toward Eighth Street when, at the corner, a small, stocky man in a shabby suit and scuffed brown shoes suddenly appeared, seemingly out of nowhere. Bentley was taken aback. Brown merely nodded and introduced the man as "Timmy." Timmy had a car parked around the corner, an old Dodge sedan, and the three of them got in and drove over to Fourteenth Street, where Brown got out and caught the subway. Then Timmy swung the car around and headed downtown. He knew a restaurant on lower Second Avenue, an out-of-the-way little place where they could sit and talk over dinner.

On the drive over, Bentley stole glances at Timmy, sizing him up. He was a short, homely man, probably in his late forties, with broad

shoulders, large hands, and a short, thick neck. He had a high, wide
forehead and small, close-set eyes that seemed fixed in a perpetual
squint. His nose was small for his face, his mouth generous, with full,
shapely, womanish lips. There was a hint of the Slavic in his high
cheekbones and his soft, rounded jaw. He was not, she thought to
herself, an impressive-looking man. But she soon discovered that he
was impressive in other ways. As they sat and talked through a two-
hour dinner, she saw that he had a quick, sharp mind. He had a way
of listening that was thoughtful yet intense and alert, a way of paying
attention that made her feel that what she said was important. So she
said a lot. She told him not just about the Italian Library of Information and her work there but also many personal details, including her
odd experiences with Glazer, Eckhart, and Marcel. He listened, his
eyes guarded. He asked incisive questions.

After they had lingered as long as they could, Timmy suggested
they take a drive and continue their conversation. As he maneuvered
the big sedan uptown and then through Central Park, he told her of
the misery and suffering he had seen in Europe, and of the new society that he hoped would replace it. Everywhere the communists were
working to create a better world, a more humane place. But it was
very hard work, and many people, although they started off as good
communists, just weren't strong enough to stay with their commitment, to weather the hardships. Timmy was giving her a pep talk,
but he seemed also to be giving one to himself.

"Our movement is like a buggy overcrowded with people going
up a steep and rocky road," he told her. "At every curve someone
loses his hold and falls off."

Bentley felt as if this man, this stranger, could see right through
her. Was she one of those people who would fall off? Did she have
what it took to be part of this great new enterprise?

Now Timmy was telling her that her Library of Information job
was "vitally important to the party." That's what *she* had thought.
That's why she hadn't given up trying to find a contact. You must
stay there at all costs, he told her. Watch what goes on. Bring out any
documents you can.

Timmy was overplaying his hand, but Bentley didn't know that. Her Library of Information job was not really all that significant. The material she might manage to bring out would be unlikely to provide the party with vital intelligence. What was important to Timmy was not Bentley's current position but taking advantage of the situation, capitalizing on an opportunity that had been handed to him. He needed to encourage this woman, who seemed bright and more than willing to work for the good of the party. She had initiative and guts. He could see that clearly. She had not only taken it upon herself to spy for the party, she had kept at her self-appointed task without any support. She was definitely worth cultivating. And so he told her to report back to him at regular intervals. He told her to contact him through a third party. He gave her a number and detailed instructions.

"You are now no longer an ordinary communist," he told her. "You are a member of the underground." He told her that she must cut herself off completely from her old communist friends. No more socializing, no more cell meetings, no more going to demonstrations or rallies or fund-raisers. If she happened to run into someone who knew her from the party, she was to say that she had dropped out. She was to avoid progressive causes, stay clear of anything that smacked even of liberalism. Her only contact with the party would be through him.

Bentley wasn't sure what to think. It was thrilling to be singled out like this, to be selected, to be told she was of special value. Timmy was telling her that she could play a new role in this struggle for a new society. He was telling her she was too important to be merely a party drudge who went to meetings and carried placards. He was telling her that on that overcrowded buggy that was going up the steep and rocky road, she had a place up front. This appealed equally to her ego and her idealism. It also sounded exciting. She should have stopped to consider what going underground would mean emotionally and psychologically, how it would feel to give up the warmth and camaraderie of the party, the comfort and sense of belonging. But she didn't. Here was a mysterious, older man who looked at her with almost more intensity than she could handle. He had seen things. He had lived. And he believed in her commitment, in her strength, her perseverance. It seemed she should, too.

"I know this is going to be hard for you," he was saying. "You will be completely alone except for me. Your fellow comrades may even think you're a traitor. But the party would not ask this sacrifice of you if it were not vitally important."

There was something that appealed to her about this, too, this notion of a tough job that called for self-sacrifice. Wasn't this part of old-fashioned Christian ideals? Wasn't this part of her New England upbringing? Didn't her ancestors make sacrifices for what they believed in? Timmy pulled the car over in front of her apartment building and watched her as she thought this through. Then his hard look softened, and he smiled. Bentley found herself drawn to him.

"Good night," he said. "Sleep well." Of course, she didn't.


In the weeks after they were first introduced, Bentley and Timmy met often, always at her initiative. She would call the number he gave her, and, as instructed, leave a message if a woman answered but hang up if she heard a man's voice. She had no idea where she was calling. She had no idea who Timmy was—of course Timmy wasn't his real name, she was sure of that—or what he did. She suspected, from how politically savvy he seemed to be and how intensely curious he was about world affairs, that he might be a journalist of some kind. But the mystery didn't bother her. In fact, it intrigued her.

They met in out-of-the-way restaurants, then drove around the city in his old sedan. She would tell him what she found out that week—who visited the library, who called, what packages had arrived—and hand over any material she had taken out. Patiently, like a teacher coaching a student with little experience but much potential, he would point out what was important and what was trivial and tell her what to look for in the future. One time she told him that she was eavesdropping at doors and going through wastepaper baskets. No one does that except in spy novels, he told her. That's not the way to operate. Instead, he instructed her to concentrate on impressing her superiors at the library with her trustworthiness so that she would be taken into their confidence. Pretend to be a fascist, he told her. Infiltrate. She listened carefully.

She was beginning to admire Timmy more and more. He was self-assured without being arrogant. He was kind without being soft. He knew so much. He had seen so much. He didn't tell her details—he kept almost everything about himself secret—but he talked sometimes about the conditions in Europe, about Russia before the Revolution, about the fate suffered by comrades working for a new society. She saw in him both gentle empathy and steely strength. He seemed to work hard and live simply, with what she saw as a pure and unswerving loyalty to the cause. He was, she thought, a man of honor and vision who cared more about the human condition than he did about himself. He was a hero.

On a blustery night in December, perhaps a month and a half after they first met, Bentley and Timmy came out of a restaurant to find Timmy's car wedged in a snowdrift. They labored together in the dark, digging snow from around the wheels with their hands, scooping snow from the windshield, rocking the car back and forth to find traction. They were exhausted and drenched when they finally got in the car. Her hat was dripping wet. Let me shake that off for you, he said, reaching over for it. Their hands accidentally touched. They stared at each other. It was like one of those bourgeois romantic movies the communists all made fun of. Then they were in each other's arms.

"Let's drive for a while," he said.

He drove, faster than he should have, through the snowy streets, onto Riverside Drive, through the city and north along the Hudson. They passed town after town, Riverdale, Yonkers, Dobbs Ferry, Irvington, Tarrytown. Neither of them talked. They were too involved with their own thoughts, too busy working through what had just happened and how they felt about it. Bentley had enjoyed liaisons with older men before, but she had never been in love. Was this love? How could she be in love with a man she knew so little about? But maybe she knew enough. She knew that, despite his small stature, he towered over every other man she'd ever met. To her, he was the

ideal communist, the ultimate self-sacrificing, self-disciplined revolutionary, a true believer.

Finally, near dawn, he stopped the car, and they watched as the
winter sky lightened in the east. He held her hand and told her he
loved her. And he did. But it was love leavened with need. He
needed someone young and enthusiastic, someone whose idealism
was untempered by the realities he knew too well. He needed to
mold and teach, to create, Pygmalion-style, a worthy compatriot, a
true comrade, a revolutionary soulmate, not just someone to help
him but someone to whom he could talk and in whom he could confide. And, maybe, despite his selfless devotion to the cause, he
needed someone to admire him. He needed to feel like the hero he
had been once, in simpler times. He was not an old man, only forty-
eight, in fact, but he was slowing down. He had not taken good care
of himself. His health was poor. He needed an infusion of energy, a
transfusion, new blood. Elizabeth Bentley was it.

Before she had a chance to say anything, he told her that although
this should be a happy moment for them, it wasn't.

"It would be simple if we were two ordinary communists, moving
in party circles," he said. "Then we could live together as good comrades do." But they were not ordinary comrades, he reminded her,
they were underground operatives. And for those in the underground, the rules were different. We are forbidden to form close
friendships, he told her, and especially to fall in love. "You and I have
no right, under communist discipline, to feel the way we do about
each other." Bentley didn't know what to say.

"I should give you a new contact and walk out of your life forever,"
Timmy continued. But he couldn't do it, as good a communist as he
was. He loved her, and he needed her, or someone like her, too much.
There is a solution, he told her. They would keep their relationship
secret. They would not be seen in public unless they were meeting on
business. They would not live together. And she would have to take
him completely on faith, not knowing who he was or where he lived
or what he did for a living. But they could love each other. They
could, somehow, with nuance and innuendo, in stolen moments,
forge a relationship. She agreed. She had no other choice.

In the months that followed, they continued to meet as contacts in public places—a park, a street corner, a restaurant. They had dinner. They talked. Sometimes they took a drive, nowhere special, just an opportunity to be alone together. Occasionally, they would manage to get away for a weekend, drive upstate to a little inn or motel, and pretend for a few days that they were just a couple in love.

Bentley knew Timmy for almost six months before she accidentally discovered his real name—or at least the name he took for himself when he joined the party. They were sitting on a bench in Madison Square Park, conducting one of their business meetings. After she had given him her regular report on the doings at the library, he handed her two tickets he had gotten to a show. He couldn't make it. Perhaps she'd like to go with a friend. Bentley glanced at the tickets in her hand. On the top of one she noted the word "Golos." There must be a mistake, she told him. This ticket is for someone else. It says "Golos." He blanched, then got up and walked away, leaving her there alone on the bench.

Later, when they met up at a restaurant for a prearranged dinner, and she casually addressed him as Timmy, he blew up.

"Why are you pretending you don't know my real name?" he said. "Don't put on an act. You know perfectly well I am Jacob Golos." He said it so fiercely and with so much conviction that it was clear he believed she knew exactly who Jacob Golos was. But the name meant nothing to her. She knew, because Comrade Brown had told her, that the man she was introduced to as Timmy was important in communist circles. But, at her previous level of party involvement, she knew little of the people and personalities that played roles in its tangled history.

Slowly, his story emerged. The first thing he told her was that, as Jacob Golos, he was the head of a company called World Tourists, a Fifth Avenue travel agency that specialized in steamship tours between the United States and Russia. Founded in 1927 with $50,000 supplied by the Communist Party of the United States, the agency was supposed to arrange and promote travel tours, including securing travel documentation, ship passage, railroad tickets, hotels, and other amenities. World Tourists was the only U.S. company able to make travel arrangements in Russia, thanks to an exclusive licensing contract between the New York company and Intourist, the Soviet Union's state-owned tourist agency. Amtorg, the Soviet trading company, and other Soviet agencies in the United States steered their business to World Tourists, and the party used its services extensively. Golos had taken over World Tourists in 1930 when it was in financial trouble and had managed to turn it into a healthy, profitable venture.

By the time Golos met Bentley, the business was at a high point, offering a wide range of travel adventures, from one-week package tours of Leningrad to one-month, ten-city grand tours with three days on the Volga River. There were southern tours, "Great City" tours, tours of the Crimea, and tours of the Ukraine. Passage was arranged on one of several French ocean liners with stopovers in either London or Paris. But World Tourists was not a disinterested commercial agency concerned merely with arranging Russian vacations for adventurous Americans. It was a propaganda enterprise, its main purpose—barely hidden in the didactic brochures the agency produced—the "selling" of the Soviet Union.

"From the moment of his arrival the visitor from abroad comes across entirely new human relationships, and realizes he is in a society that has never before been known, a society whose members are bound together by the common idea of refashioning their own backward fatherland," read the copy in a 1935 brochure. The brochure touted public education, collective agriculture, the "reeducation of the old," science, and art, and the "palaces of culture" as must-sees for all those who wanted to see firsthand the triumphs of the new Soviet Union.

World Tourists operated for at least two other purposes. Its profits helped support various East Coast communist enterprises, including the *Daily Worker,* and it provided Jacob Golos with a "cover," a legitimate job that masked his other, less-than-legitimate activities. For Golos was not just—as Comrade Brown had originally told Bentley—a good communist and a high-ranking functionary in the party. He was, as she now knew, an underground operative, a man who dealt in the currency of secret information. As head of World Tourists, he secured American passports for members of the party and the Comintern, assuring easy international movement for operatives and others. By bribing foreign consular officials and U.S. passport agency workers, he obtained fraudulent passports, naturalization papers, and birth certificates, generally belonging to people who had died or permanently left the country. Although Golos had intended to keep himself a mystery to Bentley, as much to protect his new lover as to shield himself, this turned out to be an unworkable plan. He never told her everything, but he told her more than he knew he should have. He loved her. And ultimately, he trusted her.

Eventually, he told her an abbreviated, edited version of his life story. Born into a Jewish family in the Ukraine in 1890, he was, at the age of eight, arrested for distributing anticzarist literature, and at seventeen, sent to Siberia for operating a clandestine Bolshevik printing house. Two years later, he escaped on foot into China and from there made his way to Japan and finally to the United States. By 1915 he was a naturalized American citizen, but when the Russian Revolution broke out, he went home to support the Bolsheviks, serving as a foreman in a Siberian coal mine and, he told Bentley, joining the Cheka, the powerful political police of the Soviet state and predecessor to the KGB. Back in America, he became active in the Socialist Party, a broad-based, contentious group that seemed to quarrel more with each other than with its political adversaries. Golos belonged to the especially quarrelsome left-wing faction, which was expelled from the party in 1919. This group then split again to form two rival communist parties, with Golos a founding member of one of these groups, the Communist Party of America. In 1921, Golos's party merged with the other splinter group to become the sole communist party in the United States.

Golos became a full-time functionary of the party in the early twenties, first working as an editor for one of the party's Russian-language journals, then serving as an organizer in Detroit and Chicago, and later acting as chief administrator of the Society for Technical Aid to Soviet Russia, an organization that recruited U.S. technicians for work in Russia. Then, as Bentley now knew, he was asked to take over World Tourists. When they met, he was walking a tightrope, inhabiting a dangerous and ultimately untenable position as both an open party member—he served on the three-man Central Control Commission, a powerful and often feared disciplinary committee that kept American comrades in line—and as a clandestine operative. This was precisely what he had told Bentley she could no longer do. When one worked for the underground, one *went* underground, disappearing from the public life of the party. Golos, probably because of his importance in both spheres and his impeccable revolutionary pedigree, was the exception.

Bentley may not have understood the subtleties, but she felt she understood the man. It was clear to her that he had worked many years for little recompense, going where the party needed him, doing what needed to be done, living cheaply, caring little about material comforts. His very shabbiness was a badge of honor. Everything that Golos said about himself made Bentley respect him more. Here was a man who had lived history, a man who came to his political beliefs from harrowing personal experience, a man with high ideals.

That much she knew about Golos. But there were important things she did not know. She did not know that when they first met and began their affair he already had a mistress, a woman named Caroline Klein, whose apartment on West 13th Street he shared. She did not know that he had a common-law wife and a son, whom he had sent back to live in Russia three years before. He had met Celia, a comrade in his party unit, in the early 1920s. The arrangement may not have been a love match, but the couple had lived together for more than a decade and had produced a child. By the time Bentley found out about his other intimate associations, it didn't matter. She was in love, convinced that Golos was the only man she would ever need or want.

Their union had all the excitement of an illicit affair—the secret rendezvous, the stolen moments, the forbidden sex—and few of the responsibilities of a real relationship. By being together, they were not just breaking society's code but also party regulations and espionage tradecraft. It was a heady combination. She was drunk on it. He called her *golubushka,* a Russian endearment that means "little dove." She called him Yasha, the Russian diminutive of Jacob. They were living, as someone later put it, in bourgeois sin and Leninist bliss.

# Chapter 7

# Tradecraft

*I*N MARCH 1939, after five months at the Italian Library of Information, Bentley was fired. Someone, probably a coworker—she never found out who—apparently went to some lengths to unearth a 1935 article published in the Columbia University student newspaper, which made it clear that Bentley was an antifascist. In the story, written back when she was trying to complete her master's degree in Italian, Bentley claimed she had not received a scholarship from her department because of her affiliation with the American League Against War and Fascism. Perhaps someone at work had noticed her amateur attempts at spying. Or maybe someone just didn't like her. At any rate, when the director was presented with a copy of the newspaper story, he fired her on the spot.

Now that her self-initiated stint as an undercover agent was over, she assumed she would be sent back to the open party to rejoin her unit and take up the comradely life she had left behind the previous fall. But Golos told her no. He said she would be of more use working directly for him. As a woman in love probably more than as a communist eager to serve, she was delighted. It would mean she would have the opportunity to see him more often. He told her to give up her place in the Columbia University neighborhood, where he felt she was too well-known to the party and would risk running into old comrades on the street, and take an apartment in Greenwich Village. She first found a place on Grove Street, and then a few months later moved to an apartment in a brownstone at 58 Barrow. During the day, she worked at a series of temporary and part-time secretarial and translation jobs. In off-hours, she did research for Golos, compiling biographical data on various American politicians, researching the history of the U.S. labor movement, and providing background on the elections in Mexico. He told her the information was for use in articles in the *Daily Worker* and *The Masses*.

Golos appreciated Bentley's work, but he had other things in mind for her. With party membership becoming increasingly Americanized in the late 1930s, the Soviets were interested in having their U.S. espionage efforts follow suit. Golos told Bentley that the Russians wanted to make their agents look, act, and sound more American, and they wanted to enlist more native-born Americans, rather than Russians or immigrants, into their covert operations. Golos, the Russian immigrant, saw the possibilities for Bentley, the Connecticut Yankee. He noted her industriousness, her desire to please, and her deepening attachment to him, and he began to trust her with minor tasks. She became a "mail drop" for Golos, receiving at her address letters meant for him mailed from Canada and cablegrams sent from Europe. Every week she handed them over, unopened. That way Golos could shield his own whereabouts and still be in communication with communists outside the country. She also began to function as a mail courier, traveling to Brooklyn once a week to pick up letters intended for Golos that had been sent by a high-ranking Mexican communist to another mail drop. This gave Golos another degree of separation, which became important when the Mexican letter-writer was later implicated in the plot to assassinate Trotsky.

Meanwhile, he began training her for bigger things. He instructed her in the tricks of the spy trade. First there was the use of phones. She should always use a pay phone when calling him or conducting any covert business, he told her. She should always listen carefully for buzzing or clicking sounds that might indicate that the phone on the other end was bugged. Even if she thought the line was clear, she should never say anything important over the phone. Calls should always appear purely social. They should be used only to set up meetings at which the actual conversations could take place. Then there was the issue of sensitive material. If she had to store documents in her apartment, he told her to put them in a locked trunk and then wind a thin black thread around the lock so that if someone opened the trunk in her absence, she would know. Before she left her apartment, she was to place a book behind her front door. If the book was out of place when she returned, she would know someone had broken in. He cautioned her to never, under any circumstances, put letters or documents in the trash. If she needed to get rid of them, she should burn them or flush them. One of the advantages of her Barrow Street apartment was its wood-burning fireplace.

There was other tradecraft to learn when going out into the world, and Golos taught her that, too. He told her that when leaving the apartment on covert business, she should never carry anything that marked her true identity, from a driver's license in her wallet to old ticket stubs in her purse to labels on her clothing. He taught her how to recognize if she was being followed, and cautioned her to react coolly. The idea was to not let on that you knew you were under surveillance. She should cross and recross the street, surreptitiously taking note of the actions of anyone behind her. She should memorize the license plate number of any automobile she thought might be on a stakeout. And then, as nonchalantly as possible, she should try to lose the tail. That might mean ducking into a crowded store, especially one with more than one exit, or dodging into a darkened movie theater or a strategically located ladies' restroom. Golos insisted that she make a tour of the city to identify places where she could most conveniently elude surveillance. If she thought a car was following her, she was to walk to the nearest subway station and take a ride, or walk the wrong way down a one-way street.

Bentley was an eager student, and Golos was an experienced teacher not above using their relationship in the service of the cause.

I want you to work hard, he told her. It is because I love you that I want to be especially proud of you, he said. To disappoint him would be to risk losing that love. He was her teacher in other ways, too, now that she was cut off completely from the party. He gave her party literature, explained party politics, and discussed public affairs, taking over the functions generally performed by various comrades in an open unit. She depended on him to interpret the world for her through the communist lens.

On an August evening in 1939, Bentley and Golos were listening to the radio in her apartment. Their public rendezvous were still in out-of-the-way places, and they took care to appear as business associates, not lovers. But lately, Golos was visiting Bentley at her apartment more often and sometimes staying the night. That night, sitting on the couch, they heard the news that Stalin had signed a nonaggression pact with Hitler. Communists and Nazis making deals with each other? Bentley didn't understand—and neither did thousands of other antifascist liberals in the party. She was distraught. How could this be, she asked Golos? How could the Soviet Union, the leading force in the struggle for a better world, align itself with all the evils we are fighting against? For a good many writers and intellectuals, this moment signaled the end of their infatuation with communism and the end of their membership in the party. But Bentley was isolated from the foment in the party ranks. She no longer had any comrades. She had no one to go to with her fears or doubts other than Jacob Golos, proud Russian, dyed-in-the-wool Bolshevik, a man whose entire life was the Revolution. He *had* to believe that the Soviet Union had not betrayed its high ideals. So he calmed her that night with rationalizations. The Soviet Union was justified in doing whatever it had to do to stay alive, he told Bentley. The communist dream must be preserved at all costs, he said. She needed to believe him, and she did. A month later, when Russia invaded Poland, and Golos told her that the Soviet army was, in fact, liberating the Polish people from a regime more oppressive than the czars, she believed that, too.

Golos told her she could help the cause against Nazism by getting a job at McClure Newspaper Syndicate with Richard Waldo, the owner and president. The party suspected Waldo was a German agent and wanted to keep tabs on him. At first, she balked at the idea. She was all for fighting Nazism, but her experience at the Italian Library had shown her that working undercover could be nerve-racking. She would have to play a role again. She would have to watch what she said and did. She would have to be hypervigilant without seeming to be so. When Golos saw her hesitancy, he was quick to lecture her about being a good Bolshevik, about acquiescing to the will of the party. I wanted so much to be proud of you, he told her, once more playing the relationship card, and instead you are letting me down. She couldn't bear to do that, and he knew it. But there was something besides love and ideology that made her put on a good dress and go down to the syndicate office the next morning. True, undercover work was disquieting, but it was also, she had to admit, something of a thrill. She might feel anxious about it, nervous, a little jumpy, but that wasn't all bad, was it, for it also made her feel more alive. And it was certainly more exciting than reporting to yet another temporary typing job or scanning old magazines in the library for Golos.

She told the people at McClure's that she'd been sent by an employment agency. Waldo interviewed her and, to her surprise, hired her as his personal secretary. Golos was delighted. He told her to watch Waldo as closely as she could to determine who was contacting him and to whom he was in contact, either by letter or phone. She found the job particularly grueling. It was not just because she had to be constantly on the alert and not just because she had to figure out how to smuggle out documents and correspondence without getting caught. It was also because Richard Waldo was a terrifying boss. He had a sharp tongue, and he flew into fits of rage. Everyone in the office was constantly on edge. Bentley had to handle the stress of the job itself in addition to the anxiety of the undercover work. Golos was sympathetic and encouraging at first, but, as time went on and he determined that the information she brought out had little value, he lost interest. Both of them were probably relieved when, four months later, in the midst of one of his frequent explosions, Waldo fired Bentley. Golos had other work for her anyway.

When leading Canadian communists came to New York to confer with him, Golos asked Bentley to help. The meetings had to look like social occasions. The rendezvous were set for restaurants, and the men brought along their wives. It was Bentley's assignment to keep the wives occupied and engaged in conversation while Golos conducted business with the men. But there were also more exciting opportunities. One time, she drove with him to Brooklyn where they staked out a dentist's office. It seemed that the dentist's car had been used by a man wanted by the Russians, a diplomat who had fled to the United States with $50,000. Golos told her all about it. He had tailed the diplomat from Hoboken, where his boat docked, into Manhattan. He lost him on Canal Street but not before noting the license plate number on the car he was driving. Another time Golos tried to enlist Bentley's services to soften up a man named Jaffee—an enemy of the underground movement, he told her—who was living in a Manhattan hotel. Golos told her, pointedly, that the man was "susceptible to women." He proposed the assignment to her as he would have to any operative. But she wasn't any operative. She was his lover. Bentley wanted to be a good Bolshevik, but being asked to seduce another man by the man she considered her life's partner was too much to ask. She told Golos she didn't want to have anything to do with the assignment. He was probably relieved and dropped the matter quickly.

Meanwhile, she continued operating as a mail drop and a mail courier. But, because of her connection to Golos and because of Golos's standing both in the party and in the underground, Bentley was not just another worker bee. She was, although it took her some time to realize it, near the center of the hive. Through Golos, she was introduced to a number of important people and heard about many more. Several times, she and Golos visited Earl Browder, head of the Communist Party, at his summer home in Monroe, New York. Her position was clearly privileged.

By the end of October 1939, Bentley was still performing various tasks for Golos, and the two were meeting regularly, even chancing being seen together at the Fifth Avenue offices of World Tourists. But on October 20, the U.S. Attorney General's Office, the State

Department, and the U.S. Marshals Service served Golos with a subpoena demanding that he turn over all World Tourists' records to
a grand jury. The Justice Department suspected (correctly) that
Golos's company was really a front for the Soviets and was engaged
in a variety of illegal activities. The plan was to prove that World
Tourists, along with the *Daily Worker* and a communist publishing
enterprise, were agents of the Soviet Union. The government hoped
the subpoenaed documents would nail the case.

With guards stationed at the door to prevent the removal or
destruction of records, Golos was stuck. He was compelled to hand
over nearly two truckloads of documents, including all the telephone
number indexes in his office. "Some of that material is going to
involve our comrades badly," he told Bentley. He was right. As federal agents soon discovered, World Tourists' records showed that
Earl Browder had traveled abroad under a pseudonym and with the
aid of faked papers. He was arrested for passport fraud. Golos himself
made more than twenty appearances before grand juries in New York
and Washington, D.C. He was on the stand hour after hour for days,
and the strain began to show. His face was pale. His shoulders
sagged. He was short of breath. He began having chest pains when
he climbed stairs. Bentley was worried about him but could do nothing. He made her keep her distance.

In March 1940, the grand jury returned indictments on various
violations of espionage and neutrality laws. But ten days after the trial
hearings began, Golos was allowed to plead guilty to a lesser charge
of failing to register as an agent of a foreign power. His attorney had
orchestrated the plea bargain, with the Central Committee of the
Party urging Golos to accept. He was incensed. He told Bentley that
the deal his attorney worked out sacrificed him while the other communist organizations under investigation walked away unscathed.
But he was a good party man, so he went along. The government
came away with a quick victory. Golos came away with a suspended
sentence and a $500 fine.

Overnight, World Tourists became the place to avoid. Customers,
alarmed by press accounts of the long investigation and wary of
becoming involved with an organization publicly labeled a Soviet

front, took their business elsewhere. Golos sat in his quiet, empty
office, exhausted, angry, and as close to self-pity as a good Bolshevik
would let himself get. But this was only the beginning of his problems. The FBI was now on his tail, literally, with federal agents keeping him under close surveillance and a Soviet double agent regularly
reporting on his activities to the Bureau. It was not just the Justice
Department investigation that put Golos on the FBI radar screen.
It was also the Bureau's surveillance of an official at Amtorg
(the USSR's state-run trading company that legally operated in the
United States), Gaik Ovakimyan, who, it turned out, was actually the
chief of scientific intelligence in the United States for the KGB.
Agents noted with interest that Ovakimyan met with Golos a number of times "under suspicious circumstances." In fact, Ovakimyan
was at the time Golos's direct link to Moscow.

On top of that, Golos discovered in December 1940 that he was
the target of another investigation, this one by a congressional committee nosing around the edges of Soviet espionage. When the
so-called Dies Committee—the precursor to the House Un-American
Activities Committee—turned its attention to Golos, it was clear to
him that another subpoena was on its way. He quickly culled through
piles of remaining documents and threw the most sensitive in a carton
that he carried over to Bentley's apartment on Barrow Street. That
night, she helped him burn the documents in her fireplace. There
were many letters and pamphlets in Russian, and thirty or forty American passports. There was also a small folder with Golos's photograph
and signature on one side and, on the other side, in Cyrillic letters that
Bentley could now translate, the initials OGPU. The OGPU was a
predecessor to the KGB. Bentley was seeing Golos's secret police credentials. Now she knew for certain what she must have suspected during her year with Golos: He worked not just for the party but directly
for the Soviets.

In fact, at the time he met Bentley and took her underground,
Golos was in charge of a network of spies in New York and Washington, D.C. His sources, men—and some women as well—fed him sensitive political, scientific, and technical information that he, in turn,
passed along to Ovakimyan who forwarded it to Moscow. Now it

seemed, to add to his troubles, that Moscow was not very happy with him. He was an independent-minded, pre-Bolshevik Revolution revolutionary who, although he generally toed the party line, made no secret of his sometimes dissident opinions. Certainly he was not a loose canon, but in the late 1930s, the years of the Great Purge in the Soviet Union, one did not have to be much off the mark, or off the mark at all, to be under suspicion for "tendencies." What Moscow lacked in evidence, it more than made up for in paranoia. Within Soviet intelligence circles, there was some fear—but no proof—that Golos was a Trotskyite. Others in Moscow thought he was too casual, too informal—too *American*—to manage such an important spy network. To others, his visibility in the open party was a sore point. And now, after the conviction in the World Tourists case, there was grave concern that he was far too visible to American counterintelligence. Unbeknownst to Golos, the KGB had debated for two years whether to recall, arrest, or execute him. In the end, the political tide turned in Moscow, the purges and paranoia receded, and what remained—what Golos was just now becoming aware of—was an internecine struggle over the control of his network. His place in the espionage scene, once secure, now felt tenuous.

All these worries were exacerbated by—and probably contributed to—his deteriorating health. Early in 1941 it became clear to Bentley that her lover was quite ill. In March he began suffering again from shortness of breath, this time so severe that Bentley took him to several doctors. He had refused medical attention in the past, and she had to cajole and nag to get him into a doctor's office. The diagnosis was heart disease and arteriosclerosis. One month later, in April of 1941, Golos suffered a heart attack.

# Chapter 8

# *Konspiratsia*

$G$OLOS RECOVERED, BUT he realized he would always be a sick man. The seemingly inexhaustible well of energy he had tapped for the last thirty years was, in fact, exhaustible. At fifty-one, he was an old man, weary in body and spirit, hunted by the FBI and haunted by the fear that the Soviet secret police no longer valued him. The World Tourists case was over; the Dies Committee had moved on to someone else, but Golos was sure that federal agents would not forget him. That put everything in jeopardy. What should he do about World Tourists, which was not just his livelihood but a significant source of income for the party, not just his job but his cover? What should he do about his network of contacts in New York and Washington, his *konspiratsia*—the concealed spy apparatus he had developed? These were men and women he'd been cultivating for years who might now be exposed because of him. And what should he do about Elizabeth Bentley, his lover, his protégé, his work-in-progress? He needed her more than ever now, but the greater his need, the greater her peril.

When the FBI began its surveillance of Golos, agents couldn't help but notice the matronly looking brunette Golos often met for dinner. Bentley first realized she was being tailed in May 1941. She was leaving the World Tourists office late one evening to meet with the editor of *Hemisphere,* a pro-communist Latin American newsletter, when she noticed two young men stationed on either side of the next street corner. She kept her head. First, she walked by them as casually as she could and went into a candy store where she intended to call Golos. But when one of the men slipped into the phone booth next to hers, she quickly abandoned that plan. She thought of walking back to World Tourists, but that might alert her pursuers that she knew she was being tailed, something Golos had told her never to do. So she headed up Broadway, thinking on her feet. Penn Station was not far away. She knew that the ladies' room there was a good place to lose a tail. You could enter it from an upper waiting room, go down the stairs, and then leave from the lower level. That's what she did. When she left, she didn't see the men. But to make sure, she walked to the public library on 42nd Street and Fifth Avenue, went in one door and out another. No one was following her when she left.

But the surveillance continued. During the next few weeks, Bentley became accustomed to the FBI's tails and began to master the art of vanishing. Paying for a seat in a movie theater and then quickly leaving by the fire exit was a particularly successful strategy. Late that spring, agents also began monitoring her mail, but by this time Bentley's address was not a mail drop, so nothing came of the effort. She was also convinced that the FBI was tapping her phone, although she was wrong about that. In fact, after a flurry of interest that spring, the FBI ceased to pay any attention at all to Elizabeth Bentley, much to the Bureau's later embarrassment. At the time, the FBI employed only two thousand agents nationwide, and they were spread thin. Government investigators had been interested in "The Reds" since the Russian Revolution and especially since the founding of the Communist Party in America. But since the outbreak of war in 1939, the FBI's attention had been focused on "potentially dangerous" German, Italian, and Japanese nationals, along with American citizens whose activities might be suspected of aiding the Axis powers. The Russians, on the other hand, were allies. But with the passage of the Smith Act in 1940, which made it a crime to advocate the overthrow of the American government, the FBI began paying renewed attention to Russia and the communists. The Bureau, however, had not yet figured out how to deal with what Hoover called a "tremendous increase in duties" and "growing demand for services." However it happened, the Bentley file slipped through the cracks.

But Golos was still under surveillance, and he knew he had to do something to protect himself and the work he and Bentley were doing. Concerned both about his health and the continued presence of the FBI, he thought it prudent to find Bentley an alternate Russian contact. Right now, the only one she could report to was him. That's how espionage networks were supposed to work, with solitary contacts to protect exposure. No one was supposed to know anyone but the next person in line. But Golos was afraid that something would happen to him, and Bentley would be left out in the cold. And so, late in 1941 a meeting was arranged through intermediaries, at noon in front of a drugstore on Ninth Avenue in the Fifties. There, Bentley, who was to be known only as "Miss Wise" rendezvoused with a Russian secret police agent, whom she was to know only as "John." Now she had an alternate channel of communication. Now she was one of a handful of Americans reporting directly to the Russians.

Golos also moved quickly to establish a new company in World Tourists' stead. With his conviction and the branding of World Tourists as "Red," the business was a shambles. He needed a new cover for himself, and Bentley, if she was to be available to him for spy work, needed a day job. For years, he had entertained the idea of setting up a business that would handle not just passengers but also all the freight traffic between the United States and Russia. Now he actively pursued it. What the company needed was an ultrarespectable businessman with good connections to the financial community and no visible connections to the party—a front man to deflect suspicion.

He found the ideal candidate in John Hazard Reynolds, a retired millionaire Wall Street broker who was married to Grace Fleischman, heiress to the Fleischman yeast fortune. Reynolds was perfect. He had a fine pedigree. His family was old money, and his father had distinguished himself as a New York State Supreme Court justice. Reynolds, who had made his own fortune as an investor, served in the military in World War I and had come out a major. He had it all: money, status, and free time. And he was a sympathizer. He had flirted with socialism in the 1930s. He had known communist party pioneers John Reed and Scott Nearing. He called himself a Marxist, but he was not a party member. Reynolds not only agreed to head the new company, which would be called United States Service and Shipping Corporation (USS&S), he also invested $5,000 of his own money to get it started. Earl Browder, on behalf of the Communist Party, put up another $15,000, but the paperwork was managed in such a way as to make it appear that Reynolds was the sole owner. The new company rented office space on the nineteenth floor of 212 Fifth Avenue, just a block from the building that housed World Tourists.

The only hitch was that Reynolds rejected all the men Golos suggested for the position of vice president. None of them had the "right background," he said, which was probably code for a family tree well-rooted in American soil and Ivy League credentials. But there was one person Golos mentioned whom Reynolds did find acceptable: Elizabeth Bentley. When the company was chartered in the spring of 1941, she was listed as vice president. For a woman accustomed to scrounging for part-time secretarial jobs, this new position was particularly welcome. The munificent salary of $250 a month—at a time when the average worker was making a third of that—meant she no longer had money worries.

Reynolds had important connections at the Chase National Bank and hired top-notch accountants and impeccable lawyers to get the company off the ground. USS&S was, because of this, above suspicion. Although the company, like World Tourists, would contract for business directly with the Soviet government, the State Department ruled that USS&S did not have to register as an agent of a foreign power. Golos's strategy had paid off. In fact, the plan finessed the whole World Tourists problem. Now World Tourists could stay in business, rehabilitated as a subagent of USS&S.

The timing couldn't have been better. A month after the new company was established, Germany invaded the Soviet Union, and pro-Russian sympathies soared. Business immediately boomed when USS&S announced it would ship any useful items to the Soviet fighting forces without import duty. Reynolds worked hard the first few months, establishing a firm footing for the company and taking an active role in its operation. But he soon began to lose interest in day-to-day supervision and administration, and Bentley took up much of the slack.

She had to take up the slack for Golos, too. Fearing that any trips outside New York would be closely monitored by the FBI, he asked Bentley to act as his courier to the Washington, D.C., sources with whom he had been working. There would be new contacts, too, for after the German invasion of the Soviet Union, Golos received orders from his superiors to develop additional sources within the federal government. "Moscow must be kept completely informed about what is going on behind the scenes in the American government," he lectured Bentley.

The task was easier than it seemed, for since the early 1930s there had been an espionage network operating in Washington, D.C., the brainchild of an Austro-Hungarian-born communist known in the Party as "J. Peters." A communist cell known as the Ware Group was funneling information to the Soviets from various agencies in the federal government as early as 1933. Through the 1930s, the New Deal added thousands of new jobs to the federal workforce and attracted liberals and progressives to government service, some of whom joined the Popular Front and were subsequently tapped for underground work.

By the end of the decade, when Golos's underground duties began to include the handling of sources, the *konspiratsia* had spread to the State Department, the Treasury Department, the Bureau of Standards, and the Aberdeen Proving Ground in Maryland. Soon there were sources in the Office of Strategic Services (OSS), the Justice Department, Interior Department, Army, Navy, and, after the United States entered the war in the winter of 1941, the Office of War Information. Many of these sources did not think of themselves as spies. After all, the USA and the USSR were allies, united in battle against the Nazis. And Russia, it seemed, was bearing the brunt of the war, suffering almost unimaginable casualties. Those in positions to know felt that the U.S. government was not giving its communist ally the same helpful information it was giving Great Britain, information that might save lives or shorten the war. It was their duty, many thought, to intercede, to pass that information to Moscow through intermediaries like Golos and Bentley. Others, of course, were ideologically motivated. They saw themselves as part of an underground resistance movement, a revolutionary force, secretly waging war against what they considered to be an oppressive government: their own.

Whatever the motivation, for the most part, they operated unmolested throughout the 1930s and into the war years. The U.S. government was not well prepared to deal with espionage at this level. The response was hobbled by a hodgepodge of internal security laws and no clear executive order on what constituted government secrets. The FBI was busy keeping tabs on the German American Bund. The various counterintelligence agencies didn't talk to one another or share information. Compared to the hundreds of thousands who worked in some way for the federal government, the number who passed information during those years was miniscule—not the legions that Joe McCarthy would later claim. But they were often in the right place at the right time. The war years were, for all those reasons and more, the golden age of Soviet espionage, and Golos—and now Bentley—were at its center.

Bentley made her first trip to Washington as Golos's substitute in July of 1941. Her job was not just to gather information from a number of sources and ferry it back to New York but also, as Golos instructed her, to collect party dues and distribute party literature. She was, he told her, to "treat them as communists," to be their link to the party just as Golos was hers. But she soon learned that her duties were more expansive. As a "handler," she had to keep an eye on everyone, calming those who were nervous about the work they were doing and assessing the stress levels of others, paying attention to their sometimes messy private lives and making sure their problems would not compromise their work. At Christmastime, she bought them presents.

But her main objective was the acquisition of information. The KGB was looking for anything and everything. Moscow wanted to know about "interesting information and activities" in virtually every cabinet-level department, the Congress, the national committees of the Republican and Democratic parties, the OSS, FBI, trade unions, and U.S. foreign embassies and missions. Moscow was interested in political and diplomatic information, like internal debates on policy, America's relations with Britain, the attitudes of U.S. officials toward Russia, the personalities of policymakers, and Capitol Hill gossip. And, after the United States entered the war, Moscow wanted technical and military information, such as production figures on planes and tanks and the deployment of forces. Through the latter part of 1941 and into the early war years, the gathering of this information along with the careful tending of sources kept Bentley very busy.

She made contact with a few sources in New York, most notably a Long Island City chemical engineer named Abraham Brothman, who knew her only as "Helen." Perhaps ten times, the two met at their prearranged rendezvous, the corner of 32nd Street and Fifth Avenue, and walked to a restaurant. During the course of dinner, Brothman would hand her a thick envelope with folded blueprints, which she then delivered to Golos. She didn't look at the blueprints, and even if she had, she wouldn't have had the technical expertise to make sense of them. Brothman told her they had something to do with commercial vats, filters, and shafts used in the manufacture of chemicals.

But most of her sources were in Washington, D.C., and through the early 1940s, she took the train down every two weeks, sometimes more often, to see them. As Golos added more sources or as an established source suggested a potential one, her list of contacts grew. At first it was possible to spend just a day taking care of business in the capital, but before long, she had so many people to meet and so many documents to collect that she was spending several days at a time on each trip. She had to act casually; she had to stay calm. But each trip was a tightly controlled performance, often an exercise in fear and always a test of how much stress a person could take while remaining outwardly unruffled. Conscious of the possibility of being followed, Bentley often took several different taxis from the train station to somewhere near her first meeting. She always stopped the cab a few blocks from her actual destination and walked the rest of the way, zipping in and out of stores, crossing and recrossing streets, taking roundabout routes, watching closely for tails. Her sources worked for the federal government, but she never met them at their offices. They rendezvoused on park benches, in drug stores, and sometimes in restaurants. They knew nothing about her, not even her real name. She was Helen Johnson or Helen Grant, or sometimes Myrna or Mary. Some sources she never actually met. They handed their material to others who in turn reported to her.

At first she carried a large purse to transport the documents she collected. A briefcase might have called attention to itself, but a woman with a purse was just a woman with a purse. Soon, however, the material became too voluminous to stuff in a handbag, and she had to switch to an oversized knitting bag or a shopping bag, always with a department store name on it. She would rush to see her contacts all over the city, arranging dozens of clandestine meetings, and then come back to New York Friday night on the Congressional Limited, a woman seemingly returning from a shopping spree, a woman quietly knitting a scarf, a woman with a bag full of secrets.

It was mentally exhausting, emotionally draining work, yet it was also undeniably thrilling. It was like living in a spy novel, like playing a part in a movie. She was Ingrid Bergman in *Casablanca*. She was Hedy Lamarr in *Comrade X*. She was living a big life. She was making her lover proud. And she was also doing something important—helping the communist cause she had come to believe in, helping Mother Russia win the war. Fueled by love, by ideology, and by a sense of drama and excitement, she went about her work efficiently. Under Golos's tutelage, Elizabeth Bentley was now essentially in charge of the most extensive espionage network in the United States, not a single apparatus but several groups and a number of individual agents linked to Soviet intelligence through her.

One of her first important contacts was Mary Price, personal secretary to the highly influential syndicated newspaper columnist Walter Lippmann. Golos, as "John," and Bentley, as "Helen," had first met Price in New York at the Schrafft's on 13th Street and Fifth Avenue in the spring of 1941, where they arranged for Bentley to visit Price every two weeks in Washington. Walter Lippmann wrote political commentary that Golos found quite interesting. He wanted to get his hands on Lippmann's background material, his sources, anything in his files that might reveal behind-the-scenes intelligence the Russians would be interested in. Price, a good communist, was willing to go through her boss's files on weekends or while he was away on business, making copies of his notes or other documents. When Bentley came back with a haul from Lippmann's files, Golos declared it "extremely valuable" and pressed for more. Price was also important to Bentley because it was at her apartment on Eye Street that Bentley often stayed during her trips to Washington, sleeping on a bed in the enclosed back porch. Price's other significant contribution to the Bentley-Golos apparatus was her connection to a man named Duncan Lee who offered direct access to the OSS, America's newest and most important foreign intelligence unit.

A direct descendant of General Robert E. Lee, Duncan Lee had distinguished himself at Yale, both undergraduate and law, and had been a Rhodes scholar at Oxford, where he became involved in the Communist Party. Fresh out of law school, he secured a position with a prominent New York firm where he became the protégé of General William Donovan, head of the firm. When Donovan left to take over the helm of the OSS, Lee went with him and became part of his staff. There he met Mary Price's sister, Mildred, who was also on staff, and through her, Mary, with whom he began a messy extramarital love affair. When Bentley came on the scene, Lee was already passing Price bits of information from the OSS.

He never took out documents or committed anything to paper. He related the information orally and never let Price take notes. Both because their personal relationship jeopardized the operation and because Price was not getting much out of Lee, the Russians, through Golos, asked Bentley to take over. She added him to her list, arranging to meet at Price's apartment or a Georgetown pharmacy or a downtown luncheonette. They did not have an easy time together. He was one of the most nervous people she had to deal with, ever fearful of being exposed, acutely aware of his sensitive position at the OSS, concerned that the rival FBI might be making a special attempt to keep him in its sights. But the information he gave her was worth the trouble. He told her about the anti-Soviet work the OSS was involved in, diplomatic activities in Turkey and Romania, operations in China and France, secret negotiations with the Balkan bloc. He told her about the location of OSS personnel in foreign countries and the nature of their activities.

Lee was important, but he was not Bentley's only source at OSS. There was also J. Julius Joseph, a communist of long standing who had been an employee of the Social Security Board. At some point in 1942, Joseph made contact with Communist Party headquarters in New York, where his potential was recognized, and Golos was asked to establish contact. The first thing Golos did was suggest that Joseph find a position at a more "interesting" agency, the OSS perhaps. This he did, and as it turned out, his job gave him access to sensitive information from the agency's Far East and Russian sections, which he passed along to Bentley. Also at the OSS, in the Spanish division, was Helen Tenney, an attractive New York heiress and longtime communist whom Golos had used as a source when she was employed by a New York organization called Short Wave Research, a covert affiliate of the OSS. When that organization folded, he persuaded her to find a job with the OSS in Washington, D.C. From there she was able to pass on to Bentley secret reports from agents in Spain.

Yet another OSS source was Maurice Halperin, head of the Latin American Division. A Communist Party member since his days as a graduate student at University of Oklahoma, Halperin had lost contact with the Party when he moved to the capital in the early 1940s. But he soon got in touch with the editor of the *New Masses,* who alerted Golos, who assigned him to Bentley. Bentley considered him the ideal source: a stable, happily married man with a lovely home, a lovely family, and no public association with the party. He was also in an enviable position at the OSS, with apparently unlimited access to daily cabled intelligence summaries compiled by the State Department. He handed these over to Bentley in two-week accumulations, along with copies of sensitive U.S. diplomatic dispatches furnished to the OSS, and bulletins and reports prepared by the agency on a variety of topics.

The list of contacts went on. There was Hazen Size of the Canadian Film Board who fed Bentley gossip overheard at the Canadian and British embassies. And there were three men from the Council of Inter-American Affairs (CIAA): Joseph Gregg, who had access to naval intelligence and FBI reports on suspected communist activities in Latin America; Robert T. Miller, who also passed along summaries of information appearing in OSS and FBI files; and Bernard Redmont, a former newspaper reporter working for the press division of the CIAA.

Redmont had been introduced to Bentley by another source, a man she had been meeting regularly since early 1942, a man who would figure prominently in her life for years to come. His name was William Remington, and if ever there was an example of "the best and the brightest," he was it. A tall, handsome, sandy-haired young man whom Bentley and Golos referred to as their "infant prodigy," he had been a brilliant student of economics at Dartmouth and Columbia and, in the early 1940s, appeared to be headed for a brilliant career in government service. A mutual acquaintance at the *New Masses* introduced Golos to Remington, and, after an innocuous luncheon at Schrafft's during which Golos and Bentley, using aliases, traded pleasantries with Remington and his wife, it was decided that Bentley would meet Remington in Washington during her biweekly visits.

"This is Helen," she said when she called him at his office, which she did perhaps a dozen times during the next two years. They would arrange to meet at the Whelan Drugstore on Pennsylvania Avenue or in front of the Mellon Art Gallery or on a park bench somewhere. Their contacts were brief, Remington usually dashing out of his office during lunch hour, leaving just enough time to hand her scraps of paper on which he had jotted down notes. He worked at the War Production Board during those years and had access to military intelligence that interested the Russians. He told Bentley about aircraft production schedules, airplane and high octane gasoline tests. He told her of a process he'd heard about for the manufacture of synthetic rubber. And he was a font of political information as well, commenting on the personalities and opinions of those he knew in government.

As important as all these men and women were to the Bentley-Golos apparatus, there was no one more significant than a man named Nathan Gregory (Greg to his friends) Silvermaster, a charming, well-read, articulate, Russian-born economist who had held various posts in New Deal agencies since the mid-1930s. A good-looking man with a full head of dark hair just going silver at the temples, he was one of the most prominent agricultural economists in the nation, first with the Farm Security Administration, then the Department of Treasury, then Commerce. His wife, Helen Witte, also Russian-born, was the daughter of a Baltic baron who had been an influential counselor to the czar. She was tall and stately and held herself like the patrician she was. Together they made a winning couple, erudite and multitalented, given to hosting musical salons and weekend parties.

In June 1941, when three million Axis troops invaded the Soviet Union, various executive departments, including State, Treasury, and War, were working actively through diplomatic and clandestine channels to help the British, French, and Russians slow the Nazi onslaught. It was against this backdrop that Silvermaster approached Communist Party chairman Earl Browder and offered to supply the party with information that might aid the Soviet war effort. Silvermaster had been a communist since 1920 and had served as one of Browder's assistants during the San Francisco general strike of 1934. It was through Browder that Silvermaster met Golos, who, in turn, dispatched Bentley. She met the Silvermasters at their Washington, D.C., home in August of 1941. Before long, she was visiting them every two weeks, usually midweek to avoid their Saturday-night social gatherings. There, in the late afternoon, she would chat with Helen Silvermaster, who never quite trusted her, and then adjourn to the living room to talk business with Greg and his friend and house-mate William Ludwig (Lud) Ullmann. A Harvard Business School graduate who worked in the economics section of the Treasury Department, Ullmann was a short, mild-mannered man with large, soulful eyes and oversized, Bing Crosby ears. A confirmed bachelor, he had been living with the Silvermasters for years, an arrangement that some in the party understood to be a ménage à trois, while others considered it quite innocent.

On a typical visit, Ullmann and Silvermaster would refresh their recollections from small pieces of paper stuffed in their pockets, and dictate information to Bentley. They always passed along documents, or carbon copies of documents, the quantity and quality of which were staggering. There were reports on weapons, aircraft, tank, and artillery production; analyses of American military industrial capacity; data on the German war industry; U.S. diplomatic cables; U.S. embassy reports; OSS reports; and technical manuals and pilots' operating manuals for American fighter planes and bombers. The volume of material became so great that, despite the capaciousness of Bentley's oversized knitting bag, it was too much for her to handle. Ullmann solved the problem by buying a high-quality camera and setting up a darkroom in the Silvermasters' basement to microfilm the documents. Soon Bentley was carrying home as many as forty rolls of undeveloped microfilm in her bag every two weeks.

Not all this material came from Silvermaster and Ullmann, although both were well-placed and highly motivated sources. Much came from others who reported to Silvermaster, forming a loose assemblage of like-minded government employees, a network within Bentley's larger apparatus. Bentley never met any of the other members of the "Silvermaster Group"—with the exception of one accidental sighting—but she knew of their existence from her many conversations with Silvermaster and Ullmann. There was Solomon Adler, a Treasury Department agent in China; Norman Bursler at the Department of Justice; Frank Coe, an assistant director of the Division of Monetary Research in the Treasury Department; Bela Gold in the Agriculture Department and his wife, Sonia, who worked in Coe's division at Treasury; William Henry Taylor, also in Treasury; and Abraham George Silverman, an economic adviser in the Air Force. More loosely associated with the group was Lauchlin Currie, a New Deal hero, a senior government economist and a special assistant to President Roosevelt, who, Bentley was told, helped other members of the Silvermaster Group secure jobs in "productive areas" or get transfers.

Even more highly placed was a man named Harry Dexter White, the undersecretary of the Treasury, and as such, Henry Morganthau's right-hand man. Bentley never received material directly from White. She never met him. But she understood from her talks with Silvermaster and Ullmann that he was a contributing member of the group. The son of Lithuanian immigrants, White distinguished himself at Stanford and Harvard and was tapped for government service early in the New Deal. He came to Washington in the summer of 1934, a liberal progressive, openly sympathetic to some of the ideals of international communism but not a party member. He was, like many left-of-FDR New Dealers, a "fellow traveler," a man who could reconcile his sincere patriotism with his equally sincere enthusiasm for the communist experiment. White rose quickly in the Treasury Department and, by the early 1940s, he was one of the most influential men in international affairs at Treasury, entrusted by his boss, Secretary Morganthau with vast responsibility and discretion. White handled virtually all matters relating to foreign affairs for Treasury and managed a $2 billion stabilization fund that helped control currency rate fluctuations between the Allies. He was the dominating figure at the groundbreaking Bretton Woods Monetary Conference and was considered by many to be the real author of the so-called Morganthau Plan for the pastoralization of Germany after the war.

Bentley understood from Silvermaster that White was supplying a variety of reports concerning the financial activities of the U.S. government in relation to foreign governments, and that he also contributed memos and documents that came across his desk from other departments and agencies. But White's most valuable asset, Bentley learned, was his ability to place people in the Treasury Department.

It was said that he found jobs for Ullmann, William Taylor, and Sonia Gold, thus facilitating espionage by sponsoring the employment of Soviet-friendly sources. He also used his position to protect Silvermaster when his friend came under scrutiny for communist leanings. Bentley came to think of White as one of the most important members of the Silvermaster Group because he was in a position to influence U.S. policy in a pro-Soviet direction.

With the Silvermaster Group, William Remington, Mary Price, and all her other individual sources, Bentley found herself taxed to the limits. It was sometimes hard to keep it all straight, the appointments, the rendezvous spots, the cover stories. She had different relationships with the sources she met, each involving different fabrications. Some sources knew her only as Helen, a researcher for left-wing journals. Some knew she was a communist; others did not, or claimed later they did not. Some sources believed the material they passed along to Bentley went to the U.S. Communist Party headquarters. Others were aware it went to Moscow.

Throughout the early 1940s, Bentley kept it all going—and without much help from the ailing Golos. She may have started as his stand-in, but she had quickly became a top handler in her own right. Maintenance of the entire apparatus was now her responsibility, and she was paying the price in exhaustion and a mental weariness that segued into depression. She found herself falling asleep on buses, on trains, even standing up. Each morning she would awake already tired and trudge through the day, doubting that she could make it to bedtime. Each day it became harder and harder to concentrate on anything other than the task of the moment. It was an effort to remember what happened the week before. And all of it was made worse by what was happening to Golos.

It seemed increasingly obvious, by early 1943, that the Russians were intent on pushing him aside. He found himself struggling with several professional Soviet agents for control of the network he and Bentley had built. The men were new arrivals whom Golos thought culturally ill-equipped to work with his American contacts. These Russians didn't know how to talk to Americans. They didn't understand what it was like to live in America and be a communist. They couldn't fathom the delicate balance of bourgeois culture and communist ideology, of patriotism and collaboration. Golos would come home from his meetings with these men weary and beaten, alternately pacing the floor and sitting immobile with his face in his hands. He told Bentley that the Russians were pressuring him to turn over Mary Price. Not only that, they wanted the Silvermaster Group to report directly to a Russian agent and not to Golos through Bentley. And they wanted Bentley, too. They wanted her to report to a Russian operative, not Golos. But out of pride, out of a sense of responsibility for the people he brought into his apparatus, and out of a firm belief that the Russians would do damage to the network, Golos held on tightly. In May he wrote to his old friend Pavel Fitin, head of intelligence at KGB headquarters in Moscow, explaining how difficult espionage work was in the United States. But "we are producing quite a lot," he wrote to Fitin, not bragging but rather trying to defend his position and hold on to his leadership role. Still, he was pressured by his superiors in New York and Washington, D.C., to hand over the reins.

"I don't understand what's happening," he told Bentley. "They're trying to sabotage my work. They want to get rid of me." Bentley listened, but what could she do? The only way she could help Golos was to keep on doing what she was doing, to make sure the information kept flowing from Washington to Moscow. She must maintain the apparatus. It was the only way to keep his position viable. So she put herself on the train every two weeks, and she met her contacts on park benches, and she came home with a secret stash to give to Yasha, her gift. He was still her hero. He stayed at her apartment more often now, and at night, she lay awake listening to the sound of his ragged breathing.

# Chapter 9

# Clever Girl

BENTLEY AND GOLOS celebrated Thanksgiving Day 1943 with a late-afternoon dinner at a restaurant opposite London Terrace, followed by an early movie. It should have been a relaxing time, a quiet interlude in their otherwise hectic and stressful lives—maybe even a romantic moment—but it wasn't. They were nervous and distracted. Bentley kept stealing worried glances at her lover. He looked worse than ever, pallid, short of breath, unsteady. She had reconciled herself with his illness—he was not going to recover from heart disease—but that didn't make it any easier to watch him growing weaker, to see the man she admired more than anyone in the world growing more frail. Yet, sick as he was, she knew he would not slow down, whatever she said, for Golos was struck with the sense of urgency that a dying man has about time. He was increasingly obsessed with work. He worried about his agents. He needed to know what was going on, to keep track of them, to touch base, to tie up loose ends. Even as they celebrated Thanksgiving that afternoon, he was distracted by thoughts of an agent he needed to contact. As they walked the block from the bus stop to Bentley's apartment, he insisted she stop at a phone booth to place a call to the source. Bentley was overwhelmed by his sense of loyalty.

She didn't know it, and neither did he, but that intense and unwavering loyalty was, at the same moment, being recognized in Moscow. After his tenuous position during the Purge years and his more recent battles for control of his sources, it seemed that the KGB was finally appreciating his value. Just the day before, November 24, Pavel Fitin, head of intelligence for the secret police, had recommended in writing that Golos be awarded the Order of the Red Star in recognition of his many years as a "talent spotter, personal data gatherer, group controller, and recruiter." But there was such a thing as too much loyalty, Bentley must have thought as she helped Golos climb the one short flight of stairs to her apartment. His breath came sharply. Loyalty was killing him.

Once inside her apartment, he stretched out on the living room couch, exhausted, and fell asleep fully clothed. She changed into pajamas, set her hair in pincurls and then fit her body next to his on the sofa, lying still, dozing on and off. The scene could not have been more prosaic.

She awoke suddenly an hour later with the sense that something was wrong, but for a long, disconcerting moment, she couldn't figure out what. Then she knew: It was Yasha. He was making strange, guttural sounds in his sleep, a rattle deep in his throat. She tried to shake him awake. "You're having a bad nightmare," she told him. "Wake up." But he didn't wake up. The living room was filled with the sounds of him choking. She ran to the kitchen and returned with a bottle of brandy, which she tried to pour down his throat. But he couldn't swallow. It took a moment for it all to register. Yasha was not having a nightmare. He was having a heart attack. She was in a panic. She called for an ambulance. She rushed back to the bedroom, pulling the pincurls from her hair. Then she sat by Yasha, helpless, listening to his strangled breathing, then listening to his silence. By the time the medics from St. Vincent's Hospital arrived a few minutes later, there was nothing that could be done for him. Yasha was dead.

We'll just have to wait for the police, the medics told her. The police? A switch flipped somewhere in Bentley's brain. She was in shock. She was trembling and teary. But part of her knew there was business to attend to. In Yasha's pockets were the coded telephone numbers of most of his agents and who knew what else that must not fall into police hands. When the medics left her alone for a few minutes to move the ambulance, she bolted the door behind them and systematically rifled through Yasha's pockets, transferring their contents to her purse. A few minutes later, the police arrived, and she told them the only story she could tell them: "He was a business associate of mine," she explained. "And he had a bad heart." He was in the neighborhood when he began to feel ill, she told them, so he came up to my apartment. The scene looked innocent enough. They had little reason to doubt her. But there was a dead body, and there had been no doctor in attendance, so they questioned her closely. Where did this man work? What did he do? What did she do? How long had she known him? Who was his doctor? Did she know of any close relative? Did she know any of his friends?

It took all of Bentley's concentration to answer each question, revealing about Golos only what might be known by a business associate, allowing herself to be upset—after all, a man had just died in her living room—but not overcome, not inconsolable, like a woman who had just lost her lover. When asked about Golos's friends, she named no names, for all of his friends were party members or in some way connected to his espionage activities. She would not get them involved. She would not give these local police any reason to suspect that Golos was anything other than a Manhattan businessman with a fatally bad heart.

The scene played itself out slowly. Bentley phoned Golos's doctor, who refused to interrupt his Thanksgiving to travel across town just to sign a death certificate. The police called in the medical examiner who arrived complaining that a holiday was a "hell of a time to die." Bentley threw back a slug of brandy to quiet her nerves. At some point—she had no idea when, the evening was endless—Lem Harris, a friend of Bentley's who was a prominent New York Communist Party functionary, happened to call the apartment. She explained the situation tersely. Don't say anything more, he told her. I'll help with the arrangements. A while later, undertakers from the International Workers Order, a party-friendly union, arrived. They carried Golos out of the apartment in a canvas sling.

Alone, finally, Bentley collapsed in a chair in the living room. She knew she should try to get some sleep, but the effort of walking into the next room, of pulling down the bedspread, of turning off the light . . . it was all too much. Everything seemed too much. She sat, unthinking, staring across the living room, staring across the couch where Yasha had died, but she saw nothing. Time passed. When her eyes focused again, she saw by the clock that it was five A.M., the beginning of a new day. She had much she had to do, much that Yasha had counted on her to do. She forced herself to get up, run a comb through her hair, and put on her coat and hat. Before inertia could pull her back, she was out the door.

The elevator operator at the World Tourists building wondered why she was coming to work so early. She told him her alarm clock had gone off by mistake. She made her way to Golos's office, opened the safe, and quickly but methodically removed every incriminating document she could find, stuffing them in a suitcase Golos had left in the office for such an emergency. Among the papers, she found almost $12,000 in cash. Golos had told her many times that any money in the safe should go to Earl Browder, head of the party. But that would have to wait until she disposed of the documents. In the gray dawn, she trudged down to the subway and back to Barrow Street where, page by page, she burned the documents in her fireplace. At 10 A.M. she was in Browder's office, handing over the money and seeking his advice. She didn't know what to do about all of Golos's contacts. Should she turn them over to a Russian go-between, as he was being pressured to do, or should she carry on, as he did? Browder told her to carry on, that he would help her fight the Russians for control of the sources. That sounded good to her. It was what Yasha would have wanted her to do, she was sure. A few hours later, Bentley was back at the World Tourists office, dealing with the press. The *Daily Worker, Freiheit, New Masses*—everyone wanted details. Golos was one of the old-timers, a legend. Bentley fielded the questions and provided some basic facts, revealing nothing about Golos's secret work. She handled it because she had to, because there was no one else. And she handled it without dropping her guard.

The funeral was that Sunday. Browder made the arrangements, although he did not attend. The service was held in the Gramercy Park Funeral Parlor on Second Avenue, the small chapel filled with comrades and party functionaries. There were no religious rites, only long speeches and testimonials in Golos's behalf. Bentley did not speak, although she knew Golos better than any of them did. It was all she could do to sit there quietly, showing only as much emotion as would be appropriate.

As she struggled to keep herself under control during the days after his death, Bentley felt herself split in two: She was his *golubushka,* his little dove, the woman he would have married had marriage not been deemed a bourgeois indulgence. Yasha was the only man she had ever loved, and his passing left an enormous hole in her life. But she was also *umnitsa*—"Clever Girl"—the code name the KGB used for her. She was a spy, a trusted underground colleague with important responsibilities. She may not have been a stone-cold professional, but she was accustomed to calculating her moves, to watching her back, to pretending she was someone other than she was. And in those days after Golos's death, it was necessary for *umnitsa* to take over. It was the only way she could get through it. She could not share her sadness with anyone. She could not publicly grieve. She could not hope for consolation. The best thing she could do, she told herself, was to carry on as Yasha would have wanted her to do.

The day after the funeral, Bentley met the man who would take Golos's place as her KGB contact. The rendezvous involved the usual subterfuge, with a go-between meeting Bentley in a newsreel theater on East 42nd Street and taking her, by cab and on foot, to Janssen's restaurant on Lexington. There she was introduced to a tall, slender man in his late thirties, a meticulous dresser with only the faintest Russian accent. She was to call him "Bill." She didn't know that his real name was Itzhak Akhmerov, that he was the lead-

ing KGB operative without diplomatic cover in the United States—
he was, in fact, considered one of the most important Soviet wartime
agents—and that he was married to Earl Browder's niece.

What she did know was that she didn't like him. The handkerchief
that poked out of his jacket pocket was color-coordinated with his tie
and his socks. She noticed this right away, and she immediately
thought of Golos's shabby brown suits and scuffed shoes. *That*
was how a revolutionary should dress, not like some suave midtown
executive. This new man was an affront to Golos, an insult to the
principles of the party. When he ordered caviar and an oyster cock-
tail, she couldn't believe it. What indulgence. Was this what Golos
had died for? "Bill" was polite and well-spoken, but he quickly got to
the main point of the meeting: He wanted Bentley to hand over
Mary Price, Walter Lippmann's private secretary who had been passing information to Golos via Bentley. Price should report directly to
him, "Bill" told her. And so immediately, this dapper dresser, this
caviar-eater, challenged Bentley's authority and challenged the legacy
Golos had left her. This would be the first of many such affronts, the
first of many such demands "Bill" would make when they met every
two weeks at Alexander's or Schrafft's or one of the other restaurants
he liked to frequent.

Bentley may have left that first meeting disgruntled and disgusted,
but Akhmerov left with a good impression. Bentley was "intelligent"
and "sober-minded." She was a "sincere person," he reported back
to Moscow. His opinion was important, for the Russians were just
realizing how central Bentley had been to their operation. Apparently Golos had downplayed her significance to his superiors. Probably to protect her but perhaps also to preserve his own power, Golos
had given the impression that Bentley was merely a courier. But now,
after his death, it was becoming clear she was something much more.
She was, as New York station chief Vassily Zarubin wrote to Moscow
after Golos's death, "his closest assistant from whom he had no
secrets."

A week after Golos's death, she was on her way to Washington to
check in, as usual, with her sources. Her responsibilities at World
Tourists and USS&S had kept her so busy that she was barely able to

catch the last train of the evening. It was after midnight when she arrived at Union Station. The next morning, sitting around the Silvermaster's kitchen table sipping tea, she listened gratefully as Helen, Greg, and Lud praised Golos and his work. She needed to hear stories about him. She needed to hear how much he had been respected. She needed to hear his name. But then it was back to business as usual. Lud Ullmann handed her documents and microfilm. She put them in her big bag and left.

Bentley met several times with Earl Browder in the weeks after Golos's death, and continued seeing him regularly after she returned from her Washington, D.C., forays every few weeks. She was determined to carry on with the work Golos had entrusted to her, and Browder appeared supportive. She brought him political and economic material she thought might interest him. She continued to see Akhmerov every two weeks, and, although he never stopped pressuring her about Mary Price, he seemed to accept her role as network handler and liaison. One of Akhmerov's colleagues, New York operative Gaik Ovakimyan, seemed pleased, too. In a report to Moscow, he referred to Bentley as a "genuine American Aryan," which was clearly meant as a compliment. But to Ovakimyan and Akhmerov and their superiors at the KGB, this was all just a temporary situation. They saw Bentley's role as transitional. Although they valued her work, they wanted direct Russian control over the American sources.

American sources were necessary, of course. They provided the access to confidential information. But American *handlers* were not. That's what the Russians were now thinking. With espionage enjoying a wartime heyday, the material was flowing, and the networks were productive. But the operation, it seemed to the KGB, was amateurish. American handlers like Bentley were not trained professionals. They weren't running their affairs as cleanly or as clinically as the secret police now wanted them run. For example, Bentley both collected intelligence information and supervised her sources' secret participation in the party, a practice now considered risky at best. The Silvermaster Group knew each other socially, a dangerous and potentially compromising situation that would never be allowed if true tradecraft were being followed. Duncan Lee, one of Bentley's OSS sources, and Mary Price were lovers. Worse, Lee's wife knew of his secret work and had been present at meetings between her husband and Price. Should Lee's wife discover the affair and want revenge or need leverage, she had it—at the expense of two important sources. Another contact in the OSS who reported to Silvermaster apparently belonged to a second spy network as well, another incautious and amateurish blunder.

It might have been acceptable to run the apparatus this way back in the 1930s and early 1940s when the government was largely unaware of Soviet espionage, and the FBI wasn't paying close attention. But now that the U.S. intelligence community was beginning to catch on, the Russians felt it was imperative for KGB-trained taskmasters to take American sources in hand. For the moment, however, it was expedient for the Russians to continue using Bentley. She busied herself at World Tourists and USS&S. She made her biweekly trips to the capital. She spent long hours buying Christmas gifts for her sources—vodka and caviar, baskets of fruit, bottles of rye and Canadian Club whiskey—the value of each present commensurate with the usefulness of that person to the Soviet enterprise.

Early in 1944, Browder urged Bentley to approach a group of federal government employees who had previously been active intelligence sources but had become a "lost tribe" in wartime Washington. Some of the group, including its putative leader, Victor Perlo, had been members of the Ware Group, the original espionage apparatus established in the early 1930s, but the network had been moribund for some years. In November 1943, just before his death, Golos had made contact with the leading figures. Now Bentley was being asked to follow up. In the early spring, at a meeting set up by Browder, Bentley went to the Central Park West apartment of labor lawyer John Abt where she met Perlo and three other members of the group. Their group had been neglected, they told her, and they were eager to be useful again. Bentley quizzed them on the positions they held in government and the type of information to which each had access. They talked about the other members of the group who were not at the meeting and what they might contribute to the effort. At one point, Perlo asked if "Joe" would be getting this information, a reference to Joseph Stalin that everyone in the room clearly understood. Bentley also set up a meeting schedule and discussed collecting party dues from the group and providing them with literature, just as she did with the Silvermaster people. She left the initial meeting impressed with the group. They were, she reported, reliable party members who were "politically highly mature."

The network consisted of Victor Perlo, a Columbia University–trained mathematician and economist who was, at the time, a statistician with the War Production Board. A slender, sharp-featured man with an angular face and a penetrating gaze, Perlo was the son of Russian immigrants. At the first meeting, Bentley also met Edward Fitzgerald and Harry Magdoff, both War Production Board employees like Perlo, and Charles Kramer, an economist with the Senate Subcommittee on War Mobilization. John Abt, whose apartment served as the rendezvous spot, was the longtime legal council for the Amalgamated Clothing Workers Union and a member of the original Ware Group. She learned that the group also included Harold Glasser, a Treasury Department employee on loan to the War Production Board; Donald Wheeler, an Oxford-trained OSS employee whom the Soviets considered the group's most valuable member; Allan Rosenberg with the Foreign Economic Administration; and Solomon Lishinsky and George Perazich, both employed by the United Nations Relief and Rehabilitation Administration.

Like the Silvermaster network, the Perlo Group was less a phalanx of trained spies than a loose association of men who knew each other through their work. Under Bentley's similarly loose guidance, they operated with the kind of off-hand American informality that drove Akhmerov crazy. It was not just that the members met each other regularly, coming together every other week in one person's apartment to discuss the materials they had gathered. It was not just that their wives knew of their clandestine activities, often typing their notes for them. But on top of that, the group appointed a different representative each time to take the documents to New York and hand them over to Bentley. Although Perlo was more often than not the one who made the trip, a number of the others did as well, which meant that, in flagrant violation of professional tradecraft, at least six members of the group knew that Bentley was their handler. Whoever would be in charge of the materials that week—often it was whoever was slated to make a business trip anyway—would rendezvous with Bentley at the apartment Mary Price now rented in the West Village not far from Bentley's own Barrow Street place. Price had left her job with Walter Lippmann and moved to Manhattan, but as in Washington, her apartment served as a regular meeting spot.

After years of inactivity, the group was eager to be of use and almost immediately began to provide Bentley—and her KGB contact, Akhmerov—with a wealth of information on the American war industry. Perlo and his friends brought complete, up-to-date information on aircraft production and distribution by countries and theaters of action. They brought minutes of the War Production Board and its different committees, interdepartmental economic summaries, plans and proposals for the occupation of postwar Germany, documents on trade policies after the war, and reports on commodities in short supply in the United States. Kramer contributed Capitol Hill gossip; Glasser supplied Treasury Department information; and Wheeler provided copies of OSS reports about worldwide political development. Virtually the entire range of OSS analytical and planning documents on Nazi Germany came across Donald Wheeler's desk—and made it to KGB headquarters in Moscow. Bentley thought the group was "really going to town."

But just as the operation was at its most productive, Akhmerov had to tell Bentley to put a halt to Perlo's visits. It seemed that Katherine Perlo, Victor's ex-wife, had written a letter to President Roosevelt exposing her husband's activities and mentioning by name a number of his associates. They had recently gone through a bitter divorce, and there was an ongoing custody battle for the children. It was exactly the kind of messy situation that reinforced Akhmerov's opinion of undisciplined American communists. Yet he needed Perlo and his group. He needed the American sources Golos and Bentley had developed in Washington. But Perlo would have to be put on ice, at least temporarily, and the delicate job fell to Bentley. "He must not realize we are removing him from work. . . ." Akhmerov told her. "He will be very upset by it." Bentley handled the situation competently, but her position as a top handler was anything but secure.

At almost every meeting, Akhmerov brought up the question of Mary Price. Bentley continued to put him off, but the whole business was becoming increasingly unpleasant. At one point, he lashed out at her, demanding that she turn over Price immediately, threatening, even calling her a traitor. But the more he wanted Price, the more reasons Bentley found to stand up to him. She was not sure Price was in good enough physical or psychological shape to continue with clandestine work, an argument she made to both Akhmerov and Browder. But more than that, she knew that the Russians had been pressuring Golos to give up his contacts, and she knew he had resisted, believing that his former countrymen were incapable of dealing with American sources effectively and sensitively. So, protecting sources like Price from the Russians was one of Golos's legacies, a fight Bentley felt compelled to carry on. It was also part of a complex chess game she was being forced to play, a battle over the territory she and Golos had carved out. To give in was to be checked, and later checkmated. And the game was the only thing she had.

Bentley managed to finesse the Price situation, neither giving her up nor keeping her. Instead, she persuaded Browder—who persuaded Akhmerov—that Price was suffering from both ill health and nervous exhaustion and should be retired from espionage work. Although the Russians were somewhat dubious about this, by mid-1944, Price was taken out of commission and soon thereafter moved to political work. No sooner was this resolved than Bentley faced pressure from Akhmerov to turn over the entire Silvermaster network, the group she had been handling with considerable success since 1941. Again, she balked. She was undoubtedly motivated by a sincere concern for the people who had essentially entrusted her with their professional lives and reputations. And she genuinely liked Greg and Helen Silvermaster. But, as with the Mary Price situation, she was also motivated by self-interest. If the Soviets stripped her of her work, of the work Golos had trained her to do, of the work they had done side-by-side, who exactly would she be? What would she do with her life?

So she put up a fight. Her dealings with Akhmerov became so contentious that Moscow, when alerted, began to doubt Bentley's usefulness. From KGB headquarters, Pavel Fitin suggested to his state-side colleagues that Bentley might be "unbalanced." He criticized her inconsistency. While she professed loyalty to the cause, she was refusing to obey orders. But Akhmerov, despite the difficulties he was having with her, remained steadfast in his support. "I think she is undeniably one hundred percent our woman," he wrote to Fitin. "With a tactful attitude and friendly treatment and firm businesslike relations, it is possible to correct her behavior." Akhmerov continued the pressure and also enlisted Earl Browder in his campaign. Browder had been loyal to Golos and Bentley, but he understood better than most who had the real power in this situation. He sided with the Russians. Between Browder and Akhmerov, they managed to wrest the Silvermaster Group from Bentley's control in the late summer of 1944. She allowed it to happen, but Bentley was not a happy comrade. She was, Akhmerov wrote to Fitin, "very much taking to heart [our] direct contact with Silvermaster, evidently supposing that we do not trust her."

Now the tide had turned, and there was no way Bentley could stand against it. That fall, she was forced to give up the newly acquired Perlo Group. In December, she was told to hand over six of her solo agents, including Helen Tenney, Duncan Lee, and Maurice Halperin. It was for her own protection, her KGB contact said. Helen Tenney, she was told, had shared a taxi with a man who turned out to be with military intelligence. J. Julius Joseph, another of her sources, had been associating with a man who turned out to be an undercover counterintelligence agent. Maybe this was true. Maybe it wasn't. It very well could have been part of Akhmerov's plan to squeeze Bentley out with the greatest of tact and consideration. The sources themselves were also left in the dark. Bentley was instructed to tell them that she was anticipating going into the hos-

pital for an appendectomy and that during the time she was incapac-
itated they would be contacted by another individual. They had no
idea that Bentley's role had been terminated.

To further exacerbate her sense of insecurity, she was also being
shuffled from one KGB contact to another. In the fall of 1944,
Akhmerov ("Bill") handed her off to "Jack." She was instructed to
go to a drugstore on Lexington Avenue in the Fifties, carrying a
copy of *Life* magazine and wearing a red flower. There she met a
husky man in his late thirties, an American of Lithuanian descent,
whom she would meet at various venues in Manhattan during the
next few months. Later "Jack" would turn her over to "Al," whom
she was told to identify, in case she was asked, as a Czech businessman working in Washington, D.C. He was really Anatoly Gorsky,
head of KGB operations in America and first secretary at the Soviet
Embassy.

Bentley was hurt and angry and scared at the turn of events, and
she often lashed out verbally at her Russian handlers. But she had not
given up hope that there might be a place for her in the organization. She had told Akhmerov that summer that she didn't have any
other interests besides her work and that she loved Russia more than
anything else. This may have been a ploy to keep the Soviets from
taking away even more from her, but it was also true—at least the
part about not having any other interests. "Her life will lose its
meaning without this work," Akhmerov reported to his Moscow colleagues after one of his meetings with Bentley. He was right.

The situation was confusing for Bentley. Clearly, the Russians were
forcing her out, but they were also being particularly solicitous. Her
new KGB contacts offered her a salary—Bentley had never been
paid, only reimbursed for travel expenses—and later a fur coat and an
air conditioner. She declined the offers. In fact, they offended her.
Loyalty was not for hire, as far as she was concerned, and money
cheapened the whole enterprise. Still, in their way, the Russians were
communicating that she was a valued member of the organization.
But if she was valued, why was she simultaneously being relieved of
her responsibilities? Her confusion only deepened when, in the fall of
1944, "Jack" told her that Gorsky had some good news that he

wanted to deliver personally. "You will be very thrilled by it," "Jack" said. "I do not want to spoil the surprise."

Gorsky traveled up from Washington to meet her in front of the Edison Theater on Broadway and 103rd. As they started walking toward Riverside Drive, he told her with great formality that the Supreme Presidium of the Union of Soviet Socialist Republic had awarded her the Order of the Red Star in recognition of her extremely valuable services to Russia. This was a great honor, he told her, bestowed on only the most devoted and worthy workers for the cause. He showed her a picture of the award he had torn from a magazine. He told her that the award carried certain benefits, like a monthly salary, preferential living quarters in Moscow, and free vacations. "This is a memorable day," he told her.

Whatever she might think of the Russians, whatever trouble she was having with them, Bentley nonetheless must have felt deeply honored. She assured Gorsky that she would work "indefatigably" to justify the award. But what was she to make of all this? With one hand they took away; with the other, they gave.

Behind the scenes, the KGB was also helping Bentley keep her lucrative USS&S job. The Soviet foreign-trade commissar was apparently considering authorizing another company to perform services similar to those of USS&S, such as shipping parcels to the USSR. But the KGB warned him off. The new proposal would "directly threaten the existence of [Bentley's] cover." And it was not only her professional life that the KGB was taking an interest in. Akhmerov and later Gorsky also discussed with their Moscow superiors the idea of finding Bentley a husband. "She is alone in her personal life," Akhmerov cabled his boss in Moscow. "Why not send someone from home? Send him as a Polish or Baltic refugee to South America or Canada. We'll arrange the rest." Fitin apparently considered the request seriously, cabling back, "The question of a husband for her must be thought over." But the matter was apparently dropped. Six months later, when Bentley made what her new contact Gorsky interpreted as a romantic overture—she told him he reminded her of Golos—he immediately fired off a cable to Moscow saying that it was urgent to find her a husband. But again there was no follow-through.

The Russians seemed to care about her. Her contacts—first
Akhmerov, then "Jack," then Gorsky—treated her well when they
weren't busy demanding that she give up control of her sources. She
was being offered money and gifts and awards, and, unbeknownst to
her, being taken care of in other ways, yet the fact was that barely a
year after Golos's death, she had lost virtually all her power. By the
end of 1944, she was no longer the leader of the two most productive spy rings in America. She was no longer what Golos had made
her. The game, she was beginning to realize, was over.

# Chapter 10

# Russian Roulette

HER SOVIET SUPERIORS undoubtedly knew of Bentley's romantic involvement with Golos. Even if they had been blind to it during Golos's lifetime, they would have seen it in Bentley's words and actions after his death: her intense loyalty to him, her staunch defense of his work, her desperation to keep things as they were before he died, the obvious fact that she had nothing in her life besides her work. But the KGB's concern for her emotional health was transient. What the Russians most cared about was building a more professional, highly disciplined spy operation. That meant pushing Bentley out while not making an enemy of her. It meant taking away what she and Golos had built while not angering her so much that she would turn against them. It was a delicate matter that they handled with singular indelicacy.

In early 1945, after she'd reluctantly—and often truculently—handed over all her agents, Bentley was dealt another blow. Gorsky demanded that she move from her lovely Barrow Street brownstone in the West Village. His reasoning was sound. Some of her contacts knew her address, others had visited the apartment, and most knew her phone number. That was just bad tradecraft, as far as the KGB was concerned. But that didn't make the demand any more palatable, or any easier, for Bentley. The apartment was rich with memories for her, not just the painful memories of her lover's death, but memories of long evenings in front of the fireplace talking and drinking, stolen weekends spent as quiet homebodies, listening to the radio, eating breakfast together like an ordinary married couple. The apartment was one of her last tangible links to Golos. Leaving it was finally, irrevocably, leaving him. As she packed her belongings into boxes, she never felt more alone or more adrift.

To make matters worse, the move itself was logistically difficult. Manhattan was still suffering from a wartime housing shortage, and Bentley had trouble finding a new apartment. It may have been that she couldn't bring herself to look very hard or that, as depressed as she was, she had little energy to devote to the effort. Whatever the case, she found nothing. Finally, she put her furniture in storage and took a room at the Hotel St. George in Brooklyn Heights. This made the move all the more wrenching, as she was leaving not only the apartment, but the neighborhood she'd called home for almost seven years. It meant she would be commuting into work every morning. And the weekly rate at the hotel was quite a bit more expensive than an apartment rental. But she felt she had little choice. Anyway, she could afford the extra expense. She was still making good money at USS&S.

But now that part of her life was threatened, too. It seemed the Soviets wanted her out of that enterprise as well. Gorsky told her he had received an inside tip that the FBI was looking into the affairs of the corporation. The ties between USS&S and the party might easily be discovered. Worse, Gorsky told her, the FBI might come to understand that the company was a front for illegal activities, thus compromising far more than Elizabeth Bentley. That was true, but Gorsky was also reacting to reports from his other American agents that Bentley's associates at USS&S knew of her intelligence work, that she was, in other words, mixing her legal and illegal activities. To Gorsky, it was just another example of Bentley's amateurism. He felt completely justified urging her to give up her position. But to Bentley, it was far more than a job, just as the apartment had been more than a place to live. USS&S was the business she and Golos had founded. They had worked side by side. Her job there was truly her last tie to her life with him.

So she stalled Gorsky. She said she was concerned about John Reynolds, titular head of the company, who knew he was fronting for the party but did not know his business was providing a cover for espionage activities. If Bentley was gone, and the Russians moved in, wouldn't that compromise Reynolds? And what about the money Reynolds had personally invested to get the business going? Would the Soviets buy him out? Reynolds was a friend and colleague. She liked him. But she was undoubtedly worried more about her own future. The position at USS&S was an interesting, challenging, well-paid executive job, an unusually impressive attainment for a woman. The job was both her identity and her livelihood.

But she had to do as the party asked. In February, her New York contact, "Jack," told her he had found a replacement for her. In March, Bentley resigned the lesser of the two positions she held in the company, and a woman named Ray Elson took over as corporation secretary. Two months later, she handed over the vice presidency to Elson, drew six weeks of salary, and left for an extended stay in Old Lyme, Connecticut. But she couldn't quite leave the job behind. Through the summer months, she traveled to Manhattan a number of times to help straighten out USS&S business. She continued to be involved in the operation despite the KGB's direct orders. In August, Gorsky insisted she come down to Washington for a meeting, the purpose of which was to tell her, again and in no uncertain terms, to stay out of USS&S. Still, Bentley resisted. When she returned from her summer in Connecticut, she started going to the office regularly again. Reynolds didn't like Ray Elson. He had complained to Bentley all summer that her replacement wasn't doing a good job. On the other hand, he viewed Bentley as indispensable. That's all she needed to hear. In the fall, she resumed her position as vice president. Gorsky must have been astonished. How often was it that an agent, a loyal agent, a woman, defied the orders of a top-ranking officer of the KGB? He and "Jack" and their Moscow superiors were coming to fully understand just how stubborn and independent-minded—and perhaps, given the situation, reckless— their "Clever Girl" really was. She was becoming a handful. The Russians would have to find a way to manage her.

One approach was to keep her close even as they pushed her away. And so, as her KGB contacts pressured her out of active espionage work, out of her apartment, and out of USS&S, they did not let her stray too far. Moscow instructed Gorsky to make extensive use of Bentley as a talent-spotter and recruiter, loading her up so much that "she didn't have time to think too much." Bentley was told she was being taken out of circulation for only a limited time. It would be just a matter of six months to a year before she could resume her clandestine work. And these new duties, her contact "Jack" promised her, would be significant. Your apprenticeship has been served, he told her early in 1945. You are now ready to move on, he said. He told her of a KGB plan in which six sources would each report to six different messengers. Three of these messengers would report to one courier, three to another. The two couriers, in turn, would report to a single individual who would oversee the entire operation and know everyone's identity. This last person, unknown to any of the six original sources, would normally be a Russian, "Jack" told her. But because of her experience and loyalty, she would be entrusted with this position.

He couldn't have been serious. Gorsky had a low opinion of Bentley's tradecraft and had reason to question her loyalty. She had played an extended game of tug-of-war with him over her sources and was now disobeying direct orders by staying at USS&S. Why would she be tapped for more sophisticated clandestine work? The promise had to have been an empty one, an enticement meant to keep her in line. There were other promises as well. Gorsky, determined to pry her out of her position at USS&S, promised that the KGB would set her up in some small business in Philadelphia, Baltimore, Washington, D.C., or somewhere on the West Coast. She could operate a hat shop or a dress shop or a travel agency for six months and then be recalled to active espionage duty. Meanwhile, to his Moscow colleagues, Gorsky was suggesting that Bentley be relocated to another country.

Bentley didn't know she was being manipulated. All she knew was that her world was falling apart. She was confused and worried, depressed, scared, and angry. And, like a good American, a citizen born with the constitutional right to make noise, she did. Talking back to the KGB was as dangerous and foolhardy as disobeying orders, yet she couldn't keep quiet. She may not have fully understood how precarious her position was. She may have felt her citizenship protected her. Or she may not have cared. Whatever the case, she criticized the Russians to their faces. When she was first being pressured to hand over her sources, she told Akhmerov just what she thought of her Soviet comrades: They cared little for Americans or America. The USSR was the only country they loved and worked for. Akhmerov was taken aback by her bitterness. And this wasn't an isolated incident. Reading various reports of Bentley's intransigence, Moscow decided she suffered from "shattered nerves" and an "unsettled private life."

It all came to a head in late September when she returned from her summer in Connecticut and met with Gorsky at Alexander's in New York. She had just come from a liquid lunch with John Reynolds and had made the decision to go back to her position at USS&S. Emboldened both by that defiant move and by several dry martinis, she told Gorsky that she never wanted to deal with the Russians again. "All of them are gangsters and care only about Russia," she told him. The American communist party was "a gang of foreigners," she said. Gorsky promptly reported to Moscow that Bentley was hostile, unreliable, and untrustworthy, and that she "drank in order to tell in a drunken state that which she did not dare discuss sober." He saw her now as a "serious and dangerous burden for us," someone who could "damage us here very seriously." First, he suggested that she be "taken home"—that is, sent to the Soviet Union. But soon he was suggesting something more drastic. "[There is] only one remedy left," he wrote to his Moscow superiors. "Get rid of her."

But Moscow answered with surprising restraint, perhaps because

Bentley was still of some use to the KGB. Just a few weeks after her drunken meeting with Gorsky, she identified a new OSS employee who would be willing to pass along confidential material. People's Commissar for State Security Vsevolod Merkulov wrote to Gorsky to "take all precautions with regard to yourself and other agents known to [Bentley]." Get her out of our business, he told Gorsky, but keep her under Soviet influence and maintain "an appearance of our complete confidence in her. . . ." Merkulov wrote that he didn't think Bentley would soon betray the Soviets but that her threats should be taken seriously. He counseled Gorsky to arrange a friendly meeting with her, to calm her down, to remind her of the good work she had done and offer her financial assistance.

In late October, Gorsky wrote back that he and Bentley had met again. Among other things, the two had discussed the recent defection of a man named Louis Budenz, an American communist journalist who knew Bentley by her real name and knew of her involvement in espionage. Budenz had publicly renounced the party and had gone to the FBI, which meant Bentley could be in serious trouble. Gorsky was surprised that she didn't seem nervous or concerned about this turn of events. Otherwise, the meeting went well. Bentley was sober, cordial, and apologetic. But Gorsky was far from mollified. In late November, almost two years to the day after Golos's death, he wrote to Moscow, once again recommending Bentley's liquidation. In a long and chilling memo, Gorsky discussed various ways of eliminating this troublesome American. Shooting was too noisy, he concluded. Arranging an accident was difficult; faking a suicide was too risky. He had contrived a plan for another agent to kill her, but that option didn't look promising right now because Bentley was, he told Moscow, strong and healthy, and the agent in question was not feeling very well. In the end, Gorsky concluded that a slow-acting poison would be the best method. Agent X could put it in her food or dribble a little on her handkerchief.

# Chapter 11

# Closing In

BENTLEY WAS UNAWARE of the KGB plot to kill her, but she had other reasons to be frightened during the first half of 1945. It turned out that Gorsky had been right: The FBI was taking an active interest in USS&S. Hoover had prodded the New York field office in late 1944 to pick up the investigation that had been dropped back in 1941 when agents had targeted Golos and World Tourists. Now Bentley's company—the one she would not leave despite Gorsky's warnings and direct orders—was under intense scrutiny. Confidential informants at New York City banks were feeding agents detailed information on the financial activities of both World Tourists and USS&S. It wasn't long before the New York field office had a complete record of all deposits and withdrawals transacted by the two companies. Other informants helped local agents compile a personnel dossier on USS&S. The FBI now knew who had been and still was working for the company, and began to dig into their pasts. John Reynolds, identified as the principal shareholder in the company, was first on the list. The agents could find no evidence of communist or anti-American activity—his unblemished record, after all, was the reason he had been chosen to head the company. They wanted to interview him, but Hoover called them off, saying that this would tip the FBI's hand.

Bentley began to suspect that agents were nosing around. One day, as she was packing her belongings at the Barrow Street apartment, her landlady came by to tell her that a man had been asking questions about her. A few days later, a tall, dark, athletic-looking young man knocked on her door and started inquiring about someone who used to live in the apartment. There was something about his looks and his demeanor that had "FBI" written all over it, Bentley thought. And the questions were odd. No one else had lived in this apartment for years. It may have been nothing. It may have been a coincidence. But Bentley was spooked. When she met Gorsky in a Washington, D.C., movie theater later that spring, he reinforced her suspicions about the proximity of the FBI, warning her that her situation was "extremely dangerous" and that she should take a "vacation" immediately, in Mexico or Canada.

And there were other reasons for Bentley to be nervous. In the spring, security officers from the OSS began investigating how portions of a secret report had come to be printed in *Amerasia,* an obscure left-wing journal on Pacific affairs whose editors were close to the Communist Party. The FBI raided the magazine's New York offices in June and discovered 1,700 secret or confidential documents from the Navy, the State Department, and the OSS. The publisher of *Amerasia,* a wealthy, pro-Soviet, greeting-card entrepreneur, and five others were arrested on charges of conspiracy to commit espionage. But authorities had failed to get search warrants for much of the evidence, which was then ruled inadmissible in court. The upshot was a plea bargain in which two *Amerasia* editors were found guilty of theft of government property. To those watching closely, those like Elizabeth Bentley, it was a close call. The authorities were closing in on espionage operations. She could be next.

Bentley also had reason to fear her own American comrades. She had received threats from an officer in the Communist Party who said that if she didn't return the money Earl Browder had put up to help bankroll USS&S she would be "blown to hell." Bentley had no way to evaluate the seriousness of the threat. It could just be someone spouting off, an angry remark meant merely to intimidate, or it could be that her comrades really had it in for her. She didn't know the party anymore. Her ties to the organization, except through Browder himself, were severed years back when she went underground. It had now been seven years since she had felt the warmth and camaraderie that had initially attracted her to the party. The threat confused and frightened her and added to her growing disillusionment with the life she had chosen for herself.

"The effect of Mr. Golos was wearing off," she said later, trying to make sense of this moment in her life. She had idealized Golos as a selfless revolutionary with a lifelong commitment to the betterment of the common man. No one could live up to that. All of her Soviet contacts since Golos's death had been disappointments one way or the other. They dressed too well. They spent too much money. They offered her gifts. They made threats. They seemed disdainful of Americans, often cynical, and, most disturbing, they seemed completely uninterested in American communism and its goals. She had now been exposed to three different KGB operatives—two of them, Akhmerov and Gorsky, of the highest standing—and the experience had been jarring. These men were not utopian progressives interested in bringing social justice and economic equality to America. They were professional espionage agents, trained members of the Soviet secret police intent on gathering intelligence that would aid their country. Bentley had been ferrying information to them for years, but she had been protected from the reality of the situation by Golos. He had stood between her and the operatives who now, after his death, defined communism for her and who now controlled her fate.

She was coming to see these men as selfish and corrupt, partially because they were, indeed, ruthless and self-interested, and partially because they failed to measure up to her Yasha. They were cheap little men pulled by strings from Moscow, she thought. They were no better than gangsters, with their threats and bribes. As her eyes were being opened to the reality of the KGB, she was also learning that what she thought she knew about the Soviet Union—the inspiring stories of a new and glorious society that she had read about in party literature, tales of full employment, education for all, new hospitals, productive farms, happy workers—might not be the truth, or the whole truth. American Communists like Bentley were almost completely ignorant of the excesses of Stalinism, of the purges, the violence, and the repression. The Soviet propaganda machine had done an excellent job of hiding the internal politics of the country from American eyes. But now that story, incident by incident, was leaking out. One day a Lithuanian Jew came into World Tourists to arrange for the shipment of parcels. He told Bentley that when the Nazis invaded, they decimated the Jewish population and killed most of his relatives. But, he said, "as bad as the Nazis were, the Red Army was worse."

Bentley was further disillusioned when she met Gorsky at Bickford's restaurant on 23rd Street and Eighth Avenue in the fall of 1945. It was their first meeting since her drunken outburst the month before, when she called the Russians "gangsters" to Gorsky's face. In the interim, Gorsky had been instructed by Moscow to treat her gently, to arrange a friendly meeting that would give Bentley the idea that the Russians had complete confidence in her, the strategy being that you keep your friends close but your enemies—or potential enemies—closer. Gorsky was very pleasant that day. He assured her that he didn't hold her responsible for her outburst at their last meeting. There were great pressures in this job. It was not uncommon for someone to let off steam. But Gorsky wanted her to know how very much Moscow appreciated her work. He handed her an envelope containing one hundred twenty-dollar bills, $2,000 in cash, "as a gratuity for past services and a token of friendship," he said. There were no strings attached, he told her. He hoped the money might help her in case she encountered financial difficulties, given the FBI's investigation of USS&S.

At another time, in another state of mind, Elizabeth Bentley might have seen the money as a compliment. She *had* done good work. She *had* been useful—no, more than useful, *integral*—to the success of Soviet espionage in wartime America. The money could be considered a token of esteem, a reward for years of selfless work, an earned but unexpected bonus. Certainly that's what Gorsky tried to communicate as he turned over the envelope to her. He was, of course, far from sincere. Given his increasing distrust of Bentley and the fact that he had been plotting to liquidate her, the money he handed her was not a reward for services but rather an attempt to keep this difficult woman in line. If she could be made to feel indebted to the Russians, she would be less likely to cause trouble. Bentley was smart enough to see the envelope stuffed with bills for what it really was: an attempt to buy her loyalty, like the fur coat or the air conditioner—a bribe. It made her angrier than ever.

But what exactly was she to do about her situation? She was in no shape to make a decision about her life. Through the spring and into the summer of 1945, as she experienced more and more stress, both her mental and physical health suffered. She was sleeping poorly, battling either insomnia or terrifying nightmares about firing squads. She was losing weight. Her face looked thin, tense, and drawn. She hardly recognized herself in the mirror. And she was drinking. At the Hotel St. George, where she now lived, she was regularly being treated by the house physician, a Dr. Herbert Mann, for what she called aches and pains, but what he recognized as severe hangovers. The drinking was making her sick, but it was also blunting her anxiety and taking the edge off her isolation.

One lonely evening in the spring of 1945 Bentley found herself at the hotel bar again, drinking alone and to excess. That night she picked up a man. It may not have been the first time. This man was an ordinary-looking fellow, perhaps forty years old, with thinning reddish hair and glasses. He looked a little like Yasha, she thought. He said his name was Peter Heller and that he was a New Yorker, but he was vague about the details of his life—perhaps because, as Bentley would learn much later, he was married with several children. Bentley got the impression that he was a lawyer or an investigator of some kind. It really didn't matter. At least not then, not at that moment in the bar. She took him up to her room. But Heller was no one-night stand. He and Bentley began to see each other often, and Bentley began to eye him as potential husband material. Then,

abruptly, Heller stopped calling and disappeared from her life, resur-
facing several weeks later with a tale about being a "big-shot government spy."

Bentley knew the FBI was nosing around USS&S, and she had
suspected an agent was making inquiries about her at her old apartment. Maybe this was a trap. Was Heller employed by a federal
agency? Had he been hired by the Russians to spy on her? One
night, while he slept, she went through his wallet, where she found
an identification card with a shield on it, like the police or the FBI
might issue. But she couldn't make out the name of the agency. It
seemed to be purposefully obscured. She told her New York contact,
"Jack," about Heller, and "Jack" told Gorsky, who felt sure Heller
was an FBI agent. Bentley was advised to discontinue the liaison
immediately, cutting off contact diplomatically so as not to arouse
Heller's suspicion.

But she didn't cut it off. She was too lonely, and he was too willing. It was easier for her to compartmentalize her suspicions, dissolve
them in alcohol, and keep seeing him. If she could no longer enjoy
the camaraderie of the party, if she could no longer enjoy the emotional intimacy she had with Yasha, at least she could have a warm
body in her bed at night. They saw each other often that spring, and
together they played a dangerous game. Her lips loosened by drink,
she probably told him tales of her espionage activities, or at least
broadly hinted at them. It made her an exciting person, an extraordinary character, something more than a plain-faced, thirty-seven-year-
old woman living in a hotel room in Brooklyn and picking up men in
bars. Heller may have fashioned an elaborate response to her tales to
keep up with her or to keep his real life secret from her. At one point,
Heller apparently told her that he had taken part in investigations of
communists and that he knew the Russian language.

When Gorsky warned her again to end it, she defended her new
lover, telling the Russian that Heller would be an ideal husband.
Heller, however, was apparently not as taken with Bentley as she was
with him. To him, she was little more than a sloppy drunk who was
generous with her favors. But the relationship satisfied them both
enough that they kept it going. And so Bentley's loneliness was tem-

porarily relieved even as her situation worsened. Now Gorsky was more than ever concerned that his "Clever Girl" was an accident waiting to happen. And Bentley, although she tried to repress it, was now more than ever paranoid that someone was after her.

That summer, the summer of 1945, she left the city to spend several months in Connecticut, commuting into Manhattan from time to time to help at the USS&S office and traveling down to Washington to see Gorsky. But mostly she kept to herself, walking and thinking and drinking, alternately trying to make sense of and forget the frightening situation in which she found herself. Later, when she needed to create a sympathetic picture of herself, she would tell a story about her epiphany in Old Lyme, the small, picturesque town on the shores of Long Island Sound where she spent part of that summer. It was here, she said, that she got back in touch with her New England self and with the values of the sturdy and independent people who lived there. The story, as she told it, went this way: One summer day, walking the streets of the town, she found herself inexplicably drawn to the pretty, white-steepled Congregational church. She went in. It was quiet and peaceful. She sat down in a back pew and suddenly, without thought or volition, she began to pray. She cried out for help and, in response, the words of the Twenty-third Psalm filled her head. Yes, she was indeed walking through the valley of death. She was fearing evil. And now God was coming to the rescue; God would walk beside her. She heard the voice of her own conscience—*You must make amends*—and when she walked out into the bright sunlight, she knew what she must do. She must come clean. She must renounce her past. She must go to the FBI.

It made for a powerful tale of faith and redemption, of patriotism lost and found, and she wrote it later in lush, melodramatic prose. But it wasn't the truth. Or at least it wasn't the whole truth. Elizabeth Bentley might have had a revelation. She might have been transformed in one shining moment from Elizabeth Bentley, Communist Spy, to Elizabeth Bentley, God-fearing, New England Patriot, sitting in that back pew. But it is more likely that the metamorphosis was a longer and far more painful process than that, owing more to fear and paranoia than divine intervention.

Sometime during the summer of 1945 Bentley did indeed decide to go to the FBI. But if she did it because God and her conscience spoke to her in a church in Old Lyme, she also did it because she was afraid the FBI would get to her first. She did it out of anger at the Russians, out of a desire for revenge against those who had taken away all that was exciting and meaningful in her life, out of disgust with those who degraded the principles for which Golos had died. Bentley may have been a woman enlightened. But she was also a woman scared and a woman scorned.

# Part Two

# The Reality

# Chapter 12

# In from the Cold

BENTLEY KNEW SHE couldn't go to the FBI's New York field office on Foley Square. The KGB would be watching, she was sure. And Washington, D.C., was out of the question. She couldn't chance being seen by any of the people she knew down there, all her erstwhile sources and contacts. FBI headquarters would be staked out, anyway. For all she knew, the capital might be crawling with KGB. But she didn't panic, and she didn't rush. Her years underground had taught her to think like a chess player, to examine every move and imagine every countermove, to spin scenarios until she came up with the right one, to play the game in her head until she knew it well enough to play it for real. The move that made the most sense was to find a small field office in an unobtrusive location not far from New York. She found what she was looking for in New Haven, Connecticut. Connecticut was home turf, and she was not unfamiliar with the town. It turned out that the field office was located on the ground floor of an ordinary downtown office building. Perfect.

The night of August 22 was hot and humid. It was almost 80 degrees at midnight, the air thick and heavy, the pavement still radiating that sluggish, enervating heat that drives New Yorkers out of the city in the late summer. But when Bentley awoke in her hotel room in Brooklyn the next morning, a front had moved in, bringing clouds and unseasonably cool temperatures; a break. Good traveling weather. She took pains not to be followed as she negotiated the subway into Manhattan. Once in the city, she went through the repertoire of evasive moves she knew so well, ducking in and out of stores, crossing and recrossing streets. By the time she boarded the train at Grand Central, she was satisfied that no one was following her. But in New Haven, she checked again, cautiously making her way to the building that housed the field office, taking an indirect route, passing it on foot and doubling back. She took the elevator to the third floor, then walked down the service stairs and slipped into the office.

Bentley was scared. But the fear didn't make her stupid. It made her smart. She had a plan. Before she considered saying anything to the FBI about her communist activities, she wanted to know what the Bureau knew about her. She wanted to know how close the FBI was to nabbing her. She wanted to know if her lover, Peter Heller, was part of some scheme to keep her under surveillance. But more than anything, she wanted to know—or at least get some instinctive sense about—whether she could trust the FBI any more than she could trust the Russians or the party. Golos had hated the FBI on general, ideological grounds and, more specifically, because of the crackdown on World Tourists. But Bentley had to trust someone. She had to extricate herself from her old life while she still had the choice, while she was still in control. Later, because it would put her in the best light, Bentley would write that she went to New Haven that August and "told the highlights" of her story. But she didn't. She played the whole scene close to the vest, like a poker player with a good hand who doesn't know if the guy sitting across the table might have a better one.

In the New Haven field office, she was interviewed by Special Agent Edward J. Coady, who listened with interest as she talked about having "associated" with a Peter Heller who claimed, she said, to be a government investigator and a government spy. This man Heller had told her to keep her eyes open at her place of employment, United States Service & Shipping, which did business with the Soviet Union. He suggested that there might be information about the Russians she could pass along to the U.S. government through him, and she was willing to go along with the scheme, she told Coady, if Heller was legit. Was he? Or was he impersonating an agent?

Heller was, in fact, an investigator. He worked for the New York State Division of Parole in the Executive Clemency subdivision, examining the records of prisoners under consideration for release or pardon by the governor. But, as the FBI quickly discovered, he had no connection with the Bureau, the OSS, or any counterintelligence group, although he was a lieutenant in the Amy Reserves. Mostly, he was a man involved in an extramarital affair with an unstable woman. Heller spun his story to keep Bentley interested but also to keep her off balance, to keep her wary of him so she didn't make demands. Bentley believed Heller might be a threat to her, but she also thought the impersonating-an-agent story would be a good cover for her initial personal investigation of the FBI.

But Special Agent Coady was not so easily fooled. Why, for example, would a New Yorker take a 75-mile train trip to Connecticut to report her suspicions about another New Yorker? And what would a prim and proper, obviously educated woman be doing "associating" with a man who claimed to be whom Heller claimed to be? It didn't make sense. All through the two-hour interview, Coady was not sure what to make of Bentley or her story. When he tried to ask questions about her own activities—wasn't she hinting that she was or had been involved in something questionable?—he got nowhere. She would not veer from the Heller story. Yet he also got the distinct impression that she was observing him, taking it all in, attempting, subtly but perhaps not subtly enough, to find out if the name Elizabeth Bentley meant anything to him. The interview was, he concluded later, a "fishing expedition." When it was over, neither Bentley nor Coady was satisfied with the catch.

She had made a bold move in going to the FBI, but it was not bold enough. She hadn't learned what she needed to know, and she hadn't come clean. She was still in limbo, still unsure how close the FBI was to knocking on her door. So she stepped back. She continued seeing her KGB contact. She continued working at USS&S, despite intense pressure from Gorsky to quit. She continued sleeping with Peter Heller. Weeks went by. She heard nothing from the New Haven office, no word of the investigation of Heller. Then, in mid-September, news broke in the New York papers about Igor Gouzenko, a Soviet agent employed as a code clerk at the Soviet Embassy in Ottawa. Earlier that month he had defected, taking with him a thick batch of incriminating documents. Based on that material and a number of follow-up interviews, Canadian intelligence and the FBI were in the midst of discovering a North American spy network centered on atomic espionage with operatives in both Canada and the United States. Bentley was not connected to this network, but one exposure could easily lead to other exposures, one crack could fissure into many. Undoubtedly people in the now-uncovered network knew Golos. Hadn't Bentley, years before, collected mail from Canada for Golos? The Gouzenko defection must have been, at the very least, disconcerting.

Then, in early October, came the defection of Louis Budenz, which threatened to touch Bentley directly. Budenz had known and worked with Golos and had met Bentley several times. He knew, at least by implication and association, about her clandestine work. If the FBI had somehow missed her before, surely these two investigations, Budenz and Gouzenko, would point fingers in her direction. If she needed more motivation to get back in contact with the FBI, she had it.

Almost immediately after learning about the defection of Budenz, she wrote a letter to the New York field office repeating her concerns about Peter Heller. Perhaps she could get more out of these agents than she had out of Coady. It was worth a try. Her letter resulted in an appointment on October 16 with Special Agent Frank C. Aldrich. She would have to go down to Foley Square for the interview, which did not please her, but at this point, it was a risk she'd have to take. At first, Bentley told Aldrich that she wished to make a complaint about an individual representing himself as an FBI agent, but as the interview went on, Aldrich saw that this was not exactly why she was there. It seemed she was more interested in getting information than giving it. When she switched gears and told him that she thought she was being followed, and that it was her impression that it was the FBI, he knew she was fishing. He tried, like Coady before him, to turn the conversation to Bentley and her background, and if he had a bit more success than his New Haven colleague it was only because Bentley was more ready to be honest.

But not ready enough. She told Aldrich that she was "closely tied in" with people about whom she "had suspicions" and whom she "believed to be Russian espionage agents." She made vague references to "contacts with communists." She talked about the possibility of arranging a meeting with a Russian agent that could be monitored by the FBI. When he pressed her for details, she refused to elaborate and retreated into generalities. She talked a lot, probably because she was nervous and because she was hiding much more than she was revealing. The less she said, the more words she used. Aldrich was outwardly courteous and noncommittal. As he listened to her rambling on, it occurred to him that he might be sitting across the desk from a certified nut case. But if she wasn't, if she was on the level, then something was going on here. He didn't quite know what, but he meant to find out.

He took down a phone number where Bentley said she could be reached. Then, as soon as she left, he called Special Agent Edward W. Buckley, the office's Soviet expert, and told him of the strange interview. Buckley thought there might be something worth looking into. A few days later, he called the number Bentley had left with Aldrich—it was her office phone at USS&S—but she was not there. He persisted, calling several times in October and early November, but she was apparently home with the flu. When he finally got through to her on November 6, she said she was upset and had a great deal on her mind and that she was undecided whether she should come forth with the information in her possession. She was still struggling with her conscience, still weighing her fear of the Russians against her fear of the FBI. If she came forth, there would be no turning back. She would be saving herself, but she would also be closing the door forever on the most exciting period of her life. Maybe those days had ended when Golos died, but she could still remember the passion she once felt for communist ideals, the sense of belonging to something big and important. She felt it now like a phantom limb, but she felt it nonetheless. Buckley told her that if she had any information regarding un-American activities, the Bureau needed to know it. If she was troubled or concerned, Buckley could offer guidance and assistance. She agreed to come in the next day.

On November 7, just after lunch, Elizabeth Bentley, dressed in a dark suit and matching hat, was ushered into Ed Buckley's office in the FBI building in lower Manhattan. It had been almost two and a half months since her enigmatic visit to the New Haven field office, and now, finally, it seemed that she was ready to talk. Buckley had made all the arrangements and was intending to conduct the interview by himself, but that morning he ran into fellow agent Don Jardine in the hallway and asked him to sit in. Jardine was then in the midst of developing a file on a writer for the *Daily Worker* whom the Bureau suspected of espionage. If anyone was familiar with the New York communist scene, it was Jardine.

Buckley's office was a small, drab, uncarpeted room, sparsely furnished with the obligatory, government-issue steel desk and two hard-backed office chairs. It was not a comfortable place for a conversation, but then being questioned by the FBI was not supposed to be comfortable. However, Buckley and Jardine were quite aware that Bentley had come forward voluntarily, and they planned to treat her gently. The interview would not be adversarial. They would do nothing to scare her off. They told her that they were glad to see her and that they appreciated her arranging her schedule to come in. They chatted for a while about nothing, as strangers do when they are otherwise busy taking stock of each other. Buckley and Jardine could see she was nervous and tense. They began by asking her broad, open-ended questions that allowed her to talk as little or as much as she wanted, revealing as little or as much as she wanted. Tell us about yourself, Buckley asked. Tell us how you got mixed up in all this, Jardine added.

Bentley began to chart for the agents her journey into communism, talking first of her visits to Italy in the early 1930s and the experience of living under Mussolini's rule. She told them how she had returned to America wanting to stop fascism and build a better world. As she filled them in on her personal history, Jardine became increasingly fascinated. How could a woman from stable stock, with the benefit of a top-notch education, swallow the communist line, he wondered? She was so well-spoken, so obviously intelligent. He was supposed to be a hard-bitten G-man, but Jardine found himself almost immediately sympathetic to Bentley. Maybe it was because she was a woman. He wasn't taken in by her feminine wiles—Bentley didn't have many—but rather by the idea that as a woman she was a victim, not a perpetrator. A product of his time, Jardine saw Bentley as someone taken advantage of rather than someone in charge. She wasn't a criminal, he decided. She was an idealist, a misguided idealist who had gotten in over her head.

No stenographer was in the room, and as Bentley began to offer more and more details about her life as a communist and as a spy, the agents furiously scribbled notes on lined yellow pads. She talked of her mentor Golos, hinting they were something more to each other. She gave details about World Tourists and USS&S. And she began to name names. Some of the people she named were civil servants in positions of responsibility, even power: Silvermaster and Perlo, Wheeler, Halperin, Fitzgerald, Kramer, Ullmann and Harry Dexter White. The names came quickly. Once she decided to open the tap, she opened it all the way. When she first contemplated going to the FBI, she wrestled with her conscience about turning in her contacts, some of whom she had considered friends. But she convinced herself that she was doing them a favor. She was "saving them." If she turned them over to the authorities, they would no longer be useful to the Soviets. They would be out of the spy business, whether they liked it or not. And maybe they would see the light, as she had seen the light.

The reasoning might sound like pure self-justification, a skewed logic that allowed her to expose others and not feel guilty about it. But her motives for coming forth and for naming names had an underlying simplicity. She was a woman who needed to believe in something greater than herself. She needed to be connected to a noble cause that gave her a part to play. For ten years, that cause had been communism. Now, because of what she'd learned about the Soviets, because of how she'd been treated, because Golos was dead, because she was scared, her cause would be anticommunism. As sincerely as she had been a party member, a steeled Bolshevik, a courier, and a spy, she would be a warrior on the other side, *for* the other side. Her own immunity from prosecution was not discussed. It was assumed.

She talked through the afternoon and into the evening. Buckley sent out for sandwiches, and they kept going. Four hours, six hours, eight hours, and they were still at it. The agents listened eagerly as Bentley pulled back the curtain and allowed them a glimpse of the Soviet spy apparatus. She recounted a complex web of relationships and interactions, code names and cover stories, secret meetings with people she knew by first name only, late-night calls made from telephone booths, microfilm carried in knitting bags. The agents marveled at her memory. She remembered the names of three different hotels where a minor contact had stayed in 1936. She remembered in which drugstore on what corner she had met a source three years before. She remembered what people ate for dinner, the color of a man's tie, the shoe size of a woman she knew only by a code name. She was able to recount employment histories, educational backgrounds, family histories. Jardine would mention the name of a person the FBI already had in its files, and she would know it and be able to respond with a wealth of details that would later be confirmed in the record. She talked about her KGB contacts, "Bill" and "Jack" and "Al," and how "Al" had asked for her help in placing someone in the FBI, "the only government agency that they could not crack"—a comment the agents noted with particular pride.

When Bentley finally left, taking the subway home, in the dark, unescorted, Buckley and Jardine remained in the little office hunched over the metal desk hammering out a seven-and-a-half page summary of the interview. At 1:30 in the morning, they sent it by teletype to their boss, J. Edgar Hoover, at FBI headquarters. Eighteen hours later, Hoover had a complete seventy-page statement covering the eight-hour interview, hand-delivered by an agent who flew down from New York. The director could not contain his enthusiasm, and neither could his agents in New York. Early in the interview, Jardine had thought to himself: This lady knows what she's talking about. We hit pay dirt here. He was right. And it was only the beginning.

Two days later, Bentley was back. And the day after that, and the day after that. She was interviewed fourteen times in November by the two New York special agents who took over her case, Joseph M. Kelly and Thomas G. Spencer. She came in at least every other day, and, during a particularly grueling stretch in the middle of the month, she was interviewed six days in a row. The logistics were challenging. She continued to work at USS&S during the day, both because it was the way she made her living and because quitting might have tipped off the Russians that something was going on. That meant she came in for her interviews in the late afternoon or in the evenings or on weekends. Often she walked or took a cab down to Foley Square after work, but sometimes the agents met her elsewhere for her convenience, like a hotel closer to her office.

At each interview, she mentioned more names and remembered more particulars, clarifying relationships, chronicling rendezvous, and explaining, in calm and precise detail, how the system worked. Her initial nervousness was gone. She was composed and self-possessed now that she had made the decision to tell all. Mostly, the agents let her talk, allowing her story to unfold as she told it. Of course, they would follow up on any names she mentioned, pressing for details, but they rarely brought up names themselves. They did show her photographs of officials and employees of the Soviet Embassy to see if any of the Russians she knew by code name could be further identified. That's how she learned that her contact "Al" was really Anatoly Gorsky.

As Agents Kelly and Spencer sat and listened to Bentley through November, they became increasingly convinced that she was telling the truth. Her delivery was clear, concise, and clinical. Whatever emotions she may have been experiencing, she kept to herself. She was poised and in control, just what the agents would have expected from someone who operated at her level with her responsibilities. The stories she told were internally consistent and, based on what the Bureau knew or suspected, they sounded logical. They were too rich with potentially verifiable details to be mere concoction. And the stories were beginning to check out. After every interview session, the agents would comb the FBI files to find references to the people Bentley had just mentioned, and time after time, they were there. Some of the people she named, like Silvermaster, already had thick files with the Bureau. Each time the agents found confirmation, even of the smallest detail, Bentley's stock went up.

Of course, the FBI immediately began a background check on Bentley herself, going through her Vassar and Columbia records, calling Foxcroft, checking with Macy's personnel department and various banks and credit unions. And, in mid-November, while she was being interviewed at the New York office, FBI agents were dispatched to her Brooklyn hotel to do what was called in the trade a "black-bag job." Without a search warrant—which presumably would have alerted anyone watching her room, like the KGB—the agents "surreptitiously entered," that is, broke into her room and searched it thoroughly, looking for anything that might reflect on her credibility, that might either prove or disprove the stories she was telling. They found nothing out of the ordinary.

The agents' major concern now was that Bentley could not support her story with any documents. If she had handled the volume of material she said she had, where was the proof? Why didn't she have a copy of some confidential government memo or a few pages of a secret report or even ticket stubs from her many train trips to Washington? Of course, it was explainable: The whole idea of living a clandestine life was to leave no documents behind, no traces of that life, to arrange it so there was no whiff of who you were and no hint of what you did. Her tradecraft may have been a bit sloppy for the Russians' taste, but she was a good enough spy to adhere to basic rules. One of those rules was that you did not keep incriminating material in your possession. It was a testament to how well she did her job that she could not prove, in black and white, that she had indeed done it. She had been a good communist, and she would never have thought to squirrel something away, some bit of evidence, "just in case," or for insurance, to be used against her comrades sometime later. And by the time Bentley seriously considered going to the FBI—at which time she might have thought about what proof she could bring—it was too late. It had been months since she last met with any of her sources, as much as half a year since she gathered material from one of her networks.

Perhaps Bentley sensed that the agents needed more. Perhaps her newly awakened Yankee conscience was bothering her. Whatever the case, on November 17, when she met Kelly and Spencer at a Manhattan hotel for her sixth interview, she brought with her the money Gorsky had given her the month before. Immediately on entering the room, even before she took off her coat and hat, she opened her purse, took out a fat envelope, and threw it on the bed. She was clearly enjoying the drama of the moment. "Here's some Moscow gold," she told the agents. More to the point, here was what could be considered tangible proof of the story Bentley had told the agents during her initial November interview when she first mentioned "Al" and what she considered his efforts to buy her loyalty. The agents took the money and stored it in a safe deposit box at a Manhattan bank. For weeks, the joke around the office was that the cash in the envelope was "the only money we've ever gotten back, or ever will get back, from the Lend-Lease program."

Bentley also proved her credibility to the FBI in another way. She had arranged a November 21 meeting with Gorsky the month before, at the end of their October rendezvous. When Bentley told the Agents Kelly and Spencer about it, they urged her to keep the appointment, and then set the Bureau's wheels in motion. In the capital, agents tailed Gorsky from his home to Washington National Airport, watching him board an Eastern Airlines plane for New York. New York agents picked up the trail when he arrived in town, and stayed with him despite his vigorous efforts to lose them. Three agents took note of the Gorsky-Bentley rendezvous outside Bickford's restaurant late that afternoon and watched as the two of them walked a half block east to Cavanaugh's and went in. The agents did not attempt to eavesdrop on the two-hour conversation that took place, but they didn't have to. The point was made: Bentley said she met with top Russian functionaries, and she did.

By the end of November, when the FBI assembled a final 107-page statement for Bentley to sign, she had named eighty-seven American citizens, from prominent party functionaries to prominent government officials, from sympathizers and fellow travelers to dues-paying comrades, from people she knew personally to those she had only heard about from others. The list was longer still if one counted Russians and other foreign nationals—more than a hundred names. Bentley seemed to be a one-woman encyclopedia of espionage. Her statement was so dense with names and details that the agents appended a seven-page index to it.

Of all those she named, the Bureau was most immediately and fervently interested in the federal employees Bentley said had provided her with confidential information, several of whom were already under suspicion. That list included some mostly invisible, midlevel bureaucrats, New Dealers toiling away in alphabet agencies, but it also included Harry Dexter White, the undersecretary of the Treasury, and Lauchlin Currie, former assistant to FDR, and Duncan Lee, a protégé of and top aid to OSS founder William Donovan. Twenty-seven of the government employees she named were, the FBI soon determined, still employed in Washington, D.C., including seven people at the State Department, ten at Treasury, two at Commerce, and two in the OSS. There was someone at the Department of Justice, someone at the Office of War Mobilization, several people at the Foreign Economic Administration. These people still had access to sensitive information.

Bentley's allegations were the biggest thing to hit the FBI since agents had gunned down John Dillinger in front of the Biograph Theater in 1934. The information the Bureau now had, courtesy of a woman who had just walked in the door one day, was almost overwhelming, both in quantity and in its potential significance. If she was right, the Russians had managed to burrow deep into the U.S. government using U.S. citizens as moles. If she was right, widespread espionage was more than paranoia, it was reality. And the Soviet Union, our temporary, tenuous wartime ally, would certainly now have to be considered our most powerful enemy. Her November statement touched off a torrent of memo-, letter-, teletype- and report-writing by the director, including communiqués to the White House, the attorney general, the State Department, the Civil Service Commission, the War Department, and others. Hoover moved into high gear. There would be no undeveloped leads in this case.

# Chapter 13

# Hoover's Turn

J. EDGAR HOOVER COULDN'T have been more pleased when he got word of Elizabeth Bentley's allegations from the New York field office. What a treasure to fall in the FBI's lap just as one war was ending and another, more subtle one, was about to begin. With fascism defeated, it was time to deal with the enemy the United States had embraced for wartime convenience, the Soviet Union. And the fight against communism didn't have a more willing warrior than Hoover. Bentley's revelations buttressed his belief that there was a communist conspiracy in America—men and women actively working for the Soviets and against the best interests of the United States—and gave him ammunition he was eager to use. The Bentley interviews were yielding hundreds of leads. The information she gave would reinvigorate scores of languishing investigations. It would fatten the files of men like Silvermaster and White, who were already under suspicion.

But Hoover saw something more in the Bentley revelations. He saw opportunity. He immediately grasped the political importance of

her allegations, seeing them as way to extend the power and influence of the FBI. What could be more threatening than spies in our
own government working for the demise of the American way of life?
Hoover wanted—and with Bentley's help could now demand—a
bigger budget to fight this evil, more agents, more field offices, more
power, more independence of action. Not only that, he now had,
courtesy of Elizabeth Bentley, ammunition against his chief rival in
the counterintelligence business, the OSS. Several of the sources
Bentley named worked for the OSS. That meant the organization
had been infiltrated and could no longer be trusted. That meant the
field would be clear for the expansion of Hoover's personal and
political power.

On November 8, the day after Bentley's first substantive interview
in New York, Hoover fired off a letter, a "preliminary flash," he
called it, to Brigadier General Harry H. Vaughn, military aide to
President Truman. Bentley's statement was incomplete, unsigned,
and based on the scribbled notes of two agents, rather than the work
of a trained stenographer. But the information was too hot. Hoover
couldn't wait. According to a "highly confidential source," he wrote
General Vaughn, a number of federal government employees had
been passing sensitive information to outsiders who then transmitted
it to Russian espionage agents. Hoover repeated sixteen of the names
Bentley had mentioned the day before, including several who
worked for the OSS. The investigation, Hoover assured the general,
was being vigorously pursued. But, he wrote, hardly containing his
eagerness, "I thought the President and you would be interested in
having the preliminary data immediately."

Six days later, in the early evening, President Truman called
Hoover personally and asked him to brief Secretary of State James F.
Byrnes on the Bentley affair. At 9:30 the next morning, Hoover presented himself at Byrnes's office where he summarized the information the Bureau had gotten from Bentley, telling the secretary that
the allegations had not been fully corroborated yet—after all, the
investigation was only a week old—but that he believed they had
"some substance." Many of the people Bentley mentioned were
already in the FBI's files, he said. Then he named names: Silvermas-

ter, Ullmann and White, Lauchlin Currie and Duncan Lee, Victor
Perlo and several in his group, Mary Price and Helen Tenney. He
named eighteen people that morning, all federal employees. The secretary and the director apparently saw eye-to-eye on the importance
of convincing the public of the existence of Soviet espionage. From
Hoover's perspective, it was a very successful meeting. That afternoon, he wrote a letter to his assistant directors summarizing his session with the secretary and asking for a detailed report on the
Bentley situation that he could forward, as soon as possible, to
Byrnes.

In New York, agents Kelly and Spencer were still busy interviewing Bentley, having her statements typed up after each session so
she could review and sign them at the next session. By the end of
November, the New York field office had spliced together one,
all-encompassing, 107-page statement, which Bentley signed on
November 30. Four days later, Hoover sent out a 71-page report
titled "Soviet Espionage in the United States," based almost entirely
on Bentley's allegations. Copies went not only to the secretary of
state and General Vaughn, but also to the attorney general, the secretary of the Navy, the secretary of the Treasury, the president's chief
of staff, and several others. Hoover left no doubt that the Bentley
case was the Bureau's single most important priority.

As news of Bentley's defection made its way through government
channels, the FBI geared up for what would become one of the
longest, most expensive investigations in its history. In mid-
November, while Bentley was still being interviewed, Hoover took
the case away from the FBI's Soviet Espionage Squad in New York,
arguably the group that knew the territory best, and assigned it to
the Bureau's elite Major Case Squad, which had been working on
German and Japanese espionage during the war and now had little to
do. Hoover put his faith in thirty-eight-year-old Thomas J. Donegan, head of the Major Case Squad, a small, intense man who, like
Hoover, was so focused on his work that he was almost oblivious to
the rest of life. At the office, Donegan had earned the nickname
"The Hat," because he was often so busy coming and going that his
colleagues rarely saw him without a fedora on his head. Hoover told

Donegan that he wanted the Bureau to devote all its energy to following up Bentley's leads and that there would be "no limit" on the number of agents he could use. Donegan began immediately, focusing the investigation on fifty-one of the more than a hundred people Bentley had named, with special attention to the twenty-seven still employed by the federal government. Tracking Bentley's statements from day to day, Donegan began the investigation in earnest on November 17, when the Bureau requested wire taps from the attorney general on Perlo's, Bela Gold's, and Maurice Halperin's telephones. That same day, agents were assigned to tail Silvermaster. William Remington's phone was tapped. Perlo, Ullmann, and Donald Wheeler were put under surveillance, and New York agents were told to locate and follow Mary Price. Then Harry Dexter White was put under round-the-clock surveillance, his phones tapped and his mail intercepted and read. Written summaries of White's phone conversations were forwarded to the squad, and when he moved to a new apartment, FBI agents rented the adjoining unit and installed microphones next door. Following Bentley's meeting with Gorsky in mid-November and her subsequent identification of him from FBI photos, agents in Washington were assigned to tail him night and day. Then, based on Bentley's November 21 statement, Donegan put thirteen additional people under surveillance. By the third week in November, Hoover had reassigned six Philadelphia and six Newark agents to the Washington office to join the twenty-five agents already there on the job. Eventually, more than two hundred agents would work the case.

Herman Bly was one of them, a thirty-two-year-old, five-year veteran of the Bureau when he was assigned to dissect Bentley's statement, line by line, checking and cross-checking every detail with existing material in FBI files and elsewhere. At one point, agents worked assiduously to verify a meeting that Bentley said took place. She remembered that it was a rainy Sunday in March, and she remembered that one of the men at the meeting, Harry Magdoff, had been off work recovering from an operation. Agents combed Magdoff's personnel file at the Department of Commerce and found confirmation that he'd been on sick leave following gallbladder sur-

gery and was not set to return to work until March 7. A check with
the Weather Bureau established that it had rained in New York on
Sunday, March 5. Bingo. At another point in the investigation,
agents from four different field offices fanned out to interview scores
of people, search city directories, and dig into newspaper archives,
police reports, and hospital records in what turned out to be a futile
attempt to identify a man known to Bentley only as "Charlie."

Much of it was monotonous work, but it was also the most exciting assignment Bly and his fellow agents had ever had. They were
electrified by the Bentley material, astounded at the richness of
detail, amazed at the number of leads, and absolutely convinced that
this was the breakthrough that would halt Soviet espionage in the
United States. As the initial investigation gained momentum, it
looked as if they might be right. The details were checking out. The
diverse people Bentley named matched the descriptions she gave,
which was the first good news. Then the surveillance on White
showed that he had frequent contact with Silvermaster and several
others in the alleged network. And a search of the Silvermasters'
home revealed a photo lab in the basement, just as Bentley had said.
Things were looking good.

As the investigation continued, so too did the interviews with
Bentley. But Donegan wanted her to do more than talk. He wanted
her to act as a double agent. Bentley was not just amenable; she was
eager. Here was a chance to prove her rekindled patriotism, a chance
to go back to the exciting life she had lived before the Russians
stripped her of her duties and took away her networks. She would be
squarely back in the game, although, of course, on the other side.
Bentley was asked to stay on at USS&S and keep her eyes open. She
was asked to maintain contact with Communist Party leader Earl
Browder. It was suggested that she attempt to renew her Washington, D.C., contacts and resurrect her moribund career as network
handler. Toward this end, the FBI asked Bentley to schedule another
meeting with Gorsky, her KGB contact.

They met on November 21 at their usual spot in front of Bickford's
restaurant on 23rd Street and had a long and seemingly friendly conversation over dinner. Gorsky talked mostly about USS&S and the

problems still to be ironed out there. Meanwhile, Bentley made a few apparently not too subtle attempts to get him to discuss the relationship between USS&S and the Communist Party, and the party and the KGB. Gorsky's antenna immediately went up. *What was she fishing for?* He kept the conversation going, not allowing his suspicion to show while he chose his words carefully, answering without really answering. Bentley told him she was restless and dissatisfied with her routine duties at USS&S, implying that she was ready to be reactivated or at least take on additional responsibilities. Gorsky was wholly unresponsive to her hints, not because he didn't get them but because he did. When she tried to elicit from him what, if anything, he had in mind for her, he was noncommittal. The meeting netted nothing for Bentley in her new role as a counterespionage agent. But it had served to alert Gorsky. His suspicions were further aroused when he left the restaurant and realized he was being tailed. It would be their last meeting.

Bentley could not contact her old sources without Gorsky's involvement. She had been forced to break off ties with them many months before, and since then Silvermaster and Perlo had been reporting directly to the Russians. Any attempt to reinsert herself in the apparatus would have been far too suspicious. But the FBI did ask if she would get in touch with Helen Tenney, one of her old OSS contacts. Tenney had been hospitalized for a nervous breakdown, and the FBI probably considered her the most likely candidate for "weak sister," the fragile link in the chain, the unstable one who might break under questioning and give the Bureau what it needed: corroboration for Bentley's story. Bentley traveled to Washington to meet with Tenney, who had no idea her former handler had defected. Tenney seemed amenable to reestablishing contact—too amenable for the Bureau's purposes. She indicated no dissatisfaction with the Russians, no desire to get out of the game. There was no hint that she was ripe for turning.

Bentley's efforts at counterintelligence were doomed anyway—as were the FBI's surveillance and phone-tapping operations—because by the third week in November, the KGB was not only aware of her defection but was also receiving regular summaries of her interviews with Bureau agents. The leak was in London, in British Intelligence, which received frequent FBI reports both as a professional courtesy and to aid counterintelligence efforts in that country. The mole was Harold "Kim" Philby, a senior British agent who was also a Soviet spy, recruited into covert work while a student at Cambridge in the late 1930s. When Philby read the FBI report on Bentley, he notified the KGB's London station chief who immediately reported the news to Moscow. Two days later, on November 22—the day after Gorsky had met with Bentley and had his suspicions aroused—he and his counterpart in New York received urgent cables from Moscow telling them of Bentley's defection and instructing them and other KGB operatives in the United States to cease all contact with her. On November 24, Vsevolod Merkulov, People's Commissar for State Security, notified Stalin, Molotov, and Beria of Bentley's betrayal. The FBI had no idea there was a leak and kept sending summaries of the Bentley interviews to British Intelligence, where Philby conscientiously forwarded them to Moscow, which in turn kept its American operatives duly informed. It was a smooth, continuous communications loop, a dandy system for everyone but the FBI.

A few of Bentley's former sources heard directly about her defection. Silvermaster was told the news by Akhmerov in early December. Some of the twenty-seven federal employees she had named undoubtedly picked up hints at work. Hoover had alerted so many people so early that rumors, if not truth, were probably circulating through Treasury, State, and the OSS, at the very least. Other sources may have caught on to the fact they were being tailed. With scores of agents in New York and Washington on the streets conducting close physical surveillance, it was likely that someone at some time noticed them. The clicks and taps and buzzes on phone lines would have alerted others.

So even if Bentley had been skillful and subtle and well-trained in the art of counterespionage—which she wasn't—circumstances were such that she would have failed as a double agent anyway. The same leak that sunk her efforts then began to sink the FBI's investigation. Agents following paper trails were still finding success, matching people with descriptions, pinning down details. But surveillance efforts and wiretapping were netting nothing. Gorsky and Akh-merov, Silvermaster and Perlo, everyone stopped doing what they had been doing. There was nothing for the agents to observe. There was nothing to overhear.

The interviewing wasn't going very well for the FBI either. Agents had hoped to uncover a "weak sister," but they encountered instead men and women strident in their declarations of innocence, who offered universal, unequivocal denials. Akhmerov had discussed with Silvermaster what his response would be if Bentley fingered him. "Naturally, he will deny completely any allegations of his connection and cooperation with us," Akhmerov assured his Moscow superiors. Ullmann, when interviewed, admitted meeting Bentley at the Silver-masters a number of times but denied that anything untoward took place. He told agents he and the Silvermasters considered Bentley a "hysterical, highly emotional nuisance." Remington said he knew Bentley only as "Helen" and thought she was a newspaper reporter. He gave her only press releases and published articles, he told the FBI. Some of those interviewed gave evasive answers. Others flatly refused to talk.

But even if there had been more cooperation—*any* cooperation—in developing an espionage case, the government still faced formida-ble obstacles. For a charge of espionage to stick, it had to be shown not only that the accused persons passed confidential information relating to national defense but also that they engaged in these acts with an intent to do injury to the United States to the advantage of a foreign nation. In other words, the sources who passed the informa-tion had to know it was going to Russia. Some of them undoubtedly did. Perlo had joked with Bentley about "Uncle Joe" Stalin getting the information from his network. If Silvermaster didn't know before Akhmerov took over from Bentley in late 1944, he certainly knew afterwards. But a number of the other sources had connections only with Bentley, who was also their liaison to the party, and believed, or allowed themselves to believe, that the information they were passing went from her to Earl Browder and stopped there. Maybe they knew better, maybe they suspected otherwise, but it would be difficult to prove in a court of law. A case of perjury was no simple matter either.

To prove that someone lied, you needed the direct testimony of two witnesses or one witness plus corroborating evidence. But Bentley was the only witness talking. And she had no documentary evidence.

The case itself may not have been progressing as the FBI had hoped, but there was little doubt that Bentley's defection was having a major effect. In fact, the double whammy of Gouzenko's defection in Canada and Bentley's in the United States led Moscow to order a freeze of virtually all intelligence activities by the KGB in North America for more than two years, until late 1947. On November 23, Moscow instructed Gorsky to sever connections with a number of sources who knew Bentley, including Harold Glasser, Charles Kramer, Donald Wheeler, Victor Perlo, Allen Rosenberg, Lauchlin Currie, Helen Tenney, and Maurice Halperin. Further, Gorsky was to tell Perlo and a few others, under strict secrecy, that Bentley was the cause of the new orders. Two weeks later, Akhmerov broke with Silvermaster, telling him that Bentley's defection meant they would have to "stop our work totally." Then, one by one, the KGB functionaries who had dealt with Bentley over the years were called home. Akhmerov and his wife, Catherine, both of whom had met with Bentley a number of times in New York, were ordered back to Moscow in early December. Vassily Zarubin, Akhmerov's colleague in New York, also had to leave. Gorsky, Bentley's Washington, D.C., contact, was replaced as station chief and ordered home at the same time. All of a sudden, because of one loose-lipped woman, it was the end of the golden age of Soviet espionage. Bentley had delivered what the head of KGB intelligence called "the most tangible blow to our work."

Espionage activity ceased, and lives were changed forever. The FBI, disappointed that the surveillance and wire-tapping operations had not been productive, decided to go after some of the people Bentley named, the twenty-seven still employed by the federal government, in more subtle ways. The Bureau quietly alerted the appropriate officials in the appropriate departments, and internal pressure was applied. When William Remington was about to be tapped for a White House staff position, two FBI agents paid a visit to the assistant to the president, informing him that Remington was a principal figure in an ongoing espionage investigation. Remington's name was quickly removed from the list. When the Bureau let it be known to Naval Intelligence that Remington was under suspicion, he was discharged from the Naval Reserves. Within the various government departments, some positions were abolished, some people were forced out, and some were allowed to resign. Silvermaster left the Treasury Department in mid-1946. Ullmann and Perlo followed nine months later. Halperin and Wheeler resigned from their State Department positions. Magdoff and Fitzgerald left their Commerce Department jobs. Glasser was forced out of his high-ranking Treasury post. During the course of the next year and a half, twenty-four of the twenty-seven, most of whom were career civil servants, left the employ of the federal government.

Bentley's defection was felt at the highest levels. Responding to the alarms set off by Hoover, as well as to the director's growing power and influence, the Truman administration began to take the threat of espionage more seriously. In March of 1947, the president issued a sweeping executive order that established a security-checking program for all federal employees. The new program empowered the FBI to investigate any hint of disloyalty among those working for the government. During the next few years, more than twenty-five thousand people were referred to loyalty boards for investigation.

Removing people from their positions, plugging the leaks, and stemming the flow of information to the Soviets was all fine. But Hoover wanted convictions. He wanted those who had spied to pay for their disloyalty with more than just their jobs. So the investigation continued, with every independently verifiable fact checked, every lead pursued, scores of agents on the streets, hundreds of people interviewed. There was some external corroboration for Bentley's story—Katherine Perlo's letter, for example, and a 1939 report by ex-communist Whittaker Chambers—but it was not enough. The Perlo letter could be dismissed as the ravings of a distraught woman who wanted to harm her former husband to gain the upper hand in a custody battle over their children. And Chambers, who had left the Party in 1938 and had named Harry Dexter White, Lauchlin Currie, and others in a debriefing with FDR's assistant secretary of state, was, like Bentley, an informer. Juries didn't like informers. They didn't trust them.

But two years into the investigation, Hoover got the break he was looking for. Back in 1943, Carter Clarke, the head of the Army's intelligence service, had ordered the Army's elite cadre of code-breakers to start examining ciphered Soviet diplomatic cables sent between the United States and Moscow. Clarke's fear was that Stalin, then an ally, might actually be undermining and endangering the United States by trying to make a separate peace with Hitler. But the code was more difficult to break than he thought, and by the time the first messages were deciphered, it was 1946, and the war was over. In any event, it turned out that the decrypted cables had nothing to do with the relationship between the Soviet Union and Germany. Venona—as the top-secret decryption project was code-named—had instead yielded what was unarguably the counterintelligence coup of the century: a detailed chronology of Soviet spying activities in the United States. Soon the government had evidence from the decrypted cables that more than three hundred citizens, immigrants, and permanent residents of the United States, including some high-ranking government officials, had covert relationships with Soviet intelligence agencies.

But the identities of those mentioned in the cables were obscured by code names. It fell to a select group of FBI agents, working in total secrecy, to comb Bureau files, check the personnel and travel files of other agencies, pull confidential documents, and study Elizabeth Bentley's statement in an effort to match the code names with the people. It was careful, exacting, tedious work, but it began to pay off. A picture began to emerge: The code name "Clever Girl," which showed up a number of times in the cables, was the name given to Elizabeth Bentley. "Eck," it turned out after much cross-checking and investigation, was Perlo; "Pal" was Silvermaster. Harry Dexter White was referred to as "Lawyer" or "Richard." Lauchlin Currie was "Page"; Helen Tenney was "Muse." By matching details in the cables with details in the files—personal information, travel dates, positions held, changes in assignments, access to certain material—the FBI was able to identify almost 150 people, including a number of those named by Bentley. In addition to Perlo, Silvermaster, White, Currie, and Tenney, the FBI managed to identify Duncan Lee, Harold Glasser, Bela and Sonya Gold, Mary Price, Maurice Halperin, Donald Wheeler, Edward Fitzgerald, and others. Bentley herself was the subject of more than a dozen Venona cables.

Time and again, the Venona cables confirmed the details of Bentley's story, identifying her sources and contacts, mentioning information and documents they passed along to her, detailing how sources were handled, who was valued, who was causing concern, who might be tapped for undercover work. This was the corroboration the Bureau had been searching for. If the FBI had harbored any doubts about the veracity of Bentley's statement, Venona wiped them away.

But would the Bureau—*could* the Bureau—use Venona to go after those named by Bentley? It was not as easy a decision as it seemed. The advantage was obvious: The material could very well help convict a number of people accused of espionage whose "continued freedom," one FBI official wrote to another, "is a sin against justice." But the disadvantages were, according to Hoover and his top assistants, "overwhelming." To use the material was to make it public. But the history of Venona was one of utmost secrecy and security. Almost no one knew about it, just the code-breakers themselves, the FBI team working on code names, and top brass at army intelligence and the FBI. Hoover saw to it that the CIA, the new kid on the block, the agency that had replaced the OSS, remained in the dark. There were even plans, at first, to keep the president out of the loop. The elite of the intelligence community whose professional lives were all about secrets guarded this one like no other. As proud as they were of what they had accomplished, they were prouder still that they were the only ones privileged to know about it. Knowledge was power, as Hoover knew well, and it was to be guarded jealously. Going public with Venona went against the whole culture of the FBI and the intelligence community.

And there were compelling reasons to keep the project secret. Venona would embarrass the U.S. government. After all, the decrypted messages were *diplomatic* cables intercepted while the

Soviet Union was an ally. Was this the way the United States treated its allies? What might this disclosure mean to future U.S.–Soviet relations now that the war was over? But even more important, if Venona was made public, Hoover believed it would compromise ongoing counterintelligence operations. The Russians would know that the United States had broken one of their very toughest codes. That would make code-breaking even more difficult in the future and would most certainly mean that the Russians would reexamine how and to whom any messages were sent from now on. That was too high a price to pay for the conviction of a handful of no-longer-active spies. The integrity of the project itself and the future counterintelligence activities were simply more important than punishing the wrong-doers.

Underpinning the decision, too, was the FBI's concern that Venona might be viewed as problematic evidence in court. A judge could rule it inadmissible, viewing it as "hearsay." Neither the originators of the messages nor the recipients would be in court to testify to their veracity. The messages themselves were incompletely decrypted, with words or entire passages missing. And the identities of the people mentioned, those who presumably would be on trial, were cloaked in code names. What if the FBI introduced Venona in court, compromising its own counterintelligence operations and endangering international relations, only to have the evidence thrown out? The risk was too great. Venona stayed secret. It would remain secret for the next fifty years.

But the decision to keep Venona under wraps did not mean the FBI was willing to halt its pursuit of the people Bentley named. And so, the investigation continued. The interviews continued. The surveillance continued. Then, early in 1947, Hoover asked E. P. Morgan, one of the Bureau's top lawyers, to evaluate the evidence to determine if prosecution was possible. Morgan's conclusions were grim. Despite a widespread and intensive investigation, all the FBI really had was the uncorroborated statement of one informer. If Bentley's espionage network had existed, there was no proof that it existed now. And, although the investigation had uncovered the fact that many of the people Bentley named knew each other and socialized together, there was no proof of any other kind of relationship. Moreover, the subjects in the case were bright, successful, unusually well educated, and included some very prominent people. "It can be expected that some of the finest legal talent in the country would be retained for their defense," the FBI lawyer wrote in his report. And, with the evidence available—which did not include the Venona revelations—the case was little more than Bentley's word against theirs. "The likely result," Morgan concluded, "would be an acquittal under very embarrassing circumstances." The FBI had hit a wall.

# Chapter 14

# Red Spy Queen

As THE FBI investigation dragged on into 1947, Bentley struggled to find her footing. She had imagined that the break with her past would be clean: She would confess, say her mea culpas, and move on. She would close the door on her past. The clouds would part, the seasons would change, and Elizabeth Bentley would walk forth in sunshine to begin the rest of her life. She was, after all, only thirty-seven years old. But that was not the way it was happening. The investigation seemed to have no end, the case no closure. Bentley signed her final statement at the end of November 1945, but her involvement was far from over. In fact, for much of the next year, she was virtually on-call for the FBI, coming in for dozens of interviews as agents tirelessly went back over details, followed up leads, and presented her with photographs to identify.

She was out of the spy business, but she wasn't. She was no longer an underground operative, and her attempts at counterespionage had been short-lived, yet her life was now more secretive and solitary than ever. Back when she was handling the networks and checking in with her sources, back when she was juggling multiple rendezvous and traveling at least twice a month to Washington, she was out in the world, in regular contact with a wide range of people. She dined with them, talked with them, and if they couldn't be considered friends, they were at least compatriots, partners in the cause. They were, in large part, the people who made up her life. Now, of course, they were gone. Even before she fingered them for the FBI, she had lost them to the Russians. And now that she was a committed anti-communist, she could not go back to the acquaintances she had made years before as an open party member. Nor could she talk to or confide in her colleagues at work, as she had—much to the dismay of the Russians—when she was involved in espionage. Several of her coworkers at USS&S had known about her espionage work, but they could not know this even bigger secret, that she was now an FBI informer. She had broken off with Peter Heller. Her isolation was almost complete. The only people talking to her now were federal agents.

Bentley was stuck between the life she used to live and the one she would have to reconstruct. It was a lonely and uncomfortable place, and a frightening one, too. The FBI offered confidentiality—Bentley's identity was masked by the code name "Gregory," in all reports—but the Bureau offered her no physical protection. If there was a leak, and the press found out what she was doing, she would be pilloried by the left-wing newspapers, just as turncoat Louis Budenz was now being roasted. If the Soviets found out—Bentley didn't know that they already knew—she feared she would be killed.

In fact, her friends in Moscow were still considering liquidating her as late at mid-1947. That's when KGB officials ordered the Paris station chief to meet with Joseph Katz, who had been an agent in Washington, D.C., and knew Bentley but was then living in France. Two years earlier, when the KGB had first learned of Bentley's defection, Katz was the one selected to poison her. That was Gorsky's plan, which Moscow didn't buy. Now Moscow wanted the Paris station chief to round up Katz and have him "review the prospects" for killing Bentley. A week later, Paris wired back that Katz was ready, willing, and able. But once again, Moscow demurred, for reasons that can be imagined but never known. Officials there may have figured that Bentley had already done all the harm she was going to do, and that killing her now would not only be useless but impolitic. They may have reasoned that the less Moscow showed its hand to the American intelligence community, the better. They may have considered that Bentley's death could serve to validate her story and seal her credibility, which would only mean more trouble for Moscow.

Although she knew nothing about the KGB plot to kill her, Bentley knew enough about the KGB to be concerned for her own safety. But she had no alternative other than to continue on as if living a normal life. In between frequent visits to the New York field office, Bentley kept working at USS&S. The FBI had asked her to stay on, but she would have kept the job anyway. She had stood up to Gorsky for months when he tried to pressure her to quit. She was not about to quit now. The job was not only the one source of stability in her life, it was also her only source of income. And the money was considerable. By 1946, her monthly salary had climbed to $600. By the end of that year, she was earning $800 a month. That Christmas, she received a $2,000 bonus. But the company was in trouble. It had been under FBI investigation, on and off, since the early 1940s, and Hoover was once again pushing for action. The shipping business, at an all-time high during the war years, was waning. Tourism was falling off, too, as the era of good feeling between the United States and the Soviet Union came to an abrupt postwar end.

John Reynolds, titular head of USS&S, began closing down operations at the end of 1946. Bentley claimed he promised her $9,600 in severance pay, a year's salary, when the firm shut down. But in mid-January, after she drew a check from the corporate coffers for half that amount and deposited it in her own account, she received a call from the manager of the bank informing her that Reynolds had told him several days before that all checks had to be countersigned by Reynolds himself. This was news to Bentley who, as vice president, had always had check-signing privileges. Not only that, but she had essentially functioned as the chief operating officer of the company for years, with Reynolds at first relatively uninvolved in daily operations and then away from the office entirely when he served in the military. Bentley was shocked and upset. Reynolds had valued her work and had depended on her. Now it looked as if he was attempting to renege on his promise of severance pay. When she phoned him at home, his wife wouldn't put the call through. She said he was confined to his bed, suffering a nervous collapse. It may finally have dawned on him that his company had been involved in activities that would, at the very least, compromise his reputation.

Bentley promptly took her problem to the FBI. It was the first time—but it would hardly be the last—that she would take advantage of her importance to the Bureau to enlist special help. She understood her worth to the FBI, and she was smart enough and assertive enough to use it as leverage. Bentley told the agents in the New York field office that she would probably be "of no further use to the government" unless the USS&S matter was resolved promptly and to her satisfaction. They reacted immediately to the thinly veiled threat, arranging a lengthy conference with her for the next day during which they told her that Reynolds's revocation was probably not valid and offered "informal" advice about how to proceed. The following day she met with a member of the firm that handled corporation's legal matters who indicated to her that a satisfactory solution could probably be worked out after Reynolds recovered. But a few days later, the lawyer called to tell her that Reynolds not only denied ever having promised her a year's salary but insisted that the $2,000 Christmas bonus be deducted from any severance package that might be negotiated. The FBI referred her to a lawyer, and Bentley filed a civil suit against the company. Meanwhile, the corporation stopped doing business at the end of February 1947 and was officially dissolved a few weeks later.

Bentley was out of work, and with the suit still pending, her financial circumstances were tenuous. In April, she took a job as a secretary for Ameritex Industrial Company, remaining there only one month. Then she found a similar position at Pacific Molasses, Ltd., in New York City. It seemed that her life was going backward rather than forward. She had been an executive in charge of a corporation since 1941. Now she was back where she had been before the war, scrounging for clerical jobs, accepting temporary positions to pay her bills. In June, the civil suit was settled out of court, with Bentley receiving just what she said had been promised, her $9,600 yearly salary. This should have been enough to support her without worries for quite a while. But Bentley had never been a good money manager. She was still living at the hotel in Brooklyn Heights rather than in a more affordable rental apartment. She liked eating at restaurants, and she liked her martinis. She was partial to nice hats. During her years at USS&S, she had grown accustomed to having money; she spent first and thought about it later. A few months after the settlement, she treated herself to a two-week vacation in Bermuda.

By the end of 1946, after a year of investigation of Bentley's allegations, it was becoming clear that the FBI didn't have a case. The Bureau had been sending regular summaries of its investigation to the attorney general, and in November presented the case to him for possible prosecution. A few weeks later, the assistant attorney general wrote to Hoover, asking pointed questions about Bentley's viability as a witness. Would she be willing or reluctant? Did she have any drawbacks . . . alcohol, narcotics, a criminal record, mental instability? But taking the case to court in its current state was really not an option. The FBI's top lawyer had said it was unwinnable. Still, no one was willing to let go. They all felt that Bentley had given them a treasure. They just had to figure out how to cash it in.

Part of the problem was that the Bureau could send out agents to ask questions, but the Bureau could not force people to talk. The Bureau could order wiretaps and surveillance, but the Bureau could not subpoena witnesses or interview people under oath. The FBI had tried its best but could not unearth enough evidence to indict any of the people Bentley named. But there was another way. The government could impanel a grand jury. With its broad subpoena power, a grand jury might be able to further develop the case. It could shake things up, rustle the underbrush and see who might slink out. When people heard "grand jury," they sometimes got scared and started talking. A grand jury was serious business. It was also an opportunity to testify in secret, behind closed doors and away from the media's prying eyes. The grand jury system offered tremendous protection for witnesses. It was worth a shot.

The Department of Justice was also undoubtedly interested in impaneling a grand jury to see how the "star witness" performed. Bentley would be under oath and in front of an audience—there were twenty-three people on the jury—for the first time. Grand juries were not trials with adversarial lawyers and pointed cross-examinations, but they were formal, under-oath presentations of allegations to an official body. The proceedings could be better controlled than a trial. The prosecutor, who would have access to all of Bentley's FBI statements as well as the Bureau's file on the case, would know just what the witness was going to say. The whole enterprise was really the prosecutor's show: "Here is my witness . . . listen to her." But the government would see how Bentley comported herself, how well she presented her story, and how the jury reacted. The grand jury could also serve an important political purpose: It could help deflect criticism that the FBI had botched its investigation. It would show congressional Red-hunters that the hunt continued.

In late March 1947, the grand jury was impaneled to begin hearing testimony at the U.S. courthouse in Foley Square in Lower Manhattan. The Department of Justice asked Thomas J. "The Hat" Donegan to handle the case. Donegan, who had headed the squad investigating Bentley's allegations from the FBI side, left the Bureau in 1946 to become special assistant to the U.S. attorney general. A thirteen-year veteran of the FBI, an expert in espionage and a man with an abundance of apparently well-earned self-confidence, Donegan seemed the natural choice. The assistant attorney general in charge of the Criminal Division, a man named T. Vincent Quinn, was also involved. The government was lining up its big guns.

The grand jury heard testimony all through the spring, summer, and fall of that year, beginning with a two-week stint on the stand by star witness Elizabeth Bentley, who retold most of the story she had told to the FBI and named the same names. Then the government shook the bushes and subpoenaed more than one hundred witnesses, most of whom were called to defend themselves against Bentley's allegations. Former assistant to the secretary of the Treasury Harry

Dexter White testified, as did William Remington, chairman of a Commerce Department committee that allocated exports to the Soviet Union. Lauchlin Currie, former assistant to FDR and Truman, was called, as well as dozens of other government employees, including Bentley's major sources, Silvermaster and Perlo. *Newsweek* described the witness list as "an array of top New Deal talent."

Donegan was a tough cross-examiner, an intense, poker-faced man who wanted badly to win, which meant, in grand jury terms, a return of indictments against some or all of the accused. But he was having trouble with the case, the same kind of trouble the FBI had. Witnesses were revealing little more than their employment records. A few flatly denied any involvement in the Communist Party or espionage activities, but many of the major characters invoked the protection of the Fifth Amendment, refusing to answer questions on the grounds that their testimony might be self-incriminating. Lauchlin Currie swore under oath that he had no affiliation with the party and no knowledge of Bentley. Remington told the grand jury, under oath, the same story he had told the FBI: He thought Bentley was a journalist and gave her only information already available to the public. He admitted to meeting "Helen" and "John" (Bentley and Golos) several times, but he said he had no idea they were connected to the Party. Frank Coe, a Treasury Department official whom Bentley had named as part of the Silvermaster Group, testified only that he knew some of the people Bentley had named from his work in the government. William Taylor, another Treasury Department employee, denied all charges. Duncan Lee, Sonya and Bela Gold, Bernard Redmont, and Cedric Belfrage, a British intelligence officer, all denied Bentley's allegations under oath.

Abe Brothman, the chemical engineer who, Bentley claimed, passed secret blueprints to her, testified that he gave her only harmless information, notes about common industrial processes and simple chemical formulas for the purpose of obtaining a business contact with the Russian government. Brothman said he knew both Bentley and Golos and had met them through a fellow chemist by the name of Harry Gold. Gold, when called to testify, corroborated Brothman's story. It would be three years before the FBI discovered that the two had concocted the story together, prior to their grand jury appearances. In 1950 investigators "broke" Gold and learned that he had taken over from Bentley as Brothman's courier and had later acted as a courier for atomic spy Klaus Fuchs. Gold's new testimony led to indictments against Brothman and his secretary, Miriam Moscowitz, who were subsequently convicted of perjuring themselves during their grand jury appearances. But this was in the future. What Donegan had in 1947 was Bentley's accusations countered at every turn by denials under oath, assertions of complete innocence, or invocations of the Fifth Amendment. On April 6, 1948, when the grand jury heard its final witness, Donegan knew he was in trouble. He was, as would be expected, close-mouthed to the media. Federal officials were "refusing to guess" whether the jury would indict or clear a "large group of American citizens" who stood accused of passing information to the Russians, reported a *Newsweek* story in the fall of 1947. But Donegan didn't have to guess. He knew. What he had, after thirteen months of grand jury investigation, was little more than what the FBI had back in 1945: one woman's story.

The media, sniffing around the edges, caught the scent. From New York and Washington came "inside" stories—leaks—that the jury would be dismissed without handing down any indictments, that the espionage case was "all washed up." There was even speculation in some quarters that the case reached so high in the federal government that it was politically "too hot" to pursue. To Donegan, the grand jury's failure to indict would be a significant professional setback in what had been thus far a highly successful career. More than that, it would be an embarrassment to the Department of Justice, which had vigorously mounted the case, and a repudiation of the FBI, which had devoted so many resources to investigating it. It wouldn't kill, but it would certainly wound, the growing anticommunist cause. So Donegan, with the approval of Attorney General Tom Clark, decided to take another tack. He asked the jury to wait while he prepared a new case. This one would accuse the American communist party of conspiring to advocate the overthrow of the government by force and would call for the indictment of the top party leaders. The idea behind this new strategy, Donegan told the

FBI, was that the failure in the Bentley case would become "much less significant." If the jury were to stay in session and hand down indictments in the new case, the resultant publicity "would not be unfavorable."

The Smith Act of 1940 provided just the foundation Donegan and his staff needed to build the case. The law made it a crime "to print, publish, edit, issue, circulate, sell, distribute, or publicly display any written or printed matter" advocating the violent overthrow of the U.S. government. Using the incendiary, often overblown language of standard Marxist literature, like *The Communist Manifesto* and the program of the Third International, as well as the writings and speeches of various American party leaders, it should not be difficult to persuade the grand jury that the party—at least on paper—called for the overthrow of the government. And, if Bentley told the grand jury what she had told the FBI about the connection between the party and Moscow—how former leader Earl Browder helped identify possible espionage agents from among party ranks, for example—that would strengthen the case even more.

Donegan's idea worked. On July 20, 1948, with what the media called "boom and sizzle," the grand jury handed down sealed indictments against the twelve-man national board of the American communist party. While this was hardly as dramatic, or important, as espionage indictments would have been, the news made headlines big enough to obscure the fact that the grand jury had been, essentially, a flop. The indictments—which resulted in guilty verdicts for all twelve of the accused—were, more than anything else, a face-saving device for the government. But to most Americans, who knew nothing of Bentley's allegations or the lengthy FBI investigation or the secret grand jury proceedings, the indictments looked like the successful conclusion to a government investigation of those who would harm their own country. The Department of Justice, the FBI, and especially Elizabeth Bentley knew better.

Bentley was bitterly disappointed with the outcome. None of the people she named were indicted. Her endless sessions with the FBI, her 107-page signed statement, her testimony before the grand jury, the disruption, the isolation, the secrecy, the guilt over naming names, the risks she had taken, the stress . . . it all meant nothing. She had come forth. She had told everything. But that wasn't good enough. Those she accused of passing confidential information would not be prosecuted. Her story would remain untold, hidden in a top-secret FBI file and in the never-to-be-published proceedings of the failed grand jury. It could be that her sense of justice was outraged. As a born-again patriot and staunch anticommunist, she would have had a hard time seeing the people she accused—the men and women she knew to be leaking secrets to the Soviets—go not just unpunished but unexposed. But it was also a matter of pride and of ego. Remington had, in essence, called her a liar. So had Duncan Lee and Frank Coe and William Taylor. Ullmann had told the grand jury that she was a neurotic and a nuisance. How could she let that stand? How could she, in the face of testimony that contradicted everything she said, take pride in her conversion, in the work she had done with the FBI, in herself? How could she feel she was playing a major role when the show went unproduced? The failure of the grand jury would also have scared her, as her best protection from Soviet reprisal was in her story becoming public. Once the story was out, it would be harder, riskier—and of little use—for the KGB to harm her.

She had been worrying about the jury's silence, and what it would mean to her, all spring. Maybe she should go public with her own story, she thought, and write a book about her experiences. Or maybe she could get someone else to do the work. In early April, she contacted Nelson Frank, a New York *World Telegram* staff writer and labor reporter who had interviewed her in the past for a story on the customs duties Russia charged on relief packages sent by Americans. As the vice president of USS&S, she was a logical source for the story. At the time, she learned that Frank had dabbled in communism himself. And so, that spring, she phoned the newspaper office and made an appointment to see him and his newsroom colleague, Frederick Woltman, the paper's Pulitzer Prize–winning expert on communism.

"I want some advice," she told the two reporters when they met
the following day. "The men of the FBI are very friendly, but they
don't feel free to talk to me." She told them briefly, with few details,
about the stalled grand jury. What will happen to the testimony I
gave, she asked, if the jury returns no indictments? Will my story be
forgotten? Frank's nose for news began to twitch.

They talked for three hours that day, with Bentley outlining her
espionage activities. Frank and Woltman knew immediately that they
had banner headline material. Within days, Donegan found out
about Bentley's meeting with the reporters, which he considered
an "ill-conceived act." The FBI called Bentley in for questioning,
reporting for the file that she was "nervous and distraught." Donegan didn't care about her mental health. His chief concern was that
she keep quiet. This would have been just the time he was switching
gears to mount the case against the Communist Party. The last thing
he needed was a loose cannon, a troubled witness who could blow
his chances of rescuing the grand jury from failure. He couldn't prevent her from meeting with the reporters—which she did on and off
for the next three and a half months—but he could make it very clear
to the powers that be at the *World Telegram* that the Department of
Justice would not appreciate a story at this time. The newspaper may
also have worried about possible contempt charges had it published
what could be considered secret grand jury testimony.

Nelson Frank continued to research the story through the late
spring, checking in several times with Donegan and his assistant,
Vincent Quinn, to see if he could squeeze them for information
about what was happening with the grand jury. Early in the summer,
Frank met Quinn in Washington, D.C., where the reporter picked
up hints that something might be breaking soon. He went back to
New York and started preparing a series of articles highlighting the
"exclusive details" he had gleaned from interviews with Bentley.
Then, he waited. It wasn't until July 20, 1948, sixteen months after
it was first impaneled, that the grand jury concluded its work by
handing down the indictments against the twelve leaders of the
Communist Party. The newspapers, just as Donegan had hoped, carried the "good news" of the jury's successful outcome with little

mention of the failed espionage investigation or the woman who started it all.

But the next day, July 21, the *World Telegram* ran its big story on page one under a half-inch-high banner headline that announced: RED RING BARED BY BLOND QUEEN. In a lengthy story that ran across the top of the page, the paper focused the journalistic spotlight clearly on Elizabeth Bentley, although her name was withheld. "The sparks that touched off yesterday's indictment," went the lead of the story, ". . . originated a year ago in the gnawing pangs of conscience suffered by a svelte striking blonde." It was the "beautiful young blonde" whose story of espionage was "so fantastic that even veteran FBI officials scarcely could believe [it]" who was behind the indictments and who had an even bigger story to tell. That story was one of espionage and intrigue, of secrets turned over to the Russians, of government officials—from "a personal adviser to President Roosevelt" to "a man high in the councils of the Office of Strategic Services"—who worked with the blonde to sabotage the country of their birth.

It was a dramatic story, fancifully told, in which Bentley, a plain-featured, matronly brunette in her late thirties was transformed by Nelson Frank into a captivating Mata Hari. Clearly, svelte blondes made better copy. But the fictional description also shielded Bentley's identity, which may have been one reason it was concocted. An FBI secretary, a young blonde, had been assigned to escort Bentley to and from her court appearances, the only time she would have been within sight of the press. The svelte blonde description might have been an attempt to throw a curve to the rest of the press, purposely confusing the secretary with the witness.

The next day, the *World Telegram* went with the second in Nelson Frank's series, another front-page story, this one titled, SUPERSECRECY VEILED RUSSIA'S SPY CELLS HERE. Once again, the "good-looking blonde spy ring leader" was center stage as she revealed a vast espionage network that "systematically milked" the government of "much of its top secret information." The story went on to mention a "top subordinate to a cabinet member," "a secretary to a Senator," and other well-placed federal government employees who were part of the network. The third story, published July 23, took a new approach, attempting to explain to readers how Americans could end up as Russian spies.

Bentley had explained the process, and her own motivations, somewhat disingenuously to Nelson Frank, portraying herself as a victim of manipulation, tricked by the party into spying for Russia. "Like many other communists who worked in these networks, I didn't fully realize how I had been tricked," she was quoted as saying in the story. Of course, this wasn't true. Bentley knew a long time before she took control of the Silvermaster and Perlo networks for whom she was working. She had discovered Golos's true identity early in their relationship and, after his death, had been reporting directly to Russian agents. But in the front-page story headlined CIT-IZENS TRICKED INTO SPY RING BY U.S. REDS, Bentley and her sources were portrayed as, if not innocents, then unwitting participants. It was a comfortable fiction, a reasonable explanation for a seemingly unreasonable act. Bentley could be understood—and sympathized with—as a victim of forces greater than herself, a woman whose desire to build a better world was used to manipulate her into doing things she would not normally do. There may have been some truth to this version of her past, but clearly Elizabeth Bentley was beginning to rewrite her own history. She needed to explain herself publicly in the most solicitous terms. She needed to explain herself in a way she herself could understand and live with.

The *World Telegram* stories were a journalistic coup that made New York and Washington papers sit up and take notice. Some derided the revelations. The *World Telegram* had not done itself any favors with its screaming headlines and tabloid tone. But other news media picked up the story and began to make it their own. *Newsweek,* echoing the *World Telegram* series, presented Bentley as a "tall, thin blonde . . . of old American stock and full of the idealism which had flowered at Walden Pond and Brook Farm." And editors were not the only ones paying attention. The morning after the first story appeared, Nelson Frank got a call from the legal counsel of a Senate investigating committee eager to delve into this issue of communist spies in the federal government. This mysterious blond spy in the story, would she be a good witness to appear before the committee? Yes, said Frank, she would. In fact, he could personally arrange for her appearance.

Bentley hadn't wanted her story to die. She hadn't wanted it to languish in confidential files and top-secret documents. She was getting her wish.

# Chapter 15

# The Lady Appears

IT WAS SUMMER, and Congress was in recess. But President Truman, in a fiery acceptance speech at the Democratic National Convention in July, summoned the legislators back to the hot, steamy capital for a special two-week session to pass bills stalled in the regular session. In retaliation, Republicans in the House and Senate convened hearings on subversion in the federal government. It was an election year—Americans would be voting for president in just four months—and both parties were busy positioning themselves. The Republicans considered Truman soft on communism. The hearings, they thought, might turn up something embarrassing to the administration, something that could help fuel a Republican victory in November. Up until now, the investigations had been conducted behind closed doors, within the confidential confines of the FBI or hidden from view in the grand jury room. There had been little publicity and no public naming of names. That was to end abruptly in the summer of 1948, when two congressional committees jumped feet first into what would soon become the single most contentious issue in American public life: the "communist conspiracy." Elizabeth Bentley was about to take her place, center stage.

The so-called Ferguson Committee—officially the Investigations Subcommittee of the Committee on Expenditures in the Executive Departments, but Homer Ferguson, its Republican chairman, was its namesake—had been investigating the somewhat prosaic subject of export policy. But now the public allegations of the Red Spy Queen gave the committee a chance to delve into a much juicier topic. In the *World Telegram* series, the anonymous Spy Queen had named William Remington as one of her espionage sources. Remington had been with the War Production Board at the time, but now it turned out that he held an important post in the Office of International Trade in the Commerce Department. So here was a man, thought Homer Ferguson, who might very well be a communist spy, in a sensitive position linked to export policy decisions. This man had access to confidential information that could affect America's economic and perhaps even political status. How could this be? How could Remington—while under investigation by both the FBI and a grand jury—be hired and promoted and placed in such an important and sensitive position? It was, of course, the fault of the Truman administration. It was the executive branch's laxity, its blindness to the communist threat—and maybe even its own pinkish proclivities—that allowed a man like Remington to serve in important positions. That's the case the Republicans wanted to make.

When the committee convened on July 30, just one week after the *World Telegram* series was published, it initiated hearings on the conduct of the executive branch in hiring employees for sensitive positions. Bentley would be the key witness, her appearance arranged by Nelson Frank, the *World Telegram* reporter. The question the committee set for itself that day was "how our government could employ or transfer from one department to another, a very important employee in a highly secret position when at the same time an investigation was being made of that particular employee on questions of espionage and loyalty." The target was William Remington.

At 2:20 in the afternoon, Senator Ferguson called the session to order in a cramped hearings room in the Senate office building.

News photographers jockeyed for space, flashbulbs popping. News-reelers lined up along one side of the room, adjusting their klieg lights and balancing their cameras on tripods. The small room became uncomfortably hot almost immediately. Ferguson, a Republican from Michigan, was, at age fifty-eight, a first-term senator. But he had the self-assurance of a man who had been a practicing attorney, a circuit court judge, and a professor of law before coming to Washington. He had already tangled with the Truman administration over concealment of facts about Pearl Harbor and was more than willing to do battle again.

Elizabeth Bentley walked into the room. This was her first public appearance, the first look the media would have of the Spy Queen. Calm and composed, she wore a simple, short-sleeved, black dress with large, ornate earrings and a flowered hat, the kind of outfit a woman of a certain age might wear to a ladies' luncheon. Much to the surprise of the media in attendance, she was neither blond nor svelte. *Time* magazine, huffy about being mislead concerning her appearance, described her as "neither beautiful nor glamorous" but, more accurately, "plump . . . with a sharp nose and a receding chin." Ferguson and his colleagues already knew what she looked like. They had questioned her in closed session several days before, treating her kindly while going over the terrain they would cover in the pubic hearing. In this, Ferguson was probably aided by FBI reports and documents leaked to him prior to the hearings, material that helped arm him and his colleagues with tough questions regarding Remington. Certainly they knew far more about him than could be found in his official records.

Bentley took her place at the witness table just a few feet in front of the raised dais where the senators sat. There were microphones everywhere, at least six in front of her on the small desk she shared with a stenographer and another half dozen placed strategically along the length of the dais. When she stood to take the oath, she was staring directly into the bank of klieg lights. She took a moment to fish a handkerchief from her purse and blot her brow. It must have been close to a hundred degrees under the lights.

The committee was gentle with her. "How old are you?" Senator Ferguson asked early in the proceedings, quickly adding, "If you do not want to answer that question, that is all right; that is a woman's privilege." He moved on without giving her the opportunity to reply and walked her briskly through her résumé, an account of the life of a privileged young woman with a high-class education and sojourns to Europe.

Led by Ferguson's simple, methodical questioning, Bentley began talking about her conversion to communism. "How did you happen to stray so far from the fold?" one senator asked plaintively. Bentley talked about meeting socialists at Vassar and Columbia, about experiencing fascism in Italy, and about joining what she called a "fringe organization"—but which Ferguson quickly dubbed a "communist front"—the American League Against War and Fascism. As Bentley began to detail her activities as a "card-carrying member" of the party and later, as an underground operative, the senators were clearly mesmerized.

The hearing was designed to focus on Remington, but the committee seemed to forget that as Bentley's story unfolded. This was as close as any of them had ever gotten to a real, live communist. They had so many questions. They wanted to know the intricacies of how things worked, what exactly was printed on the party membership card, who this man Golos was and what he did, how a mail courier operated, where and when and from whom she gathered intelligence, what agencies her sources came from, whether they were still working for the government. Bentley answered as fully as she could while not naming any names, a strategy agreed upon during her previous closed-door sessions with the committee. She answered confidently, with the calm assurance of a schoolteacher lecturing a classroom of eager but not terribly bright children. Her voice had that slightly nasal East Coast finishing school tone about it, a little pinched, a tad metallic, and very much in control. The afternoon wore on without a mention of William Remington. At one point, the chairman seemed to scold the committee. "It is not desired at this particular time to go into all of the ramifications," he told his colleagues, after they had sat spellbound, listening to Bentley's tale of intrigue. "We would like to conduct this hearing, if we can, concerning one person: William Remington." But almost immediately, Ferguson himself turned the questioning back to Bentley's personal story. And, a few minutes later, when she seemed to be rushing through the narrative, he reined her in, cautioning, "I do not want to go too fast now, on this."

Bentley offered a clinical description of her relationship with Golos with no hint of the emotional and sexual intimacy they had shared. She offered, too, the version of her past that she seemed to have convinced herself she had lived, a version that cast her as passive rather than active, someone things happened to rather than someone who made things happen. She told the senators, for example, that her underground activities began when she was "turned over" to a special contact (Golos) because she had access to material at the Italian Library of Information. But the truth was that she herself had recognized the potential importance of her position at the library and had sought out, through the Party, a contact to whom she would report. She had not been spotted as a possible operative and *taken* underground. It had been *her* idea. She had launched herself into clandestine activities. Later in the afternoon, when she was questioned about what had made her come forth and denounce communism, she answered that, in part, it was because the "effect of Mr. Golos was wearing off," as if Yasha had been a Svengali rather than a toiler in the trenches.

For more than an hour, they quizzed her on how her Washington, D.C., network operated, why she thought her sources gave her confidential information, to whom they thought it was going, who her Russian contacts were and what kind of information seemed to interest them. She answered each question carefully, articulately, often with precise details and completely from memory. She had no notes. She had no lawyer by her side. Finally, more than two hours into the afternoon session, Ferguson asked the first question about the man who was the subject of the hearing.

"Did you have a source [in the War Production Board]?" he asked Bentley.

"I had several," she replied.

"Did you have a man by the name of Remington?" Ferguson asked.

"Yes, I did," said Bentley. She then launched into the same story she had told both the FBI and the grand jury about Remington: how an editor at the *New Masses* introduced Remington to Golos, how Golos and Bentley met Remington at the Schrafft's on Fourth Avenue, how it was arranged for her to rendezvous with him during her trips to Washington, how they met in drugstores and on park benches "ten or fifteen or twenty" times, how he gave her his Communist Party dues and accepted party literature, how he passed her confidential information on scraps of paper he took from his jacket pocket. The senators wanted to know what kind of information, and she told them: aircraft production figures, internal policies of the Board, a formula for synthetic rubber. The committee focused on Remington for perhaps twenty minutes before the questions once again turned to the Russian spy apparatus and Bentley's Soviet contacts. The bigger story was just too good. They couldn't stay away from it for long.

It was Bentley who finally brought the conversation back to Remington just a few minutes before the committee adjourned. She was questioned about the purity of her motives. Did she have anything against any of the people who gave her information, any ulterior motives in exposing them? No, Bentley said, adding ". . . and I don't too much like having to do this to Mr. Remington, either." But she had done it to Mr. Remington, and this hearing would be only the beginning of his troubles.

Remington appeared the next morning, a tall, slender, sandy-haired, handsome man barely out of his twenties who wore a suit well and looked exactly like what he was: a well-heeled Dartmouth man on the way up. Remington told his side of the story that morning, a Saturday, and at another session a few days later. He could have brought along an attorney, but he didn't. He was young and smart and sure of himself. He was quick-witted and charming. He could handle this. He told the committee that just about everything Bentley had testified to was true. Yes, he was introduced to her at Schrafft's. Yes, they met a number of times in Washington at the locales she mentioned. Yes, he gave her information that came from the War Production Board, where he was employed at the time. He gave her money. He took Communist Party literature. But in each instance, he had an alternate explanation. First of all, he had no idea, he told the committee, that either Bentley or Golos were communists. He thought Golos was a Dutch journalist writing a book, he said, and that Bentley was his research assistant. True, they met under odd circumstances, but he could explain that. Bentley would always be in a hurry when she called. She'd be uptown, far from his office, and suggest they meet somewhere halfway. That's why they met on street corners and out-of-the-way drugstores. The money she said she collected from him for party dues? Those were actually contributions to an antifascist fund, he said. The *Daily Worker?* Yes, he did buy it from her, as she said, but he did it not to keep in touch with the party—he was *not* a communist and never had been, he insisted—but because he wanted to examine the stories in the paper to evaluate their accuracy. And the information she said he passed to her? It was no more than he would have given any journalist, he said. It was all publicly available material. Nothing was secret or confidential.

Remington presented himself as a young, well-meaning naïf, but the committee was having no part of it. The senators bombarded him with questions. How could he have not known—or even *suspected*—that Bentley was a communist when she was introduced to him by a famous communist editor, when every time he saw her she sold him copies of the *Daily Worker?* If he truly believed she was a journalist, why didn't he treat her like one? Why not insist on meeting in his office? If the information he gave her was publicly available, why not steer her to the government information service or published sources? Why scribble the information on scraps of paper? Remington, seemingly unshaken, weathered the storm, steadfastly maintaining his complete innocence, accusing himself only of "forgivably erroneous judgment."

"Sir," he said to Senator Ferguson, "as I look back on it, I realize I was involved in something of a very dubious nature. But at the time, it did not appear to me to be of a dubious nature." But no one could be that naïve, least of all a bright, educated man like Remington, thought the senators. They were astonished and unbelieving, openly hostile. Ferguson called his story "preposterous." The *Washington Post,* giving him the benefit of the doubt, dismissed him as a "boob."

Throughout, Remington's confidence remained unshaken. He called a press conference for that evening, telling reporters from Washington and New York that he had "very high regard for Miss Bentley." He called her "very courageous" and said the nation owed her a debt of gratitude for exposing communism. But Bentley was wrong about him. She was confused. She was remembering incorrectly, he told the reporters. And he was sure he could prove his innocence when he testified again. He was confident, too, that he made a good impression with the media. He was at ease with them, staying after the questions to chat with reporters and pose for photographs.

The hearings continued on Monday with ex-communist Louis Budenz testifying explosively that the American communist party, which he called "the Russian fifth column," had placed "perhaps thousands" of its members in government jobs. He had no particular knowledge of Remington and could only corroborate Bentley's testimony in the most general way, but his appearance served to whip up the already stormy seas. When Remington returned to testify the next day, the committee subjected him to a grueling five-hour session. He had been confident that he would prove his innocence, but he couldn't have been more mistaken. With every protestation of his own blamelessness, his own gullibility, Remington dug himself a deeper hole. By the end of that afternoon, the senators seemed more skeptical, more hostile, and more intent on developing a case against him than they had been when the hearings began. Toward that end, Ferguson demanded certain records on Remington, notably his military file. But the secretary of the Navy flatly refused the request, citing an executive order to keep such records confidential. That was all Ferguson had to hear, that the *executive branch*—the Truman administration—was standing in the way of his investigation. There was much posturing about the purity of motives on both sides, much heated oratory, much saber-rattling, but little result. The hearings closed without closure. The senate committee had no power to do what the grand jury hadn't been able to do the year before. Remington would remain unindicted. He would keep his government job. But Elizabeth Bentley and William Remington would not be rid of each other. The Ferguson hearing was merely the opening salvo in what would be a five-and-a-half-year war of words between them. It would be messy, and it would end badly.

# Chapter 16

# Un-American
Activities

THE FERGUSON HEARING was Bentley's first
public appearance, but it was not her most important. The senators had focused—to the extent that they focused at
all—on one man. But Bentley's story was bigger than that. There
were more than a hundred men and women she had alluded to in
her testimony. There were many doors yet to be opened, many
avenues to be explored, many names yet to be publicly named. It fell
to the single most controversial, most partisan committee in Congress, the House Committee on Un-American Activities—commonly
referred to as HUAC—to aggressively mine the terrain Bentley had
mapped for the senators.

The HUAC hearings began July 31, the day after Bentley's
appearance before the Ferguson committee. Like the Ferguson sessions, they were called that summer for political purposes. Conservative Republicans and equally conservative southern Democrats ran

much of the committee machinery in Congress, and they were being urged by the GOP national chairman to take full advantage of this situation. "Set up spy hearings," the GOP chairman advised the head of HUAC. "Stay in Washington, and keep the heat on Harry Truman." Keeping the heat on Harry Truman meant focusing on—and with any luck, causing him embarrassment about—communists in the government. Public testimony that accused scores of federal employees—most of them FDR Democrats—of espionage could weaken Truman, discredit the New Deal, and give the GOP the keys to the White House. This hunt for communists in the government would be the centerpiece of the GOP's strategy to recapture the presidency, and HUAC would lead the way.

The intent of the hearings that summer was not, as officially stated, "to investigate subversive activities"—the committee did not have the resources to mount an actual investigation—but rather to publicize information already known to the FBI, and most probably leaked to the committee. The intent was to give Elizabeth Bentley a chance to name names. A ranking member of the committee put it more succinctly. It's about time, he said in his opening statement before the committee, to "drive these rats from the federal . . . payroll." The congressmen were confident they could do it. After all, their committee had already enjoyed great success the previous fall driving "the rats" out of Hollywood.

The hearings in October had been one of the biggest media circuses in the history of Washington, D.C., with high-profile "friendly" witnesses like Walt Disney, Gary Cooper, and then-actor Ronald Reagan testifying that a communist conspiracy was taking over the motion picture industry. They were pitted against a group of screenwriters alleged to be party members or fellow-travelers who were accused of inserting un-American propaganda into their scripts, an example of which was offered by Leila Rogers, Ginger's mother. She testified that her daughter had turned down a role in a movie because the script would have her deliver a speech that began, "Share and share alike—that's democracy!" Humphrey Bogart, Groucho Marx, Judy Garland, Frank Sinatra, and other luminaries picked up the screenwriters' cause, and the hearings became a magnet for autograph hounds and every newsreel, radio, and television broadcaster who could shoehorn his equipment in the room. Meanwhile, the sessions devolved from polemic to melodrama to farce, ending with armed guards dragging the screenwriters from the committee room. Despite all this, or perhaps because of it, the hearings were an unqualified success for HUAC. Studio executives, who had at first opposed the House probe as an unwarranted intrusion, blacklisted the so-called Hollywood Ten. And in December, two months after the hearings, a federal grand jury handed down indictments against all of them. They stood trial, were found guilty, and, after various appeals, went to jail.

HUAC emerged from the Hollywood hearings a committee to be reckoned with. More powerful than it had ever been in its short and contentious history, it was also, simultaneously, the least savory it had ever been, its image tarnished by the incivility and extremism of its members. Although membership on the committee ensured a high profile and held the promise of bigger things to come in one's career, it was one of the least popular committees on which to serve. Of all the new and returning Democratic members of Congress in 1948, not one listed HUAC as a committee preference or even a second choice. But for a small group of conservatives motivated by their enthusiasm for hunting subversives, it was the place to be. They were not, however, the best and the brightest.

J. Parnell Thomas was the chairman. A charter member of the committee since 1938, he was an arch-conservative Republican from New Jersey who believed that government, education, the movie industry, and unions were all hotbeds of communist activity. Considered by his fellow congressmen to be arrogant and opinionated, Thomas had shown himself to be coarse and vindictive on the House floor. In the midst of the summer 1948 hearings, he was accused of operating a kickback racket with his own office staff, and was later convicted and sent to federal prison.

John Rankin, a Mississippi Democrat, was another powerful committee member who had served as chairman in the mid-1940s. A dedicated enemy of the New Deal, he equated FDR's policies with "the beginnings of a communist dictatorship the likes of which

America has never dreamed." Communism, he once said in remarks on the floor of the House, "hounded and persecuted the Savior during his earthly ministry" and "inspired his crucifixion." An ardent and unreconstructed racist, Rankin hated Jews—communism was, he said, a Jewish conspiracy—and was sympathetic to the Ku Klux Klan. The committee also included Karl Mundt, a six-term Republican congressman from South Dakota. A politically ambitious man—he would move up to the Senate in a few years—he found the executive branch contemptible, distrusted the State Department, hated the United Nations, and vehemently disagreed with Truman's postwar foreign policy in general. And then there was the junior congressman from California, Richard M. Nixon, one of the ablest and cleverest on the committee, who had made it to Washington, D.C., two years before by virtue of a smear campaign against his Democratic opponent. HUAC would give him the exposure he needed to mount a national career in politics that would end in the White House.

Thomas gaveled the session to order at 10:45 in the morning on Saturday, July 31. Rankin was particularly eager to begin. He had kept close tabs on the New York grand jury investigation and was angered that it had taken so long and produced so little. The proceedings, he thought, had been purposefully and politically delayed by Truman and his ilk. At the same time, he saw the grand jury as a threat to what he liked to think of as HUAC's exclusive possession of the hunt for subversives. And now, worse yet, the committee had been beaten to the punch by Ferguson the day before. There was no more time to waste.

The hearings were held in the Ways and Means Committee room, a vast auditorium with banks of seats on either side of a central aisle, a raised platform in the front for the committee members, each with his name etched on a bronze plaque, and, along the window side of the room, a battalion of newsreel cameras and klieg lights. The first witness that morning was Elizabeth Bentley, outfitted conservatively, as the day before, in a simple, dark dress. Although the room was much grander, the crowd much bigger, and the media even more in evidence than the day before, Bentley appeared unintimidated. She had told her story so many times now to so many people for so many years that it must have felt to her like a play for which she had over-rehearsed. But this truly was opening night—or day—and, underneath the composure, underneath the New England sangfroid, she must have felt a sense of excitement and purpose. The spotlight was clearly, sharply, brilliantly on her. She may not have sought this particular spotlight, or even imagined that her talks with the FBI three summers before would lead to something like this. But, at least for the moment, at least until the spotlight burned a hole in her life, she was enjoying the new, meaningful role she was playing. She was the most important person in that room, and she knew it.

Bentley took her place at the witness table behind the forest of microphones. She sat erect, her spine straight, her hands clasped on the desk in front of her. As in the hearings the day before, she brought no notes or documents to read from or refresh her memory, and she was not accompanied by counsel. The questions began, as they had at the Ferguson hearing, with her background and the reason she turned to communism. Bentley recounted, once again, her New England upbringing and years at Vassar but added a twist at the end: She blamed her education, which she said had included not a single course in American history, for her lack of respect for the American political system that allowed her to embrace communism. Creeping liberalism in education was a favorite target of anticommunists, and her comment interested the committee.

"So you grew up as a typical young woman, an American child in American schools, went to a very renowned institution . . . and through all those years, you were never exposed, or put into contact with what American history was, what America stands for, and what our form of government was?" one committee member asked her, making the most of his incredulity.

"No; I never was," Bentley replied.

But before the conversation could go too far afield, the committee's chief investigator, Robert E. Stripling, brought Bentley back to the real business at hand: spies in the government. Quickly and efficiently, he guided her through the naming of names. Her voice was calm and measured. Silvermaster, Perlo, Ullmann, and White, she told him. Lee, Currie, Remington, and Kramer. "Can you name any other individuals?" Stripling asked, again and again. And again and again, she did: Halperin and Magdoff, Coe and Taylor, Adler, the Golds, Henry Collins, Redmont, Price, Tenney, Silverman, Miller. The list continued. Bentley was more careful with her answers than Stripling and the committee were with their questions. Her responses were almost clinical in their precision. She seemed to parse each question the way a lawyer would, picking it apart, examining its components, making no assumptions, answering narrowly and with care. When she was asked if Silvermaster was a party member while employed at his final government position, she declined to answer— I can only tell you what he was during the time I knew him, she said—even though, knowing Silvermaster's decades-long devotion to the party, she could have easily made that assumption, or at least hinted at it.

The committee's questions, by comparison, seemed sloppy and superficial, so eager were the congressmen to air the names they knew she knew. Bentley was not often asked detailed follow-up questions about the people she named and very often not asked whether she actually *knew* them. Thus, sources like Silvermaster, Ullmann, Perlo, and Remington, whom she had met and spoken with many times and from whom she had personally received information, were not distinguished from men like Harry Dexter White and Lauchlin Currie, whom she had never met but only heard about from others. Her information might be correct—in fact, Venona later showed it was—but in the context of HUAC in 1948, it was hearsay, and Stripling and the others should have known better.

Bentley's version of her years as spy, courier, and network handler had few of the hard edges the committee expected. Her sources were not paid, either by the party or by the Soviets, she told the congressmen. And, according to Bentley, they were not traitors. In fact, in a way, their motives could be seen as noble. "They had been told it was their duty as good communists," she said to Stripling, when he pressed her about why so many people were so free with presumably confidential information. "They had been told that Russia was our ally, that she was bearing the brunt of the war, that she was not being properly treated as an ally, and it was their duty to do something about it." And throughout the morning, Bentley positioned herself, as she had since she first came forth to the FBI, as a fallen angel, a foggy-minded liberal led astray both by the idealistic rhetoric of communism and her love for one man.

Congressman F. Edward Hébert, a fourth-term Louisiana Democrat who would serve another twenty-eight years in the House, at first did not swallow this explanation, confronting Bentley with some of the toughest questions she faced that day.

"How old were you when you started this maneuvering, this espionage?" Hébert asked.

"That was about seven years ago," said Bentley.

"I want to know whether or not you were a mature individual."

"I think you may be physically mature, but many times you are not mentally mature," Bentley responded carefully.

"I do not think that Columbia or Vassar would like for their graduates to say they were not mentally mature . . ." Hébert countered.

Bentley had no good reply for this, and the congressman pressed on. Didn't it ever dawn on her during "these secret meetings, and this super-duper secret stuff" that she was performing a disservice to her country? No, Bentley replied. She was convinced she was helping to build a decent world in the future. Even if she was betraying her own government? Hébert persisted. Bentley parried: "I did not think it was betraying my own government." Bentley told him that communism was almost a religion. One did not question it; one followed its precepts on faith. Hébert clearly did not like the analogy, but he did warm to the idea that Bentley's actions were motivated by emotion rather than reason, since, as far as he was concerned, there was no rational explanation for why one would embrace communism.

"Who spurred this emotionalism on you?" he asked Bentley, guiding her just where she wanted to go anyway. "Was it this man Golos?"

"Yes," Bentley said.

"Was it that you were devoted to him so much that you followed him blindly and were blind to everything else?"

"Yes; it was," Bentley said.

"And it blinded you to your traitorous acts against your country?"

"That is right," Bentley said.

Her testimony continued through the afternoon, interrupted at various points by the political posturing of the committee. At one point, Congressman Rankin, overcome by a combustible mixture of anger and enthusiasm, demanded that every communist in the United States be shipped out "by the boatload" and that spies in the government be shot.

Congressman Nixon, on the other hand, stayed focused on the political purpose of the hearing—the attack on the Democrats. He questioned Bentley closely about exactly when she had first come forth with her story of espionage. When she told him it had been nearly three years ago—a fact he surely knew from the files to which the committee had access, both legally and through leaks—he expressed disbelief. Do you mean to tell me, he asked Bentley, that the investigative agencies of this country, the Department of Justice, were fully aware of all this testimony that you have given us today? Yes, Bentley said, that is correct. Nixon then turned to chairman Thomas.

"In other words, it is quite apparent, Mr. Chairman, that this information has been available to these government employees for a period of . . . years," he said, implying that the Truman administration had sat on the material out of lack of interest or fear or perhaps even collusion.

Congressman Mundt of South Dakota jumped in immediately. "It is also quite apparent that we need a new attorney general," he said, providing the punchline.

"Does that apply to Mr. Remington, too?" Rankin put in, not to be bested. The congressmen laughed.

When the afternoon session was over—Bentley would be back throughout August to answer additional questions—the congressmen were quick to sing the praises of their star witness. Hébert called her a "reformed saint." Congressman John McDowell from Pennsylvania, who had been silent throughout most of the day, praised her as "an American citizen who . . . has the courage . . . to place herself in a highly dangerous position." Rankin, who had been the most contentious that day, tempered his compliments. "I think you are rather late in seeing the light," he told Bentley. But he did, nonetheless, "commend the lady very highly for coming here." Chairman Thomas sympathized with her for having had a "grueling time. Your ability to stand up under it in the way you have is certainly something to be proud of," he said, thanking her again in the committee's name.

But at least one person in the room that Saturday was not quite so pleased. Robert Stripling, the committee's chief investigator, the man who had led the questioning throughout the day, found Bentley's story "too hard to believe." He had been warned by the Justice Department—which was out of the loop and knew nothing of the deciphered Venona messages—that there was no evidence to substantiate Bentley's tale, and he believed the HUAC investigation, like the others that preceded it, would go nowhere if based solely on her testimony. Nothing he had heard that day changed his mind. Yes, Bentley had presented detailed, forthright testimony. She had been calm, composed, and articulate. And certainly the congressmen were eager to believe her. But Stripling knew this was not enough. The star witness was still just a woman telling stories. In the absence of any tangible evidence that could support Bentley's story—a document, a roll of film, a receipt book, anything—Stripling needed another witness, someone who might be able to corroborate any part of Bentley's tale. That's when he remembered a man named Whittaker Chambers, a former communist and self-confessed courier for a Washington, D.C., spy network who had defected from the party in 1938 and told his story to the government the following year. There had never been any follow-up. Chambers went on with his life—he was now a senior editor at *Time* magazine—and had never been called to publicly testify. But, thought Stripling, if Chambers could tell the committee of his own work in the late thirties, perhaps there would be links connecting his activities with Bentley's. It was worth a try.

On Tuesday, August 3, when the hearings resumed, Whittaker Chambers took the stand. Unlike Bentley, with her confident, orderly air, Chambers was an uncomfortable witness, a big, shambling, disheveled man, soft-spoken and reticent, whose shyness quickly turned to nervousness in the witness chair. He got flustered. He mumbled. He perspired profusely. But Stripling led him along, and slowly his story emerged. Chambers had joined the Communist Party in the mid-1920s and had established himself as a journalist of the proletariat, working first for the *Daily Worker,* then the *New Masses,* before being recruited for secret work in the spring of 1932. From then until his defection six years later, he had served as a liaison between sources in the federal government and Soviet contacts, including the same man, Itzhak Akhmerov ("Bill") who had been one of Bentley's contacts. As it turned out, Chambers had helped develop and oversee one of the networks Bentley took over almost ten years later, the old Ware apparatus, which became the Perlo Group. Chambers was somewhat vague and circumspect about his own spy activities that day, perhaps out of nervousness, perhaps out of an unwillingness to delve into a life he had renounced almost a decade before. But because his story overlapped somewhat with Bentley's, he came up with some of the same names she did, notably Perlo, Kramer, White, Collins, and Abt.

This was good news for Stripling and the committee. The additional testimony could help strengthen the committee's stance when these men were subpoenaed to testify later in the month. But the congressmen didn't really get excited until Chambers began talking about a certain State Department source from whom he claimed to have collected secret information, a man named Alger Hiss. "Mr. Hiss," Chambers told the committee, "represents the concealed enemy against which we are fighting." And it seemed to HUAC that this was absolutely right, that Hiss, a golden boy who had sailed through Johns Hopkins and Harvard Law, a protégé of both Felix Frankfurter and Oliver Wendell Holmes, one of the bright stars in the New Deal galaxy, did indeed represent the enemy. Here was a man who had helped coordinate U.S. foreign policy, a man who had helped establish the United Nations, a man who was now president of the prestigious Carnegie Endowment for International Peace. If he was a Red, if he had been a spy, this would go a long way to discredit not just the New Deal, with its policies and agencies so hated by the conservatives, but also the direction America had taken after the war. For a moment, Elizabeth Bentley was all but forgotten, and Alger Hiss and Whittaker Chambers took center stage.

The drama was irresistible—to the committee, to the media, and to the country. Here was Whittaker Chambers, rumpled, overweight, and sweaty, telling traitorous tales about Alger Hiss, the lean, handsome, well-spoken Ivy Leaguer, cream of the New Deal aristocracy. The day after Chambers testified, Hiss appeared before the committee to deny everything. Then the committee heard Chambers again, first in executive session, then in public. A week later, they were back, first Hiss, then Chambers, both sticking to their stories. Then, on August 25, HUAC engineered a dramatic confrontation, bringing the two together in the same room to testify once again. The yes-you-did-no-I-didn't war of words that had become a public spectacle under the aegis of HUAC might never have advanced further—just as Bentley's grand jury testimony and the subsequent denials of those she named had not advanced further—had not Chambers, some months later, come forth with something Bentley never had: evidence.

It seemed that when Chambers was extricating himself from clandestine work, he had squirreled away copies of documents and rolls of film as insurance against retribution by his Soviet contacts, "life preservers," as he called them. Included in the batch of material, which was at first hidden at a relative's house and then in a hollowed-out pumpkin on Chambers's Maryland farm, were a number of secret State Department documents he claimed Hiss had given him. There were four handwritten notes, sixty-five single-spaced pages of retyped cables, and three rolls of microfilm, enough to eventually convict Hiss in what was called "the trial of the century." But that August, it was still just a war of words that captured the attention of HUAC, threatening to take over the entire hearings. As it was, nine of the twenty-one public sessions were devoted to Chambers and Hiss, including all of the final six. But through mid-August, in between the appearances of the two men, it was still Elizabeth Bentley's show.

On August 4, the day after Chambers first appeared to offer corroboration for Bentley's story, the committee subpoenaed Nathan Gregory Silvermaster. He was the first of seventeen federal government employees named by Bentley whom the congressmen would question that month, and his testimony set the tone for many of the others. After he was sworn in, Silvermaster immediately asked to read a prepared statement, which the committee examined and then allowed. In it, he called himself "a loyal American" and a "faithful government employee." The FBI had investigated him, he reminded the committee, and so had a grand jury. There had been no action taken against him. That was because, Silvermaster said, his voice rising, the charges made by Bentley were "false and fantastic" and that she was "a neurotic liar." He would, on the advice of his attorney, refuse to testify further on these matters. He would invoke his constitutional privilege under the Fifth Amendment, refusing to answer on the grounds that anything he said might tend to be self-incriminating.

Silvermaster then proceeded to stonewall the committee, refusing to answer any questions other than those pertaining to his work record. He even refused to answer whether he knew Bentley, who was sitting in the back of the hearings room and, in a dramatic moment, asked by the chairman to stand. Throughout the long and unproductive session, various members of the committee attempted to shake Silvermaster's resolve. Rankin pounded on him, equating taking the Fifth with an admission of guilt. When the witness refused to answer whether he was a member of the Communist Party, Rankin shot back: "If you were not a member of the Communist Party, it would certainly not incriminate you to say 'No.' Now why do you refuse to answer that question?"

"I have already given my responses in the prepared statement," Silvermaster said.

"In other words," Rankin countered, "you are afraid that if you answer 'No' we will prove you were a member and then you would be subject to indictment for perjury."

Mundt took a kinder, gentler tack, a folksy approach. Look, he said to Silvermaster, I'm not a lawyer, and you're not a lawyer. So just between us two laymen, why take the Fifth if answering will clear you? Silvermaster took the Fifth on that question.

Elizabeth Bentley's father, Charles Prentiss Bentley, was the son of a minister and the direct descendant of a dissident English clergyman who arrived in Boston Harbor in 1637. *(Two Centuries of New Milford History)*

Bentley spent the last two years of high school at East High in Rochester, New York, where she played sports, worked on the yearbook, and earned high enough grades to merit a scholarship to Vassar. *(The East High Orient Yearbook 1926)*

At Vassar in the late 1920s, Bentley and her privileged classmates were exhorted to live noble, self-sacrificing, meaningful lives. While a student there, she was exposed to some of the most important, most controversial ideas of the day. *(Special Collections, Vassar College Libraries)*

Jacob Golos, Bolshevik revolutionary, U.S. Communist Party functionary, and spy handler, was Bentley's mentor and lover. They lived together, someone once remarked, in "bourgeois sin and Leninist bliss." *(Russian Foreign Intelligence Service)*

World Tourists was, ostensibly, a Fifth Avenue travel agency specializing in steamship tours between the United States and Russia. But it was really a moneymaking venture for the Communist Party, supporting various East Coast enterprises, including the *Daily Worker*. The company also provided Jacob Golos with a cover. *(Hayden Peake collection)*

**World Tourists, Inc.**
175 FIFTH AVENUE • NEW YORK CITY
Telephone Algonquin 4-6656-7-8

TOP SECRET TRINE VENONA

Reissue (T910)

From: NEW YORK

To: MOSCOW

No: 687

13 May 1944


On HELMSMAM's[RULEVOJ][i] instructions GOOD GIRL[UMNITsA[ii] contacted through AMT[iii] a new group [0% in CARTHAGE][0% KARFAGEN][iv]:

[53 groups unrecoverable]

HAGDOFF — "KANT"[v]. GOOD GIRL's impressions: They are reliable FELLOW-COUNTRYMEN[ZEMLYaKI][vi] politically highly mature: they want to help with information. They said that they had been neglected and no one had taken any interest in their potentialities

[    groups unrecoverable]

STORM[SnTORM] [vii]. RAIDER[REJDER][viii], PLUMB[LOT][ix], TED[x] and KANT will go to TYRE[TIR][xi] once every two weeks in turn.

PLUMB and TED know PAL[PEL][xii]. We shall let you hace identifynig particulars later

Mo. 373                                            MAYOR[MER][xiii]

_____

Comments:
        [i] HELMSMAN: Earl BROWDER
       [ii] GOOD GIRL: Elizabeth BENTLEY.
      [iii] AMT: Presumably a mistake for JOHN ABT. See also NEW YORK to
                  MOSCOW No, 588 of 29 April 1944. [s/NBF/T118].
       [iv] CARTHAGE: WASHINGTON. D.C.
        [v] KANT: Henry Samuel MAGDOFF.
       [vi] FELLOW COUNTRYMEN: Members of a Communist Party.
      [vii] STORM: Unidentified.
     [viii] RAIDER: Victor PERLO.
      [ x ] PLUMB: Possibly Charles Kramer.
        [x] TED: Probably Edward Joseph FITZGERALD.
       [xi] TYRE: NEW YORK CITY.
      [xii] PAL: Nathan Gregory SILVERMASTER.
     [xiii] MAYOR: Probably Iskhak Abdulovich AKHMEROV.


25 July, 1968

Bentley's involvement in espionage activities was confirmed by more than a dozen Venona cables, including this one, which details the first meeting between "Clever Girl" (Bentley's code name) and the Perlo Group.

*(National Security Agency)*

FBI Director J. Edgar Hoover, one of the staunchest foes
of communism in the United States, believed Bentley's story
from the start and devoted enormous resources to try
to corroborate the details. *(Bettman/Corbis)*

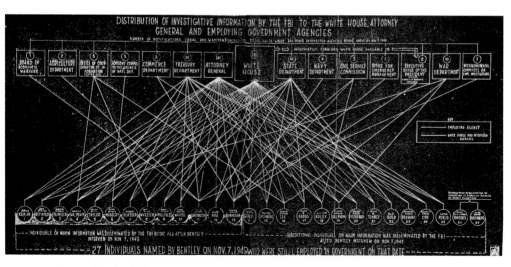

Immediately following Bentley's statements to the FBI—and before any
investigation was undertaken—Hoover and his staff began broadcasting word
of her accusations throughout the federal government. The White House,
the attorney general, six cabinet departments, and a number of other
agencies and offices were in the loop. *(Federal Bureau of Investigation)*

Bentley, flanked by two Capitol guards, awaits her turn to testify before the House Un-American Activities Committee (HUAC). To her far right is former State Department official Alger Hiss, accused by Whittaker Chambers of involvement in a wartime spy ring. *(Acme, Bettman/Corbis)*

# New York World-Telegram

**7TH SPORTS**
**FINAL**
Five Cents

LOCAL FORECAST—Hot and humid today, showers and thunder showers tonight and tomorrow  Weather Forecast on Page 17

VOL. 81—NO. 17—IN TWO SECTIONS—SECTION ONE        NEW YORK 15, N. Y., WEDNESDAY, JULY 21, 1948

# MARSHALL SEEKS BERLIN ACCORD
# TO AVERT A THIRD WORLD WAR

## Daily Worker Boss Scooped Into U.S. Net

**8 Top Reds Held, 3 More Hunted as Violence Plotters**

FBI agents today intensified a nationwide hunt for four top leaders of the American Communist party after a federal grand jury here yesterday, in one stroke, indicted the entire 12-man National Board of the party, the Communist hierarchy in the nation.

Even as the hunt was being pressed for missing Communist chiefs, John Gates, editor of the Daily Worker, official party organ, strolled calmly into the Federal Building at noon today and surrendered. He was the eighth man to be picked up in the investigation.

Another of the indicted men—Irving Potash, manager of the CIO Furriers Joint Council—will

## Red Ring Bared by Blond Queen

Foster.   Dennis.   Stachel.   Williamson.   Davis.   Winston.   Hall.   Thompson.   Potash.   Gates.   Green.

**By NELSON FRANK and NORTON MOCKRIDGE**
Copyright, 1948, by New York World-Telegram Corporation. All rights reserved.

The sparks that touched off yesterday's indictment and roundup of top American Communists originated three years ago in the growing pangs of conscience suffered by a svelte and striking blonde.

New England-born and a member of an old American family, the beautiful young blonde for several years headed one of the most intricate espionage systems ever established in this country.

If it had not been for this woman's increasing squeamishness, her growing feeling of revulsion for the spying she was doing for Russia, the federal grand jury which indicted the Communists might never have been convened.

For it was on the basis of information she supplied to the FBI, when she no longer could bear to sabotage the country of her birth, that the grand jury began its 13-month investigation.

As a result, the Communists have been indicted under the Smith Act which prohibits activities connected with the overthrow of the government by force and violence.

that more than 50 government employees of all ranks were members of the spy ring—was true.

At present it is believed the FBI still does not have enough proof to indict, but it is known that the bureau is remaining relentlessly on the track. One huge stumbling-block is that federal councils do not admit evidence obtained through wire-tapping.

The grand jury was convened in June, 1947, to hear the whole sordid tale.

The woman, a graduate of an outstanding woman's college and one of the officials of a purported relief organization during the war, had been a minor Communist party member for years, she told the FBI.

Gradually, with the outbreak of the war, she was taken more and more into the inner circles of the high command and eventually, when her immediate superior

## But U.S. Won't Be Coerced, He Warns Russia

**Some Officials Think Soviets Are Ready To Risk Hostilities**

WASHINGTON, July 21.—Secretary of State George C. Marshall said today that the United States would take all possible measures to reach an acceptable agreement with the Russians in Berlin in order "to avoid the tragedy of war for the world."

But in seeking an agreement the United States "will not be coerced or intimidated in any way," he said.

Gen. Marshall made his statement in response to a reporter's question regarding the possibility of war dangers in the Berlin impasse between the western powers and the Soviet Union.

"Are Russians reported threatening to shoot if the Allies try to force a break in the

### Local Baseball Results

**FIRST GAME:**

Indians   2 0 1   0 0 0   0 0 0 — 3   6 3
Yankees   1 0 3   0 0 2   1 0   — 7 12 1

Mossotel, Zoldak, Christopher and Hegan, Tlpton; Lopat and Berra.

With Bentley's assistance, the *New York World-Telegram* broke the story of her involvement in a secret grand jury that indicted U.S. Communist Party leaders. Bentley, who is not named in the story, is described as a "svelte and striking blonde" from an "old American family." *(Library of Congress)*

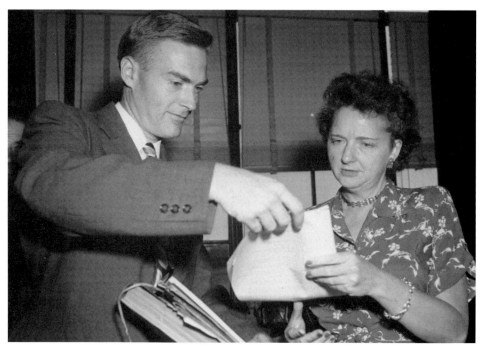

Bentley accused Commerce Department official William Remington *(left)* of giving her confidential government information, which she then passed to the Soviets. Remington, who denied all charges, became the test of Bentley's credibility through two grand juries, two loyalty board hearings, a libel case, and two criminal trials.
*(AP/Wide World)*

Nathan Gregory Silvermaster *(left)* is sworn in by HUAC chairman Karl Mundt *(right)*. Accused by Bentley of heading a ring of informers within the federal government, Silvermaster called Bentley a "neurotic liar" and then proceeded to invoke the Fifth Amendment rather than answer questions about his activities.
*(AP/Wide World)*

Former assistant secretary of the treasury Harry Dexter White, one of the major architects of America's postwar foreign economic policy, was the highest-placed government official accused of espionage activities by Bentley. White denied any involvement and offered a stirring defense of himself before HUAC. *(Library of Congress)*

President Truman, along with New Deal Democrats and other liberals and progressives, believed the congressional hearings on the communist conspiracy were "witch-hunts" devised by the Republicans to win back the White House. *(Library of Congress)*

John Brunini was the foreman of the grand jury that indicted William Remington, the man Bentley accused of passing her confidential government information. At the same time, Brunini was helping Bentley write her autobiography. *(AP/ Wide World)*

# MY LIFE AS A SPY
## BY ELIZABETH BENTLEY

*Here, for the first time, a girl from New England tells the whole story of her life and love among the Communists*

A Russian agent told me:

"I've known about your work for the last two years . . . I'm the man who sits behind the desk in Moscow and keeps track of the reports. In fact, I've been sent over here especially to see you and tell you that we all think you've done splendidly and have a great future before you." Later he told me the Russian government had awarded me the Order of the Red Star. "A great honor has been bestowed on you," he said

34

Bentley's autobiography, *Out of Bondage*, was serialized in *McCall's* magazine during the spring and summer of 1951. The four articles, like the book, presented Bentley as a well-meaning naïf who was ensnared into a life of espionage by her love for Golos. (McCall's, *1951*)

Bentley became a leading anticommunist spokesperson, delivering speeches across
the United States, appearing twice on *Meet the Press* and here, on radio,
with journalists James Reston (smoking) and Martha Rountree.
*(Acme, Bettman/Corbis)*

After her numerous appearances before congressional investigating committees and her many public speeches, Bentley announced that she would begin living a quiet life at her home in Madison, Connecticut. But, as it turned out, she wouldn't stay out of the spotlight for very long.
*(Library of Congress)*

Nixon attempted to box him in with legal thinking. "Either you know Miss Bentley or you don't," he lectured Silvermaster. "Either you know these facts are true or you don't. You have indicated in your statement these facts are false, which would indicate you have knowledge concerning Miss Bentley. Do you want to retract the statement that her statements are false, or do you want to state the facts?" Silvermaster once again took the Fifth. He could not be shaken.

For the next two days, the hearings were devoted to Chambers and Hiss, but on August 9, the committee returned to Bentley's allegations, calling Victor Perlo to the witness table. The day before, Truman had publicly denounced the HUAC hearings as a GOP tactic to distract attention from the fact that congressional Republicans were blocking his anti-inflation program. The only spy ring he knew of, he said, was in Karl Mundt's head. Truman was half-right. The air was particularly thick with partisan politics that day. But the congressmen, for all their vitriol and extremism, were half-right, too. Something had been going on in Washington, D.C., under their noses during the war years, and they would be damned if they didn't get to the bottom of it. Perlo, however, was not going to be of much help.

Like Silvermaster, he read a prepared statement in which he vigorously denied any wrongdoing. "The lurid spy charges of the Bentley woman and of Chambers are," he told the committee, "inventions of irresponsible sensation-seekers." He then, like Silvermaster, refused to answer any further questions—including whether he knew "the Bentley woman"—and, like Silvermaster, was badgered by the committee when he invoked the Fifth. Rankin was his usual acrimonious self. Nixon was far more clever, pointing out the inconsistency of Perlo denying the charges in his statement and then, when questioned, refusing to answer whether the charges were true. But neither sharp tongues nor sharp wits moved the witness. In all, Perlo took the Fifth more than forty times, his face ashen, his hands clasping his knees to keep them from shaking.

The following day, Duncan Lee appeared to answer questions, but, unlike Perlo and Silvermaster, he did, actually, answer questions.

Yes, he knew Miss Bentley, he told the committee. She had, he said, aggressively pursued a relationship with him and his wife. At first, they liked her, inviting her into their home, finding her conversation both intelligent and interesting. But then, increasingly, she became a nuisance, and her political views began to strike them as too extreme. At that point, they cut off the friendship, he said. Had he ever given her confidential information that came across his desk at OSS? Of course not. Had he ever paid party dues to her? Was he a member of the Communist Party? No. And no.

Bentley, who was sitting in the back of the room listening to the testimony, was immediately recalled and asked to repeat her story. She insisted, under oath, that Lee had, in fact, given her quite a bit of secret intelligence, including material on OSS operations in the Balkans and an OSS report on suspected communists in the government. Lee knew she was a communist, Bentley said, and was one himself. Once again, Lee took the stand.

"I am frankly bewildered, congressmen, by Miss Bentley's testimony," he said. "I know one thing . . . she has an extremely active imagination." Lee insisted that he made it a rule during his service with OSS to never discuss anything that had not previously appeared in the newspapers and that he had certainly held to that rule with Bentley. "It's hard for me to believe," he told the committee, "that Miss Bentley's statements are those of a rational person."

But it was hard for the congressmen to believe that Lee, a high-ranking officer in the OSS, could be as innocent and as clueless as he made himself out to be. He had painted a picture of a woman with strong leftist views doggedly cultivating a relationship with him. Hadn't that set off any warning bells? Why had he continued to see her? As an officer of the OSS whose job, in part, was counterespionage, why hadn't he reported her actions to one of his superiors? Congressman Mundt fired the questions at him.

". . . Surely a man who had the capacity in OSS to rise up to the rank of lieutenant colonel had the capacity to figure out that something was unusual," Mundt said. Lee remained calm and stuck to his story. Lud Ullmann and Robert T. Miller followed him that afternoon, both vehemently denying all charges.

It was, perhaps, the worst day of the twenty-one-day hearing for Elizabeth Bentley. She sat in the crowded room, face flushed, listening as Lee dubbed her a nuisance and suggested that she had mental problems, as Ullmann called her a liar and a neurotic, and as Miller referred to her as a woman with a serious drinking problem. What had she expected when she publicly testified against them and the others, that they would nod their heads in agreement and admit to everything? That they would capitulate? Thank her for easing their own consciences? She really hadn't thought that far. For three years she had been insulated by the secrecy of the FBI and the grand jury, surrounded by agents and government prosecutors and journalists who were kind and solicitous. But that was over now. The gloves were off.

The hearings continued with Charles Kramer and David Silverman, whom Bentley had named as a member of the Silvermaster Group, invoking the Fifth and then Frank Coe and Bela Gold denying any involvement in either espionage or party activities. On Friday, August 13, Lauchlin Currie, a former top-level assistant to FDR, faced the committee. He had not been subpoenaed but appeared at his own request to answer, he said, "false statements and misleading suggestions." Currie took an aggressive rather than defensive stance, not merely denying involvement but rejecting any possibility of indiscretion on his part. He stressed that he had never met or even seen Miss Bentley—which was true. He was one of the Silvermaster Group who had never directly interacted with Bentley, giving his information instead to an intermediary.

The final witness that day was the most impressive, most highly placed of the people Bentley had named, former assistant secretary of the Treasury Harry Dexter White, one of the major architects of America's postwar foreign economic policy. Bentley had never met White but testified that she knew he was part of the Silvermaster Group because the Silvermasters and Ullmann had talked about him many times. White, she said, found key positions in the Treasury Department for a number of the people in the network, implying that he played a significant role in the group's ability to carry on its espionage activities. Sonya Gold, Bentley said, was hired as a secretary in White's office to facilitate the flow of documents back to the Silvermasters, information that included departmental memos concerning foreign loan applications. White pulled strings to help members of the network when they were in trouble. He had master-minded the Morganthau Plan, which called for the destruction of German industry after the war and was seen by some as pro-Soviet, as playing into the hands of the communists whose position would be strengthened if Europe was weak.

White read the allegations in the Washington papers, proclaimed Bentley's testimony "the most fantastic thing I have ever heard of," and wired the committee asking to be allowed to respond. In his opening statement before HUAC that Friday afternoon, he called Bentley's story "unqualifiedly false," insisting that his principles would make it impossible for him to be disloyal to his country. Those principles were, he said, nothing more and nothing less than "the American creed: freedom of religion, of speech, of thought, equal opportunity for all, a government of law, where law is above any man and no man is above the law." He spoke with quiet passion and more eloquence than had been heard in that room for some time. Whittaker Chambers thought the performance was gripping.

"I consider these principles sacred," he told the congressmen. "I regard them as the basic fabric of our American way of life, and believe in them as living realities and not as mere words on paper. That is my creed. Those are the principles I have worked for . . . and am prepared to defend at any time with my life." The room erupted in applause. White then proceeded to dominate the hearings, unintimidated but not insolent, defending himself without being defensive, articulate, in control, seemingly relaxed, even witty at times. He answered all the questions patiently, affirming—not "admitting," he told Stripling, but *affirming*—that he knew most of the members of the so-called Silvermaster network but denying that he knew anything about or had ever participated in espionage activities. He was not, nor had he ever been, a communist, he said.

No other witness had comported himself so well and had managed such utterly convincing denials. By the time the questioning ended that afternoon, White appeared to have cleared his name. But the assistant secretary had, in fact, passed information, possibly sensitive documents, to Silvermaster, and he had knowingly met with Soviet underground contacts. Two years after the HUAC hearings, the FBI would positively identify White—whose code name was "Jurist"—in a number of Venona messages. But the committee knew only what they had heard that day. They had publicly scoffed at the denials of others, but they believed White. The press was friendly. His friends showered him with congratulations. Seemingly victorious, White left Washington, D.C., the next day for his farm in New Hampshire. Two days later, at age fifty-six, he was dead. There were rumors at the time that he killed himself. In a scathing editorial, the *New York Times* implied that the HUAC hearings had done him in. But the truth was that Harry Dexter White had long suffered from heart disease and had already lived through one major heart attack. He didn't survive the second one.

After White's appearance, the hearings continued off and on for another three weeks, with the focus increasingly on the stand-off between Chambers and Hiss. Truman watched from the White House, irate, convinced that the communist conspiracy was, as he told the press, a "red herring," a political invention whose purpose was brazenly partisan. The liberal left agreed, casting HUAC as an agency of bitter revenge against the champions of the New Deal, a group of rancorous, self-promoting bigots with little respect for the Constitution. But there were others who saw the committee as a group of fearless, honest, and moral men crusading against the enemies of the American way of life. Certainly, the committee cast itself in these terms, and this is how Elizabeth Bentley must have seen it as well as she alternately testified and sat through the hearings that August. She was, after all, a reformed sinner eager to confess and renounce, determined to see that those who sinned with her were exposed, and the committee gave her that opportunity. The congressmen had supported her and encouraged her, and she had done what she had to do. She had told the truth. There were, indeed, spies in the government. Communist espionage was not a figment of the Republicans' imagination. Her allegations were not the ravings of a neurotic exhibitionist.

But Bentley was not just an anticommunist witness telling her tale. She was a pawn in a political game she could not have understood. And the hearings she instigated by leaking her story to the New York *World Telegram* were more than a public forum about a serious problem. They were the beginning of one of the most controversial periods in twentieth-century history. Elizabeth Bentley had unknowingly set the stage for the abuses of McCarthyism, for innuendo and guilt by association, for the smearing of reputations and the ruining of careers, for fear and suspicion and paranoia.

# Chapter 17

# She Said, He Said

THAT SUMMER, the summer of 1948, Elizabeth Bentley transformed herself once again. She was the New England blueblood who had become a communist spy, the communist spy who had become a government informer. Now she was the shadowy figure, identified in FBI files only as "Confidential Agent Gregory," who became a headline-making celebrity. Some might dismiss her testimony before the Senate and House subcommittees as groundless, or worse, as politically motivated character assassination. But others, many others, sat up and took notice. For those who believed Bentley's story, or even a small part of it, the revelations were both startling and disturbing. It was not so much that the Soviet Union, our sympathetic, wartime ally, could now be seen, or reinterpreted, as an evil-doer. That was really not so hard to believe in the late 1940s, with the Soviet blockade of West Berlin and with the press full of news of communist aggression in Turkey, Greece, Czechoslovakia, and across Eastern Europe. What was hard to believe, what was particularly disquieting, was the idea that seemingly solid, upright

Americans, well-educated—in many cases brilliantly educated at the nation's finest schools—men with distinguished careers and upwardly mobile lives, men who epitomized what was good and right about America, that men like these could be spies. That one really didn't know whom to trust. That the enemy might be among us, invisible. This would be a theme in 1950s America, a thread woven into the fabric of everyday life. And it began in earnest that summer with Elizabeth Bentley's public testimony.

Her metamorphosis from obscurity to fame—or infamy, depending on one's politics—was partly her own doing. She had come forth, unbidden, to tell her story to the FBI. She had leaked it to the press when the grand jury hit a wall. She was a voluntary, and eager, witness before both subcommittees. She was, or thought she was, in control of her life. But that summer she became public property in a way she could not possibly have imagined. She became an item. She became a target. She was "the queen bee of the informer set," "the Nutmeg Mata Hari"—Connecticut being "the Nutmeg State"—as A. J. Liebling dubbed her in a particularly snide article in *The New Yorker*. *The Nation* and *The New Republic* reviled her. In a poem published in the *New York Herald Tribune* that summer, Archibald MacLeish wrote:

> God help that country where informers thrive
> Where slander flourishes and lies contrive.

Not surprisingly, the Communist Party was particularly displeased with Bentley and began a campaign of smears and slanders against her, including planting a story that she had spent time in a mental institution. Among themselves, American communists dismissed her as a neurotic, lonely woman who was never serious about communism in the first place and was now starved for attention. She received threatening letters in the mail. "Dear Betty," read one of them. "Congratulations on your spy story. . . . It will be the last story you will ever write. We will wright [*sic*] the last chapter." In San Francisco, police found a pile of women's clothes, a handbag, and a letter addressed to Bentley on the Golden Gate Bridge. The letter

accused Bentley of betrayal and said that the anonymous writer had
jumped off the bridge along with her baby daughter. It was a hoax,
the police discovered a few days later. But meanwhile, the story went
out across the country through the wire services. If Bentley had been
looking for the spotlight when she testified that summer, this, surely,
was not the spotlight she had in mind.

Part of what kept her in the public eye after the hearings ended
was William Remington. When she testified to the Ferguson Committee that he was one of her regular Washington, D.C., sources, she
set in motion an epic drama that would be played out at three congressional hearings, and before two loyalty boards, a grand jury, and
in two courtrooms. It would be part of her life—and great fodder for
the press—for years to come.

Remington himself was not a particularly important figure in government, like Harry Dexter White, nor was he a network leader like
Silvermaster or Perlo. But he became the test of Bentley's credibility,
just as Alger Hiss became the test for Whittaker Chambers. Remington was not like the others Bentley had named. Silvermaster, Ullmann, Perlo, and most of the rest effectively took themselves out of
the game by invoking their Fifth Amendment privilege and refusing
to answer questions that might link them with Bentley—or each
other. They were not going to be indicted for espionage, and they
and their lawyers knew it. They knew they were safe when the 1947
grand jury didn't return indictments. When it was evident that Bentley could offer no more corroboration in the congressional hearings
than she had to the grand jury, it became a simple matter of keeping
quiet and toughing it out. Silvermaster and the others had no way of
knowing that Venona could prove their involvement in espionage.
But even if they had known, it didn't matter, because Army Intelligence and J. Edgar Hoover had no intention of making Venona public. All Silvermaster and the rest had to do was not say anything that
could later be used against them in a perjury trial. All they had to do
was leave their government jobs and remove themselves from the
crossfire.

Of those who did not take refuge in the Fifth Amendment,
Lauchlin Currie disappeared to Colombia, Maurice Halperin fled to

Mexico, and Harry Dexter White, who had so eloquently stated his own patriotism before HUAC, died. Then there was William Remington, who declared his innocence, did not invoke the Fifth—and stayed to fight. He was an ambitious and self-confident young man with impeccable credentials and his whole career ahead of him. If he was going to have the career he imagined for himself, he needed to clear his name. And if Elizabeth Bentley—and by extension, the FBI, HUAC, and the whole communist conspiracy juggernaut—were to maintain credibility, Remington must be brought down.

Following the Ferguson hearings, the Commerce Department suspended Remington while a regional loyalty board—part of the government security system Truman had created under pressure—examined his case. Remington testified before the four-man panel for more than thirteen hours. "It never occurred to me," he told the board, "that she was a communist. . . . I thought of her as a vague, rather pleasant lady, a kind of sad and aimless person I befriended for a brief time." A parade of witnesses then attested to Remington's loyalty, stressing the avowedly *anti*communist stances he had taken in recent years. According to Truman's executive order, the loyalty examiners were supposed to determine whether a person was loyal to the government at the present time. But Remington's panel decided to dismiss his present activities as "self-serving" and concentrate on his past and Bentley's allegations of his conduct in 1942 and 1943. There they found much to criticize.

Like Ferguson and his subcommittee colleagues, the members of the loyalty board could not believe that Remington was as naïve and clueless as he claimed to be. "The surreptitious manner and character of the meetings [between Remington and Bentley] indicate conscious wrongdoing," the panel decided. "We think he must have known that he was imparting nonpublic information to a person closely identified with communists." On September 22, the board decided against him, determining that there was reasonable doubt about his loyalty. Remington could have opted out of the game right then by accepting the verdict and moving on to a career outside government. But he didn't. Instead, he hired a top lawyer, Joseph Rauh, an anticommunist liberal, who began the process of mounting an appeal. Rauh was convinced of Remington's innocence, calling him a "strange combination of . . . brilliance and gullibility" and "a decent boy." But Remington was lying to his lawyer just as he had misled the loyalty board and the Ferguson Committee. For one thing, there *was* communist activity in his past. More significantly, he had known Bentley was a communist, and he had indeed passed her information not intended for the public.

But his lawyer knew nothing of this. To him, Remington was a bright, personable, charmingly ingenuous young man unjustly accused. Five days after the loyalty board's ruling, Rauh filed an appeal to the federal review board. At the same time, he announced plans to file a libel suit against Elizabeth Bentley, the result of remarks she had made a week and a half earlier on the popular NBC radio program *Meet the Press.* Interviewed live by a panel of journalists, she had been challenged to repeat her allegations against any of the people she had named at the hearings.

"Now, here, Miss Bentley, you don't have congressional immunity, would you now identify William Remington as a communist?" one of the journalists asked her.

She tried to avoid answering directly, but the journalist persisted. Finally, she said, "Yes, I would certainly do that." Rauh was listening to the broadcast and thought the statement could not go unchallenged given the appeal he was mounting. He would move against Bentley on two fronts simultaneously.

While the libel case was taking shape, Rauh concentrated on presenting Remington's appeal to the loyalty review panel, a seemingly unsympathetic tribunal that included an ultraconservative attorney and the past national commander of the American Legion. Bentley's testimony, Rauh told the panel, was "charged with inconsistencies and impressions and conclusions and superficialities." Remington did nothing wrong. He was, his lawyer claimed, a young and inexperienced man "seduced by what he thought were newspapermen." Remington told the panel that he was "embarrassed" by the relationship he had with Bentley. "I was not entirely alert in my perception," he told the review board, once again casting himself as a naïf. "But I did nothing wrong." The panel then listened to a parade of impressive character witnesses, including the former president of Dartmouth, a distinguished professor from Columbia, the assistant secretary of Commerce and the chairman of Truman's Economic Council.

But the witness Rauh most wanted the loyalty review board to hear was Elizabeth Bentley, the only person to link his client to disloyal activities. He planned to cross-examine her, to blow holes in her testimony against his client, to expose her for the liar he thought she was—and to win the day. The board had granted Rauh's request to call Bentley for questioning but had no subpoena power to back it up. Bentley could be "invited," but she could not be forced. That turned out to be a moot point, because no one seemed to be able to locate her. The Spy Queen had disappeared from public view. Rauh was eager to find her, but he wasn't the only one looking for the elusive Miss Bentley. Remington's *other* lawyer, the man he had hired to handle the libel case, was also on her trail.

That case was shaping up as the loyalty review board continued its deliberations. Rauh was insistent that Bentley's radio statement be challenged. Inaction, he told Remington, might be seen by the board as an admission that Bentley's charges were true. Accordingly, Remington hired Richard Green, a libel specialist who had just won a high-profile case in New York. Before filing the suit, Green sent a strongly worded letter to Bentley—simultaneously released to the press—demanding a retraction. She did not respond. In early October, he proceeded with the case, filing a $100,000 suit against Bentley, NBC, and General Foods, the sponsor of *Meet the Press*. By late fall, the hunt for Bentley was on, with a U.S. marshal and various process servers attempting to locate her to deliver a subpoena so Remington's lawyers could take her deposition, and people from Rauh's office trying to find her so she could be cross-examined before the loyalty board. In view of her now very public persona, the press dogged the story. RED WITNESS MISSING AT 100-G SLANDER SUIT ran a headline in the *New York Daily Mirror*. A few days later, the *World Telegram* broke the news that Bentley was sequestered at a Catholic retreat in the Bronx. The story made all the newspapers in New York and Washington, D.C. Bentley, said an item in the *Wash-*

*ington Times Herald,* was "quietly pursuing her religious meditations while U.S. marshals, attorneys and process servers were frantically seeking her."

It was true. Bentley had spent most of the fall studying the Catholic faith with Monsignor Fulton J. Sheen, one of the leading anticommunist ideologues in the American Catholic hierarchy, a man who was busy making a specialty out of converting former communists. The Church itself had been a strident opponent of communism since the early 1930s, when Father Charles Coughlin, the so-called Radio Priest, had taken to the airwaves to lecture on its evils—along with the attendant and related evils of the New Deal. When Bentley came to Washington, D.C., to testify during the summer, her friend and fellow ex-communist Louis Budenz, himself a recent and well-publicized convert to the faith via the ministrations of the Monsignor, had introduced her to Sheen. After a period of private instruction, on November 5, at a church in the capital, Bentley was baptized into the faith with Budenz and his wife standing as her godparents. Afterward, she returned to New York, secluding herself at the Susan Devin Residence, a Catholic retreat.

Some thought her conversion was self-serving and its timing all too convenient. Her newfound faith could enhance her credibility at a time when it needed enhancing, and contacts within the powerful anticommunist Catholic movement could be important allies. These accusations may have been, at least in part, true. But it was also true that Bentley was an embattled woman who had lost her faith in communism and was looking for something else to replace it in her life. The decision to become a Catholic may have been both strategic and expedient, but it was also a personal, emotional response to the void Bentley felt. For whatever else communism was to her, it was also, for a while, a comforting, all-consuming dogma, absolute, unquestionable, and infallible. It was something to believe in with heart and head. It gave shape and meaning to one's life. "People who are genuine communists as I was," Bentley told the press after her conversion, ". . . they can't go into a vacuum if they give up communism. They must have something to tie to." For Bentley, at least for the moment, that was Catholicism.

On November 21, the notorious Spy Queen made her first public appearance in months, delivering a strident lecture in Rochester, New York, where she had graduated from high school more than twenty years before. Her topic: the Communist Menace. She had been asked to testify at Remington's loyalty review board in Washington, D.C., the next day but had declined, citing this and other commitments. Remington's lawyer was beside himself. He felt his case rested on cross-examining Bentley, but first he couldn't find her and then he couldn't pin her down. When the news of Bentley's conversion hit the papers, Rauh contacted high Church dignitaries, appealing directly to them to impress on Bentley the urgency of an appearance before the board. His request was declined. Now it was late fall, the case had been dragging on for months, and he was no closer to being able to question Bentley.

The hearing took place, as scheduled, on November 22, without her. Rauh presented a voluminous brief with evidence of Remington's anticommunist views and activities for the past ten years and testimonials to his loyalty. The evidence seemed very much in his favor, but the panel made no decision. That was because behind the scenes, William Rogers, counsel for the Ferguson Committee, was assuring the review board that Bentley would in fact testify. He had been instructed by Ferguson to find her and see if he could persuade her to participate. Bentley's absence from the hearing made Homer Ferguson nervous. It was her testimony before *his* committee that had first revealed Remington's name. If Remington was cleared by the review board, it was not just Bentley's credibility that would suffer, it was Ferguson's as well. Based on Rogers's promise to deliver Bentley, the panel agreed to reopen the proceedings for the purpose of hearing directly from Remington's accuser. A date of December 15 was set. But on December 13, Bentley's lawyer sent a cable to the head of the review board, saying that it would be "impossible" for Bentley to attend. She would be in New Orleans, giving another lecture.

Remington's lawyer was convinced that Bentley was refusing to appear because she was lying about his client, and her testimony would not stand up to his cross-examination. But she wasn't lying.

Remington was the one who was lying. Bentley used the excuse of being too busy when she twice refused to appear before the review board. She did, in fact, have paid speaking engagements, commitments that were important to her not just for the income—her only source these days—but for her sense of self-worth, her belief that she was now doing something good and important with her life. Still, the lectures could have been rescheduled had she wanted to testify. She could have found the time. But she didn't, even though not just the loyalty review board decision was at stake but also, by extension, the libel case. It is possible that she was just following the advice of her lawyer to keep a low profile. But it is far more likely that it was her decision alone.

The spotlight had already proved to be much hotter than she had bargained for. The press had her in its sights. There was a lawsuit against her. There had been private threats, public insults, nasty rumors, denunciations, and personal slurs. Bentley wanted and needed to feel in control of her public image, of her life. Her speaking engagements gave her that feeling. She could pick her venues, choose the friendliest of audiences, and lecture without interruption. She had in many ways been in control of her congressional appearances as well. They were orchestrated by those who believed her and believed in her, by those who had a stake in her performing well. Certain questions were asked and others were not. The questioners were, for the most part, kind and accommodating. But Remington's lawyer would be neither. He was out to disprove her story, to poke holes in her credibility, to show her up. She would be grilled. And she had every reason to believe that nothing good would come of it. She had no evidence to present against Remington, only her own recollections. She might very well be seen as an untrustworthy witness—a former communist, a former spy, and now a turncoat—impugning the reputation of a certified golden boy. Whatever happened, it would be another field day for the press. It was an intimidating prospect, even for someone who was telling the truth. And especially for someone who was struggling to find her footing, who was searching, with much apprehension, for her future.

Perhaps she was too distracted by her own concerns, the direction her life was taking, not knowing how to make sense of it or what to do next. Perhaps she thought that Remington would lose the loyalty review case without her help. He had lost the first round. And he was, she knew and he knew, guilty. Better to concentrate on her own life, to find meaning and direction in Catholicism, to hone her anti-communist image in controlled public appearances, to stay away from controversy as much as she could. For any or all of these reasons, she once again shunned the loyalty review hearing. A decision would have to be made without her. Rauh pleaded with the board to act before Christmas. The case had been dragging on for too long. His client had been on suspension from his Department of Commerce position since July. But the panel continued to take its time. It wasn't until February 10, 1949, more than four months after Remington's lawyer had begun the appeals process, that the decision was announced.

"The record here is the uncorroborated statement of a woman who refuses to submit herself to cross-examination," wrote one of the board members in his opinion, noting that the case came down to the word of a "a self-confessed spy" against a "young man whose every action in public employment showed a distinct anticommunist slant." The other members concurred, and the review panel unanimously reversed the decision of the lower board, clearing Remington of disloyalty charges and ordering him reinstated, with $5,000 back pay, in his Commerce job. Delighted and relieved, that evening Remington called a press conference at the Washington Hotel where he told journalists that he owed his clearance to "the vigor of democracy." His lawyers were doubly pleased. A clearance by the review board could have only positive effects on the libel case.

Remington's libel lawyer had been busy putting together the case against Bentley while the review board deliberated. He had hired a private investigator, a former FBI agent, to dig around, in hopes of uncovering something he could use against her in the pretrial hearing. One of the first items to surface was the rumor that Bentley had been treated for psychiatric conditions at Yale University hospital. When the FBI got wind of this, the New Haven office immediately made "discreet inquiries." Information like this, if true, could hurt not only the libel case but also cast doubt on all of Bentley's statements. The cost to the Bureau, in both credibility and status, would be enormous. But within days, New Haven agents sent Hoover an urgent teletype with good news: There was no record of Bentley ever having been admitted to the clinic. Hoover could breathe easier. But the investigation continued, with the PI tracking down Bentley's adviser at Columbia who implied that she had not been the author of her own master's thesis, and a graduate student (now a professor) who had known her in Italy and who painted a potentially damaging portrait of the young Elizabeth Bentley. She had run amok in Italy, he told the investigator, drinking to excess and carrying on promiscuously. Meanwhile, Bentley's lawyers were busy digging into Remington's past, tracking down leads about his communist activities prior to coming to Washington, D.C. Both sides were ready for a fight.

First, there was the pretrial hearing in mid-March 1949, conducted to determine whether Remington actually had a case. There, NBC's lawyers, who represented all the codefendants—Bentley, *Meet the Press,* and the network—argued that Bentley's remarks were, first of all, slander not libel, and second, that she had merely repeated the privileged testimony she gave to the Ferguson Committee, which was protected from prosecution. Remington's lawyer countered that whether the words were slander or libel made little difference. The point was that her remarks were damaging to his client's reputation and career. Nothing could be more detrimental to an economist in government, Richard Green argued, than to be called a communist. Furthermore, Bentley's remarks were actually serious criminal allegations. In accusing him of communist activities, she was also accusing him of perjury and of violating two U.S. statutes. The federal judge assigned to the case listened closely and then deliberated all through the spring and summer and into the fall without handing down a decision.

Meanwhile, Bentley had to get on with her life. She needed to find secure, gainful employment, something steadier and more reliable than the occasional public lecture. She was, as she had always been, a woman who supported herself, who had no family money to cushion her, no spouse to maintain her. But she did have—or at least she used to have years ago—a vocation. She was a teacher. She had a bachelor's degree, two master's degrees, and several years of classroom experience. However, her experience was now almost two decades old, and her current notoriety made her a poor candidate for any position dealing with young people. Finding employment would not be easy, but her new friends in the anticommunist Catholic movement could help. In the fall of 1949 she secured a position teaching political science at Mundelein College, a prestigious Catholic women's school on Lake Shore Drive in Chicago. Her Catholic friends pulled strings for her, for it was not just her shaky credentials and haunted past that stood in her way but the fact that virtually all the staff and faculty at Mundelein were nuns. Bentley hoped to get back to a more normal life, to settle into the comforting routines of academia. But with the libel suit pending, normal life was not possible.

On December 7, just before Mundelein recessed for the Christmas holidays, the judge who had heard the pretrial arguments eight and a half months before finally delivered his decision. In a sixteen-page opinion, he dismissed the arguments set forth by the NBC lawyers and ruled that Remington did, indeed, have a case. Now Bentley faced the very real possibility of a trial, which would mean a major disruption of her new life. It would mean traveling back and forth to New York to confer with her lawyers and give her deposition to Remington's legal team. It would mean traveling back for the trial, to testify and be cross-examined. It would mean headlines again.

Richard Green, eager to get on with Remington's case after such a long wait, put the NBC lawyers on notice that he planned to move ahead to trial, a tactic designed to provoke the network into settling out of court. A week later, Green and the top NBC attorney were negotiating in private. Green demanded $10,000. The NBC lawyer countered with $2,500. Green held firm, warning that the price of a settlement would only escalate. The network's lawyer parried. Perhaps a settlement was not possible, he told Green. The network lawyers were impressed with Bentley's story and would look forward to a trial. Green thought the NBC lawyer was bluffing and that he would come back with a counteroffer of $5,000, which Green would negotiate up to $7,500, and that would be the end of it.

But the NBC team was not bluffing. In fact, the lawyers thought they just might have the evidence they needed to corroborate Bentley's story. If her allegations could be proven true, then Remington would lose in court, truth being an unassailable defense in libel cases. Months before, a Knoxville attorney had written NBC offering to set up a meeting with a man who had investigated Remington many years ago and could provide proof that he had been a communist. In late December, with the out-of-court settlement stalled, the lawyers traveled to Knoxville to interview the man and left two days later with a list of eighteen witnesses who presumably knew about Remington's communist activities while he was working for the Tennessee Valley Authority. If any of this panned out, Remington would be discredited, and he would surely lose his case against Bentley. But interviewing and deposing so many people so far from New York would cost a lot of money, perhaps as much as $10,000. Bentley didn't have the money, and the insurance company covering NBC's libel policy would never approve such an expenditure. It would cost more to win the case than it would to settle it, and the insurance company cared about the bottom line, not about Elizabeth Bentley's public credibility. The NBC lawyers moved to settle.

When Bentley's personal lawyer heard about this, he was furious. He told the attorneys representing the network that Bentley would never issue a retraction and never contribute a cent to the settlement. To Bentley, he wrote that under no circumstances would he participate in any negotiations. "All along I have had complete confidence that if the matter were put to trial, you would be vindicated," he told her. *Meet the Press* producer Lawrence Spivak wrote a long and vehement letter to NBC's insurance company begging them not to settle. Spivak told the press that he did not believe a libel had been committed on his show and that the settlement was based purely on expediency.

In Chicago, the settlement took Bentley by surprise. Anticipating a trial, concerned about her ability to hold down her teaching position while making regular trips to New York and Washington, D.C., she had handed in her resignation to Mundelein. Her teaching career had lasted barely a semester. She told the press, which treated her resignation as a significant news item, that she left the college to make herself available for work in Washington. Her frequent subpoenas "did not help class morale," she said. She told the FBI she was afraid the libel suit would embarrass the school. But there were rumors of another reason. Bentley, it was said, was living with a man "openly and notoriously," and Mundelein's president, Sister Mary Josephine, thought it would be best if she left. Bentley did have a history of promiscuity. And she was alone in a new city and undoubtedly lonely. She had lived with a man in Italy and had made a life outside marriage with Golos. But she also had many detractors more than willing to concoct damaging stories. And she had a legitimate reason—or thought she did—to quit her job that winter: the Remington trial. In public, at least, Mundelein seemed genuinely sorry to see her go. "It was very hard to replace her," a member of the college staff told the *Washington Post*. "She fitted in here very well."

By early 1950, Bentley was back in New York, living temporarily at the Hotel Commodore. She was enraged at the thought of an out-of-court settlement, but there was nothing she could do. NBC's insurance company was in control. Her own lawyer was powerless. On February 17, the official announcement came: The $100,000 suit would be settled for $9,000, and, although it would have been expected in these circumstances to require one, a retraction was expressly *not* part of the settlement. When a *New York Times* article implied that the settlement had been made on the basis of a private retraction, Bentley's lawyer immediately wrote to the paper, sternly correcting the misconception and emphasizing that his client was not a party to the settlement and did not agree with it.

The settlement itself—because it was a small fraction of the amount of the suit and especially because it did not include a retraction—was neither a stirring vindication of William Remington nor a strong indictment of Elizabeth Bentley. But Remington had undeniably won two important battles against her, emerging victorious from both the loyalty review and the libel suit. The war, however, was not over. There was too much riding on Remington as a measure of Bentley's credibility.

# Chapter 18

# The Spotlight

$\mathcal{F}$OLLOWING HER DRAMATIC appearances before the two congressional committees in the summer of 1948, Elizabeth Bentley began a new chapter in her life. Driven by her desire to live a meaningful life, her need to absolve herself of past sins—and her ego—she sought out the spotlight, participating in, adding to, and in some ways orchestrating the media frenzy that now surrounded her. But the longer she stayed in the public eye, the clearer it became to her that cultivating a public persona was a double-edged sword. Publicity could be personally painful. Journalists and others could—and did—attack her in print, calling into question her motives, her memory, her integrity, even her sanity. She was a liar, a fake, a gossip, a stool pigeon. She was, her most unkind critics said, an old maid starved for attention, a frustrated spinster, a hysteric. As a woman, and as a woman alone, she was particularly vulnerable to the most personal kind of slander. It couldn't have been pleasant to read about oneself in those terms. But Bentley's new identity as a hard-charging anticommunist, and her self-worth, were tied to her public activities. She would have to learn how to live with the fallout.

In public, at least, she handled the surrounding controversy with poise and composure. Her first real test was appearing on NBC's *Meet the Press* radio program in mid-August, toward the tail end of her testimony before HUAC. She accepted the invitation knowing the format of the show, understanding that it was live and that she would face a panel of combative reporters who would pepper her with questions for half an hour. The program's announcer set the tone. "For weeks now," he began, "the front pages have been full of stories of two congressional investigations. Names were printed in bold type that shocked the nation. . . . At the roaring center of all this was an American woman. Is her fantastic story true? Could all this be a figment of her imagination? Why did she become a communist . . . Who was at fault? . . . Why did she change? Only Elizabeth Bentley can answer . . . these questions." In NBC's New York studio, Bentley fielded the first question from Frank Waldrop of the *Washington Times Herald*.

"Miss Bentley," he said, "these are pretty exciting times." He probably intended the comment to be an affable opening gambit, a nonthreatening nonquestion to ease into the session. But Bentley didn't take it that way. What did he mean by "exciting?" Was he implying that she was getting a thrill out of naming names? She didn't quite know how to respond. She was quiet for a long moment, then answered carefully, warily, "Yes, they are."

"Are you scared?" Waldrop asked. Again she paused, trying to figure out what he might mean, trying to see a trap before she fell in.

"Scared of what?" she finally answered.

"Scared about suffering reprisals from communists," he said, "scared of the publicity, scared of anything?" Now she knew what to say.

"I think you rather get accustomed to it," she answered, her voice even and calm, "although there are moments when you get a little shaky."

The reporters were understandably dubious. Bentley had told a largely uncorroborated story to the subcommittees, both of which

seemed entirely too willing to believe her. The people she accused of
wrongdoing, those who did not invoke the Fifth Amendment,
adamantly denied her accusations. Now she faced reporters, men—
and one woman, May Craig from the Portland (Maine) *Press Herald*—whose professional responsibility was to doubt, who prided
themselves on their skepticism.

"It's obvious from the testimony I've listened to that someone is
lying," Lawrence Spivak said. Spivak was a writer for *American Mercury* magazine who would soon take over as the show's moderator
and producer. "Isn't there some way that you can present testimony
that would prove beyond a doubt that the people you say are communists really are, or is there no way, and is that the reason the grand
jury was unable to take action against some of these people?"

"I'm afraid I wouldn't know, Mr. Spivak." Bentley said. "I only
know that there are my facts, which I have, and that the FBI itself
made a complete investigation." Once or twice she was a little testy,
once or twice a bit wary, but throughout the broadcast she seemed
unintimidated, even by the most pointed questions. Her answers
were measured, articulate, and generally self-confident. Her performance, live on national radio, was, in fact, astonishing. She
seemed more at ease, sharper, more verbally adept than her questioners. Her answers didn't sound rehearsed, yet it was clear she had
an agenda, the first and most important item of which was to position herself as a born-again patriot and zealous anticommunist.
When Waldrop asked her how she could have had such a poor opinion of her own country's government as to embrace communism,
she talked about the problems she saw when she returned to New
York in the depths of the Depression.

"And what do you think now?" he asked.

Her response was immediate. "I think it's the best government in
the world," she said.

Later in the program, she appealed to current members of the
Communist Party to "leave it and come forward to help." Five days
later, on a CBS radio special broadcast from Washington, D.C., she
repeated the plea. "It isn't enough," she said, "to just quit being a
communist, as I know hundreds have. Come forward now and tell

what you know while there's still time to undo the damage we have so foolishly done." Her anticommunism may have had roots in something other than ideological revelation, but it was sincere, as were these pleas to fellow party members. Of course, her entreaties served selfish purposes as well. If she could induce others to talk, her own importance would be enhanced. She would be more valuable to the government, more respected and appreciated. If she could induce others to talk, someone might corroborate parts of her story.

With both vindication and income in mind, she hit the lecture circuit, speaking in venues across the nation during the next several years. To a packed house in upstate New York, she urged patience with turncoat communists like herself. "Sometimes," she said, "the greatest sinners make the greatest saints." To 1,400 Catholic college students at a Newman Club communion breakfast in Manhattan, she stressed the importance of religious faith. Lack of faith, she told them, had made her a "pushover" for communism. Addressing 600 members of the Knights of Columbus in Brooklyn, she blamed her agnosticism and the fact that she was "surrounded by procommunist professors" for her downfall. As a guest of the Brooklyn-based Bay Ridge Catholic Action Guild, she spoke of the danger of communist propaganda spreading to young people. In Huntsville, Alabama, at a talk sponsored by the American Legion, she presented herself as a victim of brainwashing who was "molded into the communistic pattern of thought." In Hollywood, she spoke at the American Legion Auditorium, along with John Wayne and character actor Charles Coburn, at a meeting sponsored by the Motion Picture Alliance for the Preservation of American Ideals.

Bentley was a good speaker, forceful, emphatic, and articulate. She presented herself well, always conservatively dressed in tailored suits, her hair freshly curled, her lipstick carefully applied. Audiences may have come to hear the Spy Queen, thinking they would see a wild and wicked—although penitent and now reformed—secret agent, but they left understanding just what Bentley wanted them to understand: that communists looked just like everyone else, that communism was a largely invisible threat. She told her select audiences what they paid to hear: that communism was the twentieth century's greatest evil and that the enemy was still very much among us. Much in demand, she traveled to Pennsylvania, Ohio, Illinois, Iowa, Missouri, Nebraska, and Colorado to deliver lectures, charging $300 an evening. It was, for a time, the best of both worlds. She was maintaining a high profile while effectively controlling her image. She was making money while doing what she considered the most important work of her life.

Bentley was now also in demand by the government as an expert witness. She might have little more to add to her own oft-told story, but she could be tapped by congressional committees and prosecuting attorneys as an "insider," an authority on communism, the party, and the espionage apparatus. Bentley was an insider by dint of her own experiences as a courier and network handler, but in the grand scheme of things, she had been "middle management." It was her close association with Golos that gave her the real insider's view. He had been on intimate terms with American communist party leadership, with Russian nationals in the United States who worked for the KGB, and with KGB officials in Moscow. Through Golos, she met and became friendly with Earl Browder, the head of the American communist party, and came to understand the relationship between the party and espionage activities. Golos had known, or known of, just about everyone involved in espionage before and during the war. He met many people. He mentioned many names to her. Over time, he told her more than he should have. Bentley was indeed an expert.

In May, June, and August of 1949, the Senate Subcommittee on Immigration and Naturalization held hearings on proposed changes to U.S. immigration policy. Bentley was invited to appear as an expert witness to offer her opinion on amendments the senators were considering, one to bar subversives from entering the country, another to deport aliens who were involved in subversive groups or activities. She told them just what they wanted to hear—that restricting immigration would "cut the lifeline between here and Moscow" and throw the Communist Party off base. Furthermore, she said, "if you deport aliens who engage in subversive activities, you are taking away from the party the brains behind it and making it exceedingly difficult for them to operate."

Her testimony was even better than the committee hoped for. She told the senators that every Russian in the United States was potentially a Soviet spy. "I was told," she said, "that every member of the Russian embassy and consulates is working on espionage of various sorts. . . . The same is true of the Russian nationals in Amtorg [the Soviet trading commission] and in TASS [the Soviet news service]," she added. She said that agents were sent into the United States in the guise of businessmen from satellite countries like Poland and Lithuania, that agents served in the Soviet Union's United Nations' delegation and on the staff of foreign-language newspapers published in America.

Later, when the senators asked her to send them a list of the sources she had named for HUAC, she surprised them by including six additional former government employees and four others she said had been information suppliers for the Soviets during the war. But the committee seemed interested in only one man.

"Are any of these persons who you knew in the American government, who were giving information to the agents of the communists, presently in government?" the committee chairman asked Bentley.

"So far as I know," she said, "there is only one."

"And who is that person?"

"Mr. William Remington," Bentley answered.

"In what department?"

"I understand he is still in the Department of Commerce, Senator," she said.

"Remington?"

"Yes, Mr. William Remington."

The senators took note. Then they moved on.


From the late forties to the early fifties, Bentley was one of the most outspoken and one of the most knowledgeable former communists in the country. It is therefore not surprising that she was called on to play an important role in the most important trial of the Cold War period. In March of 1951, Julius and Ethel Rosenberg stood accused of espionage in connection with the top-secret Manhattan Project, which brought many of America's leading scientists to the desert of New Mexico to create the atomic bomb. It was the largest single project in wartime America and, at more than $2 billion, the single most expensive scientific endeavor in human history to date. The making of the atomic bomb was America's most closely held secret. But it apparently was not held closely enough.

Julius Rosenberg, a passionate and enthusiastic communist who joined the party before the war, an electrical engineer by trade, was accused of masterminding the theft of atomic secrets through the efforts of his brother-in-law, David Greenglass, whom he allegedly recruited into espionage and who ultimately turned against him. Ethel's participation in all of this was limited to the allegation that she typed the notes Greenglass had given her husband. Defenders of the Rosenbergs, who were legion, called the case a "hoax conspiracy" concocted to convince Americans that they were in grave and immediate danger from the communists. But to J. Edgar Hoover, it was "the crime of the century." U.S. Attorney Irving Saypol, who had just successfully prosecuted Alger Hiss, was in charge of the government's case with the assistance of the voluble Roy Cohn, who would two years later leave the U.S. Attorney's Office to serve as an aide to Senator Joseph McCarthy. Elizabeth Bentley was not the star witness by any means—that distinction fell to Greenglass. She was not the one to identify Julius or offer damning testimony about his espionage activities. In fact, she had never met him and knew nothing of his undercover work. But her role in this drama was considerable.

She was, first of all, an important guidepost on the investigative road to the Rosenbergs. Greenglass, Ethel's brother, was the accuser. But the FBI had gotten to Greenglass through a man named Harry Gold, a spy courier, and the Bureau had gotten to Gold through Abraham Brothman, the Long Island City chemist Bentley had identified as a source in her original 1945 statement to the FBI. Thus, when Bentley named Brothman, she initiated the investigation that eventually led to the Rosenbergs. But Bentley's appearance as the final witness for the prosecution was even more important.

In the course of the trial, Saypol endeavored to introduce much evidence concerning the radical politics of the defendants. Identifying the Rosenbergs as stalwart communists was important to building the case against them. But the judge ruled that the evidence was admissible only if the prosecution established some connection between communism and the offense charged, between being a member of the Communist Party and being a spy. Enter expert witness Elizabeth Bentley, the woman who understood that connection well, who had seen it operate firsthand.

Sitting on the witness stand in late March, she bore an uncanny resemblance to Ethel Rosenberg. They had the same high forehead, the same crimped brown hair, the same thin, tight lips painted dark. Bentley was eight years younger than Ethel, but the two women had aged the same way, with skin still smooth but soft jowls at the jawline. They could have been sisters.

"Miss Bentley," said Irving Saypol, guiding his witness to the key point, "had you learned what was the relation of the Communist Party of the United States to the Communist International?"

Bentley answered that the American Party was under the direct jurisdiction of the Soviets. "The Communist Party," she said, amplifying her response, ". . . only served the interests of Moscow, whether it be propaganda or espionage or sabotage."

With one sentence, she had done it. She had linked the party to spying. The thrust of her testimony was that any party member with whom she and Golos had had contact was also in the service of Moscow. The Rosenbergs had already been identified as party members. Now Bentley was used to help establish a link between them and Golos. The link was weak, but in the face of the other testimony, it did not have to be more than a seed planted in the minds of the jury.

Repeating a story she had told the FBI years before, Bentley testified that in the early summer of 1942 she and Golos were driving through the Lower East Side when he stopped the car and told Bentley to wait while he met someone at a street corner. It was dark, the car was parked some distance away, and Bentley had caught only a fleeting glimpse of the man, whom she remembered as being thin and wearing glasses. Golos told her later that the man's name was Julius and that he was one of a group of engineers with whom Golos was in contact. He told her that he had given Julius her home phone number so the man could reach him whenever he needed to.

During the following months, she told the FBI, a man identifying himself as Julius called her several times in the "wee hours," wanting to get a hold of Golos. She could not identify Julius Rosenberg as the man she had seen meeting with Golos, but the circumstantial evidence pointed to him. Rosenberg was a thin man who wore glasses, an engineer and a resident of Knickerbocker Village, which was near the location of the street corner meeting with Golos. This testimony alone would not have amounted to much. But coupled with the specific allegations of David and Ruth Greenglass, the persuasive backup testimony from Harry Gold, and the link Bentley forged between the party and espionage, it was enough to convince a jury.

The trial of the "crime of the century" lasted only fourteen court days. On March 29, the Rosenberg jury returned with a guilty verdict. And then, on June 19, 1953, after more than two years of appeals that reached to the Supreme Court, first Julius and then Ethel Rosenberg were executed in the electric chair at the federal penitentiary in Ossining, New York.


The Rosenberg case was the big show for the Department of Justice. The Attorney General's Office sent in its best men. Hoover put his considerable weight behind it, and the Bureau worked doggedly to collect intelligence. But even in the midst of such a high-stakes, high-profile case, no one could quite forget a certain small fry who had thus far escaped prosecution. He was no thief of atomic secrets. He was no government bigwig. But William Remington stuck in the craw of too many people at too many agencies to be ignored for long. Exonerated by the loyalty review board, victorious in his libel suit against Bentley, and now back at work in the Commerce Department, he was despite this—or more likely *because* of this—an accident waiting to happen.

In the spring of 1950, just before the FBI began questioning David Greenglass and piecing together the Rosenberg case, HUAC was listening behind closed doors to two self-confessed former communists who swore they had known William Remington as a communist when he worked for the Tennessee Valley Authority in 1936–37. These were the two men discovered by an investigator sent to Knoxville during preparations for the Remington libel case. The investigator, working for Bentley's attorney, had uncovered a number of leads that would link Remington to the party—important information that could win the case for Bentley—but pursuing these leads would cost just as much, perhaps even more, than settling the case. The lawyers settled the case out of court, and the matter was dropped. But not really. Very soon thereafter, perhaps even while the libel case was being negotiated in the lawyers' offices, it is probable that either Bentley herself or her attorney or someone in the loop at the FBI turned over the Knoxville information to the eager Red-hunters at HUAC. However the information made its way to the committee, in April the congressmen heard the secret testimonies of Kenneth McConnell and Howard Bridgman, admitted members of a communist cell of TVA employees.

McConnell, a former party organizer, testified that Remington had been a member of the TVA cell and had, in fact, been under "Party discipline" for, of all things, dressing more like a prep-school boy than a rough-and-tumble communist. McConnell recalled for the congressmen several party meetings he had attended where Remington was present. Bridgman corroborated, naming Remington as one of a half dozen members of the Knoxville cell and swearing that he had seen him at five or six meetings of the cell. In early May, HUAC reopened the public investigation of Remington, calling him and then Bentley to testify. Remington, who had previously sworn to the Ferguson Committee and before two loyalty boards that he had never been a communist, now sat in the hearings room listening to HUAC chairman John Wood reading the Knoxville testimony against him.

When it was his turn to testify, Remington first angrily denounced the reopening of his case, calling it "not merely double jeopardy . . .

[but] triple jeopardy." Then he vehemently denied the new evidence against him. "I am not now nor have I ever been a member of the Communist Party," he told the congressmen. "And when I say never, I mean never, whether at age three, eighteen, or thirty-two. . . ." He went on to say that any person who charged he was a communist was either "quite ignorant of the facts" or "engaged in deliberate false-hood." But it was Remington who was engaged in deliberate falsehood. He had been a communist in Knoxville in the late thirties, just as he had been a source for Bentley in the early forties.

Bentley's story—which she retold in detail before HUAC the fol-lowing day—remained uncorroborated. But now there were two wit-nesses—and perhaps others who could be located from those days—who swore that Remington had been a communist. This wasn't nearly as dramatic, or as important, as finding witnesses who swore he had passed confidential material. But it was something. It was the start of a perjury case against Remington. The FBI, heavily invested in Bentley's integrity and keenly interested in seeing Rem-ington indicted for whatever was possible, leapt at the new opportu-nity. Remington was a secondary player at best. But his lies had made him vulnerable, and criminal action against him would help dispel doubts of Bentley's credibility. The case, Bureau officials declared, would receive "continuous attention looking toward successful pros-ecution," which translated into the involvement of forty-four field offices, agents in seven foreign countries, and the special attention of J. Edgar Hoover. In Washington, D.C., a grand jury was impaneled to hear the evidence.

When Bentley testified on May 18, she repeated the story she had told the Ferguson Committee, but she also spoke more forcefully—and more damagingly—about Remington than she had in previous testimony. Remington, she said, was a "conscious agent," not, as she had implied elsewhere, a confused idealist who may not have known that he was aiding the Soviets. But the grand jury was not going to be able to indict Remington on espionage charges. The 1947 jury had not been able to do it, and nothing had changed since then. The evidence the jury was looking for now concerned Remington's affili-ation with the Communist Party. The two men from Knoxville helped build the case against him. Bentley stated, once again, that she collected party dues from him and gave him literature. But the most damning testimony came from Remington's ex-wife, who began that morning as a reluctant witness. She had assured her former husband just the day before that he had nothing to worry about concerning her testimony. But, in the hands of the government, she became, that afternoon, the agent of Remington's demise.

Ann Moos Remington was a pretty brunette with a heart-shaped face and dark, sad eyes. Active in various communist causes in the early 1940s, she was a bright but deeply troubled woman, embittered, angry, emotionally fragile, and easily intimidated. Her marriage to Remington, despite two children, had never been a strong or a happy one. Their separation a decade later had its own problems, with Ann initially encouraging her husband to find another woman and then, when he did, suing him for adultery. Still, their divorce was not as acrimonious as it might have been, and they were on speaking terms. The former Mrs. Remington had no intention of hurting her ex-husband that day, if for no other reason than because if Remington went to jail she would stop receiving alimony or child support.

Over the course of a morning and afternoon, without a break for lunch, Thomas "The Hat" Donegan, who was handling the case for the government, and a man named John Brunini, who was serving as foreman of the grand jury, hammered away at the ex–Mrs. Remington. They immediately sensed her vulnerability and took full advantage of the fact that she, like all grand jury witnesses, appeared without the benefit or protection of counsel. Brunini took an especially active role in the questioning, alternately interrogating, lecturing, and threatening her.

"I am getting fuzzy," Mrs. Remington said at one point during the long afternoon. She asked for a recess. "I haven't eaten since a long time ago and I don't think I am going to be very coherent from now on." But the questioning continued. Finally, she refused to answer. She was tired and hungry, she repeated. "Couldn't we continue another day?" But Donegan and Brunini wouldn't let her go. They were circling around a crucial question, whether Remington had told his then-wife that he was paying party dues.

"We are right down to the issue . . . now," Donegan persisted.

"Well, I don't want to answer," said Mrs. Remington. Brunini then proceeded to lecture her—incorrectly—on her rights as a witness.

"You have been asked a question," he said. "You must answer it. You have no privilege to refuse to answer the question." But in fact, she did. Brunini, who was not a lawyer, may not have known this. But Donegan certainly did. A spouse cannot be forced to testify against a spouse, and during the time under investigation, the Remingtons were married. But Donegan let Brunini continue as the jury foreman threatened the witness with a contempt citation and a jail sentence.

"We haven't shown our teeth yet," he said menacingly. "I don't want them to bite you."

Finally, Mrs. Remington answered the question. Yes, she said, her husband had told her he was paying dues. Equally as damaging was her testimony that her husband was "a communist from my earliest acquaintance of him."

Remington testified for five successive days, swearing once again that he had never been a party member. But on June 8, 1950, on the strength of Bentley's testimony and Mrs. Remington's corroboration, the grand jury indicted him for perjury, accusing him of lying about his past communist activities. Finally, the government could claim an indictment that stemmed directly from Bentley's 1945 allegations. The perjury trial was set for December.

As the trial date neared, Donegan and the FBI agents closest to Bentley began to have worries about their star witness. Bentley was nervous and jittery, even—the agents thought—paranoid. She claimed that her phone had been tapped by Remington's private detectives, and that they were tailing her as well. She began to suspect that the communists were after her. Neither suspicion was particularly far-fetched, but Bentley's disquietude seemed to border on hysteria, and her behavior appeared erratic to the agents. "This writer has no claim of being omniscient," agent Thomas G. Spencer wrote in a memo to Bureau headquarters. Spencer was one of the agents to take Bentley's statement in 1945 and had interviewed her many times since. "But it definitely appears from conversations with

Miss Bentley . . . that she may be bordering on some mental pitfall which, of course," he added unnecessarily, "would be almost disastrous to the . . . Remington case."

But on January 8, 1951, when it was her turn to take the stand, Bentley was as calm and self-possessed as she had been at all of her public appearances. Dressed smartly in a black suit and tailored blouse—which, the press still found it necessary to comment, "belied her Spy Queen label"—Bentley told her story in ninety minutes. The cross-examination, however, took two days and focused not on her testimony but on her relationship with the foreman of the grand jury that had indicted Remington, John Brunini.

Brunini, it turned out, had been helping Bentley with a book she was attempting to write on her life as a communist. Remington's lawyers had discovered the link in the months between the grand jury indictment and the trial. Donegan had learned about it around the same time, when Brunini, who was living in Bentley's hotel while helping her with the manuscript, phoned him to ask if it would be all right to accept a fee for his editorial assistance. Donegan listened in horror. His star witness and the foreman of the grand jury collaborating on a book, a book that, of course, mentioned William Remington—how much worse could it get? It got worse: It turned out that Brunini had been responsible for getting Bentley the book contract in the first place. Of course he should not accept a fee, Donegan told him angrily. Accepting money would damage the government's case. But, regardless of money, the government's case could be brought down by this absurdly indiscreet, blatantly unethical connection between Bentley and Brunini.

When Remington's lawyers found out about it, they must have thought they hit the jackpot. Bentley was forced to admit on the stand that Brunini had done "editorial work" on the book and had given her "moral encouragement." Bentley denied that Brunini acted as her literary agent, which was perhaps technically true but in fact was not. He had placed the book for her with a New York publisher. She told the jury that she had never signed a contract that named the two of them, and that Brunini was not to receive a portion of the proceeds of the book. But a former secretary from the publishing company testified that she remembered typing just such a contract.

Remington's lawyers sprung into action and moved for a mistrial. They argued that there was "gross impropriety" in the grand jury proceedings because Brunini, who not only took an active part in the questioning but was responsible for "breaking" Mrs. Remington, had something to gain by the indictment. If Remington was indicted and convicted, Bentley's stock would immediately rise. She would be a page-one heroine, the woman who brought down the only alleged spy still working for the federal government. Her book might be a best-seller. If Brunini had a piece of the action—which was the implication, although no document was introduced in evidence to prove the fact—then he benefited, too.

But the judge rejected the argument and denied the motion. Brunini was only one of twenty-three grand jurors, he said. Whatever Brunini did or did not do, he cast only one vote, and at the very least, eleven other men had voted for the indictment. (In fact, the jury had voted unanimously for the indictment.) Donegan exhaled. The trial went on. In all, thirty-seven witnesses appeared over the course of thirty days, and 107 exhibits were accepted into evidence. On February 7, after deliberating for four hours and twenty minutes, the jury returned a verdict of guilty. The judge sentenced Remington to the maximum term under law, five years. He had been convicted of perjury, not espionage, but the crime, said the judge, had involved disloyalty to the country and so should be treated most seriously.

It had taken two grand juries, two loyalty boards, a libel suit, and a criminal trial, but Bentley—and the FBI—could finally claim a small victory. Bentley was pleased that at least part of her story had now been officially, legally, accepted as truth. But she didn't feel particularly victorious. The war against Remington had taken its toll. She had given up a job for it. She had lost a measure of control over her life. Private investigators had dug into her past. Lawyers had subjected her to intense and hostile questioning. The press had dogged her. She felt tired and anxious, beleaguered and confused. And the war was not over yet.

# Chapter 19

# My Life as a Spy

BACK IN EARLY 1950 when Bentley returned to Manhattan after her short stint teaching at Mundelein, she had a phone number tucked in her purse. A Chicago acquaintance gave it to her, asking Bentley to look up an old New York friend, John Brunini. He was a fifty-one-year-old poet and essayist, the director of the Catholic Poetry Society, editor of its magazine, *Spirit,* and one of the most important, well-connected men in the New York anticommunist Catholic community. In 1948, he had been appointed foreman of a special federal grand jury convened in New York City with a mandate to investigate communist espionage. Bentley had appeared before that jury in 1949, but she and the foreman had no private contact and hadn't seen each other since. Now Bentley was interested. The two had, at the very least, their religion and their politics in common, which might not be a bad start for a friendship. Bentley phoned him soon after she returned to the city, ostensibly to convey the best wishes of their mutual acquaintance.

Brunini was undoubtedly delighted to get a call from one of the most famous anticommunists in the land, and they quickly arranged to have lunch together that day at the Commodore, where Bentley was staying.

Bentley was in poor spirits that February afternoon. She had quit her teaching position thinking she would be needed back east for the Remington libel trial. But just days after returning to New York, she found out there would be no trial. She was furious when she heard about the possibility of an out-of-court settlement, concerned about what it would do to her credibility, and very worried about money. At lunch, she told Brunini that she was broke and couldn't even afford to pay her hotel bill. The government was reimbursing her for travel expenses when she was called to testify at hearings and trials, but she had no real income. It was an old story. Bentley seemed perpetually to be in financial crisis, whether employed or not. When she had an income, she spent it all on hotel and bar bills, and on restaurants and vacations. She had not learned—and at forty-two it was not likely that she ever would—to pay close attention to her personal finances, to keep a budget, to save.

Brunini listened sympathetically. He didn't know Elizabeth Bentley personally, but he had heard her testify and, like millions of others, he had read about her in the papers. He knew she had lived an unusual life, to say the least. She had a story to tell. Why not get paid to tell it? Why not, Brunini suggested, write a book about her experiences? Bentley had considered this idea before—there was even some thought that Nelson Frank, the New York *World Telegram* reporter might help her—but nothing had come of it. She was no writer, she told Brunini, and she knew nothing about the world of publishing. Besides, she needed money right away, not months or years later. She couldn't wait for a book to be published, assuming she could write one in the first place.

But Brunini knew better. He was a writer himself, and he understood the publishing business. You wouldn't have to wait until the book was published to get money, he told her. You can get an advance for the project. Of course, she would need to put together an outline for the book and write a sample chapter, but Brunini could help her with that, he said. He knew a publisher who might be interested. He'd do some checking. And so, the two worked together that spring sketching in the outlines of the book, with Brunini helping her to begin to transform her experiences into salable prose.

A few months later, their lives intersected in another way when Brunini's grand jury—at his persistent urging—reconvened after a long recess to focus its attention on William Remington. Elizabeth Bentley would be the government's star witness. That same month, May 1950, Brunini brought Bentley to the East 26th Street offices of the Devin-Adair Company, a publisher interested in supporting the anticommunist cause. The company would later publish *McCarthyism: The Fight for America,* which featured Senator Joseph McCarthy's answers to questions posed by "friend and foe alike." At Devin-Adair, Brunini and Bentley met with Devin Garrity, the president.

"This is Elizabeth Bentley, who is going to do a book for us," Garrity told his publicity director. "And this is John Brunini who is helping her do it."

A contract was drawn up with both their names, giving Brunini a share in the profits of the book. But it was never signed. Or it may have been signed and later discarded when Tom Donegan, who was handling the case for the government at the Remington grand jury, learned about Brunini's involvement with Bentley's book. A new contract was drawn up without Brunini's name, and on June 2, six days before the grand jury indicted William Remington, Bentley signed the document.

The publishing house clearly believed in the book, offering her a $3,000 advance (close to a year's wages) and covering her living expenses during the months it would take to write it. Devin Garrity arranged for her to stay at the Westport, Connecticut, home of some friends of his while she wrote that summer and fall. In mid-June, she gave up her room at the Hotel Commodore, moved to the country, and began the task of committing her life to paper. She had told the details of her life as a communist many times—to the FBI, to the press, to congressional committees, to grand juries—but she had never told the *story,* the narrative of her life.

The book would serve two immediate purposes. It would be a much-needed source of income, and it would continue her public work, giving her yet another forum in which to warn others of the evils of communism. But writing about herself also served—or had the potential to serve—another, deeper, more personal function. It provided Bentley an opportunity for self-reflection and self-assessment, a time to delve into her own psyche, a chance to make sense of her life. Writing the book gradually became, more than anything else, an exercise in Elizabeth Bentley explaining Elizabeth Bentley to herself. And as the manuscript grew, it became apparent that there were things she just didn't want to know.

Donegan may have warned Brunini to stay away from the project, but it seems he continued to help Bentley after she signed the contract. The collaboration was not always a smooth one. Bentley had a writer's temperament without having a writer's eye. She was, said Brunini, "reluctant to write one day, willing the next," sometimes overcome with emotion as she forced herself to relive her time with Golos in order to write about it. Brunini likened her to a pregnant woman both eager to have the baby and dreading the confinement. Variously credited as a collaborator, an editor, and a ghostwriter, Brunini eventually became, as he put it, "the doctor who must perform a caesarian." Devin-Adair also assigned one of its own editors, Thomas Sloane, to the project. But later in the summer, Bentley came to New York and stormed into Devin Garrity's office, announcing that she refused to work with Mr. Sloane because he had a friend who was a communist. Mr. Sloane, she said, was under the influence of this friend and was trying to ruin her book. It was unfortunate. She needed all the editorial help she could get.

The product of her five-month writing stint was a melodramatic memoir, full of details but empty of insight, simultaneously heavy-handed and lightweight, both overwrought and underrealized. Like most memoirs, it was an account of what she chose to remember and how she chose to remember it. And like most memoirs, it was interesting both for what it said and for what it didn't say.

The book opens with Elizabeth Bentley leaning against the deck rail of the SS *Vulcania* as it steams into New York Harbor. It is the summer of 1934. She is twenty-six and just returning from a year of study in Italy. She is glad to be back home, but as she looks wistfully at the skyline, she wonders what exactly she is coming home to. She has no job, no place to live, no family. She feels "alone and frightened." And so she establishes herself, in the opening paragraph of the first chapter, as a forlorn figure, solitary and disconnected, a woman vulnerable to the forces of history.

She writes nothing of her time in Italy—except that she was appalled by fascism. There is no hint of her European adventures, her travels, her independent life, her lovers. This is not the picture she wants to paint of herself. And there is almost nothing about the quarter-century that preceded that trip. Her parents, her childhood, her girlhood, her college years—all are mentioned only in passing, as if they had little to do with the woman who finds herself looking wistfully at the skyline. It may be that she wanted to shield her family—not her mother and father, who were long dead, but aunts and uncles and cousins—from the publicity that would ensue after the book was published. But it is more likely that she had neither the wisdom nor the literary wherewithal to examine her life like this. Instead, she wrote the book from a distance, chronicling the years she was, as she now chose to perceive it, enslaved by communism as if the experience had happened to someone else, someone she had observed and knew only slightly. She titled the book, meaningfully, *Out of Bondage*.

The scenes she re-creates seem both flat and overinflated. Her emotions seem canned. When she first realizes that Golos intends to take her underground, she feels "as if someone hit me in the pit of my stomach." She hears his voice "as though from a long way off" and "waves of dizziness" swirl around her. One hundred and nineteen pages later, when Golos dies, the room again swirls around her. But with an effort, she steadies herself.

"Yasha was dead, I said to myself numbly. Never again would I hear his voice—never again would I come home to find him waiting for me. I gripped the arms of the chair and fought back a rising hysteria."

For those looking not to understand Bentley but to learn some of the details of her spy activities, the book basically recounts what she told the FBI in 1945 and testified to at hearings and trials: the clandestine rendezvous, the encounters with her many sources, the tense meetings with her Soviet contacts, the battle over the control of her networks, her conversion to staunch anticommunist. For those who had followed her testimony, who had read the front-page stories, there was nothing much new here—except the tantalizing fact that the man who had taught her tradecraft was also her lover. For those who were learning of her life as a spy for the first time, the chronicle of events was almost, but not quite, compelling, a fault not of the material but of the writer.

In the end, it is clear that Bentley wrote the book not to try to understand herself or make herself transparent to others but rather to defend herself, to justify first her embrace of communism, then her life underground, and finally, dramatically, her conversion to patriotic informer. The book ends with her sitting in the HUAC hearings room in the summer of 1948 listening as her erstwhile sources testify. "They slid and slithered around the questions," she writes. They looked old and worn, bewildered and disillusioned. She pitied them, feeling first "a terrible sadness" and then "a great cleansing anger."

"And now I looked again at these people before me in the Committee Room," she writes in the final paragraph of *Out of Bondage*. "They are spiritually dead, I thought with sudden and final release. But I am alive and speak for them. . . . Telling their story and mine, I will let the decent people of the world know what a monstrous thing Communism is."

By late 1950, *Out of Bondage* was completed, and Devin-Adair began production of the book. Meanwhile, the manuscript was submitted to *McCall's* magazine in hopes of selling the prepublication serial rights. There could be no better advance publicity for the book than having the story serialized in one of the largest-circulation women's magazines in the country. It would be tremendous exposure for Bentley and the book and would mean a considerable chunk of money for the author. A sale seemed likely. The editor of *McCall's* had reviewed the manuscript and deemed it "one of the most fascinating documents" he had ever read. The book, he thought, was destined to be a "surefire success." But some weeks later, *McCall's* got cold feet. As word spread through the New York publishing world that the magazine was considering running excerpts, someone cautioned the editor to go slow because "Elizabeth Bentley was on the verge of being discredited."

Toward the end of January 1951, the magazine's Washington representative paid a visit to FBI headquarters to have a chat with one of Hoover's assistants, a man named Tolson. Her editor loved the manuscript, she told Tolson, but what was all this about Bentley's precarious credibility? Of course, the FBI could not give her any advice about whether to publish the story, Tolson told her. But, he added meaningfully, "would it not be logical to assume that if Miss Bentley was vulnerable and if she could be discredited, would this not have occurred long before now?" The Bureau, he said, had "a great deal of respect for the veracity of Elizabeth Bentley."

That was enough. The magazine purchased the first serial rights, most likely paying Bentley three or four times what she made from the book advance. The magazine treated the series as a major publishing event, sending out a press release in mid-April that hailed Bentley's story as "a human document of tremendous interest and significance." A few days later, just as the May issue of the magazine was about to hit the newsstands, *McCall's* staged a press conference for Bentley at the Carlton Hotel in Manhattan. There she read a prepared statement—she hoped the series would be read "by as many people as possible" and that these readers "will see what communism really is like and avoid getting entangled in it"—and fielded questions from her mostly female audience. One veteran reporter was particularly unsympathetic.

"Miss Bentley," she asked, "do you think this exposé of yours will help your country as much as your spying hurt it?"

Bentley deflected the implied criticism rather neatly. "That's for the government to decide, I suppose," she responded.

A few minutes later, in response to questions about why she was drawn into the communist movement, Bentley talked about the Depression and how it seemed at the time that the American system had failed and that the communists could make a better world. The veteran newswoman's hand shot up.

"A lot of us went through the Depression, too," she lectured Bentley, "and we didn't turn communist."

When the May issue of *McCall's* appeared on newsstands and in subscribers' mailboxes the next day, the readers of the magazine may have been taken aback. On the cover, just above a picture of a cherubic toddler in a frilly yellow dress playing with an identically clothed doll—"Your Children Will Love To Play With Betsy McCall," ran the blurb—was a pink banner announcing the featured story within: MY LIFE AS A SPY . . . BY EX-COMMUNIST ELIZABETH BENTLEY. Inside the magazine, the excerpt was introduced as a "strange . . . exciting . . . tragic" story and framed for the magazine's readers as a woman's tale of love, surrender, and redemption. The introduction read: "How could an American girl with a New England upbringing and a Vassar education become a communist spy?" The editors placed this first installment of Bentley's story between an illustrated feature on Hawaiian casseroles and a fashion piece on summer suits, thus within a few pages commingling the two most resonant—and seemingly contradictory—themes of the 1950s: contented domesticity and communist paranoia.

In June, Greta Garbo was on the magazine's cover, her eyes closed under exquisitely arched brows, the slightest suggestion of a smile on her lips. Under the sweep of her chin ran the blurb: "I Joined The Red Underground With The Man I Loved." In July—a model in a bathing suit adorned the cover—the installment was titled "How I Was Used By The Red Spy Ring," Inside, the editors, showing more insight about Bentley than she had about herself, introduced the piece with this explanation: "Loneliness and disillusion drew New England–bred Elizabeth Bentley into the Communist Party during the mid-30s. The Party filled the emptiness of her existence. It gave her, she thought, a chance to bring about a better world. And, more important, it gave her a lover." For the July installment, *McCall's* had sent a photographer out with Bentley to revisit "the scenes of her communist activity in New York." There was a picture of Bentley posing in Sheridan Park, where she and Golos used to meet, one of her standing in front of the building that had housed USS&S, and another taken in front of her Barrow Street apartment. She looked uncomfortable in the camera's gaze, as if not knowing what was expected of her. Should she smile? Look contrite? Stoic? She couldn't decide. Mostly, she looked tired. The last installment appeared in August under the title "I Meet With Tragedy and Disillusion," thus completing the tale of, as *McCall's* put it, "the timid, vacillating young woman" who became "the disciplined, obedient Bolshevik."

But even as women were reading about her life, Bentley was busy adding new chapters. Soon after *McCall's* published the fourth installment, Bentley was called once again to testify in the capital, this time before the Internal Security Subcommittee (SISS), the Senate's answer to HUAC. Pat McCarran from Nevada, the subcommittee chairman, was one of the most vocal anticommunists in the Senate. The year before, he had authored, sponsored, and then pushed through over Truman's veto the Internal Security Act of 1950, which, among other things, allowed for the internment of American communists during national emergencies. Homer Ferguson, head of the committee that had first pursued William Remington, was one of McCarran's committee colleagues. In mid-August of 1951, the subcommittee directed its attention to the Institute of Pacific Relations, a privately financed research organization that the senators believed had profoundly influenced American public opinion and foreign policy on the Far East and was a tool of Soviet Russia.

The Institute (known as the IPR) was indeed a significant entity, with councils in ten countries, an international program of research and publication, generous support from both the Rockefeller and Carnegie foundations, and a number of prominent New Dealers in its ranks. Bentley was called in to provide testimony that would directly link the Institute and the Communist Party, which she willingly gave. The IPR, she told the senators, had been controlled by the party through Earl Browder who relayed the party line to the Institute's secretary. She called the IPR a communist front organization and testified that she and Golos had mined sources like Duncan Lee from its ranks. Bentley quoted Golos as saying that the IPR was "as red as a rose." As for Institute members with ties to both the party and the federal government, Bentley named the late Harry Dexter White, former Roosevelt aide Lauchlin Currie, Alger Hiss, and several others.

The senators couldn't have been more pleased with Bentley's testimony. It was hard for them to let her go. Like other congressional committees following a particular investigative path, this one could not resist veering off on side trails, with the senators quizzing Bentley about how the spy apparatus worked and, in executive session, questioning her about Canadian communists.

Bentley was barely out of the congressional spotlight when the publication of *Out of Bondage* early that fall again made her the center of critical attention. The book, on sale nationally for $3.50 a copy, was not the success the editor of *McCall's* had predicted. Sales were sluggish, and it is doubtful that Bentley made any more money from the book itself beyond the advance she had already been given. But if readers didn't flock to *Out of Bondage,* reviewers certainly did. The book was reviewed by just about every important newspaper and magazine in the country. The *New York Herald Tribune* called it "an illuminating book," the *Chicago Tribune* lauded it as a "fascinating and exciting account," and *The Atlantic* considered it "an interesting and instructive picture of a Communist secret agent."

But not everyone found the book worthy of praise. The *Saturday Review* faulted the author for her lack of subtlety and precision, concluding that Bentley was neither an acute observer of herself nor of those around her. In a lengthy and lukewarm review, the *New York Times* found that Bentley had "not a great deal more to say" in her book than she had already said in public testimony. Her account was neither interesting nor convincing, wrote the reviewer. "In fact, for a spy thriller, it is surprisingly dull."

Other reviews were downright scathing. Writing in *The Commonweal,* nationally syndicated newspaper columnist Joseph Alsop found it hard to decide whether to treat the book "as tragic, or as ludicrous, or as terrifying, or as pathetic." He found the account worthy of *True Confessions,* "with the Communist Party in the role of fascinating villain who receives his comeuppance after many a titillating scene . . . with the pretty heroine." The style of the book offended him as well, "at once so vulgar, so girlish, and so portentous." The author he deemed "obviously unstable." The reviewer for *The New Yorker* had some of the same concerns but expressed them with sharper wit. Bentley, said the reviewer, wrote "in a fashion that suggests she may have had almost as grievous a tussle with Freshman English at Vassar as she had later with her New England conscience."

Book reviewers were not the only ones keenly interested in *Out of Bondage*. The FBI was all over it, assigning agents to parse the book line by line, comparing names, dates, and details to her FBI statement and congressional testimony, an effort both to pick up new leads and to cross-validate her story. The New York agents assigned the task were happy to find some hidden clues in the book. In a three-page, single-spaced memo to headquarters, the agent in charge pinpointed eighteen instances in which Bentley had concealed a person's identity in the book, either by using a single name only or a descriptor. These were, or could be, people Bentley had not mentioned before, people the FBI might be very interested in. The Bureau seized on this as an opportunity to reinterview Bentley with the goal of compiling a list of new names to investigate.

Agents comparing the book to Bentley's other statements found that her various accounts agreed in essence but not always in detail, a problem they considered to be literary rather than substantive. Bentley had told the FBI that for her book "it was necessary to add human interest and reader appeal to a lot of characters." There were instances, she said, where she had added drama to the material and other times where she had enhanced the narrative by telescoping events or combining several meetings into one. The agents conducting the detailed analysis were not overly concerned.

Elizabeth Bentley knew she was not a writer, and she was probably not expecting literary praise for *Out of Bondage*. She was also well aware of how controversial she was. She had been publicly criticized, even pilloried, since she had first come forth to testify three years before. So the criticisms and generally bleak reviews were not altogether unexpected. But that did not make them any easier to take. She had to swallow the disappointment and move on.

The advance money and the check from *McCall's* made that easier to do. *Out of Bondage* may not have been a commercial success in publishing terms, but the project provided Bentley with more money than she had ever had before. Her income was so substantial in 1951 that she ended the year owing $3,700 in federal taxes, a sum she could not pay because, true to form, she had already spent all her money. In September 1951, a month after the fourth installment appeared in *McCall's* and within days of the publication of the book, Bentley bought her first house, a five-room cottage on several acres in Madison, Connecticut, a small town on the Long Island Sound. She posed for reporters in her new living room with a cat sprawled on her lap, an image of quiet domesticity that she hoped would become a reality. She would spend her time furnishing her new home and tending a good-sized garden, she told reporters. She hoped she might find a teaching position at some point. She intended, she said, to live a much less hectic life. Her days in the limelight were over.

# Part Three

# The Ruin

*C*hapter 20

# The Center Cannot Hold

*I*F BENTLEY THOUGHT she could retire to a quiet life in her little house by the Sound, if she thought she could become, overnight, Elizabeth Bentley: Private Citizen, she was badly mistaken. Writing the memoir may have been for her a public and dramatic way to shut the door on her previous life, but her new friends in the Department of Justice didn't hear it slam. To the FBI and the Attorney General's Office, she was still, as she had been since 1945, "a most valuable informant." After her move to Connecticut, agents from the New Haven and New York field offices continued to contact her three or four times a month, quizzing her on a wide variety of espionage matters, consulting her on loyalty cases and using her to help build dossiers on suspected subversives. She was their resident expert, their touchstone. She was, as far as they were concerned, on call permanently.

In January of 1952, she was asked to testify before HUAC for the fourth time. The congressmen were then conducting hearings on "the role of the Communist press in the Communist conspiracy," focusing that month on a woman named Grace Granich, an American communist who ran an international news agency in New York during the war years. Allegedly, the agency had been used by the *Daily Worker* and the party to obtain party information and directives from Moscow. As it turned out, Bentley had never met and knew very little about Granich. But she was able to link her with the underground, testifying that Granich and Golos had worked together. It was Granich, she said, who suggested to Golos that Helen Tenney might make a useful addition to the apparatus. (Tenney later became one of Bentley's sources inside OSS.) Her testimony that Tuesday morning in mid-January was quite brief, but it was clear that it piqued the interest of the congressmen. They rushed into executive session before lunch to question her further.

Next, SISS called on her services as expert witness. Still under Senator Pat McCarran's aggressive leadership, the subcommittee was continuing its investigation of the Institute for Pacific Relations. Bentley had previously named several people active in the IPR who, she claimed, were part of her espionage apparatus. But, as with her other accusations, there was no documentary proof. Apparently troubled by this—or perhaps reacting to criticism that careers, and lives, were being ruined on the basis of hearsay—the subcommittee used the hearings to point out just how difficult it was to *prove* that anyone was or had been a spy.

"Miss Bentley," asked the counsel for the committee, "while you were an underground agent, was there in existence documentary evidence of the fact that you were such an agent?"

"No, except in Moscow," Bentley replied.

"Did you feel that it was your business to make sure there was no such documentary evidence?" he asked.

"Definitely," she answered. "I took every possible precaution."

To hammer home the point, the counsel also questioned the former director of the CIA.

"Sir . . . what can you tell us of the likelihood that an active underground agent could be proven to be such by documentary evidence?"

"Well," replied Admiral Roscoe Hillenkoetter, "the only way you could ever prove he was an agent by documentary evidence is that he would be very stupid"—that is, stupid enough to fail to destroy evidence of involvement in such activities.

"It is common practice in connection with all underground organizations to seek to avoid documentation, is it not?" asked the counsel.

"It very definitely is," replied the admiral.

While this testimony was undoubtedly true—a good agent obscured his or her affiliation, a good agent erased his or her tracks—it was also expedient. It created an elegant loop in logic: Rather than weakening the case that someone was involved in espionage, the absence of documentary evidence actually strengthened it. Lack of proof *was* the proof. The testimony effectively explained why Elizabeth Bentley had no proof to offer other than her own word. It explained why no investigation, regardless of how thorough, into the lives of those she accused would be likely to yield documentary evidence. It made the case, quietly and forcefully, that Bentley should be believed, not just in the context of the IPR investigation but in the wider net she had helped the FBI cast.

The press didn't pick up on this point. Perhaps it was too subtle compared to the headline-grabbing revelations to which journalists had become accustomed. Certainly it was eclipsed by Bentley's statement before the committee later that day that two groups of communist spies were still operating within the federal government. She testified that her Soviet contacts had told her, back when she was engaged in such work, that there were four networks operating within the government. She had exposed two of them, the Silvermaster and Perlo Groups, which meant, she said, that there were still two out there. This seemingly out-of-nowhere disclosure—why had she never mentioned this before, during any other testimony?—was both tantalizing and impossibly flimsy. Bentley's knowledge was indirect. She had no specifics to offer. She could name no names. But

that didn't stop the committee from pursuing the line of questioning, or Bentley from making grand statements. When the counsel
asked her if the remaining communists in the government held high
offices, she did not reply "I don't know" or "I have no idea," which
was the truth. If they even existed, she didn't know who they were,
so how could she know what positions they held? Instead, she left
the door wide open.

"I assume they [hold high positions]," she replied, "because when
the Communists infiltrate the government, they don't bother with
clerks."

The FBI was quick to reinterview her following the SISS appearance, but agents looking for leads came up empty. Bentley could tell
them nothing more than what she had told the committee. But if
her revelations about postwar spy networks led nowhere, her other
testimony about the IPR proved so enticing that another congressional committee got in on the act, and the inquiry was expanded. It
was not just the Institute that was now under suspicion but the
benevolent trust funds and philanthropies that helped bankroll
organizations like the IPR. Had the Carnegie and Rockefeller foundations, supporters of IPR, been infiltrated by communists? Were
the Guggenheim, Ford, and Sloan foundations knowingly funding
subversive groups? When a House subcommittee began exploring
this terrain, Bentley was interviewed at great length at her Connecticut home. She had no direct knowledge of party infiltration of
foundations—which was, perhaps, why she wasn't called to publicly
testify—but she did provide leads on suspected communists within
these organizations. The investigation led to no indictments or
arrests, but it did add to the atmosphere of suspicion, paranoia, and
disquietude that was the leitmotif of the early 1950s.

The continued attention by the FBI and various congressional
committees, the interviews, the conferences, the frequent calls to testify, meant that Bentley could not get on with her life. She was stuck
in her past, tethered to the life she had denounced, the years she now
wanted to put far behind her, by those who needed and wanted her
to keep retelling her tale. She was an emotional—and, it was turning
out, financial—captive of her confessions. Her on-call status with the

FBI and her continuing notoriety made finding a job almost impossible, especially the kind of position for which she was most suited. Who, after all, would hire the notorious Red Spy Queen to teach their children, a woman whose name and past improprieties one could read about regularly in the press? Her Catholic friends had arranged the position at Mundelein, but she was less infamous in Chicago than she was in New York and Washington, D.C. And that position had not worked out anyway. Her other "job," her job as informant and witness, had gotten in the way.

Now, in 1952, her other job was her *only* job. But it was work for which she was not paid. Detractors had called her a "paid informant" for years, but the truth was that the only money she had ever received from the government was reimbursement for travel expenses when she was called to testify at hearings and trials. With no income, no savings—the book royalties and *McCall's* money were spent on the new house—and little potential for employment, Bentley was not just broke. She was increasingly despondent about her future. Money had been a problem before, but this time it was different. This time her lack of finances was a symptom of a larger ailment, a chronic illness, the dis-ease of being Elizabeth Bentley stuck in a life she could not escape. She had sought notoriety. Now she was its victim. Depressed and lonely, she began frequenting the offices of her publisher, Devin-Adair, where she would tell her troubles to Devin Garrity. Occasionally, he gave her money, although there were no royalties from *Out of Bondage,* and the company owed her nothing. Garrity gave her money because he felt sorry for her.

But even in these dark days, Bentley was hardly helpless. She was, despite her financial and emotional problems, a clever and resourceful woman who understood her usefulness to others sometimes better than they understood it themselves. When she was in Washington, D.C., in January testifying before HUAC, she paid an impromptu visit to her friends at FBI headquarters. At first, it seemed to be a social call. She sat in assistant director Alan Belmont's office, chatting. She wished she could see Mr. Hoover, she told him, but she knew he was a busy man. She wanted to tell the director just how highly she regarded the FBI. It was, she told Belmont, the "one stable government organization which knew what it was doing." Her praise for the work of the Bureau was effusive. The pleasantries continued until Bentley brought the conversation around to the real reason she was there.

She was, she told Belmont, very much interested in whether the Department of Justice would return to her the $2,000 she had handed over to the Bureau back in 1945. This was the money her Soviet contact "Al" had given her either in recognition of her services, which was what he said, or as a bribe, which was how she interpreted it. Whatever the motivation behind the payment, it was money given to Bentley by a Russian operative after seven years of underground work. It was astonishing that Bentley would think of asking for the money back. Even more unbelievably, the FBI took her request seriously.

Conferring among themselves the year before, Bureau agents had decided that they could consider the $2,000—which had been sitting in a safe deposit box in a Manhattan bank for five years—either as "espionage money . . . the result of Miss Bentley's activities with the Russians," in which case it should be turned over to the Treasury Department, or as Bentley's property, in which case it should be returned to her. The only reason the Bureau was entertaining the latter thought at that point was that Bentley had been particularly useful as a witness in two government trials and had received nothing other than travel expenses as compensation. The matter was discussed confidentially with Tom "The Hat" Donegan, now assistant to the attorney general, who opined that any attempt to establish ownership of the funds would lead to "some embarrassment." The New York office was more forceful. The return of the money "cannot be recommended . . . in view of the circumstances surrounding the manner in which she obtained the money."

But that decision had been made when Bentley was not desperate for funds. Her living expenses were being taken care of by her publisher at that point, and there was promise of income from the book. Now, a year later, the situation was different. Bentley was broke and racking up debts. She was begging money from her publisher. She was worried and distracted. The Bureau was becoming increasingly concerned that this would interfere with her usefulness as a witness—and Bentley did all she could to encourage that worry. She apparently convinced Belmont during their meeting in January. "Her current indebtedness . . . is jeopardizing our use of her as a source of information," he wrote in a memo to one of the other assistant directors just after Bentley left his office, hinting that the Bureau might want to reverse its previous decision. Bentley was too valuable an asset to risk losing. Two months later, Hoover authorized the deal. That spring, agents from the New York office handed Elizabeth Bentley the envelope containing the $2,000 in cash she had been paid by her Russian contact.

For Bentley, the money temporarily made life easier, but it didn't cure what ailed her. Her mood did not improve. She appeared nervous and depressed to those who saw her in public. The New York agents who met with her regularly found her emotionally volatile, alternately weepy and demanding, complaining about her health and, they thought, drinking heavily. She was going through early menopause and not having an easy time of it. But her emotional problems were more serious than fluctuating hormones—or blood alcohol levels. Her problems were, in part, the result of seven years of living an intensely stressful undercover life followed by four years of living an intensely stressful public life. Elizabeth Bentley was shell-shocked.

Stress had undone two other women from Bentley's former life. Katherine Perlo, Victor's ex-wife, had been confined to the mental ward of the Wichita Falls State Hospital on and off since 1946. In 1951 she had undergone insulin shock treatments so that she "might forget her past." Helen Tenney, meanwhile, had spent most of the past six years as a resident of the Payne Whitney Clinic, the psychiatric division of the New York Hospital. Gripped by paranoia, Tenney had suffered a complete mental breakdown, attempting suicide by taking an overdose of phenobarbital. Tenney's consulting psychiatrist thought she was suffering from "a severe case of hallucinations" because she talked of being a Russian spy.

Whatever was going on with Bentley—menopause, alcohol, stress, depression—her personal life was becoming increasingly messy. In August 1951, just as she was about to move into her Connecticut house, she hired a man named John Wright to be her caretaker. He was a rough character, fifty-two, a bit dim-witted and, unbeknownst to Bentley, a convicted felon, having served two jail sentences, one for breaking and entering, the other for assault. Their relationship was of intense interest to the good people of Madison, who whispered among themselves that the two were lovers. When the whispers became loud enough to hear, the local pastor paid a call, warning Bentley of the rumors. She insisted that Wright was a handyman and no more than that. He performed routine chores around the house and grounds, took care of the place when she was away on her frequent trips to New York and Washington, D.C., and picked her up at the New Haven railroad station when she returned. The arrangement apparently worked well until early March 1952, when Bentley discovered that Mr. Wright was charging liquor to her account at the local drugstore. She was about to fire him when she suffered a severe bout of the flu and became even more dependent on his assistance.

A few weeks later, after a brief trip out of town to deliver a speech, she called Wright from New York, requesting that he pick her up at the New Haven train station later that night. When she got into her car at the station, she immediately saw that the handyman was drunk, and ordered him out of the driver's seat. She took the wheel herself and drove off. But somewhere en route, Wright grabbed the steering wheel and struck her so hard on the side of the face that two of her teeth cut through her lower lip, and she blacked out. That's the story she told the FBI a few days later. But it was not the story Mr. Wright told when he was subpoenaed by U.S. Attorney Myles Lane a few days after that. Wright said that when he picked up Bentley at the station, she insisted on going out for drinks. The two consumed $13.50 worth of liquor—more than enough to pay for a half dozen drinks apiece—at a "respectable restaurant" in New Haven. Bentley was drunk but insisted on driving them home. When Wright became concerned over her ability to keep the car on the road, he grabbed the keys from the ignition and told her he was going to drive the rest of the way home. Bentley was infuriated, he said, and struck him across the face with her gloves, which were trimmed with buckles. At that point, Wright said, he "blew his cork and hit her with a right cross." But Tom Spencer at the New York field office, the FBI agent who knew Bentley the best, thought both versions were fishy. He figured Bentley and Wright had gotten sloppy drunk together, then had gotten into a fight that veered out of control.

Whatever the truth, the fact was that Bentley was injured. The blow to her face loosened several teeth and, by the time she saw her doctor in New York, the gashes inside her mouth where the lower teeth had punctured the soft tissue, were badly infected. And, whoever started the fight for whatever reason, Bentley was now scared of her handyman. The day after the altercation, she found him lounging in her living room. He did not apologize or even acknowledge the attack. Later that week, she noticed that a bottle of scotch was missing from the cupboard. That's when she came down to New York and told her story to Agent Spencer. Just as the FBI and the Justice Department had often turned to her for help, so she viewed the agents and the lawyers as her personal champions. Could Spencer arrange a bodyguard for her? She wanted to go back up to Connecticut, pack some clothes and get out of her house, but she was afraid to do it by herself. She was sure the FBI would want to help her. Wasn't she still an important source of information? And wasn't she set to be the star witness at yet another trial for William Remington? Surely the Bureau would want to intercede on her behalf in this matter. Surely it was in everyone's best interest that no adverse publicity should come of this unfortunate event.

It wasn't exactly blackmail, but it was close. Spencer told her that the FBI could not get involved but that he would see what he could do. Perhaps the U.S. Attorney General's Office could be of help. In fact, Roy Cohn was happy to be of service. Bentley had been a good witness for him during the Rosenbergs trial, and he needed her badly for this new trial Remington's lawyers were demanding. She installed herself at the Prince George Hotel in Manhattan and met twice with Cohn as he tried to figure out how to get her out of the mess she was in. It was Cohn's idea to threaten the caretaker with federal charges—his attack on Bentley could be construed as interfering with a government witness—and see if Wright could be scared off. Bentley got her handyman to come down to New York on a pretense. There he was served with a subpoena and forced to meet with U.S. Attorney Myles Lane, Cohn, and an FBI agent. The plan was for Lane to do the talking, to start out nice and easy but then, if Wright gave him any trouble, to "bear down" and serve him with a grand jury subpoena. Wright gave him no trouble. He quickly agreed to stay away from Bentley and her house. A short time later, Mr. Wright disappeared.

Moving to the Prince George Hotel may have helped Bentley feel safe, and it certainly solved her transportation problems now that she had no one to deliver and pick her up from train stations. But the move also worsened her already shaky financial condition. She was now paying ten dollars a night for lodgings in addition to upkeep on the Connecticut house, her considerable medical expenses—she saw her doctor at least every week—plus her equally considerable liquor bills. She had apparently already spent the $2,000 the FBI released to her just a few months before, because she complained to Roy Cohn—who seemed to offer the most sympathetic ear—that she owed $600 and had only $150 to pay her debts. Cohn told the FBI that Bentley was acting "like a spoiled child" and that her requests were "very much out of line," but he nonetheless recommended that the Bureau authorize payments to Bentley of $50 a week for three weeks.

At first, the FBI balked. Agents familiar with Bentley knew she was bad with money and saw little point in dispensing funds. But in early June, the Bureau relented, handing Bentley a check for $100 "in recognition of [her] time and assistance." Really, it was in recognition of her debt load. Then in July, Hoover authorized a $500 lump-sum payment to help settle her debts, plus a $50-a-week stipend for three months—or until she ceased to be useful in the upcoming second trial of William Remington.

The FBI had rescued her, at least temporarily, from her financial problems, but no one could rescue Elizabeth Bentley from herself. On the afternoon of August 29, while driving an acquaintance and two children from Madison to the New Haven railroad station, she sideswiped a car and drove on. The car she hit sustained only very minor damage—the repair bill turned out to be less than $25—but the other driver, understandably upset when Bentley failed to stop, swore out a complaint against her with the Connecticut State Police. Bentley's license plate number was radioed to state troopers, and within the hour, she was apprehended, charged with hit-and-run, and jailed. Bentley was belligerent and uncooperative, at first denying that she hit the other car, then refusing to identify the passengers in her car, and finally demanding to be able to call the Bureau's New Haven field office. She was, she told the commanding officer of the Connecticut State Police, "working for the FBI."

When Bentley reached the special agent in charge in New Haven and told him she was in jail, he stonewalled her. Her legal problems were not the FBI's business, he told her. She should call an attorney and take care of it herself. Bentley was upset, bordering on hysteria. No, she said, she would not get an attorney. She insisted that the Bureau intercede on her behalf. The agent told her there was nothing he could do. But when he hung up the phone, he called Tom Spencer at the New York field office, who called Roy Cohn at the Attorney General's Office, who called the Connecticut Police Commissioner. Within a half hour, Bentley was released from jail with no bail and promises to try to keep the matter out of the newspapers. Cohn had once again saved the day, but in doing so, he had encouraged Bentley's dependence and rewarded her helplessness.

Two weeks later, she was in trouble again. While driving along state route 79 in Connecticut on the way to meet with the lawyer handling her hit-and-run case, she lost control of her car, struck a boulder, and blacked out. She told the FBI that she had swerved to avoid being hit by a drunk driver, but it was more likely that she was the drunk driver. Bentley was taken home by three bystanders and then heavily sedated by a local doctor. Her 1939 LaSalle was a total wreck. A few days later, she called the New York field office to complain and make demands. Her local doctor had given her a sedative that made her sleep for more than twenty-four hours, she said, and a pill that wiped her out for another whole day. She was sick, her face was swollen, and she couldn't eat. She wanted to be treated by her own doctor in New York. And she wanted FBI agents to be dispatched to her home to drive her into the city.

Bentley was becoming a significant problem for the Bureau, and the agents didn't know what to do with her. If she was publicly discredited, if the press got hold of the stories of her drinking and her car accidents, if she came to be seen as unstable and out of control, then much of her previous testimony would be suspect. Roy Cohn may have worried about her future usefulness as a witness, but the Bureau had far more to worry about. The Bureau had a seven-year investment in Bentley. She had fingered sources, helped develop files, aided in loyalty cases, and offered so many details about so many people that the FBI was still pursuing her leads. On the one hand, Hoover did not want to get involved in Bentley's private life. He was more than happy to let Cohn handle the problems. But on the other hand, he needed to protect his investment. The agents themselves seemed to view Bentley as a burden—which she undoubtedly was—but they may also have been motivated by a kind of chivalry. She was, after all, a woman alone and in trouble, even if the trouble was of her own making.

Two agents from the New York field office were dispatched to Madison, a three-hour trek through Sunday traffic, to bring Bentley into Manhattan for medical treatment. On the drive back to the city, Bentley was rambling and incoherent, weepy and quarrelsome. The state of Connecticut was out to get her, she said. The local doctor who treated her was a quack. She fingered a small crucifix obsessively, and chain-smoked. It was apparent to the agents that she had been drinking. When they got to the Prince George Hotel, she demanded that the agents register her and call her doctor. They refused, but she created such a scene in the lobby that they made the call for her. During the next few days, she phoned the New York field office several times. The agents found her excessively talkative and "inclined to dwell on her various problems to the exclusion of almost all other conversation." They were beginning to think that it wasn't just the alcohol. Bentley was emotionally unstable even when not under the influence. She was "difficult to handle," they reported, and unable to cope with her own affairs.

A few days later, Bentley was making trouble again, this time at the U.S. Attorney's Office in Lower Manhattan. She had gone there unannounced and was engaged in what the Bureau—which was, of course, immediately notified—called a "sit-down strike." She refused to leave Roy Cohn's office until her transportation problems were solved. She had wrecked her car, and she had no money to buy a new one. She could take the train into New York or down to Washington, D.C., but how was she supposed to get to the train station? And how was she to get from her house into town for shopping? Had Cohn and her friends at the FBI not facilitated Bentley's helplessness in the past, had she not learned she could get away with just about anything as long as she continued to be politically useful—and had Bentley herself not been in the worst psychological shape of her life—this would not have been the full-blown crisis it turned out to be. But as it was, Elizabeth Bentley planted herself in the office of the special assistant to the attorney general and refused to budge. Cohn spent the afternoon mollifying Bentley as he scurried around trying to get the FBI to do something.

Would the Bureau have a New Haven agent contact Bentley twice a week to see if she needed to go into town? Cohn pleaded. Absolutely not, said the New York agent in charge. No personal services would be provided by Bureau agents. From headquarters in Washington, D.C., the response was even more adamant: the FBI "could not and would not act as a nursemaid to Bentley." Yet the Bureau "happily" agreed to have an agent meet Bentley at the New Haven railroad station and drive her home. Cohn got nowhere with the AG's Office or the FBI when he requested a car for Bentley. She wanted a car or she wouldn't leave, she told him. And he took her at her word. Quickly tapping into his anticommunist connections, he secured money from an "unidentified source" and rented Bentley a car. Once she was gone, Cohn, his boss Myles Lane, and a special agent from the New York field office met to discuss Bentley's "latest manifestations of instability and idiosyncrasies." Officially, everyone— including Hoover and his assistant directors—heaved a sigh of relief. The crisis was over. But its resolution had left Bentley that much more dependent, that much more unable to take care of her own affairs.

A few days after Cohn arranged for the car, Bentley was on the phone to the New York field office indicating that she expected the Bureau or the Department of Justice to cover her hotel bill at the Prince George. The agent in charge found the demand "entirely unreasonable" considering that her hotel stay was for personal reasons and not on government business. The topic of conversation soon switched to the $500 lump sum payment, authorized by Hoover in July, that Bentley apparently had not yet received. If it was not immediately forthcoming, Bentley said, she would feel "disinclined to cooperate" in future interviews or to make further appearances as a witness. Never before had Bentley been so bald-faced about her manipulation. But the agent in charge called her bluff, pointing out that if she stopped cooperating, she would stop receiving the $50 weekly stipends the Bureau had been paying her since the summer. Bentley calmed down, at least for the moment, but the Bureau realized there would be continued trouble ahead. Among themselves, the agents and their bosses discussed her financial woes. Apparently, she was using the $50 stipend for current living expenses and not putting any of it against her numerous debts. She owed several hundred dollars to Jolly's Drug Store in Madison—where she bought her liquor, among other things—and was behind in her mortgage, telephone, electric, and gas bills. She owed her doctor and her accountants. Her creditors were becoming increasingly insistent.

Bentley had managed to persuade the Bureau—and it was probably true—that her financial problems were so upsetting that she would be of little use to the government until they were taken care of. And, for their part, the agents allowed themselves to think that her main problem was money, that if they relieved her current indebtedness, her worries would be over, her mood would improve, and she would presumably cease to be the "neurotic" and "emotionally unstable" burden she had become. Through the fall, agents in Washington, D.C., and New York traded memos on what to do about Bentley's latest crisis. The New York field office suggested to headquarters that Bentley's weekly stipend be temporarily doubled, allowing her to begin paying off her debts. But her improvidence was too well known. There was no guarantee that she would use the extra money for that purpose. No, said headquarters. It was incumbent on the New York agents to control Bentley, to get her to understand that the Bureau was not going to continue to bail her out of her financial difficulties.

But once again, the talk was tough, and the action was not. At the end of October, Hoover authorized a lump-sum payment. Bentley would be required to submit receipted bills from the businesses to which she was indebted, and she was to be told that she "couldn't go running to us for assistance every time she finds herself in financial or other difficulties"—but she got her money. On October 28, she picked up a cashier's check for $550 from the New York field office. The agent who handed her the check observed that her mental and emotional condition was "improved to a considerable extent." She "appeared much less nervous and more reasonable in her attitude."

But something deeper remained very wrong. Bentley was a good girl who had done bad things, and she hadn't learned to live with that. She had done all she could. She had confessed. She had made amends. She had preached the anticommunist gospel. But her conscience, what she called her "good New England conscience," was permanently scarred. She was finding solace in neither the Catholic Church nor the bottle. In the past, her drinking had masked her depression and anesthetized her loneliness. Now the "cure" was itself a major problem in her life. In the past, she was independent and brave, resolute and determined. She had goals. She had, in her way, ambition. But now she was truly in limbo—financially, occupationally, emotionally, even spiritually. Her closest and most enduring ties—her only friends—were federal agents, whom she manipulated and who put up with her because they felt they had to.

On a frigid December afternoon in 1952, she had lunch, and undoubtedly drinks, with two acquaintances at the Hotel Abbey in Manhattan. When she left the restaurant, she was visibly upset. As she crossed the street, she turned to her female companion. "It doesn't seem worth the struggle," she said. "Sometimes I think I should step out in front of a car and settle everything."

# Chapter 21

# Back in the Act

$\mathcal{S}$OMEHOW, SHE PULLED herself together. It seemed that Elizabeth Bentley was made of sterner stuff than her friends at the FBI gave her credit for, or that even she herself thought. Nineteen fifty-two had been a terrible year. Her drinking was out of control, and it seemed her life was out of control, too. The questionable liaison with her caretaker, the beating, the car accidents, the sit-down strike in Roy Cohn's office—this was the behavior of a troubled woman. But she was also, despite her evident neediness and her bouts of depression, despite her officially reinforced helplessness, a woman with inner resources.

She had been, and therefore she knew she could be, independent. She had not been protected or attended to through life. She had not been cloistered by marriage or cradled by family or succored by friends. She had taken care of herself. Even during the five years when Golos was her lover, she had maintained her own apartment and held a job with significant responsibilities. She had made her own decisions. If anything, she had taken care of him, not vice versa.

Now, faced with the choice of giving in—to alcohol, to depression, to suicide—or carrying on, she found a way to carry on. A New England backbone underlay the emotional frailty.

It helped that she secured temporary employment that winter, doing research and clerical work for Alfred Kohlberg, a wealthy anticommunist bigwig. A hardliner who had founded the American Jewish League Against Communism and financed *Plain Talk*, an anticommunist magazine, Kohlberg was likely asked to employ Bentley by one of her supporters. But however the job came to be, it provided not only income but a reason to get up in the morning, something to do other than worry about having nothing to do. Along with the $50 a week she was continued to be paid by the FBI, the job now at least somewhat alleviated her financial problems. But more than anything, Bentley pulled herself together in January of 1953 because she *had* to. The Department of Justice needed her: William Remington was once again on trial.

Remington had been convicted of perjury in 1951 and sentenced to five years in prison, but his lawyer immediately appealed the decision, claiming that the trial judge had not given good instructions to the jury. The jury had been asked, among other things, to determine if Remington was lying when he claimed he was not a member of the Communist Party. But the judge had not instructed the jury on what constituted party membership. It was a technicality—but a convincing one. The court of appeals ruled in Remington's favor. The verdict was overturned, but the indictment stood, and the case was sent back to district court for a new trial.

The government, however, was not eager to try Remington again on the same charges, both because of the difficulties in establishing just what it meant to be a member of the party and because the original indictment was based, in part, on testimony gathered by the questionable Brunini grand jury. On the other hand, the Department of Justice was not about to give up. Too much had been invested in the Remington case, including the credibility of the government's star witness. And so in October 1951 another grand jury had been impaneled, and five witnesses—including Bentley—had been called. Remington was subsequently indicted on five new counts of perjury, including his denial of passing secret information to Bentley. To the ACLU, the new indictments were morally, if not technically, double jeopardy. To the leftist magazine *The Nation* they were "a mean, vengeful and subversive act." The trial began on January 13, 1953.

Unlike the first trial, the second was short, almost perfunctory, with a whittled-down witness list and a no-nonsense attitude. Now reduced to its essence, it pitted Remington against his ex-wife and Elizabeth Bentley, and the outcome would hinge on whom the jury believed. That meant Bentley had to be in top form, which meant, in turn, that the government had reason to be nervous. Based on her recent behavior—her emotional instability had been noted in numerous FBI memos—prosecutors were undoubtedly afraid of a meltdown on the witness stand. Could Bentley handle the pressure? Could she rise to the occasion? Prosecutors would also have been concerned that Remington's lawyers had discovered Bentley's recent problems and would use them in their cross-examination to attack her character and damage her credibility.

Their latter fear was unfounded. Remington's legal team had not unearthed Bentley's car accidents or her arrest for hit-and-run. But it seemed, as she took the witness stand, that their fears about Bentley herself might be justified. The star witness seemed testy and quick to anger, not her usual composed and controlled self. At one point, she was downright surly. When John Minton, Remington's new lawyer, began questioning her about her book, *Out of Bondage,* she didn't attempt to hide her disgust. "I thought that would turn up sooner or later," she said.

"Who did you write the book in collaboration with?" Minton asked, eager for the jury to hear about John Brunini.

"I sat on a Manhattan telephone directory and wrote it myself," she snapped back.

Unfazed, Minton continued: "Who is Mr. Brunini, with reference to the book?"

"Oh, again Mr. Brunini," Bentley said.

"Just what did Mr. Brunini do with you on the book?"

"Not a thing," Bentley said.

Despite this nasty interchange, Bentley did manage to repeat her previous testimony against Remington calmly and with the same directness and precision she had in the first trial. The FBI was pleased, noting that Bentley "conducted herself in a creditable fashion." The former Mrs. Remington backed her up once again, this time adding that she had been present at meetings when her husband had turned over secret material to Bentley.

Remington himself, having been through two loyalty hearings, a lawsuit, three grand juries, and now two criminal trials, was understandably less cocky. He was also more honest. He admitted being a "philosophical"—but not a "card-carrying"—communist in his younger days. And he was more penitent about his relationship with Bentley, admitting that he was "very indiscreet in . . . having this contact at all" and that he could not in all honesty say that he knew he made no mistake at the time. But he continued to lie under oath about Bentley, maintaining that he did not know she was a communist and did not pass her any sensitive information.

On January 28, after sitting through ten days of testimony and deliberating for twelve hours, the jury found William Remington guilty of two counts of perjury, including his claim that he had not given Bentley classified information. The next day, Judge Vincent Leibell sentenced him to three years in prison. Once again, Remington appealed. But this time, despite a strong dissent by Judge Learned Hand who was appalled at Brunini's behavior during the original grand jury, the verdict was upheld. A few months later, after the Supreme Court refused to hear the case, Remington began serving his time at Lewisburg Penitentiary in Pennsylvania, the same prison where Alger Hiss was being held. The government—and Elizabeth Bentley—had finally prevailed.

But the Remington verdict was a small victory after almost eight years of government investigation. Abraham Brothman, the engineer from whom Bentley had picked up blueprints on Golos's orders, had also been convicted of perjury, but none of the other dozens of sources Bentley named had even faced indictment. The FBI was ready to mothball the Bentley file and move on to more promising cases.

But not agent Bob Lamphere. An Idaho farm boy who had joined the FBI a few months before Pearl Harbor, Lamphere found himself, more than a decade later, in charge of a seven-man unit working on the top-secret decrypted Venona messages. The unit's task was to scour the voluminous Bentley file checking for names, dates, and facts, and pinpoint anything that would help the government identify those called only by code names in the Soviet cables. As he painstakingly cross-checked, the pieces began to fit together, and he became absolutely convinced that Bentley was telling the truth. Venona held the key to convicting a number of Bentley's sources, and Lamphere knew it. But he also knew that the Bureau—particularly his boss, J. Edgar Hoover—was dead set against making Venona public, which is what would happen if the information in the cables was used in a trial. Lamphere knew all the arguments: Making Venona public would expose American counterespionage operations and alert the Russians—now the sworn enemy—to U.S. intelligence activities and the success of the code-breakers. It might anger the international community, given that the United States intercepted the messages when the two countries were supposedly allies. And it might be all for naught. The Venona material was itself problematic—incompletely deciphered, full of code names—and perhaps not admissible in court. As a good Bureau man, Lamphere agreed with the arguments, but that didn't prevent him from feeling frustrated about the situation. Constrained by Hoover's policy but eager to pursue others who, he firmly believed, had betrayed the government, Lamphere hatched a bold FBI-CIA plot. Operatives would kidnap Joseph Katz, a communist spy then living in Israel, who, Lamphere believed, would corroborate Bentley's allegations. Ironically, Katz was the man the KGB had chosen to liquidate Bentley back in 1945. At the last minute, Hoover pulled the plug on the scheme.

The government's frustration deepened as congressional committees continued their unsuccessful attempts to wrest incriminating testimony from the people Bentley had accused of spying. In April of 1953, the SISS called hearings to investigate what it referred to as the "interlocking subversion in government departments," using Bentley's past testimony as a guide not only to whom to subpoena but also to what specific questions to ask. The committee, under the chairmanship of Senator William Jenner, hoped to expose "the design by which Communist agents were able to infiltrate the executive and legislative branches" and how they were able to "move with great facility from one government agency to another." Bentley was never called as a witness, but her presence permeated the hearings. Every witness called was a person she had named.

On April 16, Nathan Gregory Silvermaster took the stand, proclaiming in an opening statement that he was "a loyal citizen [who] never betrayed the interests of the United States." Using Bentley's August 1951 testimony before the subcommittee, the senators proceeded to grill Silvermaster about his alleged spy activities. But in two hours and twenty minutes of questioning, all the committee got was 148 invocations of the Fifth Amendment. Silvermaster not only refused to answer questions about his activities and associations, he also declined to tell the subcommittee the subject of his doctoral dissertation (Leninist economics) and whether he had read Whittaker Chambers's new autobiography. Once again, as they had done in the past, the senators tried to shake—or at the very least, malign—Silvermaster's use of the Fifth Amendment by insisting that an innocent man would not need constitutional protection.

"You understand that if you are not a communist, there is no need for you to invoke the Fifth Amendment?" Jenner asked him at one point.

"I refuse to answer the question," replied Silvermaster.

Jenner persisted. "You understand, do you not, that if you were not a communist at that time there is no need for you to invoke the Fifth Amendment? Do you understand that?"

"Is this a question?" asked Silvermaster.

"Yes," said Jenner, hammering away again. "Do you know that if you were a loyal American citizen at the time, if you were not a communist, there is no need for you to take refuge behind the Fifth Amendment?"

Silvermaster once again refused to answer. Lud Ullmann, his friend, former housemate, and now business partner—the two were involved in real estate development in New Jersey—followed suit.

When Victor Perlo was called in mid-May, he answered "I can't recall" and "I don't have the least idea" to those questions he did not outright refuse to answer. Helen Tenney also stonewalled the committee, declining even to answer matters of public record like whether she held a position at the OSS. The parade of witnesses that spring also included John Abt, Maurice Halperin, Donald Wheeler, Charles Kramer, Edward Fitzgerald, Harry Magdoff, Harold Glasser, and Frank Coe, all named by Bentley, all of whom consistently took the Fifth. Some of the witnesses called the hearings "witch hunts," to which Senator Jenner tartly replied: "This committee is not so much interested in witch hunts as it is in rat hunts."

That summer, the subcommittee issued its report, a fifty-page summary of three years of investigation and three and a half months of hearings: There was, indeed, the committee concluded, a communist conspiracy. Communists had infiltrated the federal government, helped each other get jobs and promotions, and protected one another from exposure. Communists had guided research and policy-making, written speeches, influenced congressional investigations, and drafted laws. Communists had stolen thousands of diplomatic, political, military, scientific, and economic secrets. The so-called Jenner Report echoed much of Bentley's past testimony, lending official credence to her allegations. But in fact, the committee had gotten nothing from its witnesses. No one had admitted anything. No one had slipped up. No indictments resulted.

For once, Bentley was not the center of attention. Neither a witness nor an observer at the hearings that spring, she was more than a thousand miles away in south-central Louisiana. Her friend Bishop Sheen had helped her find another job, this one teaching Romance languages and American government at an obscure little school, the College of Sacred Heart, in an obscure little town, Grand Coteau. The tiny school, serving fewer than a hundred students, was housed in an early-nineteenth-century convent at the center of town and had the distinction of being the nation's oldest Catholic women's college. Bentley couldn't have been more isolated. This woman who had lived most of her adult life in Manhattan now resided in a hamlet surrounded by yam fields, cut off from civilization by dense, kudzu-covered forests, 130 miles from the nearest city of any size. She was still within reach of the FBI, however. Just a few weeks after she left for Grand Coteau, the New York field office informed the New Orleans field office that the southern agents had inherited a periodically depressed, somewhat improvident hypochondriac who, "for the most part, when not beset by her real and fancied worries . . . is friendly and cooperative." New York suggested that New Orleans assign an experienced agent to contact Bentley once a month.

Settled comfortably into academic obscurity, far from the spotlight that had burned her so many times, Bentley now had the life she said she wanted. Only it seemed she didn't want it after all. Why else agree to write a six-part series on espionage based on her book for the *St. Louis Post-Dispatch,* a decision that could not help but focus attention on her again? It may be that she needed, or thought she needed, the money. Surely her teaching position didn't pay much. But how much would one need to live in Grand Coteau, Louisiana? Perhaps she was still looking for vindication and could not let go of her past. She still wanted to play a role in the unfolding Cold War drama. Despite the rocky road she had traveled, despite the public scrutiny she said she hated, she wasn't yet ready to retire.

The series, which began appearing just after Thanksgiving 1953— the tenth anniversary of Yasha's death—broke no new ground. Parts one and two focused on Harry Dexter White's influence, repeating the accusations she had made both publicly and in her original statement to the FBI. In part three, she disclosed how White and Lauchlin Currie had saved Greg Silvermaster from being fired, and then went on in part four to summarize the activities of the Silvermaster spy ring. The OSS—"one of the most sensitive United States agencies deeply infiltrated by spies," she wrote—was the subject of the fifth article. In the last of the series, she detailed her move away from communism, presenting herself as rehabilitated and "restored to the society of decent men."

The headlines were enticing—OSS YIELDED AN ENDLESS FLOW OF SECRETS, HOW WHITE USED TREASURY TO GET SECRETS FOR REDS—but the editors employed unusual restraint in presenting the articles. The paper placed the series in the editorial section of the newspaper rather than the front page, under standard-sized headlines that announced rather than screamed. The stories themselves were written with journalistic directness in a punchy, "just-the-facts-ma'am" voice that sounded nothing like the voice of *Out of Bondage*. Either she had been heavily edited or the series had actually been written by a reporter. Whatever the case, she was once again in the public eye.

The St. Louis articles led to her second appearance on *Meet the Press*—"America's press conference of the air"—which had moved from radio to television and was broadcast "live and unrehearsed" from NBC's studios in Washington, D.C. Bentley made the trip from Louisiana in December to appear as the televised program's first female guest. She looked pasty-faced and tired under the harsh lights, older than her forty-five years. Her dark hair had been too energetically permed for the occasion. It was crimped tight around her face and looked like a bad wig. She was wearing a white blouse with voluminous puffed sleeves and a very large, pointy collar—a schoolgirl's outfit.

She sat motionless, her hands clasped before her on the desk, back erect, her gaze straight into the eye of the camera, as Lawrence Spivak introduced her. She faced four journalists, including a reporter for the *Post-Dispatch,* all intent on getting her to publicly reveal more than she already had, all attempting to straddle the line between good, patriotic, communist-hating citizens who approved of Bentley and skeptical newsmen who weren't quite sure if they believed her. Sitting quiet and composed, like a schoolteacher at her desk, Bentley was intimidated by neither the questions nor the camera. She faced each journalist in turn, her gaze unblinking. They were the ones who fidgeted, uncomfortable with the lights and microphones, men accustomed to batting out stories in their local newsrooms, not sitting before cameras.

Bentley listened to each question intently, giving away nothing with her eyes or body language. The journalists struggled, phrasing and rephrasing questions, tripping over dates and places—which Bentley patiently corrected. They wanted new information. They wanted personal opinion. They wanted her to name names, to criticize Truman, to comment on the way the FBI conducted its investigations. Bentley nimbly sidestepped a number of questions and answered others as narrowly as possible, confounding the journalists' best efforts.

"Are any persons whom you did not name publicly still engaged in Soviet espionage?" one of the reporters asked her.

Bentley took a moment before she replied, in her slightly nasal and accentless voice, "I don't know offhand which ones I have named publicly and which ones I have not. That is why I cannot answer your question." Stymied, the reporter moved on.

"Why have there been no charges against those you have named?" she was asked a few minutes later. The question was clearly combative, but Bentley didn't rise to it.

"It is a question of law," she said, "and I, not being a lawyer, cannot explain it to you."

She seemed in complete control, answering what she wanted to answer and finessing the rest. The only emotion she displayed during the questioning was when one of the reporters started to ask her what had made her turn "informer."

"I dislike that term very much," she said, interrupting the question. Her voice was sharp. "I do wish people wouldn't use that term when it comes to ex-communists." She was lecturing the reporter. "We are trying to help this government, and we do not consider ourselves as tattletale people." The reporter retreated immediately, stumbling over his words as he attempted to rephrase the question.

Bentley emerged unscathed. She might have seemed a bit high-handed to those who tuned into the program, but she also seemed intelligent, alert, and articulate. Those who might have heard or read that she was hysterical, neurotic, a liar, and a Red-baiter saw only a mild-mannered, unflappable schoolteacher who spoke carefully and appeared to know what she was talking about. If Bentley had decided to say yes to Lawrence Spivak in order to enhance her reputation—which continued to suffer because of the lack of indictments against those she had named—she had perhaps modestly succeeded. If she had said yes to make nice to her friends at the FBI after giving them so much trouble the year before, she also succeeded. Bentley was "very conservative in her answers," a Bureau official noted, with pleasure, and she "did not allow herself to be trapped." She had done a "very good job in the face of loaded questions." And, most important, she had mentioned the Bureau "only briefly" and "each time remarks were commendable." If she agreed to appear on *Meet the Press* to reclaim her place in the public eye, she also succeeded. A week after her appearance, the *New York Mirror* reprinted the six-part series that had originally appeared in the St. Louis paper, and she was the talk of the town again.

The articles themselves were the same, but the *Mirror* treated them as tabloid fodder. EX-SPY QUEEN TELLS OWN STORY . . . LINE RAN STRAIGHT TO STALIN, SAYS BENTLEY ran the one-inch-high banner headline announcing the first in the series. The second article, which detailed her interactions with the Silvermaster and Perlo Groups, mentioned in passing that Bentley believed there might be other spy rings still operating. The headline read, in bold face: BENTLEY FINDS THIRD SPY RING. Publishing these stories in St. Louis was one thing; airing them in New York was another. FBI officials at headquarters, tipped off three days before the first article appeared, instructed agents in the New York office to obtain copies of the paper and forward them to Washington, D.C., for analysis. There the series was read with interest, as agents compared it, name for name, detail for detail, with Bentley's book as well as her 1945 statement to the FBI. Upon close examination, there seemed to be a few places where Bentley had expanded on the original material. Headquarters instructed the New Orleans field office to send an agent to Grand Coteau to question her about this.

Back at her teaching post at Sacred Heart after her appearance on *Meet the Press,* Bentley made herself available for three FBI interviews in as many weeks. She was as cooperative and voluble as she had been in the best of times, filling in details for the visiting agent, answering questions about Golos and her Soviet contact "Bill," adding information about a communist member of the War Production Board. But she claimed to be displeased with the *Mirror* articles, which, she told the agent, she had not actually written, although all of them appeared under her byline. She said she had been interviewed by a reporter in Louisiana months ago, and that the articles were a product of those talks, written entirely by the reporter. Bentley claimed she did not even review them before publication. The agents analyzing the newspaper articles had not found any misstatements or inaccuracies, but Bentley may have been worried that they would. She had trouble remembering what she had said to whom, which details had been made public and which had not. There had been too many grand juries, too many hearings and trials, too many speeches and interviews. She was on the record too many times for there not to be a mistake somewhere, a story she told a shade differently one time, a date she remembered, then misremembered. But the FBI concluded that "practically all" the information in the newspaper series was previously published in *Out of Bondage*.

Whatever her involvement in the series, it couldn't have happened without her participation and consent. The stories had been published in two major newspapers within a week of each other, and in between, she had appeared on national television. She had been in Grand Coteau for only a matter of months, been out of the media spotlight only since the Remington trial barely a year ago. Still, it seemed she had had enough of obscurity. Maybe she wanted it both ways: a quiet, out-of-the-way job she could settle into *and* the excitement of reporters at her door, special agents calling for interviews, NBC producers inviting her to appear on national television. Although she had been hurt by it, although it had created stress in her life that she had not been able to handle, she apparently could not give up her identity as the righteous and rehabilitated Spy Queen. As it turned out, she would not have the choice.

# Chapter 22

# Under Attack

*I*T WAS WILLIAM HENRY TAYLOR, an obscure government bureaucrat, who turned up the heat. Bentley had testified a number of times that Taylor was one of the group of federal employees who fed confidential information to Greg Silvermaster. She knew this, she said, not because she had ever met or talked with Taylor, not because she had actually seen him pass information to Silvermaster, but because Silvermaster told her of Taylor's involvement. Taylor had been anything but intimidated by the accusations. He hadn't tried to escape the spotlight by leaving the country or even, as Silvermaster, Ullmann, and so many others had done, by leaving government service. He had stayed put and spent five years defending himself. When called to testify—he had appeared before three congressional committees, five grand juries, and was in 1954 being investigated by a loyalty board—he did not plead the Fifth, and he did not skirt the issues. Again and again, under oath, he proclaimed his complete innocence and denied all of Bentley's accusations.

The war of words between Bentley and Taylor mostly stayed behind closed doors, locked away in secret grand jury testimony or the unpublished record of subcommittee executive sessions, until, in the fall of 1953, both the attorney general and the director of the FBI mentioned Taylor's name in their statements at a public session before the SISS. The press covered the hearings, and Taylor, who at the time was an assistant director at the International Monetary Fund, found himself fighting for his job. This time it was not enough to proclaim his innocence. This time he took direct action, mounting a $5 million libel suit against the *Washington Daily News* for carrying a story in which he was accused of disloyalty. In putting together the case in February of 1954, Taylor's lawyers subpoenaed Bentley. She was to give her deposition at a law office in Opelousas, Louisiana.

But Bentley wanted no part of it. She immediately called the FBI field office in New Orleans, telling agents there that she had no intention of honoring the subpoena. Taylor was on a fishing expedition, she said, and she was the fish. The libel suit was just a cover for Taylor's real purpose: He wanted to find out exactly what Bentley had told the FBI about him and what she had testified to in closed-door sessions. Meanwhile, the suit would delay his dismissal from the IMF. Bentley didn't stop there. She told the resident agent in Lafayette, Louisiana, that the suit was, in fact, a communist plot, that Taylor was being backed by the party in an effort to bring her out into the open so that a libel suit could be filed against her. This, she told the somewhat incredulous agent, was a tactic used by the party to get revenge on a turncoat. Later, Bentley reported to the agent that unknown persons had broken into the College of Sacred Heart library and then ransacked the dormitories. Bentley saw this as directly related to her troubles with Taylor.

But the New Orleans agent wasn't so sure. "It is apparent that a lot of the instances which she has related to agents of the Bureau are merely figments of her imagination," he reported to his boss in Washington. "She is merely trying to apply pressure on the Bureau to get them to intervene on behalf of her so she will not have to appear and give a deposition." The "communist plot" may have been a figment of her imagination, but she was right about Taylor's underlying motive. He named a newspaper in his suit, but he was after her. He had been trying for two years to confront his accuser in public under oath. He was hopeful, he told the press, that the libel trial would finally provide that opportunity.

But the New Orleans agent was also right about one thing: Bentley was looking for FBI protection against Taylor and his lawyers. The FBI was, she told him, "the only organization left in the government that can't be bought," and it was the FBI's duty to protect those who, like herself, had assisted the government. The Bureau had gotten her out of scrapes before, both legal and financial, and she expected the Bureau to do it again. She was being difficult and demanding—not to mention paranoiac—the agents thought, but the truculence actually masked fear. The college was expressing concern about adverse publicity. She would lose her job, a job that had not been easy to come by. She would be penniless again. And in the meantime, she would be dragged through the mud. She would have to listen, again, to people calling her a liar. She would have to read about herself in the newspapers. It was one thing when she wrote the stories herself, quite another when they were written about her. She still didn't understand, or at least had not come to terms with, the reality: In coming forth to target others, she had become a target herself. She had set something in motion that she could not stop.

But maybe her friends at the Bureau could. On the phone, the agents stonewalled her. There would be no protection. The Bureau would give her no legal advice, they said. She should hire a lawyer and attend to the business herself. But behind the scenes, they moved into action, with the New Orleans office in close contact with the assistant attorney general, a federal judge in western Louisiana, and Taylor's lawyers. It was a good thing, because Bentley was decidedly not taking care of business. She didn't hire a lawyer for herself, and she ignored the subpoena. In April, a second subpoena was issued, and once again, Bentley ignored it, this time leaving the impression with a federal judge that she was under FBI protective custody. When Hoover heard about this, he was furious. In an urgent teletype sent to the New Orleans field office, he instructed the agent in charge to make it clear to the judge that the FBI was in no way protecting Bentley. Bentley should be told that responding to the subpoena was her own business but that the Bureau would not want her to do "anything foolish which might damage her reputation and possible future value as a government witness."

Meanwhile, it seemed that Bentley was damaging her reputation with the people she needed most. In early May she presented herself at the New Orleans field office, demanding that the attorney general and Mr. Hoover provide her with immediate protection against the "corrupt [Huey] Long political machine in Louisiana" and the "communist plot" against her. She rambled and spoke in generalities about intimidations and threats, telling the agent in charge that she expected to be a "corpse" before long. Clearly rattled by the encounter, the agent sent a special delivery teletype to Hoover. Bentley appeared "irrational and illogical," he told his boss. "Her talk impressed me as being that of a demented person."

"Demented" was an overstatement, but certainly Bentley was bordering on hysteria over the Taylor affair. Regardless of what they thought of her at the moment, however, the FBI had many reasons to try to shield her from her own worst instincts. She was still a star witness and one of their most valuable informers. And the federal judge had his own reasons as well. Although Bentley was ignoring the subpoenas, he was reluctant to cite her for contempt. "She has undoubtedly performed a great service to this country," he told the assistant attorney general. And he was particularly averse to moving against Bentley if the plaintiff in the libel suit was, as she alleged, a communist.

With Bentley successfully avoiding subpoenas, and the lawyers unable to depose her, the libel case stalled. But Taylor and his attorney Byron Scott refused to be stymied. In mid-April, Scott engineered a press conference in Manhattan at which he called for a public hearing before SISS where Taylor could confront Bentley and deny her charges under oath. But Taylor and his lawyer had more in mind than that. They had spent months going through Bentley's public testimony, cross-checking her statements for internal consistency and checking the veracity of any independently verifiable facts, like names and dates. Their strategy was to find enough to discredit Bentley in general, so that her testimony against Taylor would be seen in that context. And they thought they had found more than enough.

Scott immediately went on the attack, charging that they had found thirty-seven "discrepancies" in Bentley's writings and testimony. "We are challenging the inconsistencies, the inaccuracies, and the impossibilities of her story," he told the press. Taylor was even more forthright: "Miss Bentley has lied so often and so outrageously in her testimony . . . that she can scarcely be looked at as a credible source," he later wrote.

Taylor and Scott had, indeed, uncovered a number of discrepancies. For example, Bentley had testified that she collected party dues from the Perlo Group and passed it to Golos, but Golos had already died by the time Bentley took over the group. She also testified, at various times, that Duncan Lee, her valuable OSS contact, was a member of the Silvermaster Group, the Perlo Group, and no group at all. At one point, Bentley told investigators that her Soviet contact "Al" informed her she received the Red Star in "late October," but in another statement she put the date at "mid-November." She had testified incorrectly that only two of her government sources were not native-born Americans. Taylor and his lawyer had checked: There were at least ten. She had misestimated the number of people in the Communist Party. A source no less unimpeachable than Hoover himself had used another number.

Some of the charges were so insignificant as to be silly: She had, for example, called the United States Service and Shipping Corporation the *U.S.* Service and Shipping Corporation. She had referred to the same man by two different first names (both of which she had known him by). Other discrepancies were probably errors in transcription and not in testimony. Taylor noted that Bentley told HUAC that Columbia University didn't offer classes in American government, testimony that would have been both ludicrous and patently false. What Bentley probably said was that she didn't *take* any such courses. The mistake was not hers but the stenographer's.

Most of the thirty-seven errors, mistakes which Taylor and his lawyer were trying to present as unconscionable and deliberate lies were, in fact, trivial: relatively minor mix-ups that might be expected, given how many times she had testified, always without notes, and given the sometimes convoluted questions she was asked. Taylor was certainly right that Bentley had not recalled all facts and dates accurately and that her testimony was occasionally inconsistent. But her mistakes were not only relatively minor, they did not show a pattern of fabrication. There seemed to be, in almost all cases, no intent to mislead. Even if every one of Taylor's charges were proven correct, the case against Bentley was still weak.

Regardless, the FBI took the accusations seriously, understanding Taylor's charges for what they were: the first significant effort to discredit their top informer. Except for Remington, who had hemmed and hawed his way into prison trying to explain his relationship with Bentley, everyone else she accused ducked the fight. Harry Dexter White undoubtedly would have pressed the point, but he had died soon after his initial testimony. The others opted out, refusing to testify, consistently invoking the Fifth rather than directly denying Bentley's accusations (and thus risking a perjury charge). But Taylor was clearly in for the long haul. He was angry, and he was defiant. As long as he kept his job in Washington, D.C., he was, he told the press, a constant reminder of the government's failure to make anyone believe Bentley's story.

After interviewing and reinterviewing Bentley at length, both in Louisiana and back in Connecticut where she was spending her summers, the FBI was not overly concerned with the errors themselves, most of which were deemed misinterpretations, understandable mix-ups, or minor quibbles. Even her outright errors were not so egregious as to worry the investigating agents. But the Bureau was concerned with preserving her credibility. The best tactic, it was decided, was not to counter every one of Taylor's charges but to stress the corroborating evidence for significant elements in Bentley's testimony—and to keep Bentley out of the hands of Taylor's attorneys.

In late September 1954, Taylor was called before a grand jury, where he once again denied Bentley's charges and testified at length and in detail about the thirty-seven discrepancies he had uncovered. Then, in the spring of the next year, he was called before a loyalty board that would rule on whether he could keep his job with the

International Monetary Fund. There, Taylor and his lawyer presented a 107-page brief charging Bentley with lying and accusing the Bureau of conducting a sloppy investigation of her story. A synopsis of the brief was printed in an April 1955 issue of *I. F. Stone's Weekly*, and both the tabloids and the leftist press spread the story. *The Worker*, in an article that referred to Bentley's past testimony as "lurid tales" and blamed her for the death of Harry Dexter White, said she was "tripped up" and "undone" by Taylor's accusations. The *New York Post* called her in Grand Coteau for a comment. "I have testified truthfully," she told the reporter, "and I see no point in making any reply." BENTLEY CLAMS UP ran the headline.

Then, in the midst of the Taylor case and fending off the press, Bentley heard the shocking news that William Remington had been bludgeoned to death in his bed in the honor dormitory of the federal penitentiary at Lewisburg, Pennsylvania. He had been murdered by an inmate with an IQ of 61, who told the FBI that he killed Remington because he was a "damn communist who wanted to sell us all out." Remington had less than nine months left to serve on his perjury conviction.

Bentley was no more to blame for Remington's murder than she was for Harry Dexter White's heart attack. The two men had been engaged in highly questionable activities, and she had testified honestly about them. But that was probably slim consolation to Bentley. She knew Remington as a bright and charming man, and his death must have shaken her, as she considered the part she played in his demise. Of course, she was not left alone to work through her emotions. Reporters from all over called her at home, badgering her for comment. She said nothing. What could she say?

Meanwhile, the Taylor case was still very much alive. Initially, the board examining Taylor ruled that there was reason to doubt his loyalty, but, ever the fighter, he appealed, and in early January of 1955, the panel reversed its earlier decision. Taylor's attorney told the Associated Press that his client's victory cast doubt on Bentley's credibility, and the press touted the reversal as a direct repudiation of the Red Spy Queen. But in fact, it had nothing to do with the thirty-seven discrepancies or Taylor's claim that Bentley had lied so often and about so much that all of her testimony was suspect. Instead, the reversal was based on the confused and suspicious circumstances surrounding a piece of evidence originally used against Taylor, a letter allegedly written by Lud Ullmann concerning Taylor's appointment to a Treasury post. Byron Scott, Taylor's lawyer, was able to successfully challenge the authenticity of the letter, presenting evidence that it had been manufactured. Taylor was cleared, and the lawsuit fizzled. But that was not the end of it.

Bentley told the agent in charge at the New Orleans field office that Byron Scott's comment to the press was just the "opening barrage of an attack" on her integrity. She was half right. Her integrity would continue to be attacked, but not by Taylor, who proclaimed himself "just too happy" to be in the clear or his attorney, who probably felt he had made his point. Instead, a confidential source associated with the American Civil Liberties Union alerted the FBI that one of the congressional subcommittees now had a "maniacal fixation" on Elizabeth Bentley. Benjamin Ginzberg, research director for the Subcommittee on Constitutional Rights, was an opponent of the loyalty and security programs that had been created in the wake of Bentley's—and others'—allegations. Around the time of the Taylor affair he hired someone at the Library of Congress to work full-time "studying the inconsistencies in the various testimonies of Elizabeth Bentley" and building a case against her. A few weeks later, the FBI was relieved to learn that one of the senators on the subcommittee had submitted his resignation along with the strongly worded statement in opposition to Ginzberg's investigation. The subcommittee chair assured the senator that there would be no investigation and that the Library of Congress researcher was "off the committee payroll."

But as one challenge faded, another flared. The next one came in the stocky form of a brash, garrulous, and unstable young man named Harvey Matusow. A purported genius who flunked out of high school, he had joined the Army in 1944 and the Communist Party shortly thereafter. Early in 1950, he turned informer, finding a niche for himself with the FBI as a self-proclaimed expert on communist infiltration of youth organizations. He had testified before congressional committees, and, egged on by Senator Joe McCarthy, he had named more than two hundred names. He had made headlines and had become, like Bentley, one of the darlings of the anticommunist movement. But unlike her, he used the position to enhance his social standing, bragging that he had dined with J. Edgar Hoover at the Stork Club, ridden in Walter Winchell's Cadillac, and gone out on double dates with Roy Cohn. A few years later, struggling with his conscience—and perhaps mental illness—he converted from Judaism to Mormonism, took the middle name of "Job" from the Bible, and publicly repented his sins—not the sins of working for the Communist Party but the sins of falsely accusing others of subversive activities. Matusow now said that he had lied to Congress and the FBI, that everything he told them was a fabrication. Early in 1955, his book *False Witness*—an obvious play on Whittaker Chambers's autobiography *Witness*—appeared in bookstores. Stewart Alsop, promoting it in his column, called the book "a remarkable political confession which may cause major explosions."

In his book, Matusow wrote that Bentley, Louis Budenz, and others were "hailed as heroes" and that he wanted to climb on the bandwagon. "It was the easy way up—to let the world know that I was not just another guy." He confessed that he wanted to be "in the limelight," that he loved "the headlines, the flashbulbs and the pats on the back." Seeing himself on TV and hearing reports of his doings on the radio fed his ego, he wrote. "I considered myself a success. I was a national figure." He mentioned Bentley six times in the book, five times to lionize her—the famous witness, the headliner, a member of the Big Leagues, where he wanted to be. But in the sixth reference, he cut her down to size—his size.

Called to testify before SISS in February of 1955 just before his book came out, Matusow was not the shamed and repentant soul the senators had expected. Instead, he took the offensive, accusing the committee members of creating "an atmosphere of hysteria" that encouraged lies. "You're the one responsible for my role as a witness," he yelled at Senator Price Daniel, a Texas Democrat who had been trying to trap Matusow into responses that could form the basis for a perjury indictment. But the real fireworks came when the committee counsel asked the witness if he considered Elizabeth Bentley one of the most important anticommunists.

"I consider her as the most unstable," Matusow replied.

He went on to testify about an incident he had described in his forthcoming book, his sixth reference to Elizabeth Bentley. He told the committee that he and Bentley had lunched together in a Manhattan restaurant in the fall of 1952. He remembered the date because it was his birthday. Bentley was distraught and weepy, he said. She told him she was broke and had to keep testifying to make enough money to live. The only problem was, she allegedly told him, she had run out of things to testify about. She would have to "find" additional information. In case the implication was not clear enough, Matusow added: "Miss Bentley, I believe, gave false testimony." Elizabeth Bentley was back in the headlines.

Hoover immediately fired off an urgent teletype to the New Orleans field office. Contact Bentley and detail any conversation she can recall with Matusow, he instructed his agents. See if Bentley would be willing to testify and deny the allegations. Hoover had to have been worried. He knew that Bentley had been in bad shape in 1952. His own agents had reported that she was frequently upset and often seemed depressed, even suicidal. She might have said anything to anybody. There was another reason to worry as well, for the Bureau immediately understood Matusow's allegations not just as a threat to Bentley's credibility but as part of a "carefully planned attack on the government's security program" and, even more important, on the director himself. Hoover was on record stating that all information from Bentley that was possible to check had proven correct. An attack on Bentley was an attack on the director.

New Orleans agents contacted Bentley by phone the next day, reporting back to Hoover that Bentley said she did remember having lunch with Matusow at some point but never mentioned anything about her relations with the FBI. Bentley was emphatic: Matusow was lying. She had never told him she was desperate for information, and she had never testified falsely. She assured the agent that she would be willing to go before the committee and refute Matusow's charges. Bentley may have been confident that Matusow had nothing on her, but she understood that she might be in real trouble this time. Two days after local agents contacted her, she called New York agent Lester Gallaher at his home. Gallaher had been one of the agents closely involved in her life in the early 1950s. She told him she was "considerably worried" about the allegations. She seemed most concerned about reporters, who were already beginning to hound her, and about jeopardizing her job at the college. That evening she also called Hoover's office, telling one of his office staff that the "heavy artillery" was now being trained on her. She insisted on speaking to Hoover personally. When that request was deflected, she hung up and called one of the assistant directors at home.

Bentley wanted the FBI to help establish her whereabouts on October 3, 1952, the date Matusow said they had lunched together in New York. She might have been in New York, but she might not have. She couldn't remember, and her own records weren't clear. Her friends at the Bureau promised nothing, but they quickly moved into action. They needed to disprove and discredit Matusow as fast as possible before the story got more out of hand than it already was. Any airing of that period of Bentley's life, the agent in charge of the New York office wrote to his boss in Washington, "could cause more serious embarrassment to the Bureau." For it was not just Bentley who had comported herself badly during 1952, it was the FBI as well, assigning agents to chauffeur her around on personal business, working unofficially and behind the scenes to extricate her from various scrapes.

The New York office immediately dispatched an agent to the auditor's room at the Prince George Hotel, where Bentley generally stayed when in Manhattan, to go through the handwritten registration cards for October of 1952. Yes, the agent reported back, Bentley had stayed at the hotel on the evening of October 3, thus establishing it was at least possible that she had lunched with Matusow earlier that day. Next, presumably following leads from Bentley, agents interviewed, and reinterviewed, six people who had been at lunch or dinner or parties where it was thought both Bentley and

Matusow were in attendance. It turned out that three people could confirm that Bentley and Matusow had a late dinner—not lunch—together at the Rochambeau restaurant on West Eleventh Street on the night in question.

One was a man named Llewellyn Watts who said that he saw Matusow and Bentley enter the restaurant together and that, a minute later, Matusow beckoned him over to their table, where he remained for the rest of the evening. Watts told the FBI that at no time during the evening did Miss Bentley show any evidence of tears or depression. On the contrary, she had impressed him as a "charming woman" with a "good sense of humor." There was no discussion of false testimony that Watts could remember. The only conversation he recalled was a lighthearted one about the uncommon names of Midwest towns. Apparently, a few minutes after Watts joined the table, another man, Earl Henry, sat down with them. He told the FBI that Matusow had at first introduced Bentley using a fictitious name but that he had corrected himself almost immediately. It seemed to Henry that Matusow had enjoyed playing this little joke on him. Henry, like Watts, did not think Bentley showed any signs of despondency. The thing he most remembered about the half hour he had sat with them was that Bentley didn't have a chance to say very much because Matusow monopolized the conversation. That meshed with Watts's memory that when he asked Bentley to talk about her Communist Party activities that night she was able to say very little because "Matusow was continuously interrupting to tell about his."

It had taken some effort, but the Bureau did a good job disproving Matusow's story. The statements from the other diners that night, along with Matusow's admitted history of fanciful fabrications, put an end to his attack on Bentley's credibility. He was a troubled man who made up stories. He had made up the one about Bentley as well. She was cleared, and the latest crisis was over. But once again, she had paid a price for being who she was—or who she used to be. Matusow's allegations, especially on the heels of William Taylor's attack, made her feel as vulnerable as ever, unable to escape her past, unable to maintain a normal life for herself. The press had once again trumpeted her name, and the sisters at Sacred Heart were not happy.

Harvey Matusow served five years in jail for perjury. Released in 1960, he went on to play avant-garde music with Yoko Ono, perform as a stand-up comic, invent the stringless yo-yo, and marry fifteen times—nine of them to the same woman.

# Chapter 23

# An Unsettled Woman

I T WAS BEGINNING to look as if Elizabeth Bentley was doomed to live from one crisis to another, for just as the Matusow and Taylor challenges were being resolved, just when it seemed she might go back to living a quiet life in Grand Coteau, the IRS came after her. Back in 1951, the year *Out of Bondage* was published and the year *McCall's* bought the serial rights to the book, Bentley had earned a considerable amount of money, an income many thousands of dollars in excess of her usual annual salary. Her attorney had recommended that she spread the income across a period of three or four years, paying a portion of the taxes each year, but the IRS didn't like the idea and ruled against her. The attorney, however, considered the ruling "inconsistent" and recommended that she not pay. Bentley was only too glad to comply with his advice. She didn't have the money anyway. Now, in the late spring of 1955, the IRS delivered an ultimatum: Unless Bentley paid

$1,800 in back taxes within a week, the agency would institute criminal proceedings against her.

Bentley immediately got on the phone to her savior, Roy Cohn, who, once again, began working behind the scenes. He contacted Robert Morris, who had been the counsel for SISS, and Morris in turn got on the phone to one of Hoover's assistant directors. It would be "tragic" if the IRS proceeded against Bentley, Morris told his highly placed FBI friend. The action would not only stir up sentiment against the IRS among anticommunists, it would fuel the ongoing left-wing attack on Bentley. While the Bureau remained in the loop but not directly involved, Morris took up the matter with Deputy Attorney General William Rogers. But these initial efforts were unsuccessful. In early June, the Louisiana office of the IRS attached Bentley's bank account.

Bentley immediately called the FBI, furious over what she called an "arbitrary action." Elements in the government were trying to destroy her, she said. It was "more than a coincidence," she told her FBI friends, that Matusow had attacked her, Taylor had attacked her, and now the IRS was zeroing in. She felt beleaguered and besieged, singled out for especially aggressive treatment. "I seem to be Target No. 1 for my 'old friends,' " she wrote to one FBI official. Her current problems were not a question of an individual getting into difficulties with the government over income tax mistakes, she insisted. They were a very particular attack on Elizabeth Bentley, Anticommunist, by those who didn't like what she had done or what she stood for. Moreover, the latest "attack" was having immediate and serious consequences for Bentley, which she was quick to point out to her friends at the Bureau. Three weeks after her bank account had been seized, with the attending local and national reports in the press, the mother superior of the College of Sacred Heart advised Bentley that she was being dropped from the faculty. The publicity was harming the school's reputation. The school had received, according to the mother superior, "many adverse criticisms."

Bentley may have presented herself as a victim—and she may well have been, because of her notoriety, a special target—but she was by no means helpless. There was, first, the power of her connections. She not only had Roy Cohn scrambling around for her and the Attorney General's Office paying attention, but she also had FBI agents in three states and the District of Columbia tracking her concerns. She was not shy about calling agents at home or writing personal "Dear Lou" letters to Louis Nichols, a top official at FBI headquarters. She was not shy about enlisting the help of anyone who might be useful. She made a trip to Washington, D.C., later that summer to pay personal calls on two HUAC congressmen. After hearing her tale, they promised to apply pressure on the Treasury Department to help her resolve her problem. They also said they'd mobilize others, including some powerful Senate allies.

There was also the power of the threat. Bentley told agents in New Haven that unless the Bureau got her out of her present situation, she would be forced to "blow the lid off the Administration" and "blow up the works." The threat itself was probably meaningless—it is unlikely that Bentley had any additional intelligence at this point, damning or otherwise—but the idea of Bentley as a loose canon must have been unsettling for the Bureau. She was full of bluster, too, telling New Haven agents that she would settle for nothing less than a full public apology from the IRS. With agents in Louisiana, she took another tack, threatening to call the newspapers and inform them that President Eisenhower had been allowed to spread the income from *his* book over a period of years, and the IRS hadn't raised a stink about that.

At first, it looked as if the case could be quickly resolved. Robert Morris had the ear of the deputy attorney general who made a call to the Treasury Department, reporting back in mid-June that the IRS would be "reasonable" and was willing to negotiate. Assistant FBI Director Alan Belmont got reassurances that the matter had been taken up with the IRS "at a high level" and that the agency was considering her problem "sympathetically." Meanwhile, the Bureau authorized first a $100 payment to Bentley and then an additional $50 to help her meet expenses while her bank account was frozen. Officially, she was being paid for "value received"—the help she had already given agents investigating other cases and the time she had spent going over William Taylor's allegations. But it was obvious that the FBI was helping her out of a tight spot.

By August nothing had happened. In fact, it seemed that despite—or more likely *because*—of the pressure being applied, the IRS had dug in its heels. Robert Morris called Bentley to tell her that he had learned that the agency was refusing to remove the lien on her bank account in Louisiana and, moreover, would be demanding that she sell her house in Connecticut. He had also learned that the IRS would not authorize any public apology or retraction for publication in the Louisiana newspapers, which Bentley had thought might help her save her job.

In late summer her case took on new urgency. Bentley was at her Connecticut house when a deputy U.S. marshal knocked on the door and handed her a surprise subpoena. One of the men Bentley had implicated in espionage activity years ago, Edward Fitzgerald, had just been sentenced to six months in jail for contempt because he refused to testify about the Silvermaster case, even after the government granted him immunity. Fitzgerald was not taking this turn of events quietly. He wanted his day in court, and he wanted Bentley to be there. It was because of her congressional testimony fingering him as one of the Perlo Group, a productive source in the OSS, that he was in the spot he was in. "I am very happy," he told the press after the subpoena was served, "that at long last we have succeeded in forcing Miss Bentley to come to court and put up or shut up." It was William Taylor all over again.

Bentley immediately called the New Haven field office, telling the agent there that she believed Fitzgerald's lawyers would seize on her income tax problem to attempt to discredit her. Should that happen, she warned the agent, it would reflect "most unfavorably" on the director, the attorney general, and Vice President Nixon, all of whom had publicly commented on the value and veracity of her testimony. The potential threat to Hoover's status was taken most seriously by the agency over which he had for decades ruled like a caesar. Moreover, Fitzgerald's overambitious lawyer had committed the political faux pas of having a subpoena served on Hoover himself.

Bentley was after help with the IRS, but her problem became secondary to the one at hand: protecting the director. The FBI must have moved quickly, for a week later, the judge directing Fitzgerald's contempt proceedings voided the subpoenas, ruling that the issues they raised were not germane to the case. Neither the director nor Bentley would have to testify, which was undoubtedly a relief. But it was not the outcome Bentley was looking for. She had hoped that the Fitzgerald case would provide a compelling reason for the IRS to back off. She had hoped it would give the Bureau the ammunition it needed to deal with the headstrong agency. But now that she was no longer under subpoena, the immediate threat of exposure disappeared, and the tax case dragged on.

Through the summer, Bentley became increasingly impatient and, as far as the Bureau was concerned, increasingly difficult to deal with. Others might be intimidated by an agency as powerful and seemingly untouchable as the Internal Revenue Service, but Bentley was not. She was aggrieved, angry, and defiant. She had stood up to KGB operatives and had testified before congressmen, grand jurors, and judges. She had toured the country giving speeches and appeared on national radio and television. This was a woman who, regardless of the victim role she sometimes played with the FBI, knew how to make her way in the world. And she knew the way to make this problem go away was to keep nagging the Bureau.

She was right. As Bentley was busy calling the New Haven office, demanding action and threatening to go to the press, the Bureau was busy making "discreet inquiries" within the IRS to determine if someone in particular was pushing action against her. The FBI, with its connections and power, its loyalty to Bentley, its fear of her as a loose canon—and, most important, its concern for the integrity of its director—cast a wide net. The district director of the IRS and the IRS regional commissioner were brought into the conversation, as were the chief counsel of the Treasury Department and the deputy attorney general. Privately, the IRS told the FBI that it was "unfortunate that this matter had gotten out of control" and promised to send a revenue agent who had "tact and diplomacy" to talk to Bentley. Meanwhile, hoping to help her keep her job at Sacred Heart, the

FBI, conferring privately with the assistant attorney general and several lawyers, tried to pressure the IRS to put out a news story in Louisiana that slapping a lien on Bentley's bank account had been a mistake. When that tactic didn't seem to be working, the Attorney General's Office sent the U.S. attorney in New Orleans to pay a personal visit to the mother superior to vouch for Bentley. The college relented. Bentley would have a job to come back to in the fall. But still, her tax problem did not go away.

In September, Hoover himself got involved, taking the occasion of a regular conference with the attorney general to call to his personal attention the handling of Bentley's case. The director was blunt and forceful, citing the unresolved tax problem as "indicative of the gross lack of cooperation upon the part of the Treasury Department." That may have done the trick, for finally, after months of meetings, memoranda, and sub rosa maneuverings, an agreement was reached. Bentley would arrange, over time, to pay a portion of what she owed, and the IRS would back off. There would be no fines, no prosecution for tax evasion. Bentley's bank account would be unfrozen, and the IRS would not demand that she sell her house. She would be out of the spotlight, free to resume her quiet life.


Through all the turmoil, the unwanted attention, and the negative publicity that were a constant in her life in the mid-1950s, Bentley attempted to carry on, spending her summers in Connecticut and the school year in Grand Coteau. In the summer of 1954 and again in 1955, she stayed at her Connecticut house, one summer commuting into Manhattan several times a week to take classes at Columbia. She was thinking about pursuing her Ph.D. In the fall, she was back in Louisiana teaching Romance languages again, dealing not only with the Taylor and Matusow attacks and then the seemingly intransigent IRS problem but also with an unending parade of agents, investigators, attorneys, and reporters who turned to her whenever they needed an expert in communism or espionage. She was, the New Orleans field office told Hoover, "constantly beset" and under "considerable mental strain" from the demands put on her by government agencies, congressional committees, and the press. But the FBI itself was the most insistent. Rarely did a week go by in the mid-1950s when Bentley wasn't being questioned by an agent from New Orleans, New Haven, New York, or headquarters.

She continued to be interviewed regularly about *Out of Bondage*. Agents at the New York field office had gone over the book dozens of times since its publication in 1951, and each time they found something new to ask her about: a name she mentioned in the book but not in her 1945 statement, a relationship that needed clarification, a party connection, a bit of history she could sketch in, the whereabouts of a former compatriot. She was, even in the midst of her other troubles, cooperative and forthcoming. Agents from both the New Haven and New Orleans offices regularly visited her to ask questions about ongoing espionage investigations and to show her pictures of unidentified or code-named suspects, hoping she might supply names or pertinent facts.

When a highly confidential source told the FBI that Jay Lovestone considered Bentley the only ex-communist "who had always told the truth and never been crossed up," Hoover jumped on it. Lovestone had been head of the American communist party until his expulsion by Joseph Stalin in 1929, and the Bureau had amassed a considerable file on him. Now Hoover saw the opportunity to gather additional intelligence. He ordered agents from the New Orleans office to interview Bentley immediately, sending him full details of any and all conversations Bentley may have had with Lovestone. She had been out of the game for ten years, but she was still a player.

The demands on her time were considerable, yet somehow Bentley managed to keep to her teaching schedule. She returned to Sacred Heart in the fall of 1955, thanks to the personal intervention of the Attorney General's Office, and she was glad to be back. She needed to hold onto the job to support herself, so she made every effort to manage her messy and sometimes unmanageable life with its ongoing crises and conflicting demands. But the position at the Catholic college was more than a paycheck, and teaching was more than a job. It was her vocation, her calling. She had known that since she was a little girl. It was a link to her past, to her mother, to a time before she had created a notorious life for herself, a life that in many ways continued to hold her captive. She saw this clearly as she fended off attacks from people like Taylor and Matusow, as she fielded phone calls from reporters, as she agreed to yet another interview with yet another agent pursuing yet another lead. If there was a way to escape the past, to firmly establish a new identity—or rather, to reclaim an old one—it was through teaching, through holding a respected position at a respectable academy. Teaching was the cornerstone of her new life. In the absence of family or friends, of passions or attachments, it *was* her life.

And so the news that Sacred Heart would be permanently closing hit her especially hard. The college had become too small to support itself, with only forty young women enrolled in the spring of 1956. Bentley got the news from the mother superior in late May. In June, she would be jobless once again, her future uncertain, the cornerstone crumbling. She was discouraged and despondent as she packed her bags for the move back to Connecticut a few weeks later. She had no idea what she would do. She had teaching credentials, but she also had—as she put it when she spoke to the New Orleans field office to say good-bye—a "background," a past that followed her and made it difficult to find work.

As it turned out, Bentley once again landed on her feet. She spent the summer living at the home of an acquaintance in Madison—her own house was rented—and then, probably with the help of supporters in the anticommunist movement and the religious community, she secured another teaching position. In the fall, she moved to Garden City, Long Island, to begin teaching English and Romance languages at the Cathedral School of St. Mary's, an all-girls Episcopal secondary school. It was her third job and her fifth change of address in seven years. She was, as an adult, almost as rootless as she had been as a child, when her parents moved every two years. But it was the life she had made, and she lived it as well as she could. She was lonely, of course. She was always lonely. But she found satisfaction in the work.

Things went well for her that fall. She seemed in control. There were no public incidents. If she drank, she drank at home, and alone.

There were no headline-making trials, no subpoenas, no trips to Washington, D.C., to testify, no attacks from those she had named long ago. The IRS left her alone, and the FBI hadn't quite figured out where she was. It seemed, for a moment, that the world had forgotten her.

Then, in January of 1957, four months into her tenure at St. Mary's, the *New York Herald Tribune* began running a twenty-four-part series on the FBI, which featured, one day, a photograph of top government informant and former communist spy, Elizabeth Bentley. One of the Long Island students saw the picture, and Bentley immediately became the hot topic of conversation in the hallways. Those who hired her knew of her past but her students did not and neither did their parents. The dean, sensing a catastrophe in the making, called an emergency assembly and asked the students to keep the information to themselves. Bentley, he stressed, was a heroine, a woman who had helped the government identify traitors.

But having someone like Elizabeth Bentley in one's midst was just too exciting to keep under wraps. The girls gossiped. Rumors flew. Someone must have gotten hold of a copy of *Out of Bondage*, because Bentley's eighth-grade English class all of a sudden seemed to know quite a bit about their teacher's notorious past, which, while juicy enough, was ripe for embellishment. The girls took some of the gossip home, just as the dean had feared.

"Did you know Miss Bentley was someone's mistress?" a thirteen-year-old girl in one of Bentley's classes informed her astonished mother at the dinner table one evening. "Did you know they found a man murdered in her apartment? Did you know," the girl confided, feeling very grown-up, "that her autobiography has some real 'moments' in it?" The mother, who had two daughters enrolled at St. Mary's and two sons at St. Paul's, the brother school, was scandalized. She immediately wrote the bishop in charge of the diocese but received only a curt acknowledgment. Furious, she tapped into the old girls' network, writing a pointed letter to the national chairwoman of the Daughters of the American Revolution (DAR), an organization to which she belonged and which Bentley, an authentic blueblood, would have been more than entitled to join.

"Do you think someone who inspires that sort of talk and thinking among minors . . . is the sort of person to have on a faculty?" she asked rhetorically. She called Bentley a "weak and twisted personality" who had "become a stool-pigeon to save her neck." The DAR chairwoman forwarded a copy of the letter to J. Edgar Hoover, who could not have been pleased at this turn of events. He wanted Bentley employed. He didn't want her broke and in trouble and on the phone bothering his agents. But the director chose not to become involved in the situation, and the old girls' network kicked in. A month after the letter arrived at DAR headquarters, Bentley learned that she would not be asked to return for the following school year. St. Mary's, it seemed, was "not entirely satisfied" with her as a teacher.

It was a severe blow—and not just because it meant she would be on the move again, that she would be out hunting for another job in another town. She was smart enough to realize that her dismissal from St. Mary's might mean something more serious and more troubling. It might mean that no matter how many years went by, no matter where she moved or how careful she was or how well she did her job, she could not outrun her past. She had done everything right in Garden City. She had been a competent and responsible teacher. She had lived quietly and kept a low profile. But so much was outside her control. Anyone from her former life could at any time surface and make waves. The newspapers could, for any reason or no reason, decide to turn the spotlight in her direction. That's what had happened with the FBI story in the *Herald Tribune*. She hadn't done anything to make news, but she was, by virtue of her past as both spy and informer, a story waiting to happen, a perennial public figure, fair game always in season. It was a situation of her own making, and she was trapped in it. And so, as much as she could help herself by finding a new job and a new place to live, as much as she could take control by refusing to give up or give in, by continuing to try to live an ordinary life, she must have also felt helpless.

She moved back to Connecticut that summer, back to her house in Madison, and tried once again to restart her life. It wasn't easy. She couldn't find a teaching job, so she took employment as a secretary in the office of a Hartford construction company. For a woman with degrees from Vassar and Columbia, with six years of teaching experience and several years' experience in running a company, this could not have been satisfying work. But she had a plan. That fall she started taking classes at Trinity College in Hartford, going to school in the evenings after work and on Saturdays. She would earn her Connecticut teaching certificate. Then, she hoped, a number of jobs would be open to her.

She kept to the plan through the winter and into the spring. But this time, starting over proved to be too much. In early March 1958, as she was leaving Trinity one night after class, something happened. She couldn't explain it herself. All she knew was that she got in her car to drive home and, an hour and a half later, she found herself back at the college with no memory of where she had been or what she had done, no sense that any time had passed. She called it a "blackout," but had she really blacked out, had she actually lost consciousness, it is unlikely that she would have made it back to the college unscathed. Whatever happened—transient amnesia, a momentary mental break-down, a kind of trance or stupor—Bentley thought it might be due to overwork. Certainly her schedule was taxing and left little time to relax. But her "blackout" that night could just as easily been caused by stress or depression or drinking or some combination of psycho-logical factors.

The psychiatrist whom Trinity obtained for her couldn't figure out what happened either. He put her in Hartford Hospital for observation, concluding, after a week, that her past was in part responsible for her present difficulty. She should, he counseled, "try to put her espionage activity out of her mind." But that would be difficult, for even though Bentley wanted to move forward in her new life, the FBI was always there to drag her back to her past. On May 5, a month and a half after being released from the hospital, Bentley was at the New Haven field office looking at photographs in sixty-five cases still pending. The agents there thought she was in good health, and she seemed to them both friendly and cooperative. But not far beneath the surface, things were still not going well.

She had to sell her house that spring. Although the doctor told her she could go back to work after she left the hospital, she couldn't bring herself to do it. She dropped out of school, too. The strain was too much. Still, she needed money to live and funds to pay for her medical and hospital bills, and the house was her only asset. It was also the only home she had known as an adult, the only roots she had ever put down. But it sold in April, and Bentley, homeless and jobless now, moved to New Haven where her Catholic connections helped her get back on her feet. By the time she visited the New Haven office, ostensibly in good spirits, she was living at the Highland Heights Orphanage, where the nuns gave her room and board in exchange for help with the children.

A few weeks later, New York agents called her at the orphanage, asking if she would meet with them in connection with an espionage case they were working on. She agreed, but the day before the interview was scheduled, she presented herself at the New Haven field office where she told agents she no longer wanted to be contacted by the FBI. She had felt for a long time, she said, that she must make a complete break with her past. Interviews with agents and government committees always served to keep her in a "highly nervous state," she told the agents. She was tense and on edge. She suffered severe headaches. And so, she was serving them notice: Elizabeth Bentley would no longer be available. She wanted out.

The agents were taken aback, but it was not the first time an informant had balked, and they knew what to do. They treated her gently, praising her past contributions, stressing the importance of the information she had given them, and making as compelling a case as they could for her continuing assistance. This seemed to calm her, and she agreed to come back the next day to meet with the New York agents. But when she arrived at the office, she was visibly upset. She had now definitely decided she would no longer be available for interviews, she told the agents. Delving into the past was no good for her. There was nothing more to talk about. This was, she said, "good-bye."

Still, the agents pressed her. Would she be unavailable even in "the most urgent matters affecting the welfare of the country?" Bentley couldn't quite close the door. She would have to decide "when the occasion arose," she said.

In New Haven, in New York, and at headquarters in Washington, D.C., the FBI considered what to do about Bentley. She was valuable, but she was also volatile. She had been enormously useful, but she had also been, at times, a nuisance, a burden, and a hazard. But there were cases pending. The Cold War was still being waged. The communists—abroad and at home—were still the archenemy. In the end, it was decided that the Bureau would refrain from contacting her unless there was a matter of "great necessity." No agent, no field office should contact her without prior authorization from headquarters. New Haven was instructed to keep informed of Bentley's address and employment but stay out of her life.

Meanwhile, Bentley did what she knew how to do: She survived. In the fall of 1958 she found a position teaching English and French at St. Joseph Academy in West Hartford, where she rented a room in a private home.

# Chapter 24

# The Wayward Girl
# Comes Home

*D*EAR MR. HOOVER," Elizabeth Bentley wrote in the summer of 1959, "lately it has come to my attention that there are still some unenlightened people who still believe that I am not a loyal American. This is a great handicap, especially since I am at present in search of a position." Again. For the fourth time in as many years, she was on the job market, a fifty-one-year-old woman with a spotty employment record and a checkered past. Her one-year stint at St. Joseph ended in the spring, and, for reasons unknown, she had not been rehired. Now she was spending the summer looking for work, and it was not going well. Hunting for a new position every year was exhausting and humiliating. It kept her perpetually anxious and permanently rootless. She had to do something about it. So she turned, once again, to those she had become accustomed to turning to when she was in trouble, the FBI. This time, she went straight to the top.

Bentley had never met Hoover, or even spoken with him, but she knew her name would be familiar to the director. And she knew that a letter of reference from a man who might be considered the nation's single most impeccable source could help her. Would Hoover write a letter on her behalf, Bentley asked, which would "for once and all allay doubts in the minds of school superintendents and principals and in the minds of the general public as well"?

Hoover answered three days later with a curt but serviceable note. He was a careful man, and given what he knew about Bentley's instability and past problems, he was not about to go out on a limb for her. He had not gotten as far as he had by giving much away. "Your cooperation with this Bureau is a matter of public record," he wrote, neatly finessing any personal endorsement on his part. Then he quoted from a public statement he had made before SISS in 1953: "All information furnished by Miss Bentley, which was susceptible to check, has proven to be correct." The terse letter was probably not the enthusiastic endorsement of loyalty that Bentley was looking for, but it was something, and she was deeply grateful for it. "It was most kind of you to rescue me," she wrote to the director when, using his letter as collateral, she finally secured a position for the fall.

That September, she began teaching English at Long Lane School for Girls, a job she took gladly not just because it was gainful employment but because Long Lane was a special kind of school. Located on a hill overlooking Middletown, Connecticut, Long Lane was a residential institution run by the state for girls who had gotten into trouble with the law. It was not a prison or a place of punishment—there were no bars or wardens—but rather an old-fashioned home for wayward girls that had been established in the 1860s to instill "friendless children" with moral rectitude. The girls, 175 of them between the ages of eleven and seventeen, were runaways and truants, shoplifters and petty thieves, girls who drank and smoked and ran with boys. They were girls whose "personality and behavioral disorders" were "unacceptable to the community," girls who could not be controlled by their parents or who had no parents or who suffered from, as the Long Lane mission statement delicately put it, "poor family relationships." For many, Long Lane was the nicest place they had ever lived. For Bentley, it was a place she could fit in, a misfit among misfits.

The sprawling facility included ten brick cottages set in a circle on the treed campus, each with its own fireplace, each staffed by a housekeeper who taught the girls how to cook and a housemother who greeted them in the afternoon with cups of hot chocolate. There was a working farm on the grounds, with an orchard, vegetable and flower gardens, and a greenhouse, all of which supplied the school with fresh produce in season and flowers for the dining-room tables where the girls took their meals. There was also a fully accredited twelve-classroom school building where a dozen or more teachers, supported by a psychiatric consultant, a full-time psychologist, three counselors, and six social workers, attempted to turn these girls' lives around.

"We . . . rehabilitate the young through kindly and understanding discipline," Bentley wrote to Hoover late that fall after she had settled in. She was living on campus until she could find her own place. "I am very much interested in this experiment, because I have come to believe that the best way to defeat Communism is to build up good citizens in the coming generation," she wrote.

She may or may not have been instilling patriotism in the next generation, but Bentley was teaching writing and literature, and serving as the adviser to the school's publication, *The Tower.* She was, by all accounts, a good teacher, interested in her students and particularly adept at bringing out their writing talents. But she also kept her distance. Many of the teachers became deeply involved in the lives of their students, befriending them outside the classroom, acting as surrogate mothers or older sisters, staying after school to join in extracurricular activities. They worked alongside the girls in the gardens in the spring, and ice-skated with them on a nearby pond in the winter. They stayed late to direct the choir, coach sports, and oversee any number of clubs. Bentley gave some time to *The Tower,* but then she had been hired with the understanding that she would be the adviser. Mostly she just did her job and went back to her quarters. She commuted into Hartford in the evenings and on weekends to complete her master's degree in education at Trinity College, which gave her little free time. But even after she was awarded her degree in June of 1960, she did not integrate herself into life at Long Lane. After years in the spotlight, she craved, more than anything else, solitude and anonymity.

The teachers and social workers knew of her past, and it was fodder for gossip, but no one spoke of it openly. In a place built on the understanding that good girls could go wrong, Bentley was not shunned. But neither was she sought after. She never socialized. She was, as she had always been, a loner. One of her colleagues, a woman who taught physical education, was sure she was an alcoholic. Rumor had it that Bentley kept a bottle in her desk. But however serious her drinking problem was, she didn't give in to it. She was always there for school the next morning, always prepared and always composed. Her colleagues looked the other way. No one confronted her. No one tried to help. What she did on her own time was her own business.

When she could afford it, she moved down the hill to a small apartment in a particularly shabby section of Middletown. It was an old, working-class Connecticut River town with a Main Street going to seed, a community of quarry workers and fishermen, of tough Italians down by the river, the antithesis of the picture-postcard village of Bentley's childhood. Within the year, she moved again, this time to a little house on Route 5A in East Hampton, eight miles or so from the school, where she ensured her isolation by having no telephone. But soon she was living at yet another address, a cottage on Cherry Hill Road a few minutes from the small, picturesque town of Middlefield. Surrounded by orchards and cornfields and solid nineteenth-century farmhouses, she at last settled in. She had a life, now, that she could live.

Although she had severed ties with the FBI after her "blackout," refusing to be interviewed or contacted by agents, she kept Hoover personally informed of her activities, sending him a number of letters through the early 1960s. Hoover replied politely each time, telling her that he hoped she would continue to keep him advised of her progress. Bentley probably thought she had found a friend in the director, or at least a person sincerely concerned with her well-being.

She had no one else like that in her life. But Hoover had other motives, as he was careful to point out to his associates at the Bureau, lest they thought that the director was actually taking a personal interest in Bentley. At the bottom of one of the letters Hoover sent to Bentley was typed, for the benefit of the permanent file: "It is believed that we should express interest in the continued progress of Miss Bentley inasmuch as her services may still be needed at some future date."

Meanwhile, the agents themselves kept their distance. Early in 1960, they decided not to reinterview her in connection with a loyalty case, in view of her "emotional condition." But later that year, agents did try to approach her about an ongoing espionage investigation. She refused to help, insisting once again that that part of her life was over. But her refusal was both amiable and polite. She told the agents that she had only the best feelings toward the FBI and that she and the director had exchanged several friendly letters. But just as Hoover had an ulterior motive for writing those letters, so too, it seemed, did Bentley. It happened she needed the Bureau's help getting security clearance for a job that summer at General Dynamics.

Although it was official policy to leave her alone except in extraordinary circumstances, agents from the New Haven field office contacted Bentley again in January of 1961, driving up to Long Lane to show her photographs in connection with a decade-long espionage investigation. Bentley agreed to take a quick look at the photos but was unable to identify the man in question. In November of that year, gathering evidence for a criminal case against the New York School for Marxist Studies, the FBI contacted Bentley once again. Would she be willing to testify in the case? Bentley told the New York agents that she had no information related to the matter and that she was "absolutely not willing to testify." Finally, they left her alone.

And so she settled into her job at Long Lane, becoming a fixture in that cloistered community of women and girls, feeling now that she was living up to her potential as a teacher, that she was making a real difference in the lives of her disadvantaged students. Her mother would have been proud. It was a long way from the classrooms of Foxcroft, the elite boarding school where she began her teaching career almost thirty years before, and it had been a hard journey. But finally, she had arrived somewhere. This was a job she knew she could and would keep. One school year ended and another began, then another and another. In the fall of 1963, she began her fifth year at Long Lane.

She must have known something was wrong for months, maybe even longer, before she went to see the doctor. There would have been nausea, heartburn, bloating, changes in bowel movements, and stomach pain, a lot of stomach pain. But she had suffered through a difficult and protracted menopause, and she drank more than she should, so it may have been easy for her to dismiss her growing discomfort. Or she may have suspected something was going wrong and just didn't want to know. In any case, in mid-November of 1963, she could no longer ignore her symptoms. She felt a bulge in her abdomen, a lump that shouldn't be there. Taking a leave from Long Lane, she checked herself into Grace New Haven Hospital the week before Thanksgiving, the week before Yasha's death twenty years before. After two weeks of tests and observation, on December 2, she underwent exploratory surgery.

The doctors found cancer everywhere in the abdominal cavity. There was so much that they knew they couldn't remove it all. It was so widespread that they couldn't tell where it had originated. It could have started as intestinal or colon cancer, like her mother's. It could have started in her ovaries, which might have explained her troublesome menopause. It could have started in her stomach. It didn't matter. It was inoperable, and it was going to kill her. She was sewn back up and wheeled into her room. When she awoke, the surgeon would have to tell her the bad news.

But she never awoke. The surgery may have been too much of a shock to her system. There may have been internal bleeding that went unnoticed. She could have thrown a clot. Whatever the cause, less than twenty-four hours after her operation, Elizabeth Bentley was dead. She was just one month shy of her fifty-sixth birthday.

She made headlines one last time. The *New York Times* ran the story as its lead obituary, devoting twenty-nine paragraphs to the significance of her life and concluding that her revelations helped "set the tone of American political life for nearly a decade." The *Herald Tribune* ran a six-column story that presented Bentley just as she had tried to present herself to the public: a naïve young woman snared by communism who saw the light and repented. The *Washington Post* credited her with unmasking a "web of wartime red treachery in this country." *Newsweek* noted her passing in its Transition section, explaining that she broke with the Reds because of "a good old-fashioned New England conscience." The right-wing *National Review* paid homage, calling her a courageous woman whose life should serve as a reminder of "the kind of sacrifice that can be necessary to preserve [the] country." She would have been pleased that the final spotlight illuminated a brave and loyal American. In death, at least, she was exonerated.

Elizabeth Bentley left no survivors, no close relations, no grieving friends. Her earlier conversion to Catholicism seemed to afford her little solace. She had not been in a Catholic church for years. Except for Yasha so very long ago, she had forged no strong ties. From her hospital bed, in the weeks prior to her surgery, she reached out to her only enduring connection: the FBI, the agents who had treated her well over the years. They had valued her even when she was at her most difficult. They had seen her through both emotional and financial crises. They had bailed her out, pulled strings, picked her up at train stations, drove her to doctors' appointments, listened to her troubles. She had depended on them, and on their boss in Washington, D.C., for support as much as they had depended on her for information. And the Bureau had shown its respect. She had been paid periodically for her work, like a professional. And, most important, J. Edgar Hoover himself had kept in touch. As much as anyone was, the agents were her family, from the New Haven group, who had tracked her for years, to the New York office, where she had made her closest contacts, to headquarters, where she was on a first-name basis with Hoover's top assistants. So it was to the FBI she turned in her last days.

Several times during what she could not have known were the final two weeks of her life, Bentley called the New Haven office and talked at length to the agents there, keeping them informed of her illness and taking every opportunity to express her "warm regard and affection" for the Bureau. These may have been the only phone calls she made, her most intimate contact during her most vulnerable time.

Two days after her death, on a frigid and snowy Thursday, a small service was held for Bentley at Roberts Funeral Home in Middletown. She had a cousin or two who probably attended. Some of her Long Lane colleagues would have been there. A few FBI agents showed up. Afterward, her body was transported to Cedar Hills Cemetery bordering one of Hartford's oldest neighborhoods. The cemetery was a big, sprawling, pastoral place, all rolling hills and grassy knolls, meticulously kept, bucolic, and serene. Elizabeth Bentley's grave site was across from a small pond and by the foot of a forty-foot sugar maple that would leaf out to shade her in the summer and burn a spectacular scarlet and gold in the fall. It was an idyllic place, the kind of spot one would choose for a picnic. But the day Bentley was put in the ground, the pond was a sheet of ice, and the big tree was bare, its branches stark against an ashen sky.

She was buried among her father's people. Above her and to the right, in a neat row, were the graves of her aunt May Bentley, her father's sister; and May's husband, Howard. Below her, and off to the right, in another neat row, were the graves of her mother, Mary; her father, Charles; her paternal grandparents; and two more of her Bentley aunts. She is among her father's people, but she is not *of* them. Her gravestone—the plainest of granite markers—sits off to the side, out of line, disconnected. By itself, under the big tree by the lovely pond, it is self-contained and sovereign, unfettered by the rigid geometry that surrounds it, a place for an independent woman, a Clever Girl come to rest.

# Epilogue

$\mathscr{E}$ LIZABETH BENTLEY outwitted her fate. Destined
for a tidy little existence lived quietly and anony-
mously, she instead created for herself a notorious life, a risky life, a
life of conflict and contradiction, and ultimately, a life of meaning
and importance.

She was, as the Soviets code-named her, *umnitsa*—a good and
clever girl who knew her job and did it well. But she was far more
than a KGB worker bee. She helped to change history. As head of
two of the most productive spy rings during the golden age of Soviet
espionage, she was arguably the most important American operative
working for the Soviet secret police, and certainly the most important American woman in the apparatus. When she did an about-face
and became the FBI's top informant and the government's star witness, her defection almost single-handedly halted Soviet spying in the
United States for years.

It was her statement to the FBI that provided the first link to
Julius Rosenberg. It was her headline-making accusations that forced
Truman to take the "communist conspiracy" seriously. It was her

public testimony, speeches, and media appearances that set the stage for the McCarthy era.

But she was no McCarthyite. Unlike the senator and his ilk, she knew what she was talking about. Her statements, many of which were later validated by the Venona cables and by materials in Soviet archives, were truth, not fabrication; an honest report—although perhaps occasionally muddled or exaggerated—not an overheated act of delusion and spite. And what she was talking about was *spying*— criminal activity—not just whether someone belonged to the Communist Party or a left-wing organization that might or might not have connections to the Party, not just if one had friends who appeared to be a little pink around the edges or believed in certain causes. McCarthy was about innuendo and inference. Bentley was about actions and deeds. But the same congressmen who cut their teeth quizzing Bentley under the klieg lights went on to rally behind Joe McCarthy and create the climate of paranoia and fear that permeated the early and mid-1950s. Elizabeth Bentley opened that door.

Her life embodied deep contradictions, the most basic of which was that she was a good girl who had done wrong. Her loyalty to her principles and her loyalty to a man translated into disloyalty to her government. And then her awakened conscience—plus a healthy dose of fear and a sprinkling of revenge—turned her inside out again. Sinner and saint, villain and hero, traitor and patriot, she was one or the other, to the left or the right, for more than twenty years. To herself, she was both, and the dichotomy was as hard to escape as it was to live with.

Contradictions were at the core of who she was. Her family had some of the deepest roots in America, yet she herself was rootless, a woman who never found a home or belonged to a place, geographic or spiritual. Brought up by straight-laced New Englanders to tread carefully in their sedate footsteps, she had an undeniable wild streak that led her someplace else entirely. She was an emotionally distant woman, yet she made a white-hot connection that changed her life.

She was a woman who both craved attention and ran from it, who purposely sought the spotlight and then couldn't stand the heat, who escaped into anonymity and then couldn't stand the quiet.

She was a woman who alternately gave up control—to the party, to alcohol, perhaps, even, to Golos—but who also fought fiercely, even recklessly, to keep it. She was an unwitting pawn, used by Hoover to consolidate his power, by anti–New Deal congressmen who wanted to bring down Truman and erase the Roosevelt legacy. Yet she also knew how to work the system, how to manipulate her new friends for her own purposes. Alternately helpless and indomitable, she could seem undone by life's vicissitudes and yet always found a way to take care of herself.

She was in many ways a woman ahead of her time, or perhaps a woman outside of time. She had little interest in domestic life. She never married or had children. She seldom sought the company or camaraderie of other women. She was a spy but no Mata Hari, a lover but no seductress, a teacher of children but no nurturer. Decade by decade, she ran counter to the stereotypes of both her gender and the times. In the 1920s, she was a quiet, bookish girl, not a "flaming youth." In the early days of the Depression, she enjoyed the pleasures of Europe, not the realities of the breadline. In the 1940s, while thousands of other women worked in the war industries and waited for their men to come home, she worked against the government, undercover and underground, the secret lover of a secret agent. In the 1950s, while other women of her class propelled themselves into domestic life surrounded by the spoils of postwar prosperity, she lived alone in rented rooms and moved from job to job.

Elizabeth Bentley was no feminist heroine. But she was a woman who lived life on her own terms, a woman who made her own way in the world. Without friends or family, without the ties that not only bind but support and strengthen, she fashioned and then refashioned a life. She refused to be ordinary. She refused to be intimidated. She was a troubled soul, but she refused to give in to her demons. Elizabeth Bentley was no victim. She was, for better or worse, the author of her own conflicted and tumultuous life.

# Acknowledgments

*W*ORKING ON THIS book brought me into contact with fascinating people I would never have otherwise known—surely one of the great joys of being a writer. From the octogenarian radicals who lived these times to the former FBI agents who monitored them, many people helped me tell this story.

I owe an extraordinary debt to espionage expert and author Hayden Peake, former army intelligence officer, former CIA official, current curator of the Historical Intelligence Collection library at the CIA—and an open-minded, thoughtful, and truly generous man. He answered scores of questions, engaged in lively dialogue, challenged me to understand a diversity of views, sent me lists of books, and lent me important items from his private collection. Former FBI agent Robert Lamphere, author of *The FBI-KGB War: A Special Agent's Story*, spent hours recounting these times for me. I am sorry that he did not live to see the publication of this book. I also want to especially acknowledge John Haynes, twentieth century political historian at the Library of Congress, and Harvey Klehr, Emory University political science professor, not only for the personal help they gave me fielding questions, locating documents, suggesting sources, and offering encouragement but also for the high standards they set with their own important work. Anyone who writes about or tries to understand this period is in their debt. This book would not have been possible without the extraordinary work of Allen Weinstein, president of The Center for Democracy, and his Russian colleague, Alexander Vassiliev, in the KGB archives.

I want to thank the people who talked or corresponded with me, sharing their memories of the time and place I have tried to re-create here: Jack Beckerman, Herman Bly, Shirley Coddington, Hope Hale Davis, Merrill Golden, Dorothy Healey, Don Jardine, Dorothy Sanem Levitt, Anthony Litrento, Bud Rubin, Don Shannon, Katrina Smathers, Nathaniel Weyl, and Frank Wilkinson.

In Connecticut, I had considerable help from Joan Wells, keeper of the Turrill family history; Carl DeMilia, reference librarian at the New Milford Public Library, who found important documents and kindly broke a few rules for me; and Liba Furman at the *New Milford Times*. At Vassar, I had help from special collections librarian Dean Rogers, registrar Dan Giannini, college historian Elizabeth Daniels, and Miss Sarah H. McLean (Class of 1930).

Cleader McCoy-Brooks at the FBI FOIA reading room was both efficient and good-natured. Doug Macavey at Long Lane School, Sister Carolyn Farrell at Mundelein College, Betty Robin at Foxcroft School, and Roger Desmond in Hartford were all very helpful. I am indebted to Robert Roeker who, as a master's student in the mid-1980s, singled out Elizabeth Bentley for study. Jane Marcellus and Jon Arakaki ably assisted with library research. Jackson Kessler Hager—my first-born son, who is all of a sudden both taller and smarter than me—lent important technical assistance, including digitizing many of the images reproduced in this book.

A special place in biblio heaven is reserved for University of Oregon government documents librarian Tom Stave, who either knows everything or knows almost everything. I also want to acknowledge the experts who graciously allowed me to pick their brains: University of Oregon law professor and assistant dean Margie Paris, my on-call legal expert; Dr. Peter Kovach, my medical expert; David Weiss, my man in Manhattan; and Bonnie Mann, my authority on all things Louisiana.

Special thanks to my high-octane agent, Sandy Dijkstra, for her unstinting support of my work, and to Babette Sparr for all her efforts on my behalf. I am much in debt to copy editor extraordinaire Olga Gardner Galvin, who corrected me (with utmost tact) in three languages. As for my editor, Julia Serebrinsky, I cannot adequately express my thanks—or my admiration. She is a writer's dream, the most clear-eyed and yet kindest of critics, and, in the heart of commercial publishing, a true lover of ideas. Her support and encouragement have meant more to me than she knows (until now, of course). I owe her this book.

Finally, and most profoundly, I thank Tom Hager, my sounding board, my research partner, my best and toughest first reader, my trusted colleague in all things literary and otherwise. His contributions to this book, and to my life, are immeasurable.

# Notes

CHAPTER 1: CONNECTICUT YANKEE

12 "surrounded by rolling farmlands": The history of New Milford comes from "Our Town," *New Milford Gazette,* Jan. 2, 1914; Doris Addis, "A Chronological History of New Milford" at *www.nmhistorical .org;* New Milford Trust for Historic Preservation and New Milford Chamber of Commerce brochures; and author's interview with New Milford nonagenarian Merrill Golden, Sept. 27, 2000.

12 "spinster named Mary Charlotte Turrill": The name on birth and death certificates was Mary, but family genealogy records refer to her as May, as do some of her descendants. I have chosen to use Mary to avoid confusion with Charles Bentley's sister, May Bentley. See Katherine Elizabeth Wells, *Turrill-Wells Genealogy,* pp. 56, 60; also author's correspondence with Ruth Wells Stuhl, June 30, 2001. "Turrill" has been variously spelled Tyrrell and Terrill in family records.

12 "born in the summer of 1877": The history of the Turrill family comes from Wells, *Genealogy.* See pp. 3–4, 12, 17–22, 26–28, 56, 59–60. Olmstead, *Red Spy Queen,* accuses Bentley of inventing the connection between Roger Sherman and her family to "add to the shock value of her autobiography." If the connection was invented—which is unlikely—then the invention was part of family lore long before Bentley was born.

13 "enrolling Choctaw and Sioux students": Wells, *Genealogy,* pp. 56, 60. On Northfield School, see "Northfield Mount Hermon: Long a Champion of Diversity," *US News & World Report,* May 14, 2001.

13 "Mary Charlotte's ancestor Roger Tyrrell": Wells, *Genealogy,* pp. 4, 56.

13 "the junior, but more active, partner": Biographical material on Bentley from Record of Inhabitants of Morristown, New Jersey, June 13, 1870; Wells, *Genealogy,* p. 56; *Two Centuries of New Milford,* New Milford Historical Committee Bi-centennial Celebration, 1907; commentary by C. H. Booth in C. H. Booth & Bentley advertisement,

*New Milford Gazette,* Dec. 28, 1900. Information on Booth & Bentley comes from various advertisements in *New Milford Gazette,* 1900–1910, and the Historic Resources Inventory, Connecticut Historical Commission.

14 "they named Elizabeth Turrill Bentley": Wells, *Genealogy,* pp. 56–57; Elizabeth Bentley's birth recorded by State of Connecticut Bureau of Vital Statistics. Information on Terrace Place from author's interview with Merrill Golden.

14 "a healthy dose of advertising": Information on Charles Bentley's employment comes from New Milford city directories, 1900–1911; and the *New Milford Times,* Feb. 1914–June 1915.

15 "a western Pennsylvania steeltown": Roeker, "The Story of a Communist Agent," pp. 4–5.

15 "an old-fashioned New England upbringing": Bentley notes her "overly stern New England upbringing" in Bentley, *Out of Bondage,* p. 69, and again in the 1944 autobiographical sketch she wrote for the NKVD, cited in Weinstein and Vassiliev, *Haunted Wood,* p. 88.

16 "they'd make it that way?" Bentley recounts this conversation and discusses her mother's experiences in McKeesport in Bentley, *Out of Bondage,* pp. 12–13.

16 "the Golden Eaglet, in Girl Scouts": Wells, *Genealogy,* p. 57.

16 "an eighth grade teacher": The Bentleys' employment in Rochester is mentioned in May, *Un-American Activities,* p. 78, and by Roeker, p. 5.

17 "both resolute and unhappy": Information on Bentley at East High and the school itself comes from *The Orient,* East High School's yearbook, 1926. Her senior picture is on p. 27. Additional information on Rochester comes from the good people at the local history desk of the Rochester Public Library.

17 "a position teaching school, like her mother": Bentley, *Out of Bondage,* p. 5.

17 "enroll in the fall": Vassar tuition noted by Elizabeth Daniels in "The History of Vassar College," at *www.vassar.edu.* Scholarship information from the Vassar Student Handbook, 1926–1927, p. 42.

CHAPTER 2: SAD SACK

19 "an obligation to live a meaningful life": "Convocation Opens Academic Year," *Vassar Miscellany News,* Sept. 25, 1926, p. 1.

19 "Vassar's most famous and generous trustee, John D. Rockefeller": The history of Vassar's buildings is well documented in Daniels, *From Main to Mudd.*

19 "life at Vassar for those who lived it fully": Edna St. Vincent Millay, a student at Vassar twelve years before Bentley, certainly experienced

it this way. Nancy Milford describes the Vassar atmosphere well in *Savage Beauty* (New York: Random House, 2001), pp. 107–130.

19 "opportunities to write for the college newspaper, the college magazine, the yearbook": Vassar rules, rituals, and activities are from the 1926–1927 Vassar Student Handbook, the 1930 Vassar yearbook, and various issues of the campus newspaper, the *Vassar Miscellany News.*

20 "neither her junior nor her senior proms": Elizabeth Bentley's name appears in no issue of the *Vassar Miscellany News* for any of the four years she attended college. The names of girls involved in various activities, including attendance at dances and proms, were regularly published.

20 "She excelled at nothing": Elizabeth Bentley's Vassar transcripts, 1926–1930, courtesy of the Vassar College Registrar.

20 "didn't have a single boyfriend": Interview with Elizabeth Bliss conducted by Hayden Peake, Oct. 28, 1987 (notes graciously provided to the author by Mr. Peake).

21 "full expression in the lecture halls on campus": On McCracken, see Daniels, *Main to Mudd,* p. 9; *Vassar Miscellany News,* Nov. 6, 1926.

21 "Scott Nearing lectured on Soviet Russia": All reported in the *Vassar Miscellany News* and listed in the online history of Vassar at the college's Web site.

21 "student progressives, socialists and communists alike": Vassar Student Handbook 1926–27, pp. 112–116.

22 "not believing in anything": Bentley makes this point in *Out of Bondage,* p. 14. Also see her congressional testimony in *Communist Activities Among Aliens,* May 13, 1949, p. 122.

22 "a struggle against disease, dirt, poverty, and ignorance": Reported in the *Vassar Miscellany News,* Oct. 6, 1928 and Feb. 9, 1929.

22 "including those of Elizabeth Bentley": Bentley, *Out of Bondage,* pp. 9, 15.

23 "she enrolled in two more drama classes": Background on Hallie Flanagan from author's interview with Elizabeth Daniels, Oct. 23, 2000; Daniels, *Bridges to the World,* pp. 192, 197, 200, 202; *Vassar Miscellany News,* Jan. 15, 1927 and Nov. 16, 1927. Bentley discusses Flanagan's influence in *Out of Bondage,* p. 15.

23 "four months shy of her fifty-second birthday": Mary Bentley death certificate, New York State Department of Health.

24 "good education for these young women of Vassar": Vassar yearbook 1930, p. 55.

24 "a shipboard fling with a British engineer": Noted by Bentley in her 1944 autobiography written for the NKGB. See Weinstein and Vassiliev, *Haunted Wood,* p. 88.

24  "an aristocratic girls' boarding school in Virginia": FBI report [date illegible] No. 65-56402-25.

CHAPTER 3: AWAKENINGS

26  "a number of pillows and a clown's red nose": Information on Foxcroft and Bentley's time there comes from *Tally-Ho,* the 1932 yearbook; author's correspondence with school archivist, Betty Robin; Foxcroft catalogs and recruiting brochures and the school's Web site, *www.foxcroft.org.*

26  "He was an experience she had to have": Bentley notes her amorous experiences in her 1944 autobiography written for the NKVD. See Weinstein and Vassiliev, *Haunted Wood,* p. 88.

27  "that helped to pay tuition bills": Bentley, *Out of Bondage,* p. 3.

27  "sponsored by the Institute of International Education": Information about Bentley's graduate education is from her signed statement to the FBI, Nov. 30, 1945, p. 2, Bentley FBI file No. 65-56402-220. See also Roeker, *The Story of a Communist Agent,* p. 7, and Hayden Peake's afterword in Bentley, *Out of Bondage,* 1988 edition, p. 224.

27  "a naughty young woman with a sometimes foul mouth": This according to information dug up by private investigator working for William Remington's lawyer. See "Memorandum of Conversation with Dr. Lombardo," Oct. 6, 1950, Joseph Rauh papers. See also May, *Un-American Activities,* pp. 78–79. Peake got confirmation of this during an interview with FBI Special Agent Jack Danahy, Peake's correspondence with author.

28  "number of their live births was announced to all": Piers Brendon, *The Dark Valley: A Panorama of the 1930s,* New York: Knopf, 2000; Victoria de Grazia, *How Fascism Ruled Women: Italy, 1922–1945,* Berkeley: University of California Press, 1992.

28  "Mussolini's successful attempts to control young people": Bentley acknowledged under cross-examination during the 1951 Remington trial that she had joined Gruppo Universitate Fascisti. But there is no evidence to support assumptions that she flirted with the ideology. In fact, given the liberal influence of her mother and her exposure to the world of progressive ideas at Vassar—not to mention what she saw in the streets of Italy—it would be most difficult to believe that Bentley found anything appealing about fascism.

28  "perhaps from one of her Italian professors": The implication was that she had slept with the professor who directed her thesis, the prominent literary critic Mario Casella—or, as one of her detractors said a decade and a half after the fact, that Casella assigned his assistant to write the paper for her. There is no way to judge the veracity

of this. This same source told other lurid tales of Bentley's days in Florence, which she categorically denied. See "Memorandum of Conversation" and May, *Un-American Activities,* p. 79.

28 "and headed home to New York": Bentley, *Out of Bondage,* p. 3.

29 "in order to support herself and pay tuition": Bentley's attendance at Columbia is detailed in FBI report [date illegible] in Bentley FBI file No. 65-56402-25.

29 "In New York City alone, 650,000 people were unemployed": New York State Department of Labor, "Annual Report of the Industrial Commission of State of New York," Albany: J. R. Lyons, 1934, p. 83; National Unemployment Census, 1937.

29 "laid off by the city in a money-saving consolidation move": As reported in the *New York Times,* Jan. 21, 1934, p. 1.

30 "It was a grim and miserable time": Details from the *New York Times* coverage of the Depression: Mar. 2–3, Feb. 6, Apr. 19, July 10, 1934. Also helpful were T. H. Watkins, *The Great Depression: America in the 1930s,* Boston: Little, Brown and Co., 1993; Hope Hale Davis, *Great Day Coming;* Murray Kempton, *Part of Our Time.*

30 "pay next month's rent, let alone that night's dinner": Bentley, *Out of Bondage,* p. 3.

31 "being forged by the Soviet Union": Nearing, *Must We Starve?* pp. v, viii–ix, 215.

31 "a clarifying experience, a crucible": This is a point most articulately made by Gornick in *The Romance of American Communism,* p. 95.

CHAPTER 4: CIRCLE OF FRIENDS

33 "only a term away from a master's degree": Bentley, *Out of Bondage,* p. 3.

34 "Fuhr would just smile": Bentley talks about Fuhr in *Out of Bondage,* pp. 3–4, 6, and in her signed statement to the FBI, Nov. 30, 1945, p. 2. See also Belfrage, *The American Inquisition,* p. 19.

34 "Would Bentley like to come to the next meeting?": This is Bentley's version, in *Out of Bondage,* pp. 6–7. Belfrage, p. 19, whom Bentley named as a spy and who had every reason to try to blacken her reputation, writes that Fuhr disliked Bentley, and that Bentley "nagged" her to go to a meeting until Fuhr "relented." There is no reason to believe this version.

34 "she was impressed": Peake's afterword in Bentley, *Out of Bondage* (1988), p. 225, concerning membership.

35 "in the face of such enthusiasm and fervor": Bentley, *Out of Bondage,* p. 7.

35  "money to spend on fancy fronts": Bentley, *Out of Bondage,* p. 10; Bentley's signed statement to the FBI, p. 2.

35  "She liked him": Bentley, *Out of Bondage,* p. 10.

36  "envious of her new friends": Bentley, *Out of Bondage,* pp. 8–9.

36  "draw good liberals into the revolutionary cause": Later, the organization would be described as a kind of "farm system" for the Communist Party (Gabriel Almond, *The Appeals of Communism,* Princeton, NJ: Princeton University Press, 1954, p. 5) and the "largest, most seductive and successful of the front organizations" (Peake's afterword in Bentley, *Out of Bondage* [1988], p. 225). Of its eight thousand or so members, perhaps ten percent were what would later be called "card-carrying" communists, according to Klehr, *Heyday of American Communism,* p. 372. The organization itself had been founded under communist sponsorship a few years earlier at the World Congress Against War held in Amsterdam. See Ralph Lord Roy, *Communism and the Churches,* New York: Harcourt, Brace and World, 1960, pp. 83–86.

38  "I am a communist": Details of this remembered conversation can be found in Bentley, *Out of Bondage,* pp. 11–18.

38  "seemed to know how to get there": Bentley discusses the attraction of communism in *Out of Bondage,* p. 21; in her congressional testimony, *Communist Activities Among Aliens,* May 13, 1949, p. 122; and in her testimony before HUAC, *Hearings Regarding Communist Espionage,* July 13, 1948, p. 540.

38  "with power and moral imagination": These are the words Gornick used to explain the appeal of communism to liberals of the day, in Gornick, *The Romance of American Communism,* p. 13.

39  "the tenets of Christian brotherhood her mother had taught her": Bentley, *Out of Bondage,* p. 23.

39  "a home for the homeless": These comments, in different form, were told to Gornick when she interviewed former and present communists for her book, *The Romance of American Communism.*

39  "nobody could become a somebody": Gitlow, *The Whole of Their Lives,* p. 236.

39  "But of course, we're not": Bentley, *Out of Bondage,* p. 19.

40  "contingent on Bentley joining the Party": Bentley reports the struggle with her decision in *Out of Bondage,* pp. 21–25.

40  "to stand up for her convictions": As recounted by Bentley in *Out of Bondage,* pp. 26–27.

41  " 'Welcome to our ranks, comrade,' she said": This is Bentley's version of the events recounted in *Out of Bondage,* pp. 28–29, and there is every reason to believe her. Peake, after a meticulous study of

Bentley's life, concluded in his afterword to the 1988 edition of *Out of Bondage*, p. 226, that Bentley joined the Party for idealistic and humanitarian reasons.

CHAPTER 5: A STEELED BOLSHEVIK

42 "seizure of power by the working classes . . .": Carl Paivio writing in *Luokkataistelu* (Class Struggle), quoted in Klehr, *The Secret World*, p. 5. Two communist parties were formed in 1919: the Communist Party of the United States of America and the Communist Labor Party. They merged as the CPUSA in 1921.

43 "united in common work for a beautiful future": M. J. Olgin, *Trotskyism*. New York: Workers Library, 1935, p. 148.

43 "a result of his unending purges": Klehr, *The Secret World*, p. 10.

43 "just twentieth-century Americanism": For more on the appeal of the party to liberals of the day, see Gornick, *The Romance of American Communism*, p. 111; Kirschner, *Cold War Exile*, pp. 285–86; author's interview with Jack Beckerman, June 24, 2000.

43 "hundred thousand by the end of the decade": Klehr, *The Secret World*, p. xxxii; Klehr and Haynes, *American Communist Movement*, p. 1.

43 "outnumbered the foreign-born members . . .": Klehr and Haynes, *American Communist Movement*, p. 86.

43 "recent immigrants from Czarist Russia": Klehr, *The Secret World*, p. 5.

43 "on the ragged fringe of American society": For example, Benjamin Gitlow, Communist Labor Party cofounder and Communist Party candidate for president in 1924 and 1928. See Gitlow, *I Confess*, pp. 4, 7–8.

44 "Will I ever be able to live up to their standards?": Details of first meeting are from Bentley, *Out of Bondage*, pp. 31–33 and Bentley's signed FBI statement, p. 3. Additional insight into what happened at unit meetings from Davis, "Looking Back," p. 13.

45 "this was the place for her": Details concerning that meeting from Bentley, *Out of Bondage*, p. 61.

45 "another meeting each week": Bentley's signed FBI statement, p. 5, and Bentley, *Out of Bondage*, p. 51.

45 "linked arms with comrades and sang 'The Internationale' ": Bentley's congressional testimony, *Export Policy and Loyalty*, July 30, 1948, pp. 4–5; also Bentley, *Out of Bondage*, pp. 44–45.

45 "without knowing in detail just what it stands for": Bentley, *Out of Bondage*, p. 67.

46 ". . . new to this clandestine life": Bentley recounts this incident in *Out of Bondage*, pp. 71–72.

46 "... the Marxist-Leninist interpretation was correct": Bentley, *Out of Bondage,* p. 68.

46 " '... the whole of their lives' to the cause": Lenin in *Iskra* newspaper, No. 1, 1900.

46 "no time to feel sorry for herself": Many communists commented on the appeal of this activity. See, e.g., Kempton, *Part of Our Time,* pp. 218–19; Chambers, *Witness,* p. 9; Gitlow, *The Whole of Their Lives,* p. 236; Gitlow, *I Confess,* p. 289. Gornick, *The Romance of American Communism,* is particularly articulate about this (p. 9).

46 "breaking the bourgeois code of behavior": See, for example, Gitlow, *I Confess,* p. 314.

47 "an Iraqi student at Columbia": Bentley listed some of her affairs in the autobiographical sketch she wrote for the NKVD summarized in Weinstein and Vassiliev, *Haunted Wood,* p. 88.

47 "Some of them undoubtedly shared her bed": From an FBI report by Special Agent John J. Danahy, Oct. 13, 1950, quoted in Yalkowsky, *Murder of Rosenbergs,* pp. 125–26.

47 " '... with a zeal for the horizontal' ": Belfrage, *The American Inquisition,* p. 19.

47 "aided by her friend, nurse Lee Fuhr": This according to Peake's interview with the FBI Special Agent Danahy. Peake thought the talk was "very likely true." Correspondence with author, Aug. 9, 2000. Also see Belfrage, *The American Inquisition,* p. 19.

47 "the very best time of her life": Bentley, *Out of Bondage,* p. 279.

47 "the old Christian ideals on which she was raised": Bentley, *Out of Bondage,* p. 22.

47 "Communism could—and should—take its place": Recounted by Bentley in *Out of Bondage,* pp. 42–43.

48 "... a communist in spirit as well as in name": Bentley, *Out of Bondage,* pp. 65–66, 69.

49 " '... if I had a quarter, I'd have eaten it' ": Bentley recounts this incident in *Out of Bondage,* pp. 39–40. See also her signed FBI statement, p. 3.

49 "demanding aid for their families": "150 in Plea for Home Relief." *New York Times,* Apr. 17, 1934.

49 "clothes for the unemployed": "7 Relief Pickets Jailed." *New York Times,* July 27, 1934.

50 "But she said yes": Bentley recounts her experiences with the Home Relief shop unit in *Out of Bondage,* pp. 35–38.

50 "she sent in her resignation": Bentley, *Out of Bondage,* p. 58.

51 "targeted as a prime recruit": On Poyntz, and Poyntz and Bentley, see Bentley, *Out of Bondage,* pp. 44–57, 72–77; Bentley's signed FBI statement, p. 3; Weinstein and Vassiliev, *Haunted Wood,* pp. 88–89;

Peake's afterword in *Out of Bondage* (1988), p. 228; and Chambers, *Witness,* p. 131.

51 " '. . . all you lost was your soul' ": Bentley's signed FBI statement, p. 6.

52 " 'No one ever leaves the organization' ": Bentley, *Out of Bondage,* pp. 89–90.

52 "KGB agents": The Soviet secret political police, the KGB, had a number of predecessor or related organizations—the Cheka, the GPU, the GRU, the OGPU, the NKVD, the NKGB, the MGB, the MVD—the names and acronyms of which are unfamiliar to anyone other than scholars of communism. For simplicity, I use KGB, an acronym well-known to Americans, to refer to the Soviet Secret Police. See Klehr and Haynes, *The Secret World,* p. xxvi.

52 "Macy's Fresh Air Fund camp": Bentley's employment detailed in her signed FBI statement, pp. 5–6; FBI report (date illegible) No. 65-56402-25; FBI memo, Nov. 1, 1950, noted in Roeker, "The Story of a Communist Agent," p. 24; Bentley, *Out of Bondage,* p. 65; and Peake in his afterword in *Out of Bondage* (1988), pp. 225, 229.

53 "Bentley went downtown to headquarters to talk to him": F. Brown was his name in the open party; Mario Alpi was his underground name. He was one of the Communist International's representatives in the United States assigned to the Italian bureau. See Romerstein and Breindel, *The Venona Secrets,* p. 149.

54 "take her and her information seriously": Details of the Italian Library experience in Bentley, *Out of Bondage,* pp. 92–93, and her signed FBI statement, pp. 7–8.

CHAPTER 6: YASHA

58 "Of course, she didn't": Very similar versions of this first meeting are detailed in Bentley, *Out of Bondage,* pp. 94–97, and Bentley's signed statement to the FBI, p. 9.

59 "She listened carefully": Bentley, *Out of Bondage,* p. 98.

59 "He was a hero": As recounted by Bentley in the autobiographical sketch she wrote for the NKGB, summarized in Weinstein and Vassiliev, *Haunted Wood,* p. 87.

60 "a true believer": Bentley, *Out of Bondage,* p. 99.

61 "they were just a couple in love": Bentley, *Out of Bondage,* pp. 98–103.

61 "leaving her there alone on the bench": "Timmy" took the name Golos—which means voice in Russian—when he originally joined the Communist Party. His real name was Jacob Raisen, although no one in the United States knew him by that name. See Haynes and Klehr, *Venona,* p. 94; Bentley, *Out of Bondage,* p. 218.

61 "personalities that played roles in its tangled history": Bentley, *Out of Bondage,* pp. 112–13.
62 "the Party used its services extensively": FBI report on World Tourists, October 1954, Bentley file No. 61-6328; Haynes and Klehr, *Venona,* p. 95; Craig, "Treasonable Doubt," p. 107.
62 "a healthy, profitable venture": Bentley discusses World Tourists in her testimony before HUAC, *Export Policy and Loyalty,* July 30, 1948, p. 505.
62 "the triumphs of the new Soviet Union": Quoted directly from World Tourist brochure, 1935, courtesy of Hayden Peake.
63 "permanently left the country": FBI "thumbnail sketch" to director from special agent in charge, New York, June 21, 1955, Bentley file No. 61-6328.
64 "a man with high ideals": Details of Golos's background come from NKVD documents discovered by Weinstein and Vassiliev, summarized and cited in *Haunted Wood,* pp. 85–87; Haynes and Klehr, *Venona,* pp. 93–96; Romerstein and Breindel, *Venona Secrets,* p. 146; Klehr and Haynes, *Secret World,* pp. 55, 246; Bentley, *Out of Bondage,* pp. 113, 207–08, 218.
64 "and had produced a child": FBI report by Harold Kennedy, New York field office, Jan. 7, 1946, Bentley file No. 65-56402-420; Bentley's autobiographical sketch for the NKVD in Weinstein and Vassiliev, *Haunted Wood,* p. 86; FBI memo quoted in Yalkowky, *Murder of the Rosenbergs,* p. 326.
64 "*golubushka,* a Russian endearment": Kempton, *Part of Our Time,* p. 221. Bentley mentions this several times in *Out of Bondage.*
64 "bourgeois sin and Leninist bliss": William Duffy in his review of *Out of Bondage,* Oct. 11, 1951, newspaper unknown, clipping in Bentley FBI file, with no file number.

CHAPTER 7: TRADECRAFT
65 "he fired her on the spot": In Bentley's version, *Out of Bondage,* p. 102, and her signed FBI statement, p. 10, she says the director "stumbled over"—which hardly seems likely—an antifascist article *she* wrote. After extensive research, Hayden Peake discovered the only article in the Columbia newspaper that mentioned Bentley by name, published Oct. 17, 1935, was written about, not by, her. See Peake's afterword in *Out of Bondage* (1988), p. 232.
65 "working directly for him": Bentley, *Out of Bondage,* p. 103.
66 "the *Daily Worker* and *The Masses*": Bentley's signed FBI statement, p. 13.
66 "native-born Americans, rather than Russians or immigrants": Bentley's signed FBI statement, p. 71.

66 "the plot to assassinate Trotsky": Bentley, *Out of Bondage*, p. 105; Bentley's signed FBI statement, p. 11; Haynes and Klehr, *Venona*, p. 98; Lamphere, *FBI-KGB*, p. 37.

67 "walk the wrong way down a one-way street": Golos's instructions on tradecraft noted in Bentley's signed FBI statement, pp. 66–69; Bentley, *Out of Bondage*, pp. 103–04.

68 "I want to be especially proud of you, he said": From Bentley's autobiographical sketch for the NKVD in Weinstein and Vassiliev, *Haunted Wood*, pp. 87–88.

68 "align itself with all the evils we are fighting against?": Bentley recounts this conversation in *Out of Bondage*, p. 106.

68 "the end of their membership in the Party": Norman Holmes Pearson, "The Nazi-Soviet Pact and the End of a Dream," in Daniel Aron, ed., *America in Crisis*, New York: Alfred A. Knopf, 1952.

68 "dream must be preserved at all costs, he said": Bentley, *Out of Bondage*, p. 106.

68 "she believed that, too": Bentley, *Out of Bondage*, p. 110.

69 "instead you are letting me down": Conversation recounted in Bentley, *Out of Bondage*, p. 108.

69 "Waldo fired Bentley": Bentley's signed FBI statement, p. 12; Bentley, *Out of Bondage*, pp. 107–08, 111, 120.

70 "while Golos conducted business with the men": Bentley, *Out of Bondage*, p. 104.

70 "the car he was driving": Bentley's signed FBI statement, p. 9.

70 "dropped the matter quickly": Bentley's signed FBI statement, p. 10.

71 "suspended sentence and a $500 fine": The World Tourists investigation is chronicled in a number of sources, including FBI memo, J. Edgar Hoover to Gen. Hoyt Vandenberg, Feb. 21, 1946, Bentley file No. 61-6328-62; Bentley's signed FBI statement, p. 12; Bentley's autobiographical sketch written for the NKVD in Weinstein and Vassiliev, *Haunted Wood*, p. 87; Bentley, *Out of Bondage*, pp. 116–18; Klehr and Haynes, *Secret World*, p. 310; Cook, *FBI*, p. 285.

72 "as close to self-pity as a good Bolshevik would let himself get": Bentley, *Out of Bondage*, p. 120.

72 "regularly reporting on his activities to the Bureau": Weinstein and Vassiliev, *Haunted Wood*, p. 91.

72 "Golos's direct link to Moscow": FBI report, New York Field Office, July 22, 1952, Bentley file No. 65-57904-37.

72 "another subpoena was on its way": Interestingly, the Dies Committee also had Bentley's old Vassar professor, Hallie Flanagan, in its sights. Flanagan had left Vassar to run a New Deal theater project that members of the Dies Committee suspected of spreading sedition from the stage. Daniels, *Bridges*, p. 207; Chambers, *Witness*, p. 72.

72  "Golos's secret police credentials": Incident recounted by Bentley in signed FBI statement, p. 15.

73  "an internecine struggle over the control of his network": Weinstein and Vassiliev, *Haunted Wood,* pp. 89–91.

73  "heart disease and arteriosclerosis": Bentley's signed FBI statement, p. 15; Bentley, *Out of Bondage,* p. 134.

73  "Golos suffered a heart attack": May, *Unamerican Activities,* p. 82.

CHAPTER 8: *KONSPIRATSIA*

75  "No one was following her when she left": FBI memo, William Whelan, New York field office, Mar. 22, 1950, in Alger Hiss papers; Bentley, *Out of Bondage,* pp. 138–40.

75  "she was wrong about that": FBI report, from director to Washington field office, Apr. 5, 1947, Bentley file No. 100-17493, p. 8; Bentley, *Out of Bondage,* pp. 140–41.

75  "much to the Bureau's later embarrassment": Hoover noted in 1944 that "there are numerous leads set forth in [the World Tourists] report which have apparently received no investigative attention whatsoever." FBI memo, Hoover to special agent in charge, New York, May 5, 1944, Bentley file No. 61-6328-17. Former agent Robert Lamphere called the lack of attention "a bad mistake." Author's interview, June 23, 2000.

76  " 'growing demand for services' ": "Report of Director" in *Annual Report of the FBI,* July 1, 1940, to July 30, 1941. Also see "A Short History of the FBI" on the agency's Web site, *www.fbi.gov.*

76  "reporting directly to the Russians": Bentley, *Out of Bondage,* pp. 145–47.

78  "Bentley took up much of the slack": Information about John Reynolds and the formation of USS&S found in FBI memo, J. Edgar Hoover to Gen. Hoyt Vendenberg, Feb. 21, 1946, Bentley file No. 61-6328-62; Haynes and Klehr, *Venona,* p. 97; Bentley's congressional testimony, *Export Policy and Loyalty,* July 30, 1948, p. 10; Bentley's signed FBI statement, pp. 14, 99–100; Bentley, *Out of Bondage,* pp. 125, 130, 133.

78  " ' . . . behind the scenes in the American government' ": Bentley, *Out of Bondage,* p. 144; Haynes and Klehr, *Venona,* p. 98.

78  "funneling information to the Soviets": Haynes and Klehr, *Venona,* pp. 60–62.

78  "the Aberdeen Proving Ground in Maryland": Chambers, *Witness,* p. 27.

78  "the Office of War Information": Penetration of these government agencies is confirmed by Venona cables. See Haynes and Klehr, *Venona,* pp. 191–207.

79 "an oppressive government: their own": Bentley's explanation of her sources' motivation during her congressional testimony, *Export Policy and Loyalty*, July 30, 1948, pp. 24–25.

79 "keeping tabs on the German American Bund": Haynes and Klehr, *Venona*, pp. 85–87.

79 "agencies didn't talk to one another or share information": Haynes and Klehr, *Venona*, p. 132.

79 "the golden age of Soviet espionage": Weinstein and Vassiliev, *Haunted Wood*, p. 340.

79 "Golos's substitute in July of 1941": Bentley's congressional testimony, *Export Policy and Loyalty*, July 30, 1948, p. 11.

79 "to be their link to the party": From Bentley's autobiographical sketch for the NKVD in Weinstein and Vassiliev, *Haunted Wood*, p. 92.

79 "At Christmastime, she bought them presents": Bentley, *Out of Bondage*, p. 210.

80 "OSS, FBI, trade unions, and U.S. foreign embassies and missions": KGB memo to Anatoly Gorsky, August 1944, quoted in Weinstein and Vassiliev, *Haunted Wood*, pp. 227–28.

80 "production figures on planes and tanks and the deployment of forces": According to Bentley's congressional testimony, *Export Policy and Loyalty*, July 30, 1948, p. 12.

80 "commercial vats, filters, and shafts used in the manufacture of chemicals": FBI report by Joseph Walsh, New York field office, April 29, 1950, in Harry Gold FBI file; also Bentley's signed FBI statement, p. 113; and Lamphere, *FBI-KGB*, p. 37.

80 "spending several days at a time on each trip": Bentley, *Out of Bondage*, p. 191.

81 "They rendezvoused on park benches": Bentley's congressional testimony, *Export Policy and Loyalty*, July 30, 1948, p. 31.

81 "a shopping bag, always with a department store name on it": Bentley's testimony before HUAC, *Communist Espionage*, July 31, 1948, p. 522.

81 "undeniably thrilling": Hope Hale Davis writes that clandestine assignments "stirred me in a way that made [my husband] shake his head" in "Looking Back," *New Leader*, p. 17.

81 "agents linked to Soviet intelligence through her": Haynes and Klehr, *Venona*, p. 93.

82 "sleeping on a bed in the enclosed back porch": Information about Bentley and Mary Price in Bentley's congressional testimony, *Export Policy and Loyalty*, July 30, 1948, p. 27; Bentley's signed FBI statement, p. 16; and Bentley, *Out of Bondage*, pp. 132, 181. Thirty years after the fact, Mary Price told an interviewer that Bentley had made

homosexual advances toward her. This may or may not be true, but it certainly makes sense that Price would be interested in discrediting Bentley any way she could.

83 "the location of OSS personnel in foreign countries": The intelligence provided by Lee is noted in various Venona cables. See Haynes and Klehr, *Venona,* pp. 105, 107. Bentley testified about her meetings with Lee before HUAC, *Communist Espionage,* July 31, 1948, p. 529; Lee testified on Aug. 8, 1948. See especially pp. 718–19. Bentley also testified about Lee at the *Institute of Pacific Relations* hearings, Aug. 14, 1951, p. 413. See also Bentley's signed FBI statement, pp. 34–36 and Bentley, *Out of Bondage,* p. 183.

83 "his job gave him access to sensitive information from the agency's Far East and Russian sections": Haynes and Klehr, *Venona,* p. 108; Bentley's signed FBI statement, pp. 30–31; and Bentley, *Out of Bondage,* p. 159.

83 "secret reports from agents in Spain": On Tenney, see Romerstein and Breindel, *Venona Secrets,* pp. 298–99; Haynes and Klehr, *Venona,* p. 112; Bentley, *Out of Bondage,* pp. 200–01.

84 "bulletins and reports prepared by the agency on a variety of topics": Information on Halperin from FBI report, Jan. 27, 1947, Bentley file No. 65-14603; Haynes and Klehr, *Venona,* pp. 101–02; Bentley's signed FBI statement, p. 33; Bentley, *Out of Bondage,* pp. 263–64. Also see Kirschner, *Cold War Exile,* especially pp. 279–80.

84 "a former newspaper reporter working for the press division of CIAA": Bentley named all these sources in her signed FBI statement: Size on p. 50, Gregg, pp. 45–46, Miller, p. 17, and Redmont, p. 49.

85 "commenting on the personalities and opinions of those he knew in government": Bentley testified about her relationship with Remington at the *Export Policy and Loyalty* hearings, July 30, 1948. Remington responded on July 31, 1948, p. 169. She offered additional testimony before HUAC, *Communism in the U.S. Government,* May 6, 1950, pp. 185–89. See also Bentley's signed FBI statement, pp. 47–48; Bentley, *Out of Bondage,* pp. 178–79; May, *Un-American Activities,* pp. 258–59.

85 "held herself like the patrician she was": Romerstein and Breindel, *Venona Secrets,* p. 152; author's interview with Bud Rubin, who knew the Silvermasters in New Jersey, Nov. 19, 2000.

85 "supply the party with information that might aid the Soviet war effort": Craig, "Treasonable Doubt," pp. 113–14.

85 "one of Browder's assistants during the San Francisco general strike of 1934": Weinstein and Vassiliev, *Haunted Wood,* pp. 157–58.

86 "he had been living with the Silvermasters for years": Author's inter-

view with Bud Rubin, Nov. 9, 2000; author's correspondence with Alice Rubin, Sept. 29, 2000; Haynes and Klehr, *Venona*, p. 136.

86 "some in the party understood to be a ménage à trois": Weinstein and Vassiliev, *Haunted Wood*, p. 164. Bud Rubin found this idea "ludicrous." Author's interview, Nov. 9, 2000.

86 "manuals for American fighter planes and bombers": Sixty-one decrypted Venona messages mention Silvermaster and the information he passed. See, especially, KGB/NY to Moscow, Oct. 17, 1944, message #1469. Other key Venona messages are #1691, #1751–1753, #1787, and #1821 (all relayed in December of 1944, all detailing documents passed by Silvermaster). See also Weinstein and Vassiliev, *Haunted Wood*, pp. 158–59; Haynes and Klehr, *Venona*, p. 136.

86 "setting up a darkroom in the Silvermasters' basement": Haynes and Klehr, *Venona*, p. 129; Lamphere, *FBI-KGB*, p. 37.

86 "forty rolls of undeveloped microfilm in her bag every two weeks": FBI memo, special agent in charge, New York to Washington field office and director, Nov. 8, 1945, Bentley file No. 65-56402-1.

86 "Abraham George Silverman, an economic adviser in the Air Force": Members of the Silvermaster Group are named in Haynes and Klehr, *Venona*, p. 129; Romerstein and Breindel, *Venona Secrets*, pp. 184–85; Packer, *Ex-Communist Witnesses*, p. 58.

87 "secure jobs in 'productive areas' ": Bentley's testimony before HUAC, Communist Espionage, July 31, 1948, p. 553; Haynes and Klehr, *Venona*, p. 346; Chambers, *Witness*, p. 247.

87 "he was a contributing member of the group": Corroboration of White's involvement can be found in various Venona cables. See, especially, Venona #1119–1121 (Aug. 4–5, 1944); also see Romerstein and Breindel, *Venona Secrets*, p. 46; Carpozi, *Red Spies*, p. 229; Rees, *Harry Dexter White*, p. 424; Craig, "Treasonable Doubt," who is otherwise sympathetic to White, makes the point clearly.

87 "Morganthau Plan for the pastoralization of Germany after the war": On White's importance, see Latham, *Communist Controversy*, p. 177.

87 "facilitating espionage by sponsoring the employment of Soviet-friendly sources": Bentley's signed FBI statement, p. 25.

87 "protect Silvermaster when his friend came under scrutiny": Haynes and Klehr, *Venona*, p. 139.

88 "he was in a position to influence U.S. policy in a pro-Soviet direction": Bentley, *Out of Bondage*, p. 164.

88 "an effort to remember what happened the week before": Bentley writes about her weariness and depression in *Out of Bondage*, p. 191.

89 "report to a Russian operative, not Golos": Weinstein and Vassiliev, *Haunted Wood*, p. 91; Bentley, *Out of Bondage*, p. 206.

89  "trying to defend his position and hold on to his leadership role":
    Letter found in the KGB archives and summarized in Weinstein and
    Vassiliev, *Haunted Wood,* p. 93.
89  " 'They want to get rid of me' ": Conversation recounted by Bentley
    in *Out of Bondage,* p. 195.
89  "she lay awake listening to the sound of his ragged breathing": Bent-
    ley, *Out of Bondage,* pp. 191–92.

CHAPTER 9: CLEVER GIRL
91  " 'talent spotter, personal data gatherer, group controller, and
    recruiter' ": Letter in KGB archives noted in Weinstein and Vassiliev,
    *Haunted Wood,* p. 93. When informed of his death, his superiors in
    Moscow decided not to award the medal posthumously.
93  "They carried Golos out of the apartment in a canvas sling": Bentley
    relates the circumstances of Golos's death and its immediate after-
    math in *Out of Bondage,* pp. 212–22. She also refers to it in the
    autobiographical sketch she wrote for the NKVD summarized in
    Weinstein and Vassiliev, *Haunted Wood,* p. 93.
93  "fight the Russians for control of the sources": Bentley, *Out of
    Bondage,* pp. 223–26; Bentley's signed FBI statement, p. 92.
93  "Golos was one of the old-timers": Bentley, *Out of Bondage,* p. 228.
94  "showing only as much emotion as would be appropriate": FBI
    report, "Re: Confidential Informant Gregory" (undated). Bentley
    file No. 65-14603 gives some details of the funeral arrangements.
    See also Bentley's signed FBI statement, p. 92; Bentley, *Out of
    Bondage,* p. 229.
94  "She was to call him 'Bill' ": Bentley's signed FBI statement, p. 74.
95  "he was married to Earl Browder's niece": On Akhmerov, see
    Haynes and Klehr, *Venona,* pp. 154–55; Weinstein and Vassiliev,
    *Haunted Wood,* pp. 35–36.
95  "Price should report directly to him": Bentley recounts the meeting
    in *Out of Bondage,* p. 233.
95  "She was a 'sincere person' ": Report in KGB archive quoted in
    Weinstein and Vassiliev, *Haunted Wood,* p. 95.
95  "his closest assistant from whom he had no secrets": KGB memo in
    Weinstein and Vassiliev, *Haunted Wood,* p. 94.
96  "She put them in her big bag and left": Incident recounted in Bent-
    ley, *Out of Bondage,* p. 235.
96  "Bentley met several times with Earl Browder": According to
    Venona 2011, KGB New York to Moscow, Dec. 11, 1943.
96  "political and economic material she thought might interest him":
    Bentley's signed FBI statement, p. 93.

96  "a 'genuine American Aryan' ": Letter in KGB archives, quoted in Weinstein and Vassiliev, *Haunted Wood*, p. 80.

97  "at the expense of two important sources": Klehr and Haynes, *Secret World*, p. 310; Weinstein and Vassiliev, *Haunted Wood*, p. 260.

97  "another incautious and amateurish blunder": Weinstein and Vassiliev, *Haunted Wood*, p. 262.

97  "the FBI wasn't paying close attention": Klehr and Haynes, *Venona*, p. 122.

97  "commensurate with the usefulness of that person to the Soviet enterprise": Bentley's signed FBI statement, p. 66; Bentley, *Out of Bondage*, pp. 210, 236.

97  "a 'lost tribe' in wartime Washington": Weinstein and Vassiliev, *Haunted Wood*, p. 223. The so-called Perlo Group probably became inactive because of Whittaker Chambers's 1938 defection, after which the members feared exposure.

97  "the Ware Group, the original espionage apparatus established in the early 1930s": Chambers, *Witness*, p. 347.

97  "Now Bentley was being asked to follow up": Haynes and Klehr, *Venona*, p. 117.

98  "collecting party dues from the group and providing them with literature": Bentley testified about this first meeting with the Perlo group before HUAC, *Communist Espionage*, August 9, 1948, p. 692, and in her signed FBI statement, pp. 51–52. See also Venona 588, KGB New York to Moscow, April 29, 1944.

98  "reliable party members who were 'politically highly mature' ": Venona 687, KGB New York to Moscow, May 13, 1944.

98  "Perlo was the son of Russian immigrants": On Perlo, see Haynes and Klehr, *Venona*, p. 116; Bentley, *Out of Bondage*, pp. 239–40.

98  "the longtime legal council for the Amalgamated Clothing Workers Union and a member of the original Ware Group": Abt's memoir, *Advocate and Activist*, pp. 150–51.

98  "Donald Wheeler, an Oxford-trained OSS employee": Weinstein and Vassiliev, *Haunted Wood*, p. 252.

98  "Solomon Lishinsky and George Perazich": Bentley identified the Perlo Group in her signed FBI statement, p. 52. The members are also listed in Romerstein and Breindel, *Venona Secrets*, p. 185; FBI memo, Washington field office, Oct. 27, 1951, WFO No. 101-3599-36 in Alger Hiss papers; Haynes and Klehr, *Venona*, pp. 117–18. The identities were also confirmed in Venona 687, May 13, 1944 and May 30, 1944.

98  "off-hand American informality that drove Akhmerov crazy": Weinstein and Vassiliev, *Haunted Wood*, p. 225.

99  "her apartment served as a regular meeting spot": Bentley testified about the details of the group's operation and meetings before HUAC, *Communist Espionage,* July 31, 1948, p. 525. See also her signed FBI statement, pp. 53–54; Weinstein and Vassiliev, *Haunted Wood,* pp. 225, 229; Haynes and Klehr, *Venona,* p. 123.

99  "information on aircraft production and distribution by countries and theaters of action": Bentley, *Out of Bondage,* p. 259.

99  "Wheeler provided copies of OSS reports": Bentley details what each group member contributed in her signed FBI statement, pp. 55–56. See also Weinstein and Vassiliev, *Haunted Wood,* pp. 227, 231–32; Bentley, *Out of Bondage,* p. 259.

99  "came across Donald Wheeler's desk—and made it to KGB headquarters in Moscow": Weinstein and Vassiliev, *Haunted Wood,* p. 253.

99  "the group was 'really going to town' ": Bentley, *Out of Bondage,* p. 259.

100  "He will be very upset by it": KGB cable quoted in Weinstein and Vassiliev, *Haunted Wood,* p. 226.

100  "demanding that she turn over Price immediately": Bentley, *Out of Bondage,* p. 238.

100  "an argument she made to both Akhmerov and Browder": Venona 1065, KGB New York to Moscow, June 28, 1944.

100  "Price was taken out of commission": Haynes and Klehr, *Venona,* p. 100.

100  "turn over the entire Silvermaster network": Weinstein and Vassiliev, *Haunted Wood,* p. 96.

101  "she was refusing to obey orders": Reports from KGB archives quoted in Weinstein and Vassiliev, *Haunted Wood,* pp. 97–98.

101  "it is possible to correct her behavior": Letter in KGB archives quoted in Weinstein and Vassiliev, *Haunted Wood,* p. 97.

101  "wrest the Silvermaster Group from Bentley's control": Bentley's signed FBI statement, pp. 13–16; Weinstein and Vassiliev, *Haunted Wood,* p. 304.

101  "evidently supposing that we do not trust her": Venona 973, KGB New York to Moscow, July 11, 1944.

101  "associating with a man who turned out to be an undercover counterintelligence agent": Bentley's signed FBI statement, p. 84.

102  "they would be contacted by another individual": Bentley's signed FBI statement, p. 79.

102  "meet at various venues in Manhattan": Bentley's signed FBI statement, pp. 75–76, 78; Bentley, *Out of Bondage,* p. 249.

102  "He was really Anatoly Gorsky": Bentley's signed FBI statement, p. 83.

102  " 'Her life will lose its meaning without this work' ": Letter in KGB

archives, June 25, 1944, quoted in Weinstein and Vassiliev, *Haunted Wood,* p. 98.

102 "a fur coat and an air conditioner": Bentley so testified before HUAC, *Communist Espionage,* Aug. 11, 1948, p. 812.

103 "Bentley nonetheless must have felt deeply honored": Bentley testified about the details of the Red Star meeting before HUAC, *Communist Espionage,* Aug. 11, 1948, pp. 811–12. See also her signed FBI statement, pp. 83–84.

103 "she would work 'indefatigably' to justify the award": Report from Gorsky to Moscow in KGB archives, summarized in Weinstein and Vassiliev, *Haunted Wood,* p. 99.

103 " 'directly threaten the existence of [Bentley's] cover' ": Venona 1673, KGB NY to Moscow, Nov. 30, 1944; see also Venona 1802, Dec. 21, 1944.

103 " 'The question of a husband for her must be thought over' ": Cable in KGB archives, quoted in Weinstein and Vassiliev, *Haunted Wood,* p. 98.

103 "it was urgent to find her a husband": Cable in KGB archives, quoted in Weinstein and Vassiliev, *Haunted Wood,* p. 99.

CHAPTER 10: RUSSIAN ROULETTE

106 "That was just bad tradecraft": Bentley's signed FBI statement, p. 84.

106 "she never felt more alone or more adrift": Bentley, *Out of Bondage,* p. 270.

106 "a front for illegal activities": Bentley's signed FBI statement, p. 84.

106 "mixing her legal and illegal activities": Weinstein and Vassiliev, *Haunted Wood,* p. 100.

107 "She continued to be involved in the operation": For the USS&S saga, see Bentley's signed FBI statement, pp. 59–61.

107 "the purpose of which was to tell her, again and in no uncertain terms, to stay out of USS&S": Bentley's signed FBI statement, p. 86.

108 " 'she didn't have time to think too much' ": Moscow to Gorsky in KGB archives, quoted in Weinstein and Vassiliev, *Haunted Wood,* p. 101.

108 "resume her clandestine work": Bentley testified about this before HUAC, *Communist Espionage,* July 31, 1948, p. 541.

108 "she would be entrusted with this position": Bentley's signed FBI statement, p. 81.

108 "and then be recalled to active espionage duty": Bentley's signed FBI statement, p. 86.

109 "Gorsky was suggesting that Bentley be relocated to another country": Gorsky to Moscow, Sept. 10, 1945, in KGB archives, quoted in Weinstein and Vassiliev, *Haunted Wood,* p. 101.

109 "Akhmerov was taken aback by her bitterness": Akhmerov to Moscow in KGB archives, quoted in Weinstein and Vassiliev, *Haunted Wood,* p. 97.

109 " 'shattered nerves' and an 'unsettled private life' ": Moscow to Gorsky, Oct. 11, 1945, in KGB archive, quoted in Weinstein and Vassiliev, *Haunted Wood,* p. 102.

109 "The American Communist Party was 'a gang of foreigners' ": Bentley's signed FBI statement, p. 86, for her description of the meeting.

109 " 'Get rid of her' ": All quotes are from Gorsky to Moscow messages in KGB archives, quoted in Weinstein and Vassiliev, *Haunted Wood,* pp. 101–02.

110 "a new OSS employee who would be willing to pass along confidential material": Venona 1464, Oct. 14, 1944.

110 "remind her of the good work she had done": Merkulov to Gorsky, Oct. 11, 1945, in KGB archives, quoted in Weinstein and Vassiliev, *Haunted Wood,* p. 102.

110 "Bentley was sober, cordial, and apologetic": Gorsky to Merkulov, Oct. 29, 1945, in KGB archives, quoted in Weinstein and Vassiliev, *Haunted Wood,* p. 103.

110 "dribble a little on her handkerchief": Gorsky memo, Nov. 27, 1945, in KGB archives, quoted in Weinstein and Vassiliev, *Haunted Wood,* p. 108.

CHAPTER 11: CLOSING IN

111 "The FBI now knew who had been and was still working for the company": FBI report, Oct. 18, 1944, Bentley file No. 61-6328-19.

112 "this would tip the FBI's hand": FBI memo, special agent in charge, New York, to director, Jan. 4, 1945, Bentley file No. 61-6328-22.

112 "No one else had lived in this apartment for years": Bentley, *Out of Bondage,* p. 271.

112 "she should take a 'vacation' immediately": Bentley's signed FBI statement, p. 85.

112 "two *Amerasia* editors were found guilty of theft of government property": On the *Amerasia* case, see Klehr and Haynes, *American Communist Movement,* p. 107; Haynes and Klehr, *Venona,* pp. 176–77.

113 "she would be 'blown to hell' ": FBI memo, H. B. Fletcher to D. M. Ladd, July 27, 1948. Bentley file No. 65-56402-3494.

113 " 'The effect of Mr. Golos was wearing off' ": Bentley's testimony before a Senate subcommittee, *Export Policy and Loyalty,* July 30, 1948, p. 44.

113 "They were no better than gangsters": That's what Bentley told a Senate subcommittee, *Export Policy and Loyalty*, July 30, 1948, pp. 21, 44; Bentley, *Out of Bondage*, p. 258.

114 " '. . . as bad as the Nazis were, the Red Army was worse' ": Bentley, *Out of Bondage*, p. 276.

114 "He hoped the money might help her": Bentley's signed FBI statement, pp. 71, 87.

115 "She hardly recognized herself in the mirror": On Bentley's mental and physical condition, see *Out of Bondage*, pp. 272, 282.

115 "what he recognized as severe hangovers": May, *Un-American Activities*, p. 138.

116 "big-shot government spy": Silvermaster file No. 65-56402-3414.

116 "not to arouse Heller's suspicion": On Bentley's relationship with Heller, see Special Agent Danahy interview in Peake's afterword to *Out of Bondage* (1988), p. 276; Bentley's signed FBI statement, p. 85; May, *Un-American Activities*, p. 84; Roeker, "Communist Agent," pp. 42–43.

116 "taken part in investigations of communists and knew the Russian language": Weinstein and Vassiliev, *Haunted Wood*, pp. 100–01.

116 "Heller would be an ideal husband": From material in KGB archives summarized in Weinstein and Vassiliev, *Haunted Wood*, p. 100.

116 "little more than a sloppy drunk": This according to a civil intelligence report on Heller found in the papers of William Remington's lawyers. See May, *Un-American Activities*, p. 84.

117 "She must go to the FBI": Bentley tells this tale in *Out of Bondage*, pp. 284–85.

117 "Elizabeth Bentley might have had a revelation": Whittaker Chambers writes convincingly about an "ah-ha" moment that turned a lifelong communist into an anticommunist in *Witness*, pp. 13–14.

118 "who degraded the principles for which Golos had died": Robert Lamphere, an FBI agent who took over the Bentley case in the early 1950s, considered revenge a primary motive. Interview with author, June 23, 2000.

CHAPTER 12: IN FROM THE COLD

122 "She took the elevator to the third floor": Bentley recounts this in *Out of Bondage*, pp. 286–88.

122 "But Bentley had to trust someone": Bentley later told FBI agents that she had come to New Haven to check them out, according to former agent Don Shannon. Author's interview, July 7, 2000.

122 " 'told the highlights' of her story": Bentley, *Out of Bondage*, p. 289.

123 "Or was he impersonating an agent?": FBI letter, New Haven field

office to New York field office, Aug. 29, 1945, Bentley file No. 65-56402; FBI memo, D. M. Ladd to Director Hoover, Aug. 24, 1948, Hiss papers.

123 "affair with an unstable woman": The FBI considered Heller a windbag and something of a nut case. FBI memo, Boardman to director, Jan. 25, 1955, Silvermaster file No. 65-56402-4189.

123 "neither Bentley nor Coady was satisfied with the catch": Details of this first interview are recapped in FBI memo, New Haven field office to director, July 30, 1955, Bentley file No. 134-4353-177.

124 "North American spy network centered on atomic espionage": On Gouzenko, see Chambers, *Witness,* p. 205; Weinstein and Vassiliev, *Haunted Wood,* p. 104.

125 "Aldrich was outwardly courteous and noncommittal": So Bentley remembered when she was interviewed on *Meet the Press* in 1953.

125 "sitting across the desk from a certified nut case": A recap of this meeting is found in FBI memo, Los Angeles to director, July 28, 1955, Bentley file No. 134-435-174. It is also mentioned in FBI memo, William O. Simon to New York, July 28, 1955, Bentley file No. 134-182-103.

126 "She agreed to come in the next day": Memos summarizing Buckley's initial involvement include: Buckley to director, Nov. 13, 1946, Bentley file No. 65-14603-40; New York to director, July 28, 1955, Bentley files No. 134-182-102 and No. 134-182-103.

127 "maybe they would see the light, as she had seen the light": Bentley, *Out of Bondage,* p. 281.

128 "Her own immunity from prosecution was not discussed": Several agents interviewed by Peake say immunity was never discussed during the interviews but rather was taken for granted. See Peake's afterword to *Out of Bondage* (1988), p. 220.

128 "a comment the agents noted with particular pride": This account of the Nov. 7 interview is based in part on author's interview with Don Jardine, May 25, 2000. Details of what Bentley talked about are found in FBI memo, special agent in charge, New York, to Washington field office and director, Nov. 8, 1945, Bentley file No. 65-56402-1 as well as, of course, her signed FBI statement.

129 "they sent it by teletype to their boss": FBI teletype, special agent in charge, New York, to Washington field office and director, Nov. 8, 1945, Bentley file No. 65-56402-1.

129 "hand-delivered by an agent who flew down from New York": May, *Un-American Activities,* p. 85.

129 "she was interviewed six days in a row": FBI report by Thomas G. Spencer, Dec. 5, 1945, Bentley file No. 65-56402-220.

129 "sometimes the agents met her elsewhere for her convenience": FBI

memo, special agent in charge, New York, to director, Jan. 4, 1951, Bentley file No. 134-435.

129 "her contact 'Al' was really Anatoly Gorsky": FBI memo, from D. Milton Ladd, Nov. 21, 1945, Bentley file No. 65-56402-52.

130 "Bentley's stock went up": The agents had a "great deal of respect for her" and considered the case "one of the great breakthroughs of the time," according to former FBI agent Robert Lamphere, who took over the file in 1952. Author's interview with Lamphere, June 23, 2000.

130 "They found nothing out of the ordinary": FBI memo, D. M. Ladd to E. A. Tamm, Nov. 19, 1945, Bentley file No. 65-56402-37.

131 "that she had indeed done it": Later, the decrypted Venona cables would confirm her involvement in espionage activities. Bentley is mentioned, by code name, in numerous cables, including Venona 2011 (Dec. 11, 1943), 2013 (Dec. 11, 1943), 278 (Feb. 23, 1944), 588 (April 29, 1944), 687 (May 13, 1944), 973 (July 11, 1944), 1065 (July 28, 1944), 1353 (Sept. 23, 1944), 1464 (Oct. 14, 1944), 1673 (Nov. 30, 1944), 1802 (Dec. 21, 1944), 954 (Sept. 20, 1944), 275 (March 25, 1945).

131 "to be used against her comrades sometime later": Whittaker Chambers, a courier in Washington, D.C., in the 1930s, hid incriminating evidence in a hollowed-out pumpkin stashed on the family farm. Years later, the "pumpkin papers" were used to corroborate his story. See Chambers's heartfelt, if overly long, memoir *Witness.*

131 "in a safe deposit box at a Manhattan bank": Bentley, *Out of Bondage,* p. 294; FBI memo, special agent in charge, New York, to director, Jan. 4, 1951; Bentley file No. 134-435.

131 "the only money we've ever gotten back, or ever will get back, from the Lend-Lease program": Author's interview with Don Shannon, July 7, 2000.

132 "Bentley said she met with top Russian functionaries, and she did": Details of the meeting and FBI involvement are found in: FBI memo, New York field office to Washington field office and director (date illegible), Bentley file No. 65-56402-56; FBI memo, D. M. Ladd to E. A. Tamm, Nov. 21, 1945, Bentley file No. 65-56402-54; Bentley's testimony before HUAC, *Communist Espionage,* Aug. 11, 1948, p. 813; Bentley, *Out of Bondage,* p. 297; Weinstein and Vassiliev, *Haunted Wood,* p. 103; May, *Un-American Activities,* p. 87.

132 "These people still had access to sensitive information": The twenty-seven named in Bentley's signed FBI statement were: Solomon Adler, Norman Bursler, Frank Coe, Edward Fitzgerald, Harold Glasser, Bela Gold, Sonia Gold, Michael Greenberg, Joseph Gregg, Maurice Halperin, Alger Hiss, Irving Kaplan, Duncan Lee, Harry Magdoff,

Robert Talbott Miller III, Victor Perlo, Bernard Redmont, William Remington, John H. Reynolds, Peter Rhodes, Allan Rosenberg, Nathan Gregory Silvermaster, William Henry Taylor, Helen Tenney, William Ludwig Ullmann, Donald Wheeler, Harry Dexter White.

CHAPTER 13: HOOVER'S TURN

135   "having the preliminary data immediately": FBI memo, Hoover to Gen. Vaughn, Nov. 9, 1945, Bentley file No. 65-14603-15; FBI memo, D. M. Ladd to director, Aug. 24, 1948, Hiss papers. See also Cook, *FBI,* p. 284, and Lamphere, *FBI-KGB,* p. 36.

136   "asking for a detailed report on the Bentley situation": FBI letter, Hoover to Ass't Directors Tolson, Tamm, and Ladd, Nov. 15, 1945, No. 65-56402-403X8 in Hiss papers.

136   "Copies went not only to the secretary of state and General Vaughn": FBI memo, D. M. Ladd to director, Aug. 24, 1948, Hiss papers.

136   "the Bentley case was the Bureau's single most important priority": FBI memo, Hendon to Tolson, Nov. 11, 1945, Bentley file No. 65-56402-38.

136   "one of the longest, most expensive investigations in its history": May, *Un-American Activities,* p. 77.

136   "Bureau's elite Major Case Squad": It was a move that "disgusted" some of those within the FBI. See Lamphere, *FBI-KGB,* p. 36.

137   "with special attention to the twenty-seven still employed by the federal government": "Special Assistant Donegan," *The American Mercury,* v. 77, no. 31 (August 1953); May, *Un-American Activities,* p. 87.

137   "That same day, agents were assigned to tail Silvermaster": Romerstein and Breindel, *Venona Secrets,* p. 156.

137   "William Remington's phone was tapped": May, *Un-American Activities,* p. 87.

137   "locate and follow Mary Price": FBI memo, Tamm to Ladd, Nov. 19, 1945, Bentley file No. 65-56402-37.

137   "installed microphones next door": National Security Electronic Surveillance File, Bentley file No. 65-56402-39; Craig, "Treasonable Doubt," p. 130.

137   "agents in Washington were assigned to tail him night and day": FBI memo, D. M. Ladd to director, Aug. 24, 1948, Hiss papers.

137   "Donegan put thirteen additional people under surveillance": FBI memo, D. M. Ladd to E. A. Tamm, Nov. 21, 1945, Bentley file No. 65-56402-54.

137   "to join the twenty-five agents already there on the job": FBI memo, Hendon to Tolsen, Nov. 19, 1945, Bentley file No. 65-56402-38.

137 "more than two hundred agents would work the case": Craig, "Treasonable Doubt," p. 112.

138 "it had rained in New York on Sunday, March 5": Haynes and Klehr, *Venona,* p. 409, fn. 2.

138 "a man known to Bentley only as 'Charlie' ": FBI report, Oct. 3, 1950, Bentley file No. 65-14778.

138 "the breakthrough that would halt Soviet espionage in the United States": Author's interview with Herman Bly, July 15, 2000.

138 "a photo lab in the basement, just as Bentley had said": Lamphere, *FBI-KGB,* p. 40.

138 "maintain contact with Communist Party leader Earl Browder": Bentley, *Out of Bondage,* p. 296.

138 "schedule another meeting with Gorsky": Haynes and Klehr, *Venona,* p. 157.

139 "It would be their last meeting": Details of the meeting in FBI teletype report, Nov. 30, 1945, Bentley file No. 65-56402-56 and Bentley's signed FBI statement, p. 88. For Gorsky's suspicions, see Weinstein and Vassiliev, *Haunted Wood,* p. 103.

139 "ripe for turning": Haynes and Klehr, *Venona,* p. 112; Bentley, *Out of Bondage,* pp. 304–05.

140 "a dandy system for everyone but the FBI": Weinstein and Vassiliev, *Haunted Wood,* pp. 104–05, 108; Haynes and Klehr, *Venona,* p. 51.

140 "Silvermaster was told the news by Akhmerov": Weinstein and Vassiliev, *Haunted Wood,* p. 170.

141 "Akhmerov assured his Moscow superiors": Weinstein and Vassiliev, *Haunted Wood,* p. 170.

141 "a 'hysterical, highly emotional nuisance' ": FBI memo, director to special agent in charge, Charlotte field office, June 3, 1947, no number, Bentley file.

141 "He gave her only press releases and published articles": May, *Un-American Activities,* pp. 90–91.

141 "with an intent to do injury to the United States": According to Chapter 4, paragraph 32, U.S. Code, 1946 edition, v. 4, Title 50 (U.S. Government Printing Office, 1948), pp. 5595–96.

142 "order a freeze of virtually all intelligence activities": Weinstein and Vassiliev, *Haunted Wood,* p. 218.

142 "Bentley was the cause of the new orders": Weinstein and Vassiliev, *Haunted Wood,* p. 106.

142 "Bentley's defection meant they would have to 'stop our work totally' ": Weinstein and Vassiliev, *Haunted Wood,* p. 170.

142 "Vassily Zarubin, Akhmerov's colleague in New York, also had to leave": Romerstein and Breindel, *Venona Secrets,* pp. 9, 189.

142 "ordered home at the same time": Weinstein and Vassiliev, *Haunted Wood*, p. 286.
142 " 'the most tangible blow to our work' ": Sergei Sarchenko in a mid-March 1950 memo quoted in Weinstein and Vassiliev, *Haunted Wood*, pp. 297–98.
143 "discharged from the Naval Reserves": May, *Un-American Activities*, pp. 87–88.
143 "twenty-four of the twenty-seven, most of whom were career civil servants": Haynes and Klehr, *Venona*, p. 128.
143 "more than twenty-five thousand people were referred to loyalty boards for investigation": Fariello, *Red Scare*, p. 17; Haynes and Klehr, *Venona*, pp. 13–14.
144 "was, like Bentley, an informer": Packer, *Ex-Communist Witnesses*, pp. 104–05; Weinstein and Vassiliev, *Haunted Wood*, pp. 35–48.
144 "had covert relationships with Soviet intelligence agencies": The best sources on Venona are the FBI's Venona file, available at the FBI's FOIA reading room; the complete cables themselves with introductions, commentaries, and explanations online at *www.nsa.gov;* and Haynes and Klehr's excellent book, *Venona*.
145 "Bentley herself was the subject of more than a dozen Venona cables": These are listed in Notes for Chapter 12 and are available in their original form online at *www.nsa.gov.*
145 "Venona wiped them away": Much later, additional confirmation of Bentley's story would come from secret documents and memos in the KGB archives that were briefly opened to western researchers in the 1990s. See Klehr and Haynes, *Secret World*, pp. 295, 312–17.
145 "the disadvantages were, according to Hoover and his top assistants, 'overwhelming' ": FBI memo, A. H. Belmont to L. V. Boardman, Feb. 1, 1956, FBI Venona file, p. 69.
147 "there was no proof of any other kind of relationship": May, *Un-American Activities*, p. 89.
147 " '. . . an acquittal under very embarrassing circumstances' ": Letter, E. P. Morgan to H. H. Clegg, Jan. 14, 1947, quoted in Haynes and Klehr, *Venona*, p. 161.

CHAPTER 14: RED SPY QUEEN
149 "But once again, Moscow demurred": This exchange was found in documents in the KGB archives, summarized in Weinstein and Vassiliev, *Haunted Wood*, p. 108.
150 "she was earning $800 a month": Bentley's testimony, *Export Policy and Loyalty*, July 30, 1948, p. 10. This salary put her in the top 3.5 percent of American wage earners, according to Current Population Reports: Consumer Income (series P-60), issue No. 1 (Jan. 28,

1948), Washington, DC: U.S. Bureau of the Census, Table 11, p. 17.

150 "she received a $2,000 bonus": FBI report "Re: Confidential Informant Gregory," Bentley file No. 65-14603.

150 "Hoover was once again pushing for action": FBI report, New York field office to director, Oct. 3, 1948, Bentley file No. 61-6328-81.

151 "the corporation stopped doing business at the end of February 1947": FBI report "Re: Confidential Informant Gregory," pp. 6–7, Bentley file No. 65-14603; also Peake's afterword in *Out of Bondage* (1988), p. 303, fn. 279.

151 "she found a similar position at Pacific Molasses, Ltd., in New York City": See Peake's afterword, *Out of Bondage*, p. 303, fn. 280, for relevant FBI documents.

152 "just what she said had been promised, her $9,600 yearly salary": FBI memo "Re: Gregory, Espionage-R," Nov. 1, 1950, p. 6.

152 "But Bentley had never been a good money manager": As former Special Agent Jack Dahany commented in an interview with Peake, whatever her skills, managing money was not one of them. See Peake's afterword in *Out of Bondage* (1988), p. 303, fn. 285.

152 "she treated herself to a two-week vacation in Bermuda": Peake's afterword in *Out of Bondage* (1988), p. 268.

152 "for possible prosecution": FBI memo, D. M. Ladd to director, Aug. 24, 1948, Hiss papers.

152 "Did she have any drawbacks . . . alcohol, narcotics, a criminal record, mental instability?": FBI memo, Theron Caudle to director, Dec. 13, 1946, Hiss papers.

153 "see how Bentley comported herself": My understanding of the grand jury system comes from University of Oregon law professor Margaret Paris.

153 "Donegan seemed the natural choice": Nelson Frank, "Special Assistant Donegan," *American Mercury,* August 1953 (v. 77), pp. 30–33.

153 "a man named T. Vincent Quinn, was also involved": FBI letter, D. M. Ladd to director, Aug. 24, 1948, Hiss papers.

153 "retold most of the story she had told to the FBI": Because grand jury testimony is secret and closed to the public unless an indictment results, much of the information about what happened during those thirteen months comes from other sources, such as later testimony before congressional committees or an occasional news magazine story based on leaked information. See, especially, *Newsweek,* Aug. 2, 1948, pp. 23–24, and *The Nation,* Jan. 30, 1954. Also Bentley's account in *Out of Bondage,* p. 308.

Lauchlin Currie repeated his grand jury testimony in his appearance before HUAC, *Communist Espionage*, Aug. 13, 1948, p. 853. For Remington's grand jury testimony, see May, *Un-American Activities*, p. 93. Coe repeated his grand jury testimony before HUAC, *Communist Espionage*, Aug. 13, p. 919. For William Taylor's testimony, see *The Nation*, Jan. 5, 1957, p. 5. For the testimony of Duncan Lee, Sonya and Bela Gold, Bernard Redmont see Packer, *Ex-Communist Witnesses*, p. 114, and Belfrage, *American Inquisition*, p. 185n.

155 "Brothman and his secretary, Miriam Moscowitz": Lamphere, *FBI-KGB*, pp. 142–43, 169–70; 172; *New York Times*, July 30, 1951, p. 1.

155 "it was politically 'too hot' to pursue": *Newsweek*, Aug. 2, 1948, p. 23.

156 "the resultant publicity 'would not be unfavorable' ": May, *Un-American Activities*, p. 94.

156 "the twelve-man national board of the American Communist Party": *Newsweek*, Aug. 2, 1948, p. 23. All were subsequently found guilty and sentenced to five years and a $10,000 fine, except Robert Thompson, a decorated soldier, who was given a three-year sentence. See Belfrage, *American Inquisition*, p. 104.

157 "it would be harder, riskier—and of little use—for the KGB to harm her": Whittaker Chambers, *IPR hearings*, May 29, 1952, p. 4784. In a Nov. 21, 1947, column by Marquis Childs, the *Washington Post* had already leaked the information that the grand jury's investigation had been prompted by "a woman of education." Bentley had every reason to be nervous.

158 "Frank's nose for news began to twitch": This and the rest of the narrative concerning how the newspaper series evolved is taken from "World Telegram Touched Off Spy Expose," *New York World Telegram*, Aug. 5, 1948, p. 1.

158 "a troubled witness who could blow his chances": FBI memo "Re: Gregory," April 5, 1948, pp. 1–2, Bentley file No. 65-14603-3847.

158 "the Department of Justice would not appreciate a story at this time": The newspaper wrote that it withheld the story "at the request of government officials." Nelson Frank and Norton Mockridge, "Super-Secrecy Veiled Russia's Spy Cells Here," *New York World Telegram*, July 22, 1948, p. 1.

159 "an attempt to throw a curve to the rest of the press": FBI Special Agent Jack Dahany had somewhat of the same idea. See Peake's afterword in *Out of Bondage* (1988), p. 275, fn. 7.

160 "full of the idealism which had flowered at Walden Pond and Brook Farm": "The Case of Mary and the Spy Ring," *Newsweek*, Aug. 2, 1948, p. 20.

161 "he could personally arrange for her appearance": "World Telegram Touched Off Spy Expose," *New York World Telegram,* Aug. 5, 1948, p. 1.

CHAPTER 15: THE LADY APPEARS

163 " '. . . an investigation was being made of that particular employee on questions of espionage and loyalty' ": *Export Policy and Loyalty,* July 30, 1948, p. 49.

164 "The small room became uncomfortably hot almost immediately": *Export Policy and Loyalty,* July 30, 1948, p. 50.

164 "the kind of outfit a woman of a certain age might wear to a ladies' luncheon": Physical descriptions and other details of the July 30 session are from coverage in the *New York Times,* July 31, 1948, p. 1; and photographs in *Life* magazine, Aug. 9, 1948, p. 23.

164 " 'plump . . . with a sharp nose and a receding chin' ": *Time,* Aug. 9, 1948, p. 14.

164 "treating her kindly": So Nelson Frank told FBI agent Joe Kelley, FBI memo "Re: Gregory," July 29, 1948, Bentley file No. 65-14603-3934.

164 "they knew far more about him than could be found in his official records": O'Reilly, *Hoover and the Un-Americans,* p. 106.

165 " '. . . that is a woman's privilege' ": *Export Policy and Loyalty,* July 30, 1948, p. 1.

165 "but Ferguson quickly dubbed a 'communist front' ": *Export Policy and Loyalty,* July 30, 1948, p. 4.

165 "slightly nasal East Coast finishing school tone about it": I thank speech pathologist Jane Eyre McDonald for listening to tapes of Bentley and offering her professional assessment.

166 " 'We would like to conduct this hearing if we can concerning one person: William Remington' ": *Export Policy and Loyalty,* July 30, 1948, p. 6.

166 " 'I do not want to go too fast now, on this' ": *Export Policy and Loyalty,* July 30, 1948, p. 8.

166 "because she had access to material at the Italian Library of Information": *Export Policy and Loyalty,* July 30, 1948, p. 7.

166 " 'effect of Mr. Golos was wearing off' ": *Export Policy and Loyalty,* July 30, 1948, p. 44.

167 "they met in drugstores and on park benches 'ten or fifteen or twenty' times": *Export Policy and Loyalty,* July 30, 1948, p. 31.

167 " '. . . and I don't too much like having to do this to Mr. Remington, either' ": *Export Policy and Loyalty,* July 30, 1948, p. 45.

168 "Golos was a Dutch journalist writing a book": *Export Policy and Loyalty,* July 31, 1948, p. 91, and Aug. 3, 1948, p. 186.

168 "That's why they met on street corners": *Export Policy and Loyalty,* Aug. 3, 1948, pp. 189–90.

168 "contributions to an antifascist fund, he said": *Export Policy and Loyalty,* Aug. 3, 1948, p. 204.

168 "he wanted to examine the stories in the paper to evaluate their accuracy": *Export Policy and Loyalty,* Aug. 3, 1948, p. 199.

168 "Nothing was secret or confidential": *Export Policy and Loyalty,* Aug. 3, 1948, p. 185.

168 "accusing himself only of 'forgivably erroneous judgment' ": *Export Policy and Loyalty,* Aug. 3, 1948, p. 190.

169 "it did not appear to me to be of a dubious nature": *Export Policy and Loyalty,* Aug. 3, 1948, p. 232.

169 "Ferguson called his story 'preposterous' ": *Export Policy and Loyalty,* Aug. 3, 1948, p. 203.

169 "dismissed him as a 'boob' ": May, *Un-American Actvities,* p. 100.

169 "he was sure he could prove his innocence when he testified again": *New York Times,* July 31, 1948, p. 1.

169 "staying after the questions to chat with reporters and pose for photographs": May, *Un-American Activies,* p. 98.

169 "had placed 'perhaps thousands' of its members in government jobs": *New York Times,* Aug. 3, 1948, p. 1.

CHAPTER 16: UN-AMERICAN ACTIVITIES

172 " '. . . keep the heat on Harry Truman' ": *New York Times,* Feb. 8, 1954.

172 "HUAC would lead the way": Insights into the political motivation of HUAC come from Carr, *The House Committee,* pp. 86–88; Cook, *FBI Nobody Knows,* p. 287; O'Reilly, *Hoover and the Un-Americans,* p. 8.

172 "information already known to the FBI, and most probably leaked to the committee": Cook, *FBI Nobody Knows,* p. 288.

172 " 'drive these rats from the federal . . . payroll' ": HUAC, *Communist Espionage,* July 31, 1948, p. 502.

172 " 'Share and share alike—that's democracy!' ": Kempton, *Part of Our Time,* p. 203. In a study made at the height of the Red Scare and using the hypersensitive standards of the time, Dorothy Jones found no trace of communist propaganda in 159 films released between 1929 and 1949 in which a member of the Hollywood Ten had screen credits.

173 "They stood trial, were found guilty and, after various appeals, went to jail": Fariello, *Red Scare,* pp. 257–58; Kempton, *Part of Our Time,* pp. 202–06; and *www.lib.berkeley.edu/MRC/blacklist.html.* The Hollywood Ten were: novelist, journalist, and Warner Bros. screenwriter Alvah Bessie; director, producer, and screenwriter Herbert Biberman; cofounder of the Screenwriters Guild Lester Cole;

director Edward Dmytryk (who later returned to HUAC as a "friendly witness"); Oscar-winning screenwriter Ring Lardner Jr.; playwright and screenwriter John Howard Lawson; Warner Bros. and Paramount scriptwriter Albert Maltz; novelist and early Screen Actors Guild board member Samuel Ornitz; screenwriter and producer Adrian Scott; former newspaper reporter and MGM scriptwriter Dalton Trumbo.

173 "not one listed HUAC as a committee preference": Carr, *The House Committee*, p. 209.

173 "coarse and vindictive on the House floor": Carr, *The House Committee*, pp. 214–17.

173 "later convicted and sent to federal prison": Cook, *FBI Nobody Knows*, p. 287.

173–4 " 'the beginnings of a communist dictatorship the likes of which America has never dreamed' ": Caute, *The Great Fear*, p. 90.

174 " 'hounded and persecuted the Savior during his earthly ministry' ": 91 Congressional Record 7737 (July 18, 1945).

174 "was sympathetic to the Ku Klux Klan": Haynes and Klehr, *Venona*, p. 149.

174 "vehemently disagreed with Truman's post-war foreign policy in general": Carr, *The House Committee*, p. 228.

174 "a battalion of newsreel cameras and klieg lights": As described by Whittaker Chambers in *Witness*, p. 539.

174 "Bentley appeared unintimidated": For reports on the hearings, see *New York Times,* July 31, Aug. 1, 4, 7, 1948, all p. 1; *Washington Post,* Aug. 3, 1948, p. 1; *Time* magazine, Aug. 9, 23, 1948, both pp. 15–16; *Life* magazine, Aug. 16, 1948, p. 26.

175 " 'No; I never was,' Bentley replied": HUAC, *Communist Espionage,* July 31, 1948, p. 549.

176 "The list continued": HUAC, *Communist Espionage,* July 31, 1948, pp. 508–18.

176 "she could have easily made that assumption": HUAC, *Communist Espionage,* July 31, 1948, p. 508.

176–7 "it was their duty to do something about it": HUAC, *Communist Espionage,* July 31, 1948, p. 526.

177 " 'That is right,' Bentley said": The exchange between Bentley and Hébert is in HUAC, *Communist Espionage,* July 31, 1948, pp. 550–51.

178 "shipped out 'by the boatload' ": HUAC, *Communist Espionage,* July 31, 1948, p. 558.

178 "The congressmen laughed": Nixon's comments and the exchange between committee members is in HUAC, *Communist Espionage,* July 31, 1948, pp. 555–56.

178 "Hébert called her a 'reformed saint' ": HUAC, *Communist Espionage,* p. 952.

179 "thanking her again in the committee's name": The congressmen's laudatory comments are found in HUAC, *Communist Espionage,* July 31, 1948, pp. 559–60.

179 " 'It was worth a try' ": For Stripling's reasoning, see Stripling, *The Red Plot,* p. 97.

180 "He perspired profusely": In his book *Witness,* Chambers spends many pages describing the agony of testifying in public. See also Cook, *FBI Nobody Knows,* p. 298.

180 " '. . . the concealed enemy against which we are fighting' ": HUAC, *Communist Espionage,* Aug. 3, 1948, p. 572.

181 "There were four handwritten notes, sixty-five single-spaced pages of retyped cables, and three rolls of microfilm": Weinstein, *Perjury,* pp. 204–35.

181 " 'the trial of the century' ": Hiss died in 1996 at age 92, still maintaining his innocence.

182 "He would invoke his constitutional privilege under the Fifth Amendment": Silvermaster's opening statement is in HUAC, *Communist Espionage,* Aug. 4, 1948, p. 590.

182 "you are afraid that if you answer 'No' we will prove you were a member": HUAC, *Communist Espionage,* Aug. 4, 1948, p. 594.

183 "The only spy ring he knew of, he said, was in Karl Mundt's head": Caute, *The Great Fear,* p. 33.

183 "inventions of irresponsible sensation-seekers": HUAC, *Communist Espionage,* Aug. 9, 1948, p. 699.

183 "inconsistency of Perlo denying the charges in his statement": HUAC, *Communist Espionage,* Aug. 9, 1948, pp. 694–95.

183 "his face ashen, his hands clasping his knees to keep them from shaking": Description of Perlo testifying is from coverage in *Time* magazine, Aug. 16, 1948, p. 19, and *Washington Post,* Aug. [date illegible], 1948, clipping in Hiss papers.

184 "No. And no": Lee's testimony, HUAC, *Communist Espionage,* Aug. 10, 1948, pp. 720–42.

184 " '. . . she has an extremely active imagination' ": HUAC, *Communist Espionage,* Aug. 10, 1948, p. 742.

184 " 'It's hard for me to believe,' he told the committee, 'that Miss Bentley's statements are those of a rational person' ": HUAC, *Communist Espionage,* Aug. 10, 1948, p. 723.

184 " '. . . figure out that something was unusual,' Mundt said": HUAC, *Communist Espionage,* Aug. 10, 1948, p. 735.

185 "a woman with a serious drinking problem": *Washington Post* coverage, Aug. 11, 1948, p. 1.

185 "Coe and Bela Gold denying any involvement": HUAC, *Communist Espionage,* Aug. 13, 1948, pp. 906–12, 916.

185 "rejecting any possibility of indiscretion on his part": HUAC, *Communist Espionage,* Aug. 13, 1948, p. 853. Venona decrypts show Currie provided sensitive White House memoranda and a report on FDR's thinking about DeGaulle. They also indicate that he met with Akhmerov in October of 1944. After Currie testified before HUAC, he left the country for Colombia, renouncing his U.S. citizenship in the mid-1950s. Romerstein and Breindel, *Venona Secrets,* p. 183–84.

186 "White pulled strings to help members of the network": Bentley's signed FBI statement, pp. 27–28; Lamphere, *FBI-KGB,* p. 284.

186 " 'the most fantastic thing I have ever heard of' ": Rees, *Harry Dexter White,* pp. 409–11.

186 "Whittaker Chambers thought the performance was gripping": Chambers, *Witness,* p. 246.

186 "The room erupted in applause": White's opening statement is in HUAC, *Communist Espionage,* Aug. 13, 1948, pp. 877–79.

186 "denying that he knew anything about or had ever participated in espionage activities": HUAC, Communist Espionage, Aug. 13, 1948, p. 882.

187 "he had knowingly met with Soviet underground contacts": This is what Bruce Craig, in his meticulously researched and quite sympathetic study of White, concludes. See Craig, "Treasonable Doubt," p. 560.

187 "the FBI would positively identify White—whose code name was 'Jurist'—in a number of Venona messages": FBI memo, D. M. Ladd to director, Venona file, p. 17.

187 "He didn't survive the second one": On White's death, see Craig, "Treasonable Doubt," pp. 430–31.

187 "a 'red herring,' a political invention whose purpose was brazenly partisan": *New York World Telegram,* Aug. 5, 1948, p. 1.

187 "fearless, honest, and moral men crusading against the enemies of the American Way of Life": Latham, *Communist Controversy,* p. 8.

CHAPTER 17: SHE SAID, HE SAID

189 "But others, many others, sat up and took notice": The FBI believed that Bentley's revelations "resulted in the awareness on the part of the public as to the extent of Soviet espionage in government circles." FBI memo, Branigan to Belmont, Aug. 13, 1959, Bentley file No. 132-435-228.

190 " 'the queen bee of the informer set' ": Cook, *FBI Nobody Knows,* p. 283.

190 "as A. J. Liebling dubbed her": A. J. Liebling, "The Wayward Press," *The New Yorker,* Aug. 28, 1948, pp. 40–45.

190 "*The Nation* and *The New Republic* reviled her": *The Nation,* Aug. 7, 1948, and *The New Republic,* Aug. 16, 1948.

190 "God help that country where informers thrive/ Where slander flourishes and lies contrive": Quoted in Lamphere, *FBI-KGB,* p. 100.

190 "a story that she had spent time in a mental institution": Bentley, *Out of Bondage,* p. 309.

190 "was now starved for attention": Author's interview with Jack Beckerman, June 24, 2000.

190 " 'We will wright (sic) the last chapter' ": Reproduced in a letter from the FBI to the U.S. attorney, Nov. 5, 1948, Bentley file No. 65-56402-3693.

191 "the story went out across the country through the wire services": Bentley, *Out of Bondage,* p. 310.

192 " 'I thought of her as a vague, rather pleasant lady . . .' ": Quoted in May, *Un-American Activities,* p. 113. I owe much of my understanding of the Remington affair to May's insightful book.

192 " 'imparting nonpublic information to a person closely identified with communists' ": May, *Un-American Activities,* p. 121.

193 " 'strange combination of . . . brilliance and gullibility' ": May, *Un-American Activities,* p. 118.

193 "Yes, I would certainly do that": May, *Un-American Activities,* p. 118.

193 " 'But I did nothing wrong' ": May, *Un-American Activities,* p. 124.

193–4 "The panel then listened to a parade of impressive character witnesses": *New York Times,* Feb. 11, 1949, p. 1.

194 "a $100,000 suit against Bentley, NBC, and General Foods, the sponsor of *Meet the Press*": *William Remington v. Elizabeth Bentley, et. al.,* 4 Civ 47-554, U.S. District Court, Southern District, New York.

194 "so Remington's lawyers could take her deposition": FBI teletype, New York office to director, Nov. 13, 1948, Bentley file No. 134-435-5.

194 "RED WITNESS MISSING AT 100-G SLANDER SUIT ran a headline in the *New York Daily Mirror*": *New York Daily Mirror,* Nov. 13, 1948.

194 "Bentley was sequestered at a Catholic retreat in the Bronx": *New York World Telegram,* Nov. 16, 1948.

195 " 'quietly pursuing her religious meditations . . .' ": "Spy Queen in Catholic Retreat," *Washington Times Herald,* Nov. 16, 1948, p. 1.

195 "along the attendant and related evils of the New Deal": See Caute, *The Great Fear,* p. 108.

195 "Bentley was baptized into the faith": FBI memo, H. B. Fletcher to
D. M. Ladd, Nov. 4, 1948, Bentley file No. 134-435-4; *New York
Times,* Nov. 16, 1948, p. 1.

195 " 'a comforting, all-consuming dogma, absolute, unquestionable,
and infallible' ": See Gornick, *Romance of American Communism,* p.
203, who is extraordinarily articulate on this subject.

195 " 'They must have something to tie to' ": *Time* magazine, Nov. 24,
1948.

196 "in New Orleans, giving another lecture": For this sequence of
events, see James A. Wechsler, "The Remington Loyalty Case," *New
Republic,* Feb. 28, 1949, pp. 18–20; May, *Un-American Activities,*
pp. 123–26.

198 "a 'young man whose every action in public employment showed
a distinct anticommunist slant' ": Quoted in May, *Un-American
Activities,* p. 129.

198 "ordering him reinstated, with $5,000 back pay, in his Commerce
job": *New York Times,* Feb. 11, 1949, p. 1.

198 "he told journalists that he owed his clearance to 'the vigor of
democracy' ": Quoted in May, *Un-American Activities,* p. 130.

199 "There was no record of Bentley ever having been admitted to the
clinic": FBI teletype, New Haven office to director, Dec. 23, 1948,
Bentley file No. 134-435-8.

199 "drinking to excess and carrying on promiscuously": "Memorandum
of conversation with Dr. Lombardo," Rauh papers.

199 "tracking down leads about his communist activities": May,
*Un-American Activities,* pp. 138, 142.

199 "deliberated all through the spring and summer and into the fall":
May, *Un-American Activities,* pp. 136–37.

200 "teaching political science at Mundelein College": FBI letter, New
York office to director, Aug. 8, 1949, Bentley file No. 134-435-14.
For an understanding of Mundelein, I thank Sister Carolyn Farrell of
that institution.

200 "Her Catholic friends pulled strings": Olmstead, *Red Spy Queen,* p.
153.

201 "Bentley would never issue a retraction": May, *Un-American Activities,* pp. 141–42.

201 "Lawrence Spivak wrote a long and vehement letter to NBC's insurance company": Godfrey Schmidt to Elizabeth Bentley, May 5,
1950, in HUAC, *Regarding Communism,* May 6, 1950, p.
1851–52. See also *New York Herald Tribune,* March 1, 1950.

202 "Her frequent subpoenas 'did not help class morale,' she said":
Newspaper clippings in FBI file: *Washington Post,* May 1, 1950,

Bentley file No. 61-6328-A; *New Haven Register,* Oct. 16, 1951, Bentley file No. 134-435-48.

202 "Sister Mary Josephine thought it would be best if she left": May, *Un-American Activities,* p. 143.

202 " 'She fitted in here very well' ": Newspaper clipping in FBI file: *Washington Post,* May 1, 1950, Bentley file No. 61-6328-A.

202 "living temporarily at the Hotel Commodore": Bentley's testimony before HUAC, *Regarding Communism,* May 6, 1950, p. 1852.

202 "his client was not a party to the settlement and did not agree with it": FBI teletype, New York office to Washington, D.C., office, Feb. 8, 1950, Bentley file No. 134-435-16; HUAC, *Regarding Communism,* May 6, 1950, p. 1851.

CHAPTER 18: THE SPOTLIGHT

205 " 'Only Elizabeth Bentley can answer . . . these questions' ": I obtained the Aug. 13, 1948, *Meet the Press* broadcast (on tape) from the Library of Congress Motion Picture, Broadcasting and Recorded Sound Division. LWO 36768.

207 " 'there's still time to undo the damage we have so foolishly done' ": "Miss Bentley Urges Ex-Reds to Testify," *New York Times,* Aug. 18, 1948.

207 " 'the greatest sinners make the greatest saints' ": *Time* magazine, Nov. 29, 1948.

207 "made her a 'pushover' for communism": *New York Times,* Feb. 14, 1949, p. 17; *Washington Times Herald,* Feb. 13, 1949.

207 "she was 'surrounded by procommunist professors' ": Newspaper clipping (name unreadable), dated April 4, 1949, Bentley file No. 61-6328-A.

207 "the danger of communist propaganda spreading to young people": Newspaper clipping from *Brooklyn Eagle,* Jan. 12, 1951, Bentley file No. 61-6328-5ASB.

207 "a victim of brainwashing": *Huntsville* (Alabama) *Times,* March 11, 1949, p. 1.

207 "a meeting sponsored by the Motion Picture Alliance for the Preservation of American Ideals": Newspaper clipping from *Los Angeles Herald & Express,* June 29, 1949, in Hiss papers.

208 "charging $300 an evening": FBI memo, New York office to director, Jan. 23, 1952, Bentley file No. 134-435-52; FBI memo, New York office to director, Sept. 26, 1952, Bentley file No. 134-435-66.

208 " '. . . you are taking away from the party the brains behind it' ": Subcommittee on Immigration and Naturalization, *Communist Activities,* May 13, 1949, p. 117.

209 "agents served in the Soviet Union's United Nations' delegation and

on the staff of foreign-language newspapers published in America":
Subcommittee on Immigration and Naturalization, *Communist
Activities,* May 13, 1949, pp. 113–14.

209 " 'Yes, Mr. William Remington' ": Subcommittee on Immigration
and Naturalization, *Communist Activities,* May 13, 1949, p. 114.

210 "the single most expensive scientific endeavor in human history":
Thomas Hager, *Force of Nature,* New York: Simon & Schuster,
1995, p. 271.

210 "a 'hoax conspiracy' ": The case was officially called *U.S.A. v. Julius
Rosenberg, Ethel Rosenberg and Morton Sobell.* The FBI's FOIA electronic reading room has online a 171-page summary of the case at
*foia.fbi.gov/roberg.html.* See also "Atomic Espionage from Fuchs to
the Rosenbergs," in Weinstein and Vassiliev, *Haunted Wood,* pp.
172–222. A number of books proclaim the Rosenbergs' innocence
See, for example, Yalkowsky, *The Murder of the Rosenbergs,* and Walter and Miriam Schneir, *Invitation to an Inquest.* More recent books,
based on the Venona cables and new information from some of the
principals, argue that Julius was, indeed, a spy. See Roberts, *The
Brother,* and Feklisov, *The Man Behind the Rosenbergs.* Weinstein and
Vassiliev in *Haunted Wood* make a strong and informed case against
Julius as well. Sources on both sides agree that Ethel had little to do
with the operation.

210 "she initiated the investigation that eventually led to the Rosen-
bergs": Former FBI agent Don Shannon, who interviewed both
Brothman and Gold, was very helpful in piecing this together.
Author's interview with Shannon, July 22, 2000.

211 " '. . . only served the interests of Moscow, whether it be propaganda or espionage or sabotage' ": This and other key testimony can
be found online at *www.law.umkc.edu/faculty/projects/ftrials/rosenb.*

211 "Now Bentley was used to help establish a link between them and
Golos": I am in debt to Peake's afterword to *Out of Bondage* (1988),
p. 260, for this clear explanation.

212 "a man identifying himself as Julius called her several times": Bentley's signed FBI statement, p. 106. Rosenberg corroborated Bentley's account of him using her as a messenger for Golos when he met
with New York operative Alexander Feklissov in December of 1945.
See Weinstein and Vassiliev, *Haunted Wood,* p. 217.

212 "an accident waiting to happen": For good summaries of the entire
Remington affair, see Packer, *Ex-Communist Witnesses,* pp. 78–80,
and Caute, *The Great Fear,* pp. 287–89.

213 "turned over the Knoxville information to the eager Red-hunters at
HUAC": This is what Carr, *The House Committee,* p. 198, suspects,
and I think he's right.

213 "naming Remington as one of a half dozen members of the Knoxville cell": Testimony quoted and summarized in the *New York Times*, May 5, 1950, p. 2.

214 "either 'quite ignorant of the facts' or 'engaged in deliberate falsehood' ": *New York Times*, May 5, 1950, pp. 1–2.

214 "He had been a communist in Knoxville": In addition to the two Knoxville witnesses, Remington's ex-wife testified that he had been involved in Communist Party activities.

214 "Bentley's story—which she retold in detail before HUAC the following day—remained uncorroborated": HUAC, *Regarding Communism*, May 6, 1950, pp. 1849–64.

214 "the involvement of forty-four field offices, agents in seven foreign countries, and the special attention of J. Edgar Hoover": O'Reilly, *Hoover*, p. 150.

214 "a 'conscious agent,' not, as she had implied elsewhere, a confused idealist": May, *Un-American Activities*, p. 167.

215 "she had assured her former husband just the day before": May, *Un-American Activities*, p. 158.

215 "she would stop receiving alimony or child support": For insights into Ann Moos Remington, see May, *Un-American Activities*, pp. 44–48, 73–76, 110.

216 "her husband was 'a communist from my earliest acquaintance of him' ": Packer, *Ex-Communist Witnesses*, pp. 86–89. The grand jury testimony was reprinted in the opinion of the dissenting Court of Appeals judge, included as a footnote in Packer, p. 88.

217 " 'would be almost disastrous to the . . . Remington case' ": May, *Un-American Activities*, p. 203.

217 "Bentley told her story in ninety minutes": *New York Times*, Jan. 9, 1951, p. 1.

217 "her relationship with the foreman of the grand jury": *New York Times*, Jan. 11, 1951, p. 1.

218 "she remembered typing just such a contract": Packer, *Ex-Communist Witnesses*, p. 85.

218 "at the very least, eleven other men had voted for the indictment": *New York Times*, Jan. 12, 1951, p. 28.

218 "the crime, said the judge, had involved disloyalty to the country and so should be treated most seriously": May, *Un-American Activities*, pp. 263–65.

CHAPTER 19: MY LIFE AS A SPY

221 "begin to transform her experiences into salable prose": May, *Un-American Activities*, pp. 155–56 for the Bentley-Brunini meet-

ing and background on Brunini. Olmstead, *Red Spy Queen,* pp. 168–69, makes an interesting circumstantial case that Brunini may have written or rewritten most of the manuscript.

221 " 'this is John Brunini who is helping her do it' ": This was the testimony given by Mrs. Collins, Devin-Adair's publicity director at Remington's first trial. See May, *Un-American Activities,* p. 236. FBI teletype, New York office to director, Oct. 16, 1950, Bentley file No. 134-435-28, states that "Brunini assisted Miss Bentley in making arrangements with [the] publisher."

221 "Bentley signed the document": Packer, *Ex-Communist Witnesses,* p. 85.

221 "Devin Garrity arranged for her to stay": FBI memo, New York to director, June 23, 1950, Bentley file No. 134-435-24; FBI memo, New York to director, Jan. 4, 1951, Bentley file No. 134-435-[number illegible].

222 "the doctor who must perform a caesarian": May, *Un-American Activities,* p. 156.

222 "Mr. Sloane, she said, was under the influence of this friend": *New York Times,* Jan. 15, 1951, p. 1.

222 "a melodramatic memoir": Bentley's book was part of a torrent of confessional literature written by ex-communists who had seen the light, like Benjamin Gitlow's *I Confess* and Whittaker Chamber's *Witness.*

223 " 'waves of dizziness' swirl around her": Bentley, *Out of Bondage,* p. 96.

223 " '. . . fought back a rising hysteria' ": Bentley, *Out of Bondage,* p. 215.

224 " '. . . what a monstrous thing Communism is' ": Bentley, *Out of Bondage,* p. 311.

225 " 'a great deal of respect for the veracity of Elizabeth Bentley' ": Information about *McCall's* reaction and the meeting with the FBI in FBI memo, Tolson to Nichols, Jan. 24, 1951, Bentley file No. 134-435-35.

225 "three or four times what she made from the book advance": *McCall's* paid top dollar for serial rights. In early 1950, the magazine paid Sinclair Lewis $25,000 for a four-part series. Even if Bentley received only half that amount, it was still many times more than she received from Devin-Adair as an advance for the book. Thanks to veteran of the New York publishing world, Robert Loomis, for the *McCall's* payment information.

225 " 'a human document of tremendous interest and significance' ": *McCall's* news release, April 19, 1951, Bentley file No. 134-435-40.

226 " 'and we didn't turn communist' ": The press conference is covered in a column in the *Washington News,* April 24, 1951, p. 23, Bentley file No. 134-435-41.

227 " 'the disciplined, obedient Bolshevik' ": The *McCall's* stories ran in May 1951, beginning on p. 34; June, p. 36; July, p. 30; August, p. 50.

227 "the subcommittee directed its attention to the Institute of Pacific Relations": SISS, *Institute of Pacific Relations,* August 1951, pp. 403–47. Also see *Newsweek,* Aug. 27, 1951, pp. 21–22 for coverage of the hearings. Bentley discusses the IPR in *Out of Bondage,* pp. 193–94.

227 "the IPR was 'as red as a rose' ": SISS, *Institute of Pacific Relations,* August 1951, p. 437.

228 " 'beyond the advance she had already been given' ": May, *Un-American Activities,* p. 280.

228 " 'an illuminating book' ": *New York Herald Tribune Book Review,* Sept. 23, 1951, p. 6.

228 " 'fascinating and exciting account' ": *Chicago Sunday Tribune,* Oct. 14, 1951, p. 4.

228 " 'an interesting and instructive picture of a Communist secret agent' ": *The Atlantic,* November 1951, p. 91.

228 "neither an acute observer of herself nor of those around her": *Saturday Review of Literature,* December 1951, p. 58.

228 " '. . . for a spy thriller, it is surprisingly dull' ": *New York Times Sunday Book Review,* Sept. 23, 1951, p. 6.

228 "The author he deemed 'obviously unstable' ": *The Commonweal,* Nov. 9, 1951, p. 120.

229 " '. . . as she had later with her New England conscience' ": *The New Yorker,* Oct. 20, 1951, p. 150.

229 "compiling a list of new names to investigate": FBI memo, special agent in charge, New York, to director, Dec. 17, 1953, Bentley file No. 134-435-95.

229 "enhanced the narrative by telescoping events": FBI memo, special agent in charge, New Orleans, to director, Jan. 14, 1954, Bentley file No. 134-182-38; FBI memo, Jan. 19, 1954, Bentley file No. 65-14603-4563.

230 "she had already spent all her money": Her lawyer suggested that she spread her 1951 income over four years to mitigate taxes, which, it turned out, greatly displeased the IRS. See FBI memo, Nichols to Tolson, May 20, 1955, Bentley file No. 134-435-146.

230 "Bentley bought her first house": FBI memo, special agent in charge, New York, to director, Sept. 29, 1951, Bentley file No. 134-435-45.

230 "She intended, she said, to live a much less hectic life": Clipping

from the *New Haven Register,* Oct. 16, 1951, Bentley file No. 134-435-48.

CHAPTER 20: THE CENTER CANNOT HOLD

233 "help build dossiers on suspected subversives": FBI report, Jan. 21, 1952, Bentley file No. 134-435-50.

234 "It was Granich": HUAC, *Communist Press,* Jan. 15, 1952, p. 2207.

234 " 'I took every possible precaution' ": SISS, *IPR,* May 29, 1952, p. 4789.

235 " 'It very definitely is,' replied the admiral": SISS, *IPR,* May 29, 1952, pp. 4790–91.

236 "they don't bother with clerks": *"Capital Reds Held Still Unexposed." New York Times,* May 30, 1952.

236 "nothing more than what she had told the committee": FBI memo, D. M. Ladd to A. H. Belmont, Nov. 23, 1953, Bentley file No. 134-435-[illegible].

237 "the only money she had ever received from the government was reimbursement for travel": FBI memo, W. A. Branigan to A. H. Belmont, Oct. 15, 1952, Bentley file No. 134-435-70.

237 "the company owed her nothing": FBI memo, director to special agent in charge, New York, March 24, 1955, Bentley file No. 100-94014.

238 "the $2,000 she had handed over to the bureau back in 1945": This meeting detailed in FBI memo, A. H. Belmont to Mr. Ladd, Jan. 15, 1952, Bentley file No. 65-56402-3944.

238 "The return of the money 'cannot be recommended . . .'": FBI letter, special agent in charge, New York, to director, Jan. 4, 1951, Bentley file No. 65-14603.

239 "hinting that the Bureau might want to reverse its previous decision": FBI memo, A. H. Belmont to Mr. Ladd, Jan. 15, 1952, Bentley file No. 65-56402-3944.

239 "handed Elizabeth Bentley the envelope containing the $2,000 in cash": FBI memo, special agent in charge, New York, to director, July 10, 1952, Bentley file No. 134-435-59.

239 "She appeared nervous and depressed": Author's interview with Nathaniel Weyl, July 31, 2000.

239 "emotionally volatile, alternately weepy and demanding": FBI letter, director to William Tompkins, March 4, 1955, Bentley file No. 134-435-134.

239 "insulin shock treatments": On Katherine Perlo, see FBI memo, special agent in charge, Dallas, to director, July 31, 1952, Bentley file No. 65-57904-37X; FBI memo, special agent in charge, Houston, to director, April 4, 1952, Bentley file No. 65-57904-35.

239 "she was suffering from 'a severe case of hallucinations' ": On Helen Tenney, see FBI report "Re: Confidential Informant Gregory," Bentley file No. 65-14603.

240 "the local pastor paid a call": FBI memo, special agent in charge, New York, to director, May 16, 1952, Bentley file No. 134-435-58.

241 "Wright said he 'blew his cork and hit her with a right cross' ": The altercation is chronicled in a series of FBI memos: FBI memo, special agent in charge, New York, to director, May 16, 1952, Bentley file No. 134-435-58; A. H. Belmont to D. M. Ladd, May 13, 1952, Bentley file No. 134-435-56; A.H. Belmont to D.M. Ladd, May 15, 1952, Bentley file No. 134-435-57.

241 "Bentley and Wright had gotten sloppy drunk together": FBI report to A. H. Belmont and W. V. Cleveland, May 8, 1952, Bentley file No. 134-435-[no number assigned].

242 "A short time later, Mr. Wright disappeared": FBI memo, Mr. Belmont to Mr. Ladd, May 13, 1952, Bentley file No. 134-435-55; FBI memo, A. H. Belmont to Ladd, May 13, 1952, Bentley file No. 134-435-56; also see May, *Un-American Activities,* p. 281.

242 "payments to Bentley of $50 a week for three weeks": FBI memo, special agent in charge, New York, to director, July 10, 1952, Bentley file No. 134-435-59; see also FBI memo quoted in Yalkowsky, *Murder of the Rosenbergs,* p. 333.

242 " 'in recognition of [her] time and assistance' ": FBI memo, special agent in charge, New Haven, to director, June 27, 1955, Bentley file No. 134-435-169.

242 "a $500 lump-sum payment to help settle her debts": FBI memo, special agent in charge, New York, to director, July 10, 1952, Bentley file No. 134-435-59; FBI memo special agent in charge, New York, to director, April 10, 1953, Bentley file No. 134-435-76; FBI memo, A. H. Belmont to Mr. Ladd, Oct. 15, 1952, Bentley file No. 65-56402-3944, p. 1.

243 "Cohn had once again saved the day": Details of the incident in FBI memo, special agent in charge, New York, to director, Sept. 4, 1952, Bentley file No. 134-435-63; teletypes, New Haven office to director and special agent in charge, New York, Aug. 29, 1952, 6:17 P.M. and 6:25 P.M., Bentley file No. 134-435-62; FBI memo, A. H. Belmont to Mr. Ladd, Aug. 29, 1952, Bentley file No. 134-435-61.

244 "She was 'difficult to handle' ": This incident is detailed in FBI memos, A. H. Belmont to C. E. Hennrich, Sept. 22, 1952, Bentley file No. 134-435-65; and special agent in charge, New York, to director, Sept. 26, 1952, Bentley file No. 134-435-66.

245 "that much more unable to take care of her own affairs": This affair is detailed in FBI memos, Thomas McAndrews, New York office, to

director, Sept. 29, 1952, Bentley file No. 134-182-6; Lester Gallaher, New York office, to director, Sept. 23, 1952, Bentley file No.
134-182-5; A. H. Belmont to D. M. Ladd, Sept. 26, 1952, Bentley
file No. 134-435-67; New York to director, Sept. 26, 1952, Bentley
file No. 134-435-66.

246 "cease to be the 'neurotic' and 'emotionally unstable' burden she
had become": Her financial problems and the Bureau's reaction are
chronicled in FBI memos, New York to director, Sept. 26, 1952,
Bentley file No. 134-435-66; New York to director, Oct. 8, 1952,
Bentley file No. 134-182-7; W. A. Branigan to A. H. Belmont, Oct.
15, 1952, Bentley file No. 134-435-70.

247 "bail her out of her financial difficulties": FBI memo, A. H. Belmont
to Mr. Ladd, Oct. 15, 1952, Bentley file No. 65-56402-3944.

247 " '. . . every time she finds herself in financial or other difficulties' ":
FBI memo, New York to director, Oct. 22, 1952, Bentley file No.
134-435-69.

247 "She 'appeared much less nervous and more reasonable in her attitude' ": FBI memo from Lester Gallaher, Oct. 29, 1952, Bentley file
No. 134-182-8.

247 "step out in front of a car and settle everything": FBI report, New
York office, March 9, 1955, p. 6, Bentley file No. 134-182-74.

CHAPTER 21: BACK IN THE ACT
249 "Alfred Kohlberg, a wealthy anticommunist bigwig": FBI memo,
special agent in charge, New York, to director, Jan. 16, 1953, Bentley file No. 134-435-72.

249 "the $50 a week she was continued to be paid by the FBI": FBI
memo, special agent in charge, New York, to director, April 10,
1953, Bentley file No. 134-435-76.

250 " 'a mean, vengeful and subversive act' ": Cook, "The Remington
Tragedy," p. 498.

250 " 'Not a thing,' Bentley said": May, *Un-American Activities,* p. 285.

251 "Bentley 'conducted herself in a creditable fashion' ": FBI memo,
special agent in charge, New York, to director, Jan. 16, 1953, Bentley file No. 134-435-72.

251 " 'very indiscreet in . . . having this contact at all' ": May, *Un-
American Activities,* p. 286.

251 "did not pass her any sensitive information": It was several years
later, in his application for parole, that Remington admitted he
"took it on [himself] to discuss information pertaining to war production with unauthorized persons on various occasions" and that
he knew Bentley was a "dedicated Communist Party member." May,
*Un-American Activities,* p. 71.

251 "The government—and Elizabeth Bentley—had finally prevailed": Details about Remington's second trial come from Cook, "The Remington Tragedy," May, *Un-American Activities,* pp. 271–92; Caute, *The Great Fear,* pp. 287–89; Packer, Ex-Communist Witnesses, pp. 78–80. Also see *United States v. Remington,* 208 F.2d 567 (2d Cir. 1953).

252 "Lamphere knew all the arguments": The arguments are well articulated in FBI memo, A. H. Belmont to L. V. Boardman, Feb. 1, 1956, Venona file, pp. 61–72.

252 "Hoover pulled the plug on the scheme": Lamphere, *KGB-FBI,* p. 279; author's interviews with Robert Lamphere, June 23, 2000, Jan. 5, 2001.

253 " 'infiltrate the executive and legislative branches' ": SISS, *Interlocking Subversion,* Part I, April 10, 1953.

253 " 'a loyal citizen [who] never betrayed the interests of the United States' ": Silvermaster's testimony begins on p. 101 of SISS, *Interlocking Subversion,* Part 3, April 16, 1953.

254 " 'I can't recall' and 'I don't have the least idea' ": Perlo testimony in SISS, *Interlocking Subversion,* Part 7, May 12, 1953.

254 "all of whom consistently took the Fifth": A secret memo from NKVD to the Comintern in 1944—unearthed when the KGB archives were opened briefly to western researchers in 1992—asks for information on Wheeler, Kramer, Fitzgerald, Magdoff, Glasser, and Perlo, an indication that they were of particular interest to the intelligence community in Russia. See Klehr, *Secret World,* p. 316.

254 "rat hunts": SISS, *Interlocking Subversion,* Part 7, May 12, 1953, p. 397.

254 "Communists had stolen thousands of diplomatic, political, military, scientific, and economic secrets": SISS, *Interlocking Subversion . . . Report,"* July 30, 1953.

255 "contact Bentley once a month": FBI memo, special agent in charge, New York, to director, April 10, 1953, Bentley file No. 134-435-76.

255 "The series, which began appearing just after Thanksgiving 1953": *St. Louis Post-Dispatch,* Nov. 30, Dec. 1, 2, 3, 4 and 6, 1953.

256 "her second appearance on *Meet the Press*": *Meet the Press,* Dec. 6, 1953. A videotape of the original kinescope is available through the National Library of Congress. My copy came courtesy of Hayden Peake.

258 "she had mentioned the Bureau 'only briefly' ": FBI memo, M. A. Jones to Mr. Nichols, Dec. 7, 1953, Bentley file No. 134-435-89.

258 "the *New York Mirror* reprinted the six-part series": The *New York Mirror* stories ran Dec. 13–18, 1953.

258 "send an agent to Grand Coteau": FBI memo, A. H. Belmont to W. A. Brannigan, Jan. 6, 1954, Bentley file No. 134-435-97.

259 "Bentley claimed she did not even review them before publication": FBI letter, New York to director, Jan. 29, 1954, Bentley file No. 65-134436.

CHAPTER 22: UNDER ATTACK

260 "denied all of Bentley's accusations": For a summary of the Taylor case, see *Charges made by William Henry Taylor on March 28, 1955, before the International Organizations Employees Loyalty Board*, pp. 1–4, William Taylor FBI file No. 100-370362.

261 "the suit would delay his dismissal from the IMF": FBI memo, special agent in charge, New Orleans, to director, June 1, 1954, Bentley file No. 134-435-116; FBI memo, Lester Gallaher to special agent in charge, New York, June 17, 1954, Bentley file No. 134-182-50.

261 " '. . . she will not have to appear and give a deposition' ": FBI memo, special agent in charge, New Orleans, to director, May 7, 1954, Bentley file No. 134-435-112. See also FBI memo, special agent in charge, New Orleans, to director, April 14, 1954, Bentley file No. 134-435-105.

262 "the libel trial would finally provide that opportunity": "Suit May Force Bentley to Be Cross-Examined," *Daily Worker*, Dec. 19, 1955, in Bentley file No. 134-182-128.

262 "the FBI's duty to protect those who, like herself, had assisted the government": FBI memo, special agent in charge, New Orleans, to director, May 7, 1954, Bentley file No. 134-435-110.

262 "she was under FBI protective custody": Letter, Assistant Attorney General Warren Olney to director, FBI, April 19, 1954, Bentley file No. 134-435-104; FBI memo, special agent in charge, New Orleans, to director, April 14, 1954, Bentley file No. 134-435-105.

263 " '. . . possible future value as a government witness' ": FBI teletype, Hoover to special agent in charge, New Orleans, April 19, 1954, Bentley file No. 134-435-105. [Different document but same number assigned as April 14 memo for reasons unknown.]

263 " '. . . a demented person' ": FBI teletype, Boswell to director, May 8, 1954, Bentley file No. 134-435-109.

263 "if the plaintiff in the libel suit was, as she alleged, a communist": Letter, Assistant Attorney General Warren Olney to director, FBI, May 13, 1954, Bentley file No. 134-435-108.

264 " '. . . the impossibilities of her story' ": "Ex-US Aide Attacks Bentley Story," *New York Post*, April 19, 1955.

264 " '. . . she can scarcely be looked at as a credible source' ": "Charges Made by William Henry Taylor," p. 4, William Taylor FBI file No. 100-370362.

264 "uncovered a number of discrepancies": For the complete listing of charges, see "Charges Made by Taylor," pp. 8–80a; for the FBI's summary, see FBI memo, L. V. Boardman to A. H. Belmont, June 6, 1955, Bentley file No. 134-435-153.

265 "no intent to mislead": One exception was, I think, her testimony that she had come forth to tell her story to the FBI in August of 1945. This is when she made her initial inquiry about Peter Heller. She mentioned nothing about her espionage activities until November. It is possible that she simply misremembered the dates. But I think it is more likely that she lied to make herself look better and to obscure her affair with Heller.

265 "the case against Bentley was still weak": I am indebted to Hayden Peake's analysis of the Taylor charges in his afterword to the 1988 edition of *Out of Bondage*, pp. 239–47.

265 "the government's failure to make anyone believe Bentley's story": Erik Bert, "Why They Shield the Queen Spy," *The Worker*, May 22, 1955, p. 7.

265 "keep Bentley out of the hands of Taylor's attorneys": FBI memo, L. V. Boardman to A. H. Belmont, April 21, 1955, Bentley file No. 134-435-[no number assigned].

265 "the thirty-seven discrepancies he had uncovered": FBI memo, W. A. Branigan to A. H. Belmont, Oct. 8, 1954, Bentley file No. 134-435-123.

266 " 'undone' by Taylor's accusations": "Where Red Spy Queen Tripped Up," *The Worker*, May 8, 1955, in Bentley file No. 134-182-94.

266 "BENTLEY CLAMS UP ran the headline": *New York Post*, April 20, 1955, in Bentley file No. 134-182-78.

266 "Remington had less than nine months left": May, *Un-American Activities*, pp. 7–9, 310, on Remington's murder.

266 "cast doubt on Bentley's credibility": FBI memo, special agent in charge, New Orleans, to director, Jan. 16, 1956, Bentley file No. 134-435-210.

266 "direct repudiation of the Red Spy Queen": For example, "Vindication for William Taylor," *The Nation*, Jan. 28, 1956, p. 63.

267 "it had been manufactured": Byron Scott, "The Letter Nobody Wrote," *The Nation*, Jan. 5, 1957, p. 5; See also Packer, *Ex-Communist Witnesses*, p. 116.

267 "just the 'opening barrage of an attack' on her integrity": FBI

memo, special agent in charge, New Orleans, to director, Jan. 16, 1956, Bentley file No. 134-435-210.

267 " 'just too happy' to be in the clear": "Testimony in Loyalty Case Eyed," *State Times* (Baton Rouge, LA), Jan. 7, 1956, p. 1.

267 "the Library of Congress researcher was 'off the committee payroll' ": Letter, FBI director to attorney general, Sept. 27, 1955, Bentley file No. 134-435-195; FBI memo, L. E. Nichols to Mr. Tolson, Oct. [illegible], 1955, Bentley File No. 134-435-[no number assigned].

268 "gone out on double dates with Roy Cohn": Fariello, *Red Scare*, pp. 97–108.

268 " '. . . a remarkable political confession . . .' ": Quoted on Matusow Web site *www.beastofbusiness.com/fats/*.

268 " '. . . I was not just another guy' ": Matusow, *False Witness*, p. 29.

268 " '. . . the pats on the back' ": Matusow, *False Witness*, p. 46.

268 " 'I was a national figure' ": Quoted in Yalkowsky, *Murder of the Rosenbergs*, p. 137.

269 "Miss Bentley, I believe, gave false testimony": Matusow testified before SISS, *Strategy and Tactics*, Feb. 22, 23, and 28, 1955, pp. 3–288; see also "Harvey Matusow Tells Senators: You Turned Me Into a Stoolpigeon," *The Daily Worker*, March 1, 1955, p. 3, Bentley file No. 134-182-71.

269 "willing to testify and deny the allegations": FBI teletype, director to special agent in charge, New Orleans, Feb. 2, 1955, Bentley file No. 134-435-129.

269 "An attack on Bentley was an attack on the director": FBI memo, A. H. Belmont to L. V. Boardman, Feb. 23, 1955, Bentley file No. 134-435-[no number assigned].

269–70 "refute Matusow's charges": FBI teletype, New Orleans to director, Feb. 22, 1955, Bentley file No. 134-435-130.

270 "jeopardizing her job at the college": FBI memo, Lester Gallaher to special agent in charge, New York, Feb. 25, 1955, Bentley file No. 134-182-59.

270 "to help establish her whereabouts": FBI memo, L. B. Nichols to Mr. Tolson, Feb. 24, 1955, Bentley file No. 134-435-135.

270 " '. . . serious embarrassment to the Bureau' ": FBI letter, special agent in charge, New York, to director, March 24, 1955, Bentley file No. 134-182-66.

270 "lunched with Matusow earlier that day": FBI memo, John Meade to special agent in charge, New York, Feb. 25, 1955, Bentley file No. 134-182-60.

271 "It turned out that three people could confirm": A 7,000-word

report was sent on to Washington. See FBI report, March 9, 1955, Bentley file No. 134-182-74.

271 "the uncommon names of Midwest towns": FBI teletype, New York to New Orleans, March 3, 1933, Bentley file No. 134-182-61.

271 "Matusow monopolized the conversation": FBI letter, James Kelly to U.S. Attorney J. Edward Lumbard, March 2, 1955, Bentley file No. 134-182-64.

271 " 'Matusow was continuously interrupting to tell about his' ": FBI teletype, New York to New Orleans, March 3, 1933, Bentley file No. 134-182-61.

272 "nine of them to the same woman": For Matusow's unusual life, see *www.ibiblio.org/mal/MO/matusow/*. Matusow claimed later to be Bentley's lover, according to Olmstead, *Red Spy Queen*, p. 184. There's no reason to assume that this story is any less fanciful than the others he told.

CHAPTER 23: AN UNSETTLED WOMAN

273 "in excess of her usual annual salary": Using the 1929 tax rate, which was not raised until 1951, and figuring backward based on how much money the IRS said she owed, it appears that Bentley earned just over $40,000 that year.

274 "Morris took up the matter with Deputy Attorney General William Rogers": FBI memo, L. B. Nichols to Mr. Tolson, May 20, 1955, Bentley file No. 134-435-140.

274 "now the IRS was zeroing in": FBI letter, director to attorney general, June 9, 1955, Bentley file No. 134-435-148.

274 "by those who didn't like what she had done": Letter, Bentley to Louis Nichols, Dec. 4, 1955, Bentley file No. 134-435-209.

274 " 'many adverse criticisms' ": FBI memo, special agent in charge, New Haven, to director, June 24, 1955, Bentley file No. 134-435-163.

275 "some powerful Senate allies": FBI letter, director to attorney general, Aug. 25, 1955, Bentley file No. 134-435-183.

275 " 'blow up the works' ": FBI memo, special agent in charge, New Haven, to director, June 24, 1955, Bentley file No. 134-435-163; also August 4, 1955, Bentley file No. 134-435-176.

275 "a full, public apology from the IRS": FBI memo, special agent in charge, New Haven, to director, June 27, 1955, Bentley file No. 134-435-169.

275 "the IRS hadn't raised a stink about that": FBI letter, director to attorney general, June 9, 1955, Bentley file No. 134-435-148.

275 "the IRS would be 'reasonable' ": FBI memo, L. B. Nichols to Mr. Tolson, June 14, 1955, Bentley file No. 134-435-155.

275 "considering her problem 'sympathetically' ": FBI memo, A. H. Belmont to L. V. Boardman, June 24, 1955, Bentley file No. 134-435-157.

276 "the FBI was helping her out of a tight spot": FBI memo, A. H. Belmont to L. V. Boardman, June 24, 1955, Bentley file No. 134-435-157; FBI memo, special agent in charge, New Haven, to director, July 9, 1955, Bentley file No. 134-435-168.

276 "would not authorize any public apology or retraction": FBI teletype, New Haven to director, Aug. 10, 1955, Bentley file No. 134-435-179.

276 "Fitzgerald was not taking this turn of events quietly": FBI memo, Special Agent Thomas McAndrews (New Haven) to special agent in charge, New York, Aug. 8, 1955, Bentley file No. 134-435-104.

276 " '. . . put up or shut up' ": "Elizabeth Bentley, FBI Spy Queen, Subpoenaed [*sic*] at Behest of Fitzgerald," *Daily Worker,* Aug. 15, 1955, p. 3.

276 "publicly commented on the value and veracity of her testimony": FBI teletype, New Haven to director, Aug. 11, 1955, Bentley file No. 134-182-110.

277 "germane to the case": FBI letter, Thomas J. McAndrews to special agent in charge, New York, Aug. 18, 1955, Bentley file No. 134-182-107.

277 "increasingly difficult to deal with": FBI memo, New Haven to director, July 2, 1955, Bentley file No. 134-435-162.

277 "a revenue agent who had 'tact and diplomacy' to talk to Bentley": FBI memo, L. V. Boardman to A. H. Belmont, June 24, 1955, Bentley file No. 134-435-156.

278 "slapping a lien on Bentley's bank account had been a mistake": FBI memo, L. B. Nichols to Mr. Tolson, June 27, 1955, Bentley file No. 134-435-161.

278 "pay a personal visit to the mother superior": FBI memo, L. B. Nichols to Mr. Tolson, July 5, 1955, Bentley file No. 134-435-165.

278 " 'indicative of the gross lack of cooperation upon the part of the Treasury Department' ": FBI memo, John Edgar Hoover to Mr. Tolson, Mr. Boardman, Mr. Belmont, Mr. Nichols, Sept. 12, 1955, Bentley file No. 134-435-192. See also FBI memo, Hoover to special agent in charge, New Haven, Aug. 8, 1955, Bentley file No. 134-435-176.

278 "an agreement was reached": FBI memo, Mr. Tolson to L. B. Nichols, Sept. 1, 1955, Bentley file No. 134-435-186. Letter, Louis Nichols to Elizabeth Bentley, Dec. 9, 1955, Bentley file No. 134-435-209.

278 "thinking about pursuing her Ph.D.": FBI memo, special agent in charge, New Orleans, to director, May 22, 1954, Bentley file No. 134-435-113.

278 " 'constantly beset' and under 'considerable mental strain' ": FBI memo, special agent in charge, New Orleans, to director, Feb. 18, 1955, Bentley file No. 134-435-128.

279 "cooperative and forthcoming": FBI memo, special agent in charge, New Orleans, to director, Jan. 29, 1954, Bentley file No. 134-435-[no number assigned]; FBI letter, special agent in charge, New Orleans, to director, Jan. 14, 1954, Bentley file No. 134-182-38.

279 "supply names or pertinent facts": FBI memo, special agent in charge, New Haven, to director, June 23, 1955, Bentley file No. 134-435-152.

279 "conversations Bentley may have had with Lovestone": FBI memo, director to special agent in charge, New Orleans, Nov. 9, 1955, Bentley file No. 134-435-204; FBI memo, special agent in charge, New Orleans, to director, Nov. 23, 1955, Bentley file No. 134-435-205.

280 "a past that followed her and made it difficult to find work": FBI memo, special agent in charge, New Orleans, to director, June 6, 1956, Bentley file No. 134-435-213.

281 "her autobiography has some real 'moments' in it": Letter [name obscured] to Mrs. Erb, May 13, 1957, in Bentley FBI file with no identifying number assigned.

282 " 'become a stool-pigeon to save her neck' ": Letter [name obscured] to Mrs. Erb, May 13, 1957, in Bentley FBI file with no number assigned.

282 " 'not entirely satisfied' with her as a teacher": FBI memo, special agent in charge, New York, to director, July 8, 1957, Bentley file No. 134-435-218.

283 "things were still not going well": Report on the blackout, hospitalization, and subsequent visit to New Haven field office in FBI memo, special agent in charge, New Haven, to director, March 3, 1958, Bentley file No. 134-435-220.

284 "room and board in exchange for help with the children": FBI memo, special agent in charge, New Haven, to director, May 15, 1958, Bentley file No. 134-435-221.

284 " 'when the occasion arose' ": FBI memo, special agent in charge, New Haven, to director, May 29, 1958, Bentley file No. 134-435-222.

285 "stay out of her life": FBI memo, special agent in charge, New Haven, to director, Feb. 25, 1958, Bentley file No. 134-435-224, and May 18, 1959, Bentley file No. 134-435-226.

CHAPTER 24: THE WAYWARD GIRL COMES HOME

287 " '. . . in the minds of the general public as well' ": Letter, Elizabeth Bentley to J. Edgar Hoover, Aug. 10, 1959, Bentley file No. 134-435-22[final number illegible].

287 " '. . . has proven to be correct' ": Letter, J. Edgar Hoover to Elizabeth Bentley, Aug. 13, 1959, Bentley file No. 134-435-229.

287 "secured a position for the fall": Letter, Elizabeth Bentley to J. Edgar Hoover, Nov. 11, 1959, Bentley file, no number assigned.

287 " 'poor family relationships' ": "Long Lane School," reprinted from the 1963–1964 Digest of Connecticut Administrative Reports to the Governor.

288 " 'build up good citizens in the coming generation,' she wrote": Letter, Elizabeth Bentley to J. Edgar Hoover, Nov. 11, 1959, Bentley file, no number assigned.

288 "teaching writing and literature, and serving as the adviser": Letter, Elizabeth Bentley to J. Edgar Hoover, May 31, 1961, Bentley file No. 134-435-232.

288 "did her job and went back to her quarters": Author's interview with Shirley Coddington, Long Lane social worker, 1959–91, Oct. 24, 2000; Roeker interview with Ethel Mecum, the woman who hired Bentley, in Roeker, "Communist Agent," p. 58.

289 "Bentley kept a bottle in her desk": Roeker interview with Florence McDermott, in Roeker, "Communist Agent," p. 58.

289 "She had a life, now, that she could live": The FBI kept tabs on her. See FBI memo, special agent in charge, New Haven, to special agent in charge, New York, Nov. 17, 1961, Bentley file No. 134-182-A-10. Her death certificate lists the Cherry Hill address.

290 " '. . . may still be needed at some future date' ": FBI letter, J. Edgar Hoover to Elizabeth Bentley, Nov. 19, 1959, Bentley file No. 134-435-231.

290 "a job that summer at General Dynamics": FBI memo, special agent in charge, New Haven, to director, July 11, 1960, Bentley file No. 134-435-[no final number assigned].

290 "unable to identify the man in question": FBI memo, special agent in charge, New Haven, to director, Jan. 19, 1961, Bentley file No. 65-57904.

290 " 'absolutely not willing to testify' ": FBI memo, special agent in charge, New York, to special agent in charge, New Haven, Nov. 17, 1961, Bentley file No. 134-182-A-10.

292 "Elizabeth Bentley was dead": My thanks to oncologist Peter Kovach for insights into the symptoms accompanying abdominal cancer and the complications that may follow surgery. Bentley's

death certificate makes note of the "exploratory laphrotomy" and the diagnosis of "carcinomatosis, primary unknown."

292 "She made headlines one last time": *New York Times,* Dec. 4, 1963, p. 47; *New York Herald Tribune,* Dec. 4, 1963, p. 28; *Washington Post,* Dec. 4, 1963, p. 35; *Newsweek,* Dec. 16, 1963, p. 60; *National Review,* Dec. 17, 1963, p. 510.

293 " 'warm regard and affection' for the Bureau": FBI radiogram, special agent in charge, New Haven, to director and special agent in charge, New York, Dec. 3, 1963, Bentley file No. 134-435-234. See also No. 134-182-A-12.

293 "the kind of spot one would choose for a picnic": My thanks to Roger Desmond for his keen eye.

# Bibliography

Abt, John. *Advocate and Activist: Memoirs of an American Communist Lawyer.* Urbana and Chicago: University of Illinois Press, 1993.

Barros, James. *No Sense of Evil: Espionage, the Case of E. Herbert Norman.* New York: Ballantine Books, 1986.

Belfrage, Cedric. *The American Inquisition, 1945–1960.* Indianapolis: The Bobbs-Merrill Co., Inc., 1973.

Belknap, Michal R. *Cold War Political Justice: The Smith Act, the Communist Party, and American Civil Liberties.* Westport, CT: Greenwood Press, 1977.

Bentley, Elizabeth. FBI File. FBI Freedom of Information Act Reading Room, Hoover Building, Washington, D.C.

Bentley, Elizabeth. FBI statement (signed), Nov. 30, 1945. Bentley file No. 65-56402-220.

Bentley, Elizabeth. *Out of Bondage: The Story of Elizabeth Bentley.* New York: Devin-Adair Co., 1951.

Bentley, Elizabeth. *Out of Bondage: The Story of Elizabeth Bentley.* With an afterword by Hayden Peake. New York: Ballantine Books, 1988.

Browder, Earl Russell. Oral History Collection, Columbia University.

Carpozi, George, Jr. *Red Spies in Washington.* New York: Trident Press, 1968.

Carr, Robert Kenneth. *The House Committee on Un-American Activities, 1945–1950.* Ithaca, NY: Cornell University Press, 1952.

Caute, David. *The Great Fear: The Anti-Communist Purge Under Truman and Eisenhower.* New York: Simon and Schuster, 1978.

Chambers, Whittaker. *Witness.* New York: Random House, 1952.

Cook, Fred J. *The FBI Nobody Knows.* New York: The Macmillan Company, 1964.

Cook, Fred J., "The Remington Tragedy," *The Nation,* Dec. 28, 1958 (vol. 185, no. 22), pp. 486–500.

Craig, Bruce. "Treasonable Doubt: The Harry Dexter White Case, 1948–1953 (Espionage)." Ph.D. dissertation, the American University, 1999.

Daniels, Elizabeth A. *Bridges to the World: Henry Noble MacCracken and Vassar College.* Clinton Corners, NY: College Avenue Press, 1994.

Daniels, Elizabeth A. *Main to Mudd, and More: An Intimate History of Vassar College Buildings.* Poughkeepsie, NY: Vassar College, 1996.

Davis, Hope Hale. *Great Day Coming: A Memoir of the 1930s.* South Royalton, VT: Steerforth Press, 1994.

Davis, Hope Hale, "Looking Back at My Years in the Party: A Memoir," *The New Leader,* Feb. 11 1980, pp. 10–13, 16–18.

Fariello, Griffin. *Red Scare: Memories of the American Inquisition: An Oral History.* New York: W. W. Norton, 1995.

Feklisov, Alexander and Sergei Kostin. *The Man Behind the Rosenbergs.* New York: Enigma Books, 2001.

Gitlow, Benjamin. *I Confess: The Truth About American Communism.* New York: E. P Dutton and Co., 1940.

Gitlow, Benjamin. *The Whole of Their Lives: Communism in America—A Personal History and Intimate Portrayal of Its Leaders.* With a foreword by Max Eastman. New York: C. Scribner and Sons, 1948.

Gold, Harry. FBI File. In possession of Robert J. Lamphere.

Gornick, Vivian. *The Romance of American Communism.* New York: Basic Books, Inc., 1977.

Griffin, Margaret, ed. *Student Handbook of Vassar College.* Poughkeepsie, NY: Vassar College, 1926.

Hamby, Alonzo L. *Beyond the New Deal: Harry S. Truman and American Liberalism.* New York: Columbia University Press, 1973.

Haynes, John Earl and Harvey Klehr. *Venona: Decoding Soviet Espionage in America.* New Haven, CT: Yale University Press, 1999.

Hiss, Alger, "Papers of Alger Hiss." Manuscript Collections, Harvard Law School Library.

Hoover, J. Edgar. *Masters of Deceit: The Story of Communism in America and How to Fight It.* New York: Holt, Rinehart & Winston, 1958.

Kempton, Murray. *Part of Our Time: Some Ruins and Monuments of the Thirties.* New York: Simon and Schuster, 1955.

Kirschner, Don S. *Cold War Exile: The Unclosed Case of Maurice Halperin.* Columbia, MO: University of Missouri Press, 1995.

Klehr, Harvey. *The Heyday of American Communism: The Depression Decade.* New York: Basic Books, 1984.

Klehr, Harvey and John Earl Haynes. *The American Communist Movement: Storming Heaven Itself.* New York: Twayne Publishers, 1992.

Klehr, Harvey and John Earl Haynes, and Fridrikh Igorevich Firsov. *The Secret World of American Communism.* New Haven, CT, and London: Yale University Press, 1995.

Lamphere, Robert J. and Tom Schachtman. *The FBI-KGB War: A Special Agent's Story.* New York: Random House, 1986.

Latham, Earl. *The Communist Controversy in Washington: From the New Deal to McCarthy.* Cambridge, MA: Harvard University Press, 1966.

Matusow, Harvey. *False Witness.* New York: Cameron & Kahn, Publishers, 1955.

May, Gary. *Un-American Activities: The Trials of William Remington.* New York: Oxford University Press, 1994.

*Meet the Press.* Aug. 13, 1948; Dec. 6, 1983.

Navasky, Victor S. *Naming Names.* New York: Viking Press, 1980.

Nearing, Scott. *Must We Starve?* New York: The Vanguard Press, 1932.

New Milford Historical Society. *Two Centuries of New Milford, Connecticut: An Account of the Bi-Centennial Celebration of the Founding of the Town Held June 15, 16, 17 and 18, 1907, With a Number of Historical Articles And Reminiscences.* New York: The Press, 1907.

Olmstead, Kathryn S. *Red Spy Queen.* Chapel Hill: University of North Carolina Press, 2002.

O'Reilly, Kenneth. *Hoover and the Un-Americans: The FBI, HUAC, and the Red Menace.* Philadelphia: Temple University Press, 1983.

"Our Town," *New Milford Gazette,* Jan. 2, 1914.

Packer, Herbert. *Ex-Communist Witnesses: Four Studies in Fact Finding.* Stanford, CA: Stanford University Press, 1962.

Radosh, Ronald and Joyce Milton. *The Rosenberg File: A Search for the Truth.* New York: Vintage Books, 1984.

Rauh, Joseph. Papers. Library of Congress.

Redlich, Norman, "Spies in Government: I. The Bentley Story," *The Nation,* Jan. 30, 1954, pp. 85–88; "Spies in Government: II. The Jenner Report," *The Nation,* Feb. 6, 1954, pp. 109–111.

Rees, David. *Harry Dexter White: A Study in Paradox.* New York: Coward, McCann & Geoghegan, 1973.

Roberts, Sam. *The Brother.* New York: Random House, 2001.

Roeker, Robert, "The Story of a Communist Agent in America." M.A. thesis, Western Connecticut State University, 1985.

Romerstein, Herbert and Eric Breindel. *The Venona Secrets: Exposing Soviet Espionage and America's Traitors.* Washington, D.C.: Regnery Publications Inc., 2000.

Schneir, Walter and Miriam Schneir. *Invitation to an Inquest.* Garden City, NY: Doubleday, 1965; New York: Pantheon Books, 1983.

Silvermaster, Nathan Gregory. FBI File. FBI Freedom of Information Act Reading Room, Hoover Building, Washington, D.C.

Steinberg, Peter L. *The Great "Red Menace": United States Prosecution of American Communists, 1947–1952.* Westport, CT: Greenwood Press, 1984.

Straight, Michael Whitney. *After Long Silence.* New York: W. W. Norton, 1983.

Stripling, Robert E., Bob Considine, ed. *The Red Plot Against America.* Drexel, PA: Bell Publishing Co., 1949.

Stone, I. F. *The Haunted Fifties.* New York: Vintage Books, 1969.

Tanenhaus, Sam. *Whittaker Chambers: A Biography.* New York: Random House, 1997.

U.S. Congress. Senate. Senate Committee on Judiciary. Senate Subcommittee on Immigration and Naturalization. *Communist Activities Among Aliens and National Groups. Part 1,* 81st Cong., 1st sess., 10, 13, 16 May, 1, 8–9, 18 June, 15–16, 27–28 July, 10–12 August 1949.

U.S. Congress. Senate. Senate Committee on Judiciary. Senate Subcommittee on Amendments to the Displaced Persons Act. *Displaced Persons,* 81st Cong., 1st sess.; 81st Cong., 2nd sess., 25 March, 8 April, 26–27 July, 4–5, 11, 17–19, 23, 25–26, 31 August, 1, 9, 16, 23, 28, 30 September, 3, 7–8 October 1949; 3, 5, 19 January, 3, 6, 14–17, 22, 24 February, 3, 7–8, 10, 13, 15–16 March 1950.

U.S. Congress. Senate. Senate Committee on Expenditures in Executive Departments. *Export Policy and Loyalty. Part 1,* 80th Cong., 2nd sess., 30 July 1948.

U.S. Congress. House. House Committee on Un-American Activities. *Hearings Regarding Communism in the U.S. Government. Part 1,* 80th

Cong., 2nd sess.; 81st Cong., 2nd sess., 30 July, 7 August 1948; 20–21, 25, 29 April, 4–6 May, 8 June 1950.

U.S. Congress. House. House Committee on Un-American Activities. *Hearings Regarding Communist Espionage in the U.S. Government. Part 1,* 80th Cong., 2nd sess., 31 July, 3–5, 7, 9–13, 16–18, 20, 24–27, 30 August, 8–9 September 1948.

U.S. Congress. Senate. Senate Committee on Judiciary. Senate Subcommittee to Investigate the Administration of the Internal Security Act and Other Internal Security Laws; Senate Subcommittee Investigating the Institute of Pacific Relations. *Institute of Pacific Relations, Part 2,* 82nd Cong., 1st sess., 9, 14, 16, 20, 22–23 August 1951.

U.S. Congress. Senate. Senate Committee on Judiciary. Senate Subcommittee to Investigate the Administration of the Internal Security Act and Other Internal Security Laws. *Institute of Pacific Relations, Part 13,* 82nd Cong., 2nd sess., 2, 4, 5, 7–8 April, 15–16, 29 May 1952.

U.S. Congress. Senate. Senate Committee on Judiciary. Senate Subcommittee to Investigate the Administration of the Internal Security Act and Other Internal Security Laws. *Interlocking Subversion in Government Departments, Part 1,* 83rd Cong., 1st sess., 10 April 1953.

U.S. Congress. Senate. Senate Committee on Judiciary. Senate Subcommittee to Investigate the Administration of the Internal Security Act and Other Internal Security Laws. *Interlocking Subversion in Government Departments, Part 3,* 83rd Cong., 1st sess., 16 April 1953.

U.S. Congress. Senate. Senate Committee on Judiciary. Senate Subcommittee to Investigate the Administration of the Internal Security Act and Other Internal Security Laws. *Interlocking Subversion in Government Departments, Part 7,* 83rd Cong., 1st sess., 12 May 1953.

U.S. Congress. Senate. Senate Committee on Judiciary. Senate Subcommittee to Investigate the Administration of the Internal Security Act and Other Internal Security Laws. *Interlocking Subversion in Government Departments, Part 10,* 83rd Cong., 1st sess., 26 May 1953.

U.S. Congress. Senate. Senate Committee on Judiciary. Senate Subcommittee to Investigate the Administration of the Internal Security Act and Other Internal Security Laws. *Interlocking Subversion in Government Departments, Part 12,* 83rd Cong., 1st sess., 12, 16, 18, 23 June 1953.

U.S. Congress. Senate. Senate Committee on Judiciary. Senate Subcommittee to Investigate the Administration of the Internal Security Act and Other Internal Security Laws. *Interlocking Subversion in Government Departments, Part 30,* 84th Cong., 1st sess., 30 August 1955.

U.S. Congress. Senate. Senate Committee on Judiciary. Senate Subcommittee to Investigate the Administration of the Internal Security Act and Other Internal Security Laws. *Interlocking Subversion in Government Departments, Report,* 83rd Cong., 1st sess., 30 July 1953.

U.S. Congress. Senate. Senate Committee on Foreign Commerce. *Nomination of Thomas C. Blaisdell, Jr., To Be Assistant Secretary of Commerce,* 81st Cong., 1st sess., 23 February, 22 March 1949.

U.S. Congress. House. House Committee on Un-American Activities. *Role of the Communist Press in the Communist Conspiracy,* 82nd Cong., 2nd sess., 9–10, 15–17 January 1952.

U.S. Congress. House. Select Committee to Investigate Tax-Exempt Foundations and Comparable Organizations. *Tax-Exempt Foundations,* 82nd Cong., 2nd sess., 18–21, 24–25 November, 2, 3, 5, 8–11, 15, 17, 22–23, 30 December 1952.

U.S. Congress. Senate. Senate Committee on Government Operations. Senate Permanent Subcommittee on Investigations; Senate Subcommittee on Government Operations Abroad. *Transfer of Occupation Currency Plates—Espionage Phase,* 83rd Cong., 1st sess., 20–21 October 1953.

Venona cables. Online at *www.nsa.gov/docs/venona/.*

Weinstein, Allen. *Perjury: The Hiss-Chambers Case.* New York: Knopf, 1978.

Weinstein, Allen and Alexander Vassiliev. *The Haunted Wood: Soviet Espionage in America—The Stalin Era.* New York: The Modern Library, 2000.

Wells, Katherine Elizabeth. *The Turrill/Wells Genealogy.* New Milford, CT: Self-published.

Weyl, Nathaniel, " 'I Was in a Communist Unit with Hiss': Revelations of a Liberal," *U.S. News and World Report,* Jan. 9, 1953, pp. 22–40.

Yalkowsky, Stanley. *The Murder of the Rosenbergs.* Self-published, 1990.

# Index